NetLaw:
Your Rights
in the Online World

Lance Rose

Osborne **McGraw-Hill**

Berkeley   New York   St. Louis   San Francisco
Auckland   Bogotá   Hamburg   London   Madrid
Mexico City   Milan   Montreal   New Delhi   Panama City
Paris   São Paulo   Singapore   Sydney
Tokyo   Toronto

Osborne **McGraw-Hill**
2600 Tenth Street
Berkeley, California 94710
U.S.A.

For information on software, translations, or book distributors outside of the U.S.A., please write to Osborne **McGraw-Hill** at the above address.

NetLaw: Your Rights in the Online World

4567890 DOC 9987

ISBN 0-07-882077-4

Publisher:
  Lawrence Levitsky

Acquisitions Editor
  Scott Rogers

Project Editor
  Claire Splan

Copy Editor
  Gary Morris

Proofreader
  Pat Mannion

Indexer
  Valerie Robbins

Computer Designer
  Peter F. Hancik

Illustrator
  Helena Charm

Series Designer
  Lance Ravella

Cover Designer
  Mason Fong
  Background painting: Charlie Owen

Quality Control Specialist
  Joe Scuderi

About the Author

Lance Rose, Esq. is nationally recognized in the field of online law. He writes regularly for *WIRED Magazine* and *Boardwatch Magazine*, and is a moderator on LEXIS Counsel Connect, an online system for attorneys. He also speaks at and helps organize various national conferences, seminars, and trade shows. Mr. Rose was co-author of *Syslaw*, published in 1992.

As an attorney, Mr. Rose has been involved in computer law since 1982, and online legal matters since 1986. His firm, Lance Rose & Associates, in Montclair, New Jersey, works with many kinds of businesses in the online world including electronic and print publishers, online services, electronic payment businesses, Internet providers, system operators, content providers, and software developers and publishers. He has a J.D. cum laude from Benjamin Cardozo School of Law, and an LL.M. in Intellectual Property/Trade Regulation from New York University School of Law.

Contents

3 Owning and Using Online Property 83

4 Dangers and Responsibilities in the Online World   119

8   *Adult Materials and Themes*   245

A   *Sample Contracts*   261

B *Electronic Communications Privacy Act* 283

C *Computer Fraud and Abuse Act* 313

Acknowledgments

There are many whose influence must be acknowledged. I'm sure I'll miss a few, so please accept my humblest apologies in advance.

- My wife Janet and daughter Julietta, who with divine patience humored me while I stole from my time with them to work on this book.

- My once-partner Jonathan Wallace, co-author of *Syslaw* way, way back in 1989. That's prescience! His sense of fairness and balance hopefully live on in the newly incarnated *NetLaw*.

- My associate and co-worker Steve Barber, Esq., who helped with the book at critical points and saved me from certain death by deadline.

- The editors and other folks at Osborne/McGraw-Hill, especially Scott Rogers, who can keep authors happy while retaining his dignity; his assistant Kelly Vogel; project editor Claire Splan; and Editor-in-Chief Jeff Pepper.

- Those who added meaningfully to my understanding of online law, business, or culture, including Joe Abernathy, John Perry Barlow, Ann Branscomb, Bill Frezza, Mike Godwin, Stacy Horn, David R. Johnson, Charles Merrill, Jerry Michalski, Henry Perritt, Jack Rickard, Neil Shapiro, Mark Stahlman, Brad Templeton, Jim Warren, Don Watkins, Larry Wood, and Ben Wright.

- Plus the hundreds of others I've chatted with or whose articles or books I've read the past few years in connection with the growth of online society, all of whose insights can undoubtedly be found mingling among the observations in these pages.

Needless to say, the errors in this book are all of my own fiendish invention, and should not be blamed on any of the gentle souls named above.

Introduction

What is Online Law?

Millions of individuals are exploring computer networks and online systems today. Did I say individuals? Look again. Everywhere on the Net, *groups* of people gather—on bulletin boards, in Usenet, in chat rooms, and other places online. They're socializing, doing business, publishing to each other on the World Wide Web. It is more than just having fun with computers and modems. It is the start of a social revolution, perhaps the most important structural advance in society in our lifetime.

The new social revolution is not about technology at all, though we needed technology to make it happen. Its essence is deceptively simple: people coming together from all points of the globe to meet on the common ground of the Net. We never had this ability before, in the entire history of civilization. We created the Net when we connected computers to telephone systems, and put those computers in a lot of homes and offices.

In the past, social groups did not function unless their members were close together. If you threw a party, your guests came in from a few miles away. Corporations kept their brass concentrated near the headquarters office. The strength of civic groups depended on how often they could get their members together in the same room. There have always been more extended parties, corporations and associations, of course, but until now they could conquer physical distance only through brute force: spending lots of time and money carting people from where they lived to where they could meet with others. It was a game only the very rich or extremely dedicated could afford to play. The rise of the voice telephone system changed things a little, but it remained almost entirely a one-on-one medium. Networks and online services, in contrast, readily support online communities of almost any size.

Now we can gather together online with ease. It is getting easier and cheaper every day. People are starting to live parts of their lives online, in discussion groups, clubs, trade organizations, virtual corporations, and so on. We can help each other and enrich each others' lives in ways previously unimagined. We are bursting out of the shared blinders worn by geographically provincial groups, to achieve new, globally informed perspectives and ways of working together.

At the same time, new opportunities for misunderstanding arise, often with people we may never meet in the flesh. The Net is revolutionary in supporting social and business groups spread across countries and continents, but it does not portend any immediate change in individual human nature. Just like in the physical world, people and businesses can hurt others on the Net in a lot of ways, both accidentally and on purpose. They can tell hurtful lies about each other, steal or wrongfully copy each others' property, reveal painful or damaging secrets, or break a promise or a deal on which someone else depends. This is not merely theoretical. There has already been plenty of real damage caused to others through the Net.

For approximately the first three decades of the Net's existence, from the '60s through the '80s, little of the damage caused online led to legal action of any kind, apart from government agents busting a few "phone phreaks" for long distance pranks, or software companies shutting down pirate bulletin boards bulging with infringing "warez." The first Net users were explorers charting the wilderness, not litigious businessmen. Besides, most injuries on the Net could not be measured in money. Since our land-based courts require significant sums as the price of admission, they were simply not involved in early Net conflicts. With courtroom resolution out of the question, those injured online had few alternatives. They could try to injure the person who injured them; they could appeal to those controlling Net resources to cut off the wrongdoer; or they could simply retire from the Net and get back to the physical world, where all the real action was at the time anyway.

Things have changed. Now there's lots of money, people, and businesses on the Net. Many billions of dollars are being invested today in its further development as a social and business environment. This in turn has opened the doors to the land-based courts, who are now becoming deeply involved in online law for at least three reasons. First, there are now a lot of rich folks and companies on the Net, who can easily afford to sue those who hurt them online. Second, the companies investing billions in Net development want to protect their hefty investment. They will readily shave off millions of dollars and fund as many lawsuits as necessary to secure their online assets and business opportunities. Third, all the attention that our society is now giving to the Net, including all the hype about the "National Information Infrastructure," the "Information Superhighway," and "telecommuting," inevitably rubs off on the courts and legal systems. Judges are more likely to recognize the Net as a place where people meet and do business, where wrongful acts can lead to real injuries deserving of a legal remedy. Again, this is not merely an academic point. We are seeing a sharp, steady rise in lawsuits based on events that took place largely or wholly on the Net.

Which leads to the question: which legal system applies to the Net? The answer may change over time, but for now, U.S. citizens should assume they can be called to appear in state and federal courts in the U.S. if they injure others on the Net. The land-based governments and courts have power over our bodies. If someone injured on the Net asks a court to decide a dispute with a U.S. citizen, the court will call that citizen in to defend the lawsuit, using marshalls and guns if necessary to back up its demand.

Once in court, another question arises: what rules or laws should apply to disputes arising on the Net? Once again, U.S. citizens should assume that in legal matters involving other U.S. citizens, state and federal laws of the U.S. will be applied. Courts today are not close to recognizing special legal jurisdictions on the Net, and it may be years or decades before they do. The reality today is that U.S. laws are applied routinely to events online, as demonstrated in several of the cases listed in Appendix K.

There is currently a partial way out of the straight application of U.S. laws to Net activities. It was pioneered many years ago by banks using online funds clearing systems, and investors using online trading systems like NASDAQ: membership agreements, where participants in an online group agree to rules that will govern their mutual affairs. U.S. courts readily treat such agreements as legal contracts, setting up self-contained legal systems with their own rules and logic. Thus, any group of people running or involved in an online system can take hold of much of their own legal destiny, simply by agreeing to set their own rules by mutual agreement.

These group agreements are limited, however, whenever they conflict with overriding state or federal public policies. Such policy limits are often not hard to divine. For instance, let's say an online membership group sets up a massive bartering market where goods are traded directly for other goods with no money changing hands, and the IRS brings group members to federal court to make them report and pay taxes on the transactions. We can expect that the courts would readily apply U.S. tax law to their activities, brushing aside any suggestion that the group's internal agreement that no money changes hands makes the Internal Revenue Code inapplicable.

It is within this existing regime—that U.S. courts and U.S. laws will regularly be applied to people and businesses who can be found in the U.S.—that *NetLaw* is set. In the chapters to follow, we will explore the subjects of greatest legal importance on the Net today. Much of what we will demonstrate is how traditional legal thinking needs to take into account the many new social and business environments found on the Net. The reference point is always U.S. law, though the techniques applying that law to the Net may be instructive to those in other countries who are working out how their own laws will apply to the Net.

At the same time, we will hopefully show how the Net is not automatically a "whole new ball game." The Net is not populated by a new set of people. Everyone using the Net is deeply entrenched in the land-based world, and sharing the heritage of thousands of years of land-based cultural and social development. We bring that history with us when we go online. Whether we view our heritage as an asset or as wasteful baggage, groups of people instinctively erect their acculturated under-standings all around them in the Net. As a result, legal scenarios online will look very, very familiar to those of us who have spent any time in the physical world.

Working with and within online law is a learning process in its very earliest stages. It is not, however, nearly as mysterious as some newcomers to the field suggest. Even without a lot of court decisions or legislation specific to the online world to guide us, we can say a lot about online law today based on what we know about existing laws and their evolution, the social goals and pressures at play on the evolving Net, and common sense. It is the goal of *NetLaw* to arm the reader with enough information in all these areas to proceed with confidence into any social or business situation on the Net. In the meantime, unanswered legal questions will remain online, just as they do in the physical world. They are a permanent condition in an evolving society.

What Is in This Book

The book has eight chapters, each covering an important legal area in the online world.

1. "Freedom, Censorship, and Control of the Online System"—Who controls online systems, and what are the limits of that control? Is it legal to censor Net users? The First Amendment guarantees "freedom of speech." We will look at how freedom of speech works online, and see how it is the most important law in the U.S. protecting the Net, its users and its providers today.

2. "Contracts and Commercial Arrangements"—How do you use contracts to manage your risks online, and set up the kinds of online relationships you want. What are the terms of basic user agreements with online services and access providers? For those who do business on the Net, what deals should they make with customers and suppliers?

3. "Owning and Using Online Property"—In the past, most information was freely transmitted on the Net. Today, information freedom is under pressure from copyright owners setting up their shops online. What are the rules covering our use of messages and files belonging to others? How do the copyright and trademark laws work online?

4. "Dangers and Responsibilities in the Online World"—There are many kinds of injury on the Net, such as libel, infringing copyrights, and trafficking in stolen credit card numbers. What legal standards of conduct apply online? What is the risk to corporate managers when their in-house LANs are connected to the Net? Should system operators be blamed for injuries caused by those who use their systems? There is a great deal of concern today over network security. What legal obligations are there to keep an online system secure from intruders?

5. "Privacy"—Our privacy is increasingly threatened, and seems to become more precious as we live more of our lives on the computer networks. Does the law protect our privacy on the Net? Can businesses rely on legal protection for their trade secrets? Encryption software is becoming increasingly popular as a way to keep e-mail entirely secret. Are there legal limits to its use?

6. "Crime and the Online System"—What counts as a crime when you're online? We look at how federal and state computer crime laws apply in the online world. We also look at what you can do when you see someone committing a crime online, and when a system operator might be held responsible for criminal acts committed on the system.

7. "Searches and Seizures"—Government agents have been known to stage raids on online systems, and carry the computer equipment away for inspection. They have also been known to make mistakes, as in the famous case of Steve Jackson Games. What laws protect online systems and materials from search and seizure, and how can system operators minimize their risks?

8. "Adult Materials and Themes"—Adult materials and services are among the most active uses of the Net today. They are also often among the most illegal; adult online services advertising nationally one month can be under criminal indictment the next. We will look at the laws regulating obscenity, child pornography and indecent speech, and the Constitutional limits against state and federal prosecution.

In addition, extensive appendixes provide a variety of resources, including sample contracts, case citations, statutory texts, and pointers to other sources of information.

How to Use This Book

This book is meant to help readers know which behavior is legal, and which illegal, when they encounter it on the Net. Most Net users and operators need such a primer today. In the physical world, we know inherently about many things that are illegal, even if we never opened a law book or talked to a lawyer: shoplifting; robbing banks; driving the wrong way down a one way street; killing or injuring people; counterfeiting money or forging checks; selling dangerous products, from cars to breast implants; breaching a contract. How do we know these things? They are presented to us continuously in the media, in school, and by our parents and friends. They are the kinds of harmful activity our society knows it will not tolerate. Those who ignore the basic teaching, who carelessly cross the clear lines of illegality, could find themselves in court defending a suit for money damages or a criminal indictment.

In contrast, most people have no such background in online law, no history of examples where people did the illegal or harmful act, then got hauled into court. We cannot rely on a common knowledge of online law threading through society and culture, because it is simply not there yet.

Even when we assume that laws born in the physical world apply online, there remains the question of *how* do they apply?

That is where this book comes in. *NetLaw* can serve as a guide to the major laws and legal events today in the online world. It is also like a first aid manual: it helps the reader identify legal risks and rights for online systems, explains the causes behind them, and suggests ways in which the reader can protect their rights, and handle or avoid the risks.

For instance, if you wonder whether your privacy rights were violated on a given online system, or if you simply want to know more about the general framework of privacy rights on computer networks, you can go right to the privacy section of this book and read up. You don't have to plow through unrelated materials on computer crime or online dealmaking to figure out the score on privacy. Or you may be concerned about your company's legal responsibility to keep the in-house system secure from intrusive hackers. To learn more about it, you can look at the sections on security and related subjects in Chapter 4.

When used in this way, the book is a practical reference to be picked up and consulted whenever you encounter new legal issues on the Net. Where it does not provide an answer, the resources listed in the appendixes will show you where you can investigate further.

If you prefer, you can read the book cover to cover for a tour of the online world as it exists today and the legal tangles to which it has been host. Reading about legal matters online is one way of tuning into the drama of the Net. It is also a way to develop an understanding how the law meshes with other aspects of online culture and society.

Scattered throughout the book are two kinds of text boxes. One kind, indicated by a picture of the scales of justice, features discussions of various trends affecting the development of online law. Very few cases involving online law—less than a handful—have been decided in the two or three years since the last revision of this book (previously published under the title *SysLaw*). However, in that same time there has been a whirlwind of activity very important to how online law will develop in the next few years: new and attempted legislation; disagreements between companies, organizations, and industry groups, which may lead to lawsuits; social and business developments with obvious legal consequences down the line. These events are only potentially significant, their precise impact too vague for them to be presented as part of online law as it exists today. However, we must still track these nascent trends to understand online law as it evolves. By placing this material in boxes, we've separated it from what might be considered the better established "law" that applies online, yet highlighted its importance to understanding how online law may evolve over time.

The other kind of text box presents to the reader various metaphors that Net users apply to different parts of the online world. Each such box is graced with a picture of one of these metaphors. The special focus on metaphors reflects the peculiar path by which legal analysis and lawyers tend to approach legal affairs on the Net: by analogizing online matters to supposedly similar past events in the physical world. This phenomenon is not limited to the legal profession by any means. How many times have we all heard references to online systems being like printing presses, telephone systems, postal systems, book stores, libraries, inns, or highways?

Whether we admit it or not, metaphors underlie some of our most strongly held convictions about the Net. It is now time to get more serious about these models, to understand where it is valid to compare them to Net phenomena and where the comparisons must end. The goal of the metaphor boxes in this book is to begin the job of inspecting the metaphors and see what light they shed in understanding online law. Even the little pictures are part of this effort. They provide a visual cue for the reader, an additional path to the reader's own rich store of mental associations which flesh out the full meaning of each metaphor as it is applied to the virtual world online.

The text boxes provide, then, yet another way of reading this book. The reader can skip from box to box as if reading a magazine, and build a collage-like sense of how law is developing online and the metaphorical world in which it operates. There is some overlap of material between the text boxes and the main text. This is deliberate. Many of the events taking place online have multiple meanings and implications for online law and society, and are best portrayed in multiple contexts. In this book, we accomplish this by referring to certain key events at different points in the discussion, and within different types of discussions.

Terminology relating to the online world is used rather loosely here, mirroring the degree to which it is still unsettled among those who use online systems. You will see "online world" used a lot here, because it's simple, attractive, and accurately portrays the sense that those who communicate online regularly feel as though they operate in a shared world. The term "cyberspace" looks at this time like it might become the word of general usage for referring to this same realm, so it is also used interchangeably with "online world" in this book. "Internet" refers to the TCP/IP network of networks that evolved out of the ARPAnet of the '60s. The term "Net," on the other hand, refers to the online world as a whole, and emphasizes the connectedness of all online points to all other points (though for any two physically unconnected networks, the connection is via the people who participate in both). If this is a bit confusing, don't worry. All these terms refer generally to the big online arena within which people are socializing and conducting businesses, and within which deals can be made and laws can be broken. Other terminology is fairly straightforward: "user" means a person using an online system; "operator" means someone running an online system or service of any kind; and "online system" means any kind of online service or operation, including BBSs, newsgroup conferencing systems, mailing lists, echo conferences, and MUDs.

Remember, the information in this book is information only, and *not legal advice*. It is for readers to add to their own knowledge of how law works in the online world, so they can perform their own legal analyses armed with more and better information. For definitive help on any given legal situation, the reader should track down a lawyer competent in the practice of online law. If one can't be found, then find a good lawyer with an open mind, and show him or her a copy of this book so they too can jump into the practice of online law.

Freedom, Censorship, and Control of the Online System

You likely picked up this book to learn the legal pitfalls awaiting those who run or use online services or networks and how to avoid them. However, before we look at the risks, we will explore your online rights. After establishing your own sphere of freedom and control in the online world, we will move on, in later chapters, to discuss how your deeds and actions can create certain responsibilities and how to handle them.

Everyone who works or plays in the online world should know his or her rights. For instance, when you hook up the in-house LAN to the Internet, your e-mail and groupware systems emerge from a realm of neatly administered corporate policies to face the wider world of networked businesses and people. Your corporate guidelines are useless for understanding or defining this world, or your system's place in it. As you confront those who preach the limits on your company's actions in the online world (and there are plenty of such people online), knowing your rights will help you guide your company on its course in this new arena. For businesses and services operating primarily online, knowing what you can do freely without interference from others is essential to the whole of your business. And those who go online only occasionally or for entertainment can travel and speak with more assurance when they know intimately the legal limits of personal freedom.

Freedom of Speech and of the Press

The single most important source of rights for electronic communications in the United States is the First Amendment to the U.S. Constitution, otherwise known as the guarantee of "freedom of speech and of the press." It assures that all users of online systems can communicate freely with others, and is defined so broadly that it applies in some fashion to nearly every online legal situation. The First Amendment's promotion of free speech is particularly valuable to system operators, as it reduces their burden of legal responsibility so they can receive and transmit messages economically through their online services. The First Amendment is the friend of the user and system operator alike.

In addition to First Amendment rights, we have the legal freedom to do everything which is not expressly forbidden. Whether you call it the right to life, liberty, and the pursuit of happiness under the Constitution, or the natural right of all people without need of legal affirmation, this basic freedom applies equally on- and offline.

The First Amendment

This is the most important source of legal rights in online systems. The First Amendment to the Constitution, ratified by the states on December 15, 1791, provides

> *Congress shall make no law . . . abridging the freedom of speech, or of the press; or the right of the people peaceably to assemble, and to petition the Government for a redress of grievances.*

Based on this single sentence, U.S. citizens and the press have broad legal powers to communicate with other citizens, without significant government interference.

Eighteenth-century newspapers and magazines were the first judicially recognized recipients of First Amendment protection. In comparison, online systems are a brand new historical development. Yet in an exceedingly short time, they have become a valuable communications resource in this country. Online systems deserve the full protection from legal interference granted by the First Amendment under its express protections of "speech," "press," "peaceable assembly," and "petitioning the government," for at least two reasons.

First, the entire business of online systems is simply to collect, organize, and redistribute the electronic speech of their users. People and companies use online systems to send e-mail, public postings, electronic newsletters, text files, classified listings, and advertisements (among other things) to other people and companies. These everyday electronic activities today qualify as "speech" as much as the spoken word or printed materials, which are universally acknowledged as protected under the First Amendment. There is no reason they should not be equally protected from the laws of government. Online systems, as the vehicles for electronic speech, must also be protected from the incursions of restrictive laws, or else the speech they carry will be unfairly restricted.

The value of speech in online systems is being dramatically demonstrated in world events. The Internet international computer network was pivotal in telling the world about the pro-democracy demonstrations at Tiananmen Square in 1989. Similarly, when Soviet hard-liners attempted to recapture the government from the leaders of reform, Internet communications, both internally and to the rest of the world, helped keep up the pressure that ultimately led to the collapse of the coup. On the home front, the anti-tobacco group SCARCNET uses an online system to focus the efforts of scattered activists to systematically combat tobacco companies in the courts and in the public dialogue. More broadly, the Internet is being seriously discussed as a potential means for broadening democratic participation in government. In an early symbolic demonstration of this, the Clinton White House and several top members of the administration have made themselves available on the Internet, publishing their addresses and receiving and answering e-mail.

Second, many of the activities of online systems and users are analogous to those of traditional print publishers. Thus, many systems and users are "press" operations in their own right. The First Amendment was enacted primarily to protect private publishers from government control. It

Media and Free Speech—Inconstant Companions

In our country's earliest days there were print newspapers that were well protected under the First Amendment. Newspapers carried the views of the day to the public. A vigorous, unfettered press was deemed necessary for a healthy democracy open to new ideas.

Surprisingly, other media have received decidedly less free speech protection in the U.S. despite the guarantee of the First Amendment, as convincingly depicted by Ithiel de Sola Pool in his landmark history of media regulation, *Technologies of Freedom*. The postal system is usually not treated as a free speech distribution system, but as a public resource subject to centralized government control. When broadcast radio and television arrived, the government declared the airwaves a scarce resource and set up the Federal Communications Commission to interfere with free speech—supposedly for the public good. Telephone systems have tra-

ditionally been considered natural monopolies, regulated as "common carriers" to enforce socially acceptable prices and access for all. This does not mean the First Amendment was stamped out of these new media altogether. Television eventually received many of the same legal privileges accorded newspapers, even while remaining under FCC jurisdiction.

Will the government treat online systems as a privileged medium under the First Amendment like newspapers, or as an arena of rampant regulation like the telephone and television systems? By rights, online systems are entitled to be free of laws and regulations that would stifle speech or press activities in any way. However, the national urge to regulate surfaced with a vengeance in late 1993, in the form of the National Information Infrastructure (NII) Task Force. This group of industry and political leaders was charged by the White House to investigate the taming of cyberspace for use by Americans, and eventually to propose Congressional regulation where it seems appropriate.

The jury is still out on the NII Task Force as this book goes to press. Hopefully, it will recommend that online regulation always be tempered by respect for the free speech values of the First Amendment. As more of our speech as a nation goes online, protecting our free speech from the government becomes increasingly important.

fostered the growth of alternative publishers with diverse points of view, instead of a single government-sponsored version of "the truth." Communication technologies have progressed since the Bill of Rights. Now the "press" also includes books, wire services like the Associated Press and UPI, broadcast radio and television, cable television, and online news services.

Like these older media, online publishers bring a great variety of information and entertainment to the public. Online publishers present an enormous variety of viewpoints and specialized information. Online systems and users who assume the role of publishers are a brand new form of the "press," and should receive at least the same level of protection as newspapers and television.

The Social Power of the Computer Bulletin Board

Sometimes large social trends are revealed in relatively small events. The Writers' Guild of America West is the trade union for Hollywood screenwriters, for both industry workers and wannabes. For many years it was dominated by its president. He continually frustrated union members with what they perceived as shortsighted arrangements with other Hollywood powers, compromising their ability to share in profits from Hollywood films. Among the great lost opportunities they cite is being denied a fair share in revenues from videocassettes and overseas distribution, two big growth areas in films in the past decade. Despite scattered objections, the membership had no effective means of counterattack, as the president controlled the publications that kept members informed, and the budget for getting things done.

When the union set up a computer bulletin board, everything changed. As members compared notes online, they realized their shared frustrations over union management. They voiced their views to others on the increasingly popular bulletin board, which mutated into an informal tool for popular governance of the union. Sensing a threat, entrenched union management first kicked the main malcontents off the system, then shut down the board. The ejected members filed a lawsuit, but the court refused to force union management to reinstate the bulletin board.

As it turned out, both the lawsuit and the judicial decision were beside the point. The writers simply started another, unofficial bulletin board for use by union members. They picked up where they left off when the other board was shut down, making plans to change union management. Union members organizing on the board were able to replace several members of their governing board, and were planning to revamp the rest of the organization in short order.

In this small story, we see the enormous power of online systems—the power to transform society through unprecedented levels of information flow between its members. Today, we see the toppling of a moribund bureaucracy at a writer's union through purely democratic processes, in the best sense of the word "democracy." Tomorrow . . . ?

It should be easy to see that online systems give us far more genuinely free speech and free press than ever before in human history. Conservative estimates place the number of privately operated public bulletin boards at roughly 60,000 and rising (not counting Internet sites without direct telephone dialups). That's 60,000 electronic printing presses newly available to the public, as near as the next phone call. Multiply that by an average of at least a few dozen callers per system, add in the roughly 4 to 5 million people currently believed to be using the larger online systems, and roughly 10 to 25 million more people worldwide said to be using the Internet today, and the number of people worldwide expressing themselves on online systems ranges from 30 to 50 million today.

Online systems powerfully fulfill the First Amendment goal of publishing and distributing diverse points of view, many of which never before had a voice. Protecting online systems and users from encroachment by government should be understood to be one of the primary missions of the First Amendment today.

> **Online systems give us far more genuinely free speech and free press than ever before in human history.**

We Are All Broadcasters

When you cut through the technology and hype, is there anything novel about the online systems that connect millions of people?

In fact, there is—a kind of mass interaction that is new to society. To illustrate this, let's classify discussions as roughly three types, depending on how many people are on each end of the line: one-to-one, one-to-many, and many-to-many (an approach that has gained some currency on the Internet). These kinds of discussions all typically occur when people get together, as at a party: Two people speaking privately near the punch bowl is a one-to-one discussion, one person standing on a chair and addressing the crowd is a one-to-many speech, and a group of people chatting in a circle makes a many-to-many conversation. With the arrival of electronic mass media, these basic discussion types have been stretched to span the continents.

One-to-one discussions were extended years ago through the telephone and tele-graph. One-to-many discussions were also extended a while back, through broadcast media like radio and television. Each advance drastically changed the quality of our lives. Telephones give us living discussions with each of our friends and associates, no matter how far away. They shrink the world to human scale. Television efficiently distributes news, entertainment, and advertising to most of the civilized world, creating international bonds of shared culture previously unattainable. Each of these media also has its limits. The telephone is a private experience, awkward for any kind of group organizing. Television is virtually a one-way medium: almost all the information is sent from the broadcaster to the public, and the public can only respond by buying or not buying the advertised goods.

Online services finally bring the third kind of discussion, many-to-many, to the electronic mass media. Where the older media of television, radio, and telephone are limited, online services shine. We can organize discussions of dozens or even hundreds of participants, unlike the telephone. And unlike television, we are not bound to listen only to the broadcasts of well-heeled entertainment companies. To the contrary, anyone can be heard by many others, either in his or her own town or across the globe. With online services, society finally has a general-purpose organizational tool that allows groups of all kinds to organize effectively, and enables those who don't fit in where they live to find hundreds or thousands of kindred souls across the world. For some, a tool for socializing; for others, the most powerful aid to true democracy yet invented.

We are at the beginning of the age of widespread group interaction, and there's no going back. The awesome power of national and worldwide networks is being demonstrated almost daily at this point, yet we're still only at the stage of fumbling about for the "on" switch. Society is truly heading online—not to disappear into cyberspace like the Lawnmower Man, but to add an enormous new dimension to our lives, a space made of our shared lives and ideas. Next time someone says this online thing is just a fad, ask her when she last had a running conversation with a bunch of friends at once across several continents. People in the online world do it every day.

Viewing online services as vehicles for many-to-many discussions also aids in legal analysis. Online services are riddled with the "speech" of their users, the kinds of spirited discussions and exchange of views that lie at the heart of the First Amendment's protection of freedom of speech. We have seen the Supreme Court confer a great deal of legal protection on newspapers and books, which are mere one-to-many communications vehicles, with little chance for the audience to talk back. How much greater, then, should be the protection we expect for online systems, the smallest of which can carry a greater number of voices than a newsstand or cable television system?

How Does the First Amendment Protect Online Systems and Users?

The First Amendment is drafted in purposely broad terms: Congress may enact "no law" limiting freedom of speech. Online systems cannot be oppressed by laws or regulations that would seriously restrict their publishing or distributing of "speech" in the U.S. In other words, system operators and system users have the Constitutional right to distribute a broad range of controversial discussions and files without threat of lawsuit or government interference.

There are three different ways, equally important, in which the First Amendment protects users, operators, and the online systems they share: (1) it holds that all speech is legal except for certain extreme kinds of speech (such as obscenity), thus promoting vigorous discussion and the spread of information on nearly every subject known to humankind; (2) it keeps the overall legal burdens on system operators light enough that they can continue running their online systems to distribute user speech and pursue their own publishing; and (3) it sharply limits the government's ability to search or seize systems, users, or their property, where such intrusive measures would interfere with their ability to publish or to distribute speech.

The right to online free speech, even radical or questionable speech, includes

- *General discussions and information.* All kinds of talk are fully protected by the First Amendment from government interference. For example, online discussions of homosexuality, radical left politics, and paranoid conspiracy theories are freely and equally permitted and protected. (An important limit: the exchanges must be limited to discussions, and not become part of illegal "acts." Acts are not considered speech, and are not protected by the

First Amendment. For example, groups of technically sophisticated computer callers may freely exchange information about computer and telephone networks that is not specifically confidential. But they cannot claim First Amendment protection for exchanging passwords or access codes, which can be considered part of the act of illegal entry into computer systems.)

- *Defamatory materials* (a false statement about a person that injures his or her reputation). Newspapers and broadcasters are not liable when they publish false and damaging statements about famous people or organizations, unless the publisher acts maliciously. System operators and users are entitled to the same protection from lawsuits.

- *"Adult" materials.* Obscene materials (as defined by the Supreme Court) and child pornography have no First Amendment protection, and cannot be legally maintained on an online system. Most adult materials, however, are not legally "obscene," and are permitted to be circulated online under the First Amendment. Federal legislation may require that the system operator verify that children are not getting access to adult materials, but publication is otherwise generally permitted.

- *Commercial information.* Real estate listings, career placement information, advertisements, computerized product support, and other business-related information are fully entitled to First Amendment protection. In the past, courts said that such "commercial" speech is less protected from government action, but more recent rulings make no such distinction.

As mentioned above, the First Amendment not only protects system users and their right to speak about nearly anything online; it also protects online systems themselves as the conduits for speech, by protecting system operators from government burdens that would make it difficult to keep running online systems. For example, the following laws and rules affecting online systems are subject to First Amendment limits:

- Any supposed legal requirements for system operators to monitor files and information passing through their systems.

- Taxes on online systems (other than income tax), such as information service taxes.

- Regulating the time, place, or manner of operating online systems, such as community zoning laws that might label an online system a "business" ineligible to operate in certain zoned areas.

Though these rules and others are limited in theory by the First Amendment, they are often still imposed as if they are legal, regardless of First Amendment rights. For instance, many states in the U.S. currently impose special taxes on information services. If these taxes are ever challenged as an illegal restraint on freedom of speech, they might be declared illegal, if it is decided that they overburden the operation of online systems by making it harder to generate a profit.

The third way the First Amendment protects online activities is by limiting our government's ability to seize online systems and users performing "press" and "speech" functions. These limits are expressed most purely in the Privacy Protection Act, discussed later in this book. Government authorities are not entitled to seize an online system that distributes news-related information just because they think illegal or dangerous activities are occurring on it. There has to be a far stronger basis for the seizure, such as information that the system operator is actually pursuing criminal activities through use of the system.

Taxing Channel One

The Channel One BBS in Massachusetts is one of the most successful and popular bulletin board systems in the country. Like most other successful systems, it grew organically from a small hobbyist system into a lucrative business, adding a few lines at a time until it reached its current levels of roughly 100 lines and 15,000 users. Despite its success, Channel One almost went under when it was hit with a state "telecommunications" tax bill of over $100,000 in 1993.

The bill was for an accumulation of taxes dating back to 1990. Channel One didn't know about these taxes; it couldn't have. The tax law used against them was a sales tax on "telecommunications services." While it was on the books for years, it always applied strictly to operations like telephone companies and hotels that charge their guests for phone services. "Information services" like bulletin boards were commonly considered exempt. They provide no phone lines, just information services like handling user messages and file uploads and downloads.

In fact, information services are technically still exempt from the tax. But the state of Massachusetts declared that unless an online service separately accounted for the "information services" part of its budget, all of its revenues would be deemed subject to the "telecommunications services" tax. An official audit of Channel One has proceeded on this basis. Channel One has fought vigorously, spending large sums on its defense and taking its story to the national news media. As we go to press, the tax claim against the company is still unresolved.

Though the stories in the press about the Channel One situation do not mention it, the tax problem it is facing may be ripe for a First Amendment challenge. It would be based on discriminatory treatment—imposing a special tax on online services not applicable to other kinds of businesses. Such taxes are generally not sustained against newspapers. In fact, newspapers and magazines often receive better tax treatment than other businesses, a fact entirely due to their aura of First Amendment protection. If the same privileged treatment can be achieved for online services, it will be a milestone in society's recognition of the important role they play.

The Publisher/Distributor Distinction

One of the fascinating things about online systems is that they have no direct forerunners among the older media, such as newspapers, radio, and television. The ability of system users to interact in a variety of ways with system operators and with other users is unprecedented in traditional mass media. So is the ability of system users to obtain valuable items, such as computer programs and literature, directly from many systems at little or no cost. The ability of individuals to run successful online systems on a shoestring is also vastly different from the traditional mass media, which generally require an enormous capital investment.

For First Amendment purposes, the lack of direct models for online systems means there is some question about how existing First Amendment law, based on older media, will apply to online systems. Nonetheless, it is possible to make an educated guess.

One can designate three major kinds of online operations today for First Amendment purposes: publishing, distributing, and shared message systems. Each kind may qualify for a different type and amount of Constitutional protection. Many online systems are involved in two or all three of the following kinds of operations. For instance, online services large and small frequently have separate publishing areas (such as a daily news service or a database search service), distribution areas (such as file transfer areas and e-mail services), and shared message areas like Usenet and Fidonet.

Online System as Publisher

Some common online operations resemble traditional print publishing. Since most messages are transmitted in text form, many people find that the publishing model, based on the print book, newspaper, and magazine businesses, has a certain intuitive appeal.

The online operations that most resemble publishing include "electronic newsletters" deliberately modeled on traditional newspapers and magazines, complete with pages and articles; electronic news services such as Newsbytes or Dow Jones News Retrieval, reporting the news of the day; public discussion areas whose contents are closely supervised and edited by active system operators; creative endeavors like group stories or poetry created jointly by online participants; World Wide Web pages, which in many cases are pure publishing operations visually resembling online magazines; and databases of facts and other information, such as historical news databases, sports statistics, stock quotes, and online catalogs, maintained by online services for their callers.

> **Some common online operations resemble traditional print publishing. What these activities have in common is editorial control by the system operator or owner.**

What these activities have in common is editorial control by the system operator or owner. The operator selects the materials and data, organizes them, and presents them to the system users. This does not mean the system operator himself writes every word, just as a newspaper editor does not write the articles himself. It is enough that the system operator regularly exercises substantial control over the contents of the "publishing" areas of the online system. In databases and online newsletters, this is accomplished by regularly supplying and correcting information. In closely moderated public discussion areas, it is done by regularly deleting unwanted material, moving certain messages to other discussion areas deemed more appropriate, freezing certain discussions, and so on, as well as by asserting ownership of the discussions resulting on the system. (Please note: we are not saying here that all public discussions moderated by system operators are "publications," only those that are so closely and regularly modified and edited by the operator that his or her role is functionally inseparable from that of a newspaper or magazine editor.) In in-house LAN systems, administrators can exercise similar control over messages for a company system.

The Online System as Print Publisher

While there are many possible metaphors for online systems, that of "publisher" seems among the most prevalent, especially among those newer to the online world. What accounts for the popularity of this particular model as a way to understand the online system?

The immediate attraction of this metaphor is based largely on superficial reasons. One such reason is that today, most online communications occur through text, especially if we don't count voice telephone. This is, of course, the official presentation medium of print publishing, and stands in contrast to the audiovisual presentations of the great alternative electronic medium, television. As multimedia's incessant growth continues, though, audiovisual and virtual reality terminal programs will proliferate, and text will become less and less dominant in the online environment. Another superficial reason is that the first effective deployment of online systems was in news and stock quote systems like Quotron used by financial traders, and searchable text databases like Dialog used by librarians and researchers—all systems which were naturally viewed as simply porting traditional newspaper and book functions to electronic delivery systems. In more recent times, however, discussions between users through e-mail, chat, and bulletin boards have been on the ascendancy in online systems. These forms of socializing do not bear any particular resemblance to print publishing.

That said, there are times when the publisher model is entirely apropos for online systems and activities. Many systems indeed function largely as repositories of databases, news, and the like, fairly close online analogues to printers of directories and newspapers. In some systems, the operators may exercise such tight control over the content and flow of user messages in public discussions that those discussions, as a whole, may become the operators' publications. There are also messages and files deliberately shaped by users to stand as electronic equivalents of print newsletters: they're full of editorial content determined by the publisher, and delivered in identical form to user e-mail boxes or file download areas, or both, in many different systems, effectively using online systems as newsstands or bookstores. World Wide Web pages and services are explicitly based on a publishing model, and the vast bulk of these rapidly proliferating systems operate primarily as publishers.

Legally, the "publisher" metaphor is not bad for online systems, but it's only second best for protecting system operators from legal problems. As we know, print publishers enjoy a great deal of protection under the First Amendment from responsibility for accidental false statements about public figures. However, they are still considered highly responsible for their publications, especially since it is presumed that every bit of a "publication" passes before the editor's eyes. In contrast, the "distributor" or "bookstore" metaphors for online systems (ex-

> plored further on) portray the system opera-
> tor as just the person forwarding the mes-
> sages, files, and transmissions of users,
> usually without cracking them open to peek
> at the contents. Since they are much less in-
> volved with the content of the materials on
> the system, distributors often enjoy greater
> protection from legal risk than publishers.

Thus, the system operator's exercise of control can make the controlled areas of the system into one or more "publications," and the system operator or owner a publisher. Each publication can be considered the voice of its system operator or other creator, with its own agenda and point of view.

Legally, such publishing operations on online systems are properly considered part of the "press" under the First Amendment. Government activities seriously restricting this function, whether through a government agent or in a court of law, are Constitutionally prohibited. The best-known restraint is the so-called *Times v. Sullivan* rule, which has been shaped for years by many Supreme Court rulings. In its current form, this ruling permits the media to comment freely, even falsely, about public figures, as long as they do not publish false facts maliciously, or with reckless disregard for the truth.

At the same time, system operators are not excused from all responsibilities simply by becoming publishers. If a publisher knowingly engages in criminal activities, he or she can be criminally prosecuted by the state without hindrance by the First Amendment. Violating someone's copyright likewise is not shielded by the First Amendment protection for publishers. And, following the law applicable to newspapers, if a system operator includes a message libeling someone in an online publication, he or she has a certain amount of protection from lawsuits under the *Times v. Sullivan* rule if the subject of the message is a "public figure," but remains fully responsible for libels of private individuals.

An interesting sidelight to this are the self-styled "First Amendment" online systems one finds around the country. The operators of these systems deliberately refrain from interfering with public message areas in the name of freedom of their callers' speech, except in extreme cases where they fear serious legal problems. It is sometimes suggested that by taking such a "hands-off" approach, these system operators don't really have to worry about most legal problems, that by letting the public message areas go their own way, the legal responsibility for messages remains solely with those who post them, and does not rub off on the online system or its operators.

This is an attractive thought, but it is unlikely the courts will follow this attitude to the conclusion that hands-off system operators are never liable. Often, the only person with the power to delete public messages is the system operator. Suppose a message wrongly damages someone's reputation or wrongfully spreads information about someone's credit card account, and the system operator knowingly refuses to remove the message. Judge and jury alike could find it hard to hold the operator blameless for damage that could easily have been prevented, but was allowed to occur in the name of "freedom of speech." No one else can prevent the damage from occurring in that case. It appears likely system operators will always be regarded as having some degree of responsibility for the messaging activities of their users, barring legislative intervention or perhaps some credible approach to industry self-regulation.

In other words, system operators should not count on achieving absolute First Amendment protection simply by refusing to exercise control over their public message areas. If they have the ability to control the messages sent by their users and are keeping track of at least some of those messages, certain situations may arise in which the law will require them to exercise that control, or

System Guilty, Operator Innocent?

That seems to be the decision reached by a federal trial judge in Boston just as this book went to press, dismissing the indictment of MIT student David LaMacchia for running a pirate BBS. LaMacchia had used an Internet feature called the File Service Protocol to create a file transfer and messaging system accessible through the Internet. He ran it on several MIT computers, without asking permission from school authorities. He also asked users to upload retail software not meant for online distribution, and cautioned them against letting the "Net cops" know about his system. Eventually, MIT officials discovered LaMacchia's extracurricular use of their computers and started disciplinary proceedings. These were superseded by a federal indictment, charging LaMacchia with wire fraud for running a covert copyright infringement operation that enabled the illegal copying of over $1 million of software.

LaMacchia's attorneys provided a ringing defense of LaMacchia's position, distributing an "issues primer" for legal laymen across the Net. LaMacchia was not criminally responsible for infringements on his system under copyright law, they maintained, because he did not personally upload or download the software (the users did this), and because he did not make money off the in-fringements (he seemed to be running the pirate system for the sheer satisfaction of doing it), as required by the criminal provisions of the Copyright Act. The government's attempt to use the wire fraud laws to make such conduct criminal anyway would, in effect, extend the criminal provisions of the copyright law beyond the limits Congress intended to set.

In other words, although LaMacchia operated a pirate BBS on stolen computer resources and encouraged users to upload infringing materials, he deserved to go free. According to LaMacchia's attorneys, he deserved the same First Amendment protection we would like to see applied to honest system operators who try to run a clean system. Otherwise, a "chilling effect" would result, discouraging other system operators from permitting the free flow of user speech through their own systems.

The judge bought the defense position and ruled in LaMacchia's favor, holding that the government tried to use the federal wire fraud statute improperly to punish copyright infringement. It is hard to understand why he reached this decision. The broad use of wire fraud laws had been accepted for years by federal courts at all levels as a way to penalize deceptive, damaging conduct not described in other criminal statutes. Why the change in direction at this late date, with the effect of rewarding a pirate BBS operator caught red-handed in the act? In addition, what "chilling effect" on free speech would really have resulted if LaMacchia was convicted? It would not chill honest system operators who discourage infringement and move infringing files offline whenever they are discovered. To them, LaMacchia would just be another pirate sysop who got busted.

The dismissal of the case against LaMacchia is part of the law for now (as this book went to press, the prosecution had not announced whether it would appeal). Unfortunately, by letting a blatant software pirate go free, it needlessly set the stage for copyright owners to push for new, harsher laws strongly regulating online systems. If they succeed, it would be a terrible blow to honest system operators, making them pay for the sins of the software pirates. In the end, it is both absurd and a shame that the court felt the First Amendment was implicated in this case, which involved little or no legal "speech" by LaMacchia or his system's users, and a lot of illegal transfers of software files.

be held responsible for the injuries caused because they didn't do so. If LAN administrators keep tight watch over employee messages on the system, they might be held responsible if those messages are damaging in some way.

As time goes on, we can expect that the online operations most similar to traditional publishing will be treated like publishers under the First Amendment. The closest the law has come to this concept to date is *Daniel v. Dow Jones*, a 1987 New York case in which a news service was sued for making accidental false statements about someone. The court compared Dow Jones' service to a print newspaper, and applied the same law that would apply to a newspaper in such a case: under both New York's common law and the First Amendment, the news service is not responsible for accidental false statements unless it has a "special relationship" with

> **System operators should not count on achieving absolute First Amendment protection simply by refusing to exercise control over their public message areas.**

the person hurt by those statements. Going further, the court emphasized the shared interest of online and print news services in the free flow of information. Beyond this fairly low-level case in a single state, though, we have not seen the equivalence of print and online press much recognized (or denied) in holdings in the more influential federal courts. Such holdings may be on the way, in cases still pending as this book goes to publication, such as the continuing case against electronic newsletter publisher Cubby (which co-defendent CompuServe escaped in its capacity as a "distributor" as discussed below).

While we're waiting for official guidance from the courts on some of the details, let's sketch out the general framework of online publisher rights and responsibilities today:

- The more editorial control a system operator or owner wields over the messages and materials on an online system, the greater the responsibility for the damage those messages and materials may cause to others.

- As the law develops, the system operator will likely not be held absolutely responsible for illegal or damaging materials posted on the online system, just as a supermarket owner is not absolutely responsible for a spilled bottle of oil that creates a slipping hazard for shoppers. The operator has a reasonable time to find out about dangerous or damaging messages or activities and deal with them. The exact amount of time considered "reasonable" would depend on the type of system, the amount of editorial control the sysop customarily exercises, and how the courts end up ruling in this area.

The Online System as Telephone Service

Some of the big successes in online services are the popular "chat" areas, where groups of users have real-time discussions in printed text. The chat area revives the "party line" common to early telephone systems, with a couple of important differences. Where the old party lines were imposed by telephone companies as a matter of necessity and tied together only a specific group of homes located close together, modern chat sessions are entirely voluntary and include anyone who wants to join the discussion, provided they're acceptable to the group. Also, the printed text format of current chat sessions requires keyboard skills; the fastest typists often dominate the discussions.

The Internet as a whole can be viewed simply as an alternative telephone system for computers. To reach many online services, you have a choice of calling direct using a standard telephone number, or using the "telnet" feature to call in through your local Internet access site. For services outside your local calling area, calling through the Internet is often cheaper than calling long distance through the telephone system, especially if you get Internet access at an affordable flat monthly rate. Of course, these are not entirely exclusive communications systems:

the traditional telephone system is still involved in every Internet call, both as the carrier of the signal between your computer and the Internet access point, and as the provider of many of the transmission services used by the Internet itself. But there are important differences as well: (1) the difference in costs for calling remote systems, often tipping in the Internet's favor as described above; (2) the two systems have entirely different switching and addressing schemes for routing messages; and (3) telephone companies are highly regulated and are required to provide universal access, while regulations of the Internet are still rare.

Legally, the "telephone system" metaphor for online services makes it easier to see why system operators and administrators should be shielded from liability for materials passing through the Internet. Online services and the Internet are merely media for transmissions between users. They should not be held accountable for the behavior of millions of users, just as telephone "common carriers" are not responsible for the billions of voice calls they carry. The comparison between online services and common carriers is not totally accurate, however. Common carriers do pay for their privilege, in a sense, through trade-offs such as being required to provide "universal access," and being forced to contrive pricing structures to make their services affordable to all, rather than make their pricing and access responsive to market conditions. Online services may not be willing to make these trade-offs to achieve industrial strength common carrier legal treatment.

Another, darker consequence of the similarities between online services and telephone carriers is illustrated by the "Digital Telephony" legislation advocated by the Justice Department and FBI for the past few years, and recently passed by Congress. This proposed federal law would force all communications service providers to install facilities making it easy for government agents to perform digital wiretaps, just in case they come up with a properly authorized wiretapping order. The proposed law in its original form would have treated online systems precisely the same as telephone companies—as potential points of surveillance, always ready to help law enforcement in its desire to eavesdrop. This is a direct result of the similarity of online services to telephone services, both in structure and as carriers of a large volume of messages and other transmissions. Luckily, online systems were relieved of the wiretap-readiness requirements at the last minute, but further attempts by law enforcement to co-opt their position in the communications stream for surveillance purposes may arise in the future.

This question of responsibility for damaging or illegal materials is explored more fully in the chapters on injurious materials and criminal laws.

Online System as Distributor

Another major function of online systems is to transmit electronic mail, computer files, and other information between users. Materials commonly found on, or transmitted through, online systems include computer programs as well as text, database, graphic image, and sound files. Some of these materials are found only on a single system, while others are spread across a number of systems around the country or even the world. The transmissions can range from real time "chat"—the online text equivalent of a widespread telephone party line—to users uploading and downloading computer files, maintained for this purpose in file library areas on the system. In the case of uploading and downloading, as well as e-mail between users, the concept of "transmission" gets a little stretched, because there may be a lag of days, weeks, or even months between one user sending the materials and the other user receiving them.

Online systems usually transmit materials sent by system users to other users unchanged, in contrast to the editorial changes they often make in publicly posted materials in their capacity as publishers as described earlier. Much of the material found on bulletin boards is not actually read or used until after callers download it into their own computers. Thus, an online system does not express its own "voice" through the e-mail and files it carries. Rather, it disseminates the expressive voices of those who created the materials.

Because system operators rarely interfere with the contents of most files and e-mail, and because the creators of many files and messages send them to many online systems around the country, online systems act more like local "distributors" of such materials than publishers. As a distributor, an online system resembles such older operations as magazine distributors, bookstores, libraries, postal services, and common carriers (such as telephone and cable companies).

Unfortunately, each of these analogies breaks down somewhere: the magazine distributor model works best when we consider online file distribution operations, while a postal service model may work best when we look at systems carrying e-mail. Note that even when online systems act as distributors, the materials they carry could still be considered "published"—for example, a newslet-

The Online System as Magazine Distributor

Consider businesses that distribute newspapers and magazines. The people working for these businesses do not create the magazines, nor do they read them, except perhaps on their lunch hour. Their job is to move them in batches, keeping printed words and images moving from publishers' presses to the newsstand for public consumption. Magazines in transit are often shrink-wrapped and boxed, and cannot be reviewed without stopping the flow of work. The basic tools in this trade are truck, warehouse, and forklift.

System operators prefer keyboards and mice, but in many ways their activities are analogous to those of distributors. The daily routine can include many mundane chores such as eliminating duplicate files, ironing out computer system problems, responding to all kinds of user inquiries, comments, and complaints, and sifting through great batches of messages and files for various purposes, with the assistance of automating software. The first priority is to keep the system running efficiently so messages, files, and information flow properly between the system and its users. Consequently, and perhaps to the surprise of some users, system operators often don't have time to read many of the fascinating discussions on their own systems.

The courts have long recognized that distributors of print magazines and newspapers are not in the publishing or speaking business, but the delivery business. They also recognize that in that delivery role, distributors have strong First Amendment protection from burdensome laws and regulations. Freedom of speech is meaningless unless those who distribute speech are allowed to bring it to the public without undue government interference. Thus, magazine distributors are not held responsible for the contents of the magazines they deliver, unless they are actually aware of those contents. Online system operators want and deserve the same kind of privileged treatment for distributors of electronic speech. The first case addressing this issue, *Cubby v. CompuServe* (discussed at length in the text), correctly recognized that online systems perform the kind of speech distribution that invokes the protections of the First Amendment. It remains to be seen how strongly future cases will support this approach, such as the $200 million libel suit against Prodigy, pending in New York as this book goes to press.

ter distributed through private file uploads or downloads, or perhaps through an Internet mailing list. The difference is that the distributed materials are published by their creators, not by the online system.

When an online system acts like a distributor instead of a publisher, it is less responsible for the materials it distributes, for two reasons.

First, the system operators of online systems in their role as distributors of files, e-mail, or other user messages do not review the contents of the distributed materials. In effect, the online system only provides "shelf space" and mail boxes to its users; users place their files on virtual shelves and their e-mail in virtual mail boxes, and other users dial in and pick them up at will. Since the operator is not aware of the contents of these materials, if any of the materials are illegal he or she would not know it. This makes it very difficult to find a system operator responsible under laws that require knowing distribution of illegal materials. This factor makes a great deal of difference under the criminal laws, and somewhat less difference under some of the civil laws, such as copyright.

The second reason online systems as distributors should have reduced responsibility is that they serve a valuable First Amendment function in acting as clearinghouses of information uploaded by their callers. They crucially promote the First Amendment goal of free expression of diverse viewpoints. There are 60,000 or more privately run online systems, and many thousands more university and institutional systems, each with its own point(s) of view, as well as the far greater number of individuals who use those online systems to distribute their own speech and viewpoints to others. How many voices are being electronically extended via online systems? Probably a significant portion of the estimated 30 or more million people who are online.

If system operators were held highly responsible for the possible illegality of users' materials flowing through their systems, then online systems' valuable function of distributing the speech of others would be greatly reduced. The movement of speech through and between online systems would be vastly slowed down, as each file and piece of e-mail is checked for copyright infringement, trademark infringement, invasion of privacy, defamation, or any of a hundred other possible kinds of illegality or danger. The overall volume of user speech going through online systems would also be reduced. Finally, with so much energy being expended to make sure no system user is misbehaving, system operators would have far less resources for expanding socially valuable publishing and distribution operations.

Many system operators facing a high risk of liability for their users' materials would just drop the distribution function altogether from their online systems. Otherwise, they face a Hobson's choice: either waste vast amounts of time and effort combing through massive quantities of computer files, or face potential lawsuits and damage awards based on the unknown illegal acts of any one of hundreds or thousands of users who might choose to commit a crime on the system. In turn, people using online systems for distributing their speech would be suddenly cut off or frustrated, as system operators close down or tightly monitor their online systems for fear of being held responsible for the acts of their users. Others would be similarly cut off from exploring this channel of speech distribution in the future. These are the "chilling effects" of imposing too much responsibility on system operators for distributing the materials of others, effects often forbidden under the First Amendment.

These considerations mean there must be a limit on system operator responsibility for distributed files and e-mail, if online distribution of user materials is to thrive as a valuable First Amendment activity. The limit is conceptually simple: online distributors cannot be burdened with legal responsibility so great that either the flow of speech through online systems is substantially restricted, or online systems with distribution functions cannot be profitably operated. This is not a new legal concept: it was recognized years ago by our highest federal courts in cases involving bookstores and magazine distributors.

In 1990, the case of *Cubby v. CompuServe* provided the first federal ruling on the First Amendment rights of distributor online systems. It upheld the principle discussed above, stating that online systems that merely distribute others' materials are not absolutely responsible for those materials.

The Online System as Bookstore

When we go into a bookstore, we are faced with rows of books neatly organized according to author, subject, and title. Each book is a package of information or entertainment to take home for a price and peruse at our leisure. Books also have a certain cachet. They are the realm of fine literature and authoritative reference works. Even trashy novels are often heard to be "better than the film" as the lights go back on in movie theaters. Books are celebrated in classroom and scholar's study as the prime agents of education in the Western world, a status dating back to the last (or first) enormous media revolution—the development of the printing press.

In attempting to describe the place of online services as part of today's computer network revolution, it is natural to reach to the book metaphor as symbol and vehicle of the last glorious advance in distributing information on a previously unimagined scale. There is some validity to the model. Much of the file traffic on online systems consists of text files, which can be considered the electronic analogue to printed books. While most of the texts are still plain, relatively unformatted ASCII, more booklike presentations are being introduced all the time. Sorting through text files can be much like skimming the spines in a row of books. Downloading a text file for later reading can be like taking a book home from the store, especially if the online service charges for the download in some form. Some providers take the book metaphor very literally. There are a growing number of actual books online in electronic text form, and a growing number of online services referring to themselves as electronic bookstores.

There are already clear limits to the metaphor. At the moment, nonlinear multimedia and hypertext works are emerging as the powerful new forms for packaging text and other information on the net, instead of the linear format of traditional books. While bookstores are the final distribution point for physical books to reach their readers, those seeking a given text online might be able to pick it up equally easily at various points in the distribution chain, including directly from the author if he or she so wishes. An online bookstore, then, cannot be just a last-stop distribution point that charges users for downloading files. To justify its price, it must provide other benefits and services to shoppers—a comprehensive, easily search-able assortment of titles, or an exclusive source for certain titles—and those benefits must clearly outweigh those provided at online "libraries," which will offer their texts for free or at very low cost. Finally, there is an ineffable quality to books that some say does not translate to the digital text: you "can't curl up in bed and read a computer screen." Today, anyway.

The bookstore analogy is a good one legally for those who run online services. Bookstores are not highly responsible for the contents of the books they sell, just as magazine distributors, discussed earlier, are not.

Their business is to order, stock, and sell books, not edit or review their content. Likewise, online services distributing text files often have no time or interest in reading through them all. Their role is to procure the texts from a variety of sources, assemble them attractively and usefully for customer browsing, and let the customers have them for a charge. As described in the text, in the *Cubby v. CompuServe* case, the federal court dismissed a defamation case against online service CompuServe in part because, like a bookstore, CompuServe only stocked the offending newsletter, it did not take responsibility for what the newsletter contained.

Will this legal approach last if online "bookstores" branch out from merely offering digital texts for sale, to offering text-related information services useful to customers? Actually, if those services are helpful to customers, they may justify stronger legal protection of online bookstores even as the analogy breaks down, because these services would be doing even more than physical bookstores to facilitate the productive distribution of speech and publishing throughout society. On the other hand, the erosion of the "last-distribution-point" status of bookstores in their online form may make some of them look more like publishers than in the past. These services may end up being held more highly responsible for the contents of an illegal text, depending on how close they are to the source of the text—for instance, if an online bookstore has an exclusive distribution right for the text in question ("illegal" here would mean anything from copyright infringement to obscenity to defamation).

The case arose when the publisher of an electronic newsletter sued a rival newsletter for making supposedly defamatory statements. The publisher added the CompuServe Information Service (a large online service) as a defendant because it made the offending newsletter available to online callers. CompuServe itself was not the editor of the defendant newsletter. It was published by a different company and made available through a subcontract arrangement with one of CompuServe's forum managers, itself an independent contractor to CompuServe.

The federal trial court in Manhattan held that under these circumstances, CompuServe was merely a "distributor" of the newsletter. It was not responsible for the contents of the newsletter, any more than a bookstore is responsible for the contents of every book on its shelves. The court reasoned that if CompuServe was held liable in this case, then it would be forced to review all messages and files passing through its system to avoid legal problems. This would be an intolerable burden on CompuServe as a distributor of others' protected First Amendment speech.

The reasoning in the *CompuServe* case applies to all online systems, great and small, that perform the distributor role. It is a great start toward recognition of the protected status of online systems as distributors of others' speech, though admittedly there is a long stretch of road to travel before this protected status is generally acknowledged.

So far we've discussed the online system as a pure distributor of others' speech. However, the world is imperfect. Few online systems perform a pure speech distribution function. Therefore, general rules are necessarily vague. The exact First Amendment status of each system can only be determined by looking at how that particular system operates.

Music Publishers Rally Against CompuServe

Just when online services drew a collective sigh of relief from the *Cubby v. CompuServe* decision, another case raising similar issues hit the courts in 1993—*Frank Music v. CompuServe*. About 140 music publishers sued CompuServe for copyright infringement, based on user transmissions of music files through CompuServe special interest forums. The federal complaint singled out the Righteous Brothers' "Unchained Melody" as heavily infringed, following its renewed popularity from the hit film *Ghost*. The suit was organized by Harry Fox Agency, a New York City-based organization that handles most of the licensing of music rights for records, television, and films in the U.S.

The music publishers seek an order both moving the offending files offline, and for substantial monetary damages from CompuServe. Their position is that copyright law makes CompuServe responsible for all files on the system. If those files are infringing, CompuServe must pay. There is an interesting, and very common, leap of logic here. The files in question were not placed on the system by CompuServe, but by its users. And they were not downloaded by CompuServe, but by other users. So if there was infringement, the most direct infringers were the

users, not CompuServe, whose role was to hold the files transmitted between users.

We can easily understand why the publishers would sue CompuServe because it has the "deep pockets" here. But why didn't they sue the individual users who sent and received the infringing files? Most likely because the publishers want to establish a legal rule that CompuServe, and all other online services, have to pay copyright owners for the infringing activities of service users. This would make online copyright enforcement as easy as "one-stop shopping." This approach is understandable for the music publishers, but does its convenience justify holding online services responsible for the accumulated sins of everyone using online services?

As in the *Cubby* case, CompuServe's most powerful defense is the First Amendment guarantee of freedom of speech. In *Cubby*, it meant CompuServe was not responsible for an undetected defamation on its system. Holding otherwise would have caused all online systems to monitor messages closely for defamatory statements, and chilled the free flow of speech through the systems. In *Frank Music*, if CompuServe does not receive a similar judicial shield from the responsibility of paying for all infringements, then all online systems will be forced to comb through every file for copyright infringement, another speech-chilling effect. The music publishers deny this, asserting copyright law permits holding even "innocent infringers" responsible. In their view, the First Amendment need to avoid the chilling effect should have no bearing on copyright enforcement.

The publishers' position fits neatly into a larger pattern of shortsightedness. Every person or company with a legal beef against an online service will say that their claim—

whether for contract, obscenity, unfair competition, trademark infringement, product liability, or a hundred other kinds of claims—does not permit a court to consider the "chilling effect" on other online systems if the claim is enforced. However, the First Amendment need to avoid chilling the free flow of speech arises *every time* a legal claim against an online service would lead them to slow down legitimate message traffic simply to avoid potential liability for unknown illegal materials. And given the great degree of respect accorded the First Amendment by the Supreme Court, it is unlikely that the *Frank Music* claim, or any other claim that online services should closely monitor messages, will escape the question of whether the claim dangerously curtails online speech.

For example, there are many system operators who actively fight the spread of computer viruses through their systems. Such operators today typically use automated virus-scanning programs to check every program file uploaded to their systems before making it available to other users. The fact that many operators routinely check for viruses suggests it may not be too demanding to legally require that all operators do the same before making files available for download. But slow down a second . . . In fact, this responsibility would not make sense for all system operators. Some systems permit transmission of files that cannot be executed on the computer system they are moving through (such as DOS-based systems permitting transmission of program files that can run only on the Next or Amiga operating systems). If the system operators cannot run virus-checking programs for these files, should they be held absolutely responsible for hidden viruses anyway? The likely result is that such system operators would simply stop letting their users transmit any file that could not be checked for viruses. Or will the First Amendment step in to permit system operators to transmit such files without liability for unknown viruses, because their assistance in distributing such files is so valuable to society that we cannot afford to squelch them through too heavy a legal burden? The jury has not yet been treated to this question.

Let's consider those system operators who already expend at least the minimal time and effort with each file necessary to check for viruses. There is another danger, the "slippery slope" phenomenon. If system operators can afford to slow down their transmissions to check for viruses, then can't they go just a little further, and see if there are other legal problems with the files? The eventual result of this "little bit more" logic could be that if system operators take on any responsibility at all to monitor the transmissions through their systems, they could find themselves held legally responsible for everything they should have noticed during those monitoring efforts. We can expect to see this argument in the future from those who are injured somehow by an online transmission, and seek at any cost to hold the system operator responsible whether or not he or she had anything to do with it. Hopefully, the courts will decline the invitation to ride down the slippery slope, helping system operators to develop coherent monitoring schemes which they can rely on to keep them safe enough from lawsuits to continue running their systems.

With only the single case described above directly addressing this area of online law, we cannot draw "bright lines" of proper system operator behavior for the moment. Those system operators who wish to be prudent in handling distribution of files and e-mail on their online systems should consider the following framework:

- A system operator is not responsible for the legality of every file or piece of e-mail passing between users of the system. Users are primarily responsible for their own materials. However, the system operator should at least monitor system activity as a whole.

- If the system operator comes across any unusual activities involving transmitted materials, he or she should follow up until either satisfied that nothing illegal is occurring, or a problem is found.

- If the system operator sees user activity that may be criminal, or may violate the rights of others, he or she should do whatever is necessary in the situation: confront the suspected troublemaker, lock him or her out of the system, and so on.

- If the system operator believes one or more users are involved in a crime, he or she should consider contacting the police. But before doing so, the system operator should take steps to make sure the police do not accidentally seize the system as evidence, or as a tool of the crime.

These points are more fully explored in the chapters on injurious materials, search and seizure, and criminal laws.

Shared Public Message Networks

These are a very important part of online activities. Such networks include Usenet (a set of discussions carried on the Internet), Internet Relay Chat (a real-time equivalent to Usenet), Fidonet, RIME, ILINK, and a host of others. They are the closest thing we have today to an online "public street," where you might bump into anybody from a gas station attendant to a Zen master, and where manners are sometimes at a minimum.

On the Internet it is easy to view each online system as a roadside stop of one sort or another.

Public message networks are organized very much like the public message area in a single online system. They are set up according to separate general interest categories (e.g., "conferences," "forums," or "newsgroups"), subjects within those categories (e.g., "subjects," "topics," or "threads"), and finally individual messages or postings within each subject, arranged chronologically and also according to the earlier messages to which they respond. These conferences typically are carried by many online systems regionally, around the country, or even around the world.

In the case of Usenet many of the member systems, called "nodes," do not have local online discussion areas beyond their involvement in Usenet. By contrast, most Fidonet nodes have "BBS" areas for their own callers, and "Fidonet" areas for participating in the international Fidonet network. These networks typically are not centralized. Messages originating in one node may spread to others by being sent up to higher-level distribution nodes, then across to other distribution nodes, and back down to lower-level individual nodes. Depending on the transmission method and frequency, messages sent into shared public message systems may show up on neighboring systems immediately, or on others as much as a day or two later.

Shared public message networks somewhat resemble both the online publishing and the online distribution examples discussed earlier. They are like online publishing where running discussions

Computer Networks as Public Streets

The early Internet was a benign scientific research network, a veritable Athens where scholars could walk with their peers and disciples down beaten paths of the communal mind. In recent years, the buzzing needs of the rest of society and commerce have barreled onto the Internet. They carved out and paved great data highways serving the needs of millions, with even more massive construction of the Information Superhighway supposedly on the way. Evolving in parallel, though on a smaller scale, are the corporate-wide area networks and electronic data interchange networks, and public conferences and e-mail systems like Fidonet and RIME, shared by thousand of computer bulletin boards.

Streets are used for going places. The data paths of the various networks certainly fill this role. On the Internet it is easy to view each online system as a roadside stop of one sort or another. A system specializing in intellectual discussions can be a cafe; another selling CDs by online order is like a record store; a large, general-purpose service is like a shopping mall or even a small town; a customer support system is like a repair shop or sales floor; and so on. Some of the new graphical interfaces for online users, such as Magic Cap, Imagination Network, and e-

World, are based on this metaphor, showing users visual streets and landmarks as a way to help them get around online.

Does the streetlike nature of the net have legal implications? Indeed it does. Data paths on the Internet enabling millions of users to get to online systems look like public thoroughfares. Not surprisingly, the federal and state governments are investigating whether the needs of society as a whole are served by those thoroughfares, and whether special regulations of the data pathways will be necessary to protect those needs. For example, the federal government is looking into a requirement that public online systems provide a certain amount of free or very cheap access to the poor, so they do not fall further behind as "information have-nots" in this increasingly wired-up world. Another example: a government advisory group recently recommended a change to the copyright laws, confirming that U.S. copyright owners have the right to prevent their own works from being imported into the U.S. against their wishes through the networks. How would such a copyright rule be enforced? By making all international data transmissions pass through customs inspections?

Streets are also destinations in themselves, especially for those to whom getting there is half the fun. Dense urban environments like Manhattan or San Francisco have streets full of invigorating spectacle and the swirl of life. This side of our physical streets is also reflected online in places like Usenet, the enormous shared discussion space on the Internet. Usenet is very much a crowded public street. There are all kinds of activities, and anyone can play because there is no price of entry (beyond the Internet's access cost, which is dropping all the time).

Usenet and other network environments, like the urban sidewalks they resemble, are legally a kind of loosely moderated anarchy. In physical cities and streets, police officers walk the beat and prowl in squad cars. Their presence keeps trouble from erupting most of the time. The cops can't be everywhere, though. When they're not around every sort of mayhem can take place, from swindling to murder. Similarly, net cop-equivalents such as Usenet moderators, systems security administrators, and real law enforcement agents online seem capable of keeping a semblance of social order on the nets most of the time. At any moment, though, the networks can be overrun by rampant infringements, obnoxious messages, or computer viruses.

This may well be the ongoing reality of the net as Street: a place of adventure and unpredictable events. There is no saying it will ever again be the benign environment of the early Internet users. For some, this will keep the net more entertaining than television. For others, it will make the net a place to observe only in transit to safe online havens, like those who drive through strange neighborhoods with their windows rolled up.

among users are presented publicly to all users on the various network nodes for viewing and participation, and there is strong "editorial" control. Bulletin board conferences or newsgroups often have "moderators" with certain powers over the conduct of the group discussions. Moderators can exercise a fairly firm hand if they wish, banning callers or even entire BBSs or nodes from future participation for failing to observe the rules.

Such moderator control, however, is not as strong as the control a system operator can exercise over his or her own system. This is because a shared public conference does not exist on a single centralized system run by the moderator. It is supported instead by all the member nodes. The moderator's only control point is from his or her own place within the larger network. A user can send a message into the network that may remain for days or weeks before the moderator can successfully eradicate it, though technical means of eradicating messages more quickly are becoming available, especially on the Internet. An exception is moderated newsgroups on Usenet, which can be completely controlled: if you want to get a message into such a newsgroup you must send it directly to the moderator, who alone decides whether or not to forward the message into the newsgroup itself.

Public message networks also resemble distributors of files and e-mail (in fact, most message networks now carry binary files as well as public messages). Each node in the network passively carries all the message traffic from other nodes in the conferences or newsgroups its operator chooses to carry. Messages sent into the network by callers normally are sent to the rest of the network without intervention by the local node operator. The nodes in a shared network all carry the same set of messages for the same conferences, except for differences due to transmission delays, and most permit their own callers to contribute to those message bases.

Some public message groups—for example, many of the "alt." newsgroups in Usenet—have no moderators. In these cases, there is no editorial control for the message group as a whole. It is a public discussion, but it is not published by anyone in particular, only distributed through the local nodes on the network.

So what is the legal responsibility of a local node operator for the messages on the shared network? The node operator has no direct control over the composition of the message traffic, so he or she does not (and cannot) perform a publishing function. Conceivably, an activist local operator can selectively delete disliked messages he or she receives from the network, but this will quickly garble the discussions between local users and the rest of the network. The main control exercisable by a node operator is broader: selecting the conferences or newsgroups carried. If the system operator does not like enough of the messages found in a given conference, he or she can drop the whole conference from the node.

The node operator's legal responsibility thus resembles that of the "hands off" or self-styled "First Amendment" sysops described earlier. By helping distribute public discussions on the networks, and by providing a local entry point for their callers to participate in those discussions, node operators perform a valuable First Amendment speech-distribution function. At the same time, they have some responsibility for the contents of the conferences.

This is where the lack of local editorial control at the node becomes important. It may not be possible or worthwhile for a local node operator to delete or edit individual messages on the conference as he or she receives them from the network. The operator may only have the option of carrying or dropping an entire conference. If a conference very rarely contains legally questionable materials, then the node operator should have little exposure to liability for an individual message. But if a conference frequently or regularly contains illegal materials, at some point the node operator may have a duty to drop the conference, or face legal problems.

So the node operator's general responsibilities would be as follows.

- The node operator is a carrier of shared network communications. His or her role is to make those communications available to callers, and transmit caller postings into the shared conferences.

- In conferences where illegal or damaging postings are rare, the node operator is not responsible for reviewing every posting. He also does not need to take steps to eliminate messages he does review or hear about unless they are clearly illegal or dangerous.

- In conferences where illegal or damaging materials are frequently found, the node operator who wants to avoid legal problems should discontinue carrying the conference. The node operator should be considered to be aware of the illegality of messages on conferences where many of the messages are illegal.

What is the responsibility of the person who moderates a conference spread across hundreds or thousands of nodes? It depends largely on the control the moderator wields. Moderators who attempt to closely regulate caller etiquette and edit materials they deem offensive are acting like full-fledged publishers. They could be held liable for illegal or injurious materials that are permitted to remain in their conferences, subject to the kind of First Amendment protection accorded to print publishers. Those who are less controlling will likely face correspondingly lower levels of liability, though we cannot expect the law to ratchet down to the precise level of liability appropriate to the exact level of control wielded by each moderator.

The legal risks do not fall to zero for any moderated conference. Even where the moderator is an entirely uncompensated volunteer on a university-

> **Moderators who attempt to closely regulate caller etiquette and edit materials they deem offensive are acting like full-fledged publishers.**

owned node, taking on the moderator role means he or she also takes on some measure of responsibility regarding illegal or damaging materials in the conference.

So generally, moderators' responsibilities are as follows.

- A moderator's legal responsibility for the messages in the conferences depends on how much control he or she wields over the conference. The more control, the greater the responsibility.

- The moderator will probably not be responsible for illegal or damaging materials that remain posted on his conference during the time it takes to eliminate them from the conference, even if it takes a few days due to the way messages are distributed.

- If a moderator finds illegal or damaging materials consistently coming from certain callers or nodes, then the moderator should block them from the conference, if possible. The moderator can be considered to be aware of the illegality of messages on conferences where many of the messages are illegal.

Growing Pains Online and Off

If all legal authorities appreciated the contour of operators' rights and government limits as we have described it, system operators and users would be operating today with a breathtaking level of freedom. The reality is that in our society, many in positions of power do not yet understand the broad First Amendment protection to which users and operators are entitled. Society is still learning about online systems and their value as a communications medium. Until the First Amendment importance of online activities is legitimized by a number of court holdings, skeptics will question whether First Amendment protection is justified. Society is going through growing pains complementing the growth of online systems. It appears some of that pain will be shared by operators and users of those systems.

Unfortunately, those who do not appreciate the full reach of First Amendment protection include a fair number of law enforcement agents and officials. In fact, many such agents, especially those who may be "computerphobic" to begin with, are barely familiar with online systems, large or small.

Small Online Systems Don't Get Much Respect

Based on various incidents (discussed in Chapter 7, "Searches and Seizures"), people in law enforcement sometimes view online systems, especially smaller ones, as merely a bunch of machines. They might seize the system as if it was a bloody knife if suspected of being used in foul play, or tax it like a store or office when the state seeks new revenue sources. Others see smaller systems in a more romantic vein, inhabiting the same dark world as computer criminals who rip off telephone companies and raid military computers.

> **The opportunity for intimate or thoughtful discussions with total strangers is one of the big attractions of bulletin boards.**

This dramatic view can be fun when playing cops and robbers, but the truth is that online systems are an emerging everyday communications medium. Online systems perform many different roles. Some are social meeting places, like an inn, salon, or bar. Others provide technical expertise or news and information in specialized areas. A great many others exist largely for swapping software and other files. In

The Online System as Local Bar

The popular TV show "Cheers" portrayed a neighborhood bar full of wacky characters who commiserated together and got on each others' nerves. A warm family of strangers passing the time and having a few laughs and beers. This kind of atmosphere is no fantasy online; it is available readily in many computer bulletin boards around the world. Indeed, the opportunity for intimate or thoughtful discussions with total strangers is one of the big attractions of bulletin boards. It is the sole reason that a lot of system operators are in the business. Run your own bar without selling or drinking any liquor, though you still may have to bounce the occasional rowdy.

This very human engagement with computers and telecommunications is startling to some people. Those who have not yet ventured online may find it hard to believe that people really relate to each other there. Then, there's the conversion experience: a newbie wanders into some chat area on an online service, or perhaps a bulletin board discussion of his or her favorite old TV show, and they're hooked. A whole new social dimension opens up, a whole new way of relating to people. There's a standard backlash, too: the claim that you don't find flesh and blood people online, just thin streams of misunderstood text and massive veils of private fantasy. Sssshhhh, don't burst the bubble—this dream is too much fun . . . .

Legally, the neighborhood bar metaphor demonstrates, differently from the distributor metaphor, that the "speech" in many online systems is the speech of users, not of the system operator. If a bar patron spouts slanderous falsehoods about his boss, it's obvious the words are his, not the bar owner's. If another customer keeps stolen software under his trenchcoat and sells it in the back room outside the barkeep's notice, that activity is the software seller's alone, and cannot imaginably be blamed on the owner of the bar. The naughty things users might do online are perfectly analogous, yet in the online context there is a continual effort to make the system operator, the online bartender, liable. In part, this is a temporary failure of visualization. As more people become more comfortable with being online, its nature as a friendly social meeting place will become increasingly obvious. System operators may then be able to gratefully recede to their proper place as managers of the partying throngs, rather than being called upon to answer for the sins of their customers.

addition, a sizable and growing number of online systems are becoming integrated into the in-house operations of large and small businesses, as in-house bulletin boards, or extensions of internal local area networks or groupware systems.

Only a small minority of online systems operate as "pirate boards" for swapping stolen software and computer access codes, spreading viruses, and so on. When these criminal boards are seized and shut down by the authorities, everyone benefits. Unfortunately, when seizures of criminal boards make the news, far greater numbers of legitimate online systems may be tarred with the same brush by reporters or defense attorneys who should know better. It is important for the robust development of online systems to fight this misimpression, making it clear that those who attempt to run clean, above-board systems are an entirely different breed from those who run pirate systems.

Larger online systems, such as corporate systems and the "Big 3" of CompuServe, America Online, and Prodigy, do not face quite the same problems. When police chase after a pedophile, infringer, system cracker, or other troublemaker online, they often handle it differently according to the size of the system. When a large system is involved, police work with the system staff to identify and apprehend troublemakers, but leave the business untouched. For small systems, the police may choose to grab the computers used to run the system, instantly shutting it down altogether, and arrest or search the owner of the system. The different treatment is entirely due to police perception of the respective systems. Larger systems appear (and are) institutional, and are presumed not to be involved in criminal activities just because some system users might be criminal. Small systems and their owners, on the other hand, are readily identified with any troublemakers on the system; if there is any trouble on the small system, the owner is almost automatically a suspect. It's not right, but that's often how it works today.

This practical principle carries right over to in-house systems and LANs: systems used by larger businesses and organizations will be respected, while those used by smaller businesses could be seized. For example, when MIT's on-campus computer system was misused by student David LaMacchia to run a software piracy operation, or when it was discovered that Lawrence Livermore Laboratories' in-house system was being used to house a porn image collection, the individuals who performed these acts were investigated and prosecuted, and the computer systems were left unscathed. In contrast, when federal agents discovered that a youthful phone hacker they were pursuing had a day job as system operator for the online system for Steve Jackson Games (as discussed at length later in this book), they wasted no time seizing the entire system and nearly wrecking the small business that depended on it. In their misguided opinion, the small business online system was inseparable from the off-hours hacker exploits of one of the business' employees.

How Do We Fix It?

How do we increase education about online systems? How do we help law enforcement agents and others understand that online systems are full-fledged, fully protected First Amendment enterprises, with no strings attached?

Some major educational efforts are now underway. Perhaps the most conspicuous are those of the Electronic Frontier Foundation, founded in 1990 to protect privacy rights, freedom of the press, and freedom from unreasonable searches and seizure in the world of electronic communications. EFF's major effort to date was its support of the lawsuit by Steve Jackson Games against the U.S. government, for wrongfully seizing that company's customer support bulletin board. The suit successfully established that the government violated free press rights and user privacy rights in doing so, and is discussed at length in a later chapter. The EFF's staff also writes extensively, both online and in print, and appears frequently in public speaking engagements across the country. The example of the EFF spawned a number of local like-minded groups: EFF Austin, in Austin, Texas; the Society for Electronic Access (SEA) in New York City; and This!Group in San Francisco. A number of international groups were likewise inspired by EFF's example.

Speaking of Education . . .

How are schools and universities doing at protecting our First Amendment freedoms online? Many do just fine, but there are some notable exceptions. One class of school censorship fairly common these days is the exclusion of certain newsgroups from campus Usenet feeds. Usually these are the "alt.sex" newsgroups, containing sexual materials. While some of these materials are arguably obscene (and thus not protected by the First Amendment), most aren't. Yet universities heavyhandedly cast them out with a flourish of self-righteous moral outrage.

Another notable occurrence is the University of Texas' barring of its student, Gregory Steshenko, from use of a student Internet account. Mr. Steshenko's sin was that he irritated and argued with a lot of people. One of his tricks that really annoyed others was contacting the employers of people he disagreed with on the net, trying to get them in trouble. Bending to a lot of pressure from Steshenko's online opponents, the university canned his account. In retaliation, he sued it for violating his First Amendment rights. As we go to press, the case is not resolved.

The theory of Steshenko's case is that university online systems are government-sup-ported. Unlike private online systems, they cannot simply banish users just because they don't like what the users are saying. But it's not a clear-cut case. Schools are not as tightly bound by the First Amendment as other government-supported operations, such as government agencies. The Supreme Court has held that a school could censor a school-funded student newspaper whenever it felt it was necessary for "pedagogical reasons." In other words, school officials were given broad authority to regulate school speech in their protective role as educators and guardians. This rule clearly carries over to online systems provided by the school. School officials remain tightly constrained against attempts to control privately funded student speech, such as privately published leaflets distributed in the halls. But this is a small consolation for students using online systems at universities, because the systems directly accessible by students are all school-run, and subject to pedagogically-driven control.

One result of the Supreme Court's position on school speech is that universities, instead of introducing students to the breathtaking freedom of speech and ideas one can find in the adult world, are permitted to use their stranglehold over campus communications to repress speech and influence student minds in any direction the local officials wish. Students finding themselves in such repressive regimes may have to go outside the university system, either contemporaneously or after they graduate, to private online systems to learn what true freedom of speech can be.

A powerful statement about the common failure to appreciate the point of the First Amendment in the modern age was the 1990 proposal by Lawrence Tribe, a leading Constitutional scholar, for a 27th (now, it would be 28th) amendment to the Constitution. Tribe's proposal, presented at the First Conference on Computers, Freedom and Privacy in San Francisco, would make it clear that all Constitutional protections, including those of freedom of the press, apply equally to all current and future communications media and technologies, including online systems.

Some argue that Tribe's proposed amendment has its heart in the right place, but we don't really need it. The broad language of the Constitution already protects free speech rights for all new media. If we press for a new amendment, it might look like an admission that online systems do not currently merit Constitutional protection.

However, the point of Tribe's proposal is not necessarily to obtain such an amendment, but to stimulate us all to discuss what the First Amendment means when we apply it to new communications technologies. His proposal has strong symbolic value: it clearly asserts that online systems and other new media are entitled to the full scope of protection already available to the traditional press under the U.S. Constitution. If society has trouble getting it clear that the new media are entitled to the same protections as newspapers and books, then maybe the Constitution itself needs to be amended so the point can no longer be argued.

In the end, system users and operators themselves will largely determine how the First Amendment applies to online systems through their own actions and attitudes. If an online system performs the valuable service of promoting public speech by its callers, it is doing its part to establish First Amendment treatment for all online systems and users in the U.S.

How do you operate as a "free speech" service or service user? It's mostly common sense. Treat the online system as a place for people to freely express their opinions, even highly unpopular opinions if that's your personal preference. Treat it as a gathering place for like-minded people (or different-minded people, as the case may be) to meet and exchange views. Take part in shared networks like Fidonet and Usenet; contribute your voice(s) to the rest of the networked world; receive the opinions of others on the nets.

Meanwhile, despite the uncertainties we face while society at large learns about online systems, we must keep our sense of perspective. The First Amendment does apply, today, to online systems. If government agents, and even news reporters, occasionally fail to see the First Amendment connection, that failure does not negate the connection. It only demonstrates how much our citizenry has to learn about its own rights in this electronic age. For a while, online systems may appear to be treated unfairly compared to newspapers, books, television, or films. However, as public understanding and reliance on online systems grows, their treatment should consistently be elevated to the same highly protected status as the other, more traditional press and speech media.

Structuring the Online System

A private system operator may freely structure the online service any way he or she wants. The opening screen, menu areas, user interface, file areas, message areas—there are no regulations for building online environments.

Such freedom may seem obvious to some, but it is really quite special. Consider other everyday living and working environments. You cannot maintain your car any old way, because it has to pass a state inspection. You cannot wire your home any way you want, because the wiring must conform to local electrical codes. In many neighborhoods, you can't build an extension to your home without a permit under the building code. If you open a bar with live entertainment and food, then your premises will have to be structured to satisfy the health code, fire safety regulations, building code, zoning, and liquor license requirements, among other things. Even a computer maker must pass FCC standards on radio emissions.

In contrast, an online system, in its role as a meeting place for its users, suffers few legal limits on its interior structure. The freedom resulting from this lack of regulation has provided a fertile ground for developing many types of online systems. To name just a few:

- General purpose messaging and file transfer systems.
- Conferencing systems devoted to group discussions.
- Special interest systems for users who share the same interests.
- Internal communication systems for businesses.
- Systems for making business and career contacts.
- Gateway and access provider systems, devoted to giving users access to other systems or networks.
- Systems to further political goals.
- Public information and educational systems.
- Customer and client support systems for businesses.

The variety of possible uses for online systems is one of the main reasons they are proving so attractive to a broad range of people with very different interests. Many more variations than those described above will certainly surface over time. Happily, the law today does not take away the vast variety and flexibility of online system setups.

Controlling User Speech: System Management, or "Censorship"?

Ralph Cramden of the old "Honeymooners" television show might enjoy running an online service, because the system operator is "king of the castle." Private system operators offering their services to the public can set up any rules they want on their systems. If users want to play by those rules, fine. If not, they can take their online explorations elsewhere. With many thousands of systems out there, the user can simply point his or her modem in another direction to find a comfortable online environment. We naturally expect all system operators to be sensitive to their callers' feelings. But part of the new online freedom is that ill-tempered grouches get to run online systems too.

Legally, private system operators are free to do what they want, provided they do not injure others. Users, meanwhile, can be barred from a system by the operator for any reason, or for no reason at all. Those who have started their own systems know this innately. They can set up the whole system and make

> **Users have no First Amendment rights whatsoever against system operators of privately operated systems.**

rules to fit their whims before a single user is invited in from the outside. Once users start showing up, the operator is not under any compulsion, legal or otherwise, to share power over the system with them. If the system operator wants to take the online system down entirely at any point, that's the operator's choice as well.

Every private system operator, then, starts out as a benevolent ruler. If he or she doesn't want to feel like a ruler, the operator can share power with other operators and with users. At any time, however, system operators can take back all power and control, unless they have made contracts with users preventing them from doing so. The unquestioned power of operators on their own systems has important consequences, not yet fully understood (or accepted) by many users in the online population. What are these consequences?

First, users have no First Amendment rights whatsoever against system operators of privately operated systems. None. Every time you hear a caller complain of being "censored" by a sysop who moved, altered, or deleted his message, it is no more than a figure of speech. Only the U.S. government is required to recognize First Amendment rights, and only U.S. government censorship is illegal (which naturally implies that public systems, operated in whole or part by the government, may indeed have to give users some First Amendment rights, as discussed in a later section).

A private system operator who is not acting on behalf of the U.S. government can freely suppress or eliminate any caller "speech" he or she wants without a legal problem. The system operator is similar to a newspaper or magazine editor in this regard. Editors can refuse to print any article submitted by their writers, for any reason or no reason, and writers have no First Amendment right to force the editors to do otherwise. Because of this, it's often wryly observed that "freedom of the press" really means "freedom of the owner of the press." This cliché applies fully to online systems. As the "owner of the press" (or as agent of the owner), the system operator or LAN administrator can permit or deny speech as he or she pleases.

Second, despite the progress we see on privacy rights in this country, users have only limited privacy rights on an online system. If the system operator makes no special rules on the subject, he or she has legal permission under the U.S. laws to look over the private e-mail of users on the system, regardless of their privacy rights. The law does step in eventually, to forbid the system operator from divulging user e-mail to anyone else. But the system operator can even override this law simply by making it known to users that there is no private e-mail on his or her system. Then, he or she can both look at e-mail, and show it to others without liability. (Privacy issues are explored more fully in Chapter 5.)

Third, a system operator's rulemaking power is more than just an excuse to run an online system according to whim (though that itself is important). It also allows system operators to adjust the amount of freedom and power they give to users, and the amount of legal risk they take on. For example, a system operator who wants users to enjoy total e-mail privacy and full uncensored speech rights on the system can give these things to users simply by making them part of the system rules. On the other hand, those using an online system to run a business may feel they have to limit their legal exposure sharply as a matter of simple commercial prudence. Thus, they may choose to permit little or no e-mail privacy and exercise broad discretion in moderating public discussions. To each his or her own.

Some system operators think of public discussion forums as their own living room, and users as their guests. If the user conducts himself in a civil manner and is considerate of others, he is permitted a lot of

> **Some system operators think of public discussion forums as their own living room, and users as their guests.**

latitude in his behavior. If he is inconsiderate or does damaging things, he will be invited to leave, just as if he was really in the system operator's living room and started hitting people or pouring beer on the furniture.

The system operator not only sets the rules initially, he or she can also change those rules at any time, and set different rules for different areas of the system. The system operator is limited only by what may have been agreed to with users in the user contract. Of course, a properly drawn user contract will point out that the system operator retains full power to change the system rules, perhaps with a week or two prior notice to callers for normal changes, and immediately for emergencies.

Some online systems do not have quite all of the rule-setting freedoms sketched out above. Corporate systems, for instance, are often an extension of the employer-employee workplace relationship. The system will be subject to the rules of that relationship, which may be found both in corporate policy manuals (which may or may not have a special section for online activities), and in the history of dealings between the employer and employees. In-house systems are also subject to state and federal laws on workplace privacy and other rights, which are constantly evolving as technology progresses.

Online systems with government involvement, either on the funding or operational side (such as an online system run by a public library, a school, a museum, a legislative agency, a regulatory agency, and so on), also face certain limits in their rule-setting behavior. Callers of such systems may indeed have strong rights to freedom of speech. Censorship may be forbidden on such systems with rare exceptions such as in matters of national security. In addition, depending on the exact nature of government involvement in the system in question, callers may have very strong privacy rights under federal and state statutes. Unauthorized system operator intrusion into caller privacy in this case might be illegal in the same sense as an illegal government wiretap on a telephone discussion.

These special-case limits on rule-setting behavior (which are discussed further in the following chapters) are the exception and not the norm. For private system operators, the sky is the limit in setting the rules of play on their systems.

So what exactly is real censorship? To put it bluntly, it is when the government shuts you up. This can be accomplished in a number of different ways:

1. Government control of message traffic on government-run online systems, as discussed above.

2. Illegal searches and seizures of online systems and their operators. This directly results in silencing not only the system operator, but more importantly, the collective discussions of all users of the system (we look at search and seizures in detail in a later chapter devoted to the subject).

3. Cutting off an individual's access to a state-operated communications service.

4. Prosecuting individuals for acts that may consist of no more than exercising their rights of free speech. Some feel this is the case with the government's ongoing investigation of Phil Zimmerman, father of the "Pretty Good Privacy" (PGP) program.

5. Singling out online services for taxation, which places a burden on businesses offering those services.

As you can see, there is no particular kind of government conduct that violates freedom of speech. Rather, a variety of different government actions can affect speech, all of which at least potentially raise First Amendment issues. This is precisely what was intended by the drafters of the Bill of Rights, when they phrased the First Amendment to read "Congress shall make no law abridging freedom of speech or of the press . . ." Any law, or the way the law is enforced, that might affect freedom of speech must withstand close scrutiny under the First Amendment.

So now we have cleanly divided the world into two regimes: privately operated systems versus government action. In private systems, user speech can be routinely restricted by the operator as a byproduct of operating the system; the government, however, must always tread carefully where laws or their enforcement might impair the free speech of U.S. citizens—users and system operators alike.

Is there a third situation, where a system might be privately operated, but still be prohibited by law from interfering with the speech of its users? Theoretically, there might be, if it turns out that an online system or group of systems becomes so all-encompassing that users no longer have a real choice of logging on elsewhere. In such a world, it would no longer be good enough to tell users they can always move on to an online system hospitable to their views, because there is no longer any choice. The system owners would effectively have entire control over a public resource, and laws could easily arise forcing them to give up at least some bandwidth to those whose views they would prefer not to carry. There is precedent for this in the regulation of television by the FCC, which imposes a variety of must-carry obligations on television providers. It also generally reviews their records of providing programming that serves a variety of diverse views before renewing licenses.

From this corner it does not appear such a scenario will unfold; we are more likely to find ourselves overrun with increasing numbers of online service providers, coming in through the cable and telephone wires, and through ground and satellite transmissions. As user choice increases, the option of fighting back with the modem or remote control becomes more effective, and user cries of "censorship" by private system operators will be heard less and taken less seriously.

Whether to Join a Network

In the last few years, virtually all online systems, except for the smallest hobby systems, have joined computer networks in at least a minimal fashion. Users these days expect to be able to send e-mail to others on remote systems, as a matter of course. Those running Novell systems in-house can hook up to the Internet and the large online services, and can obtain their own Internet domain names and e-mail addresses these days. Privately operated online systems have their choice of Fidonet, RIME, ILINK, and a host of other small system networks. Increasingly, there are gateways developing between all these networks, so that e-mail can be exchanged between callers of the different systems, with more advanced functions being made available in the very near future. Individual users also have the option of hooking up directly to the Internet through services specializing in providing such access.

> **For many system operators and users, network membership holds a greater attraction than the local service itself: the opportunity to be part of a worldwide online community.**

There are no state or federal laws regulating who gets to join a network, or what the network's rules should be. Each network has its own rules, to be sure, just as online systems have their own rules. But these rules are made up by each network and its members, not by any legislature or government agency.

In the case of the Internet, historically government-funded, there are questions about whether the First Amendment limits the scope of network rulemaking. But this is exceptional. As the Internet moves from being mostly government-funded to mostly privately funded, and as the other, privately developed networks of the world, such as Fidonet, grow larger and larger, most networks can have their rules entirely set by private agreement.

Thus today every system operator can choose whether his or her online system will join any networks, which ones it will join, and which networkservices it will carry. Online systems do not need to be involved in computer networks. For many system operators and users, though, network membership holds a greater attraction than the local service itself: the opportunity to be part of a worldwide online community.

Whether to Run an Online System for Profit

When *Syslaw* came out in 1988, there were two or three large online services, not all of them making money, and a bunch of hobbyist computer bulletin boards. Times have changed. In the past two or three years, our society has learned there is a lot of business opportunity on the "Information Superhighway." Large-scale business systems like CommerceNet and Ziff-Davis Interchange are making a splash. It seems that companies in nearly every industry are declaring themselves now to be in the "information business." They are projecting their in-house LANs into surrounding public networks, and are setting up their own online systems for private and public use. In the meantime, many computer bulletin boards and other small online systems have started becoming real moneymakers for their owners.

Hopefully, the operators of commercial online systems still have fun, though inevitably they adopt a more "bottom-line" business mentality. The growing realization that online systems can earn a system operator a living has attracted a lot of new people to the field. Is there a limit to the amount of business that can be brought into the online environment? At this time of expansion, we have not seen any.

There remains a large contingent of system operators who operate online systems for purposes other than profit or consumption. These include the civic and free systems growing up all over the country, often as part of some agenda to bring municipal or regional activities online. There are also increasing numbers of systems operated for idealistic and traditional nonprofit purposes, such as Peacenet. And there are the hobbyists, who may not be motivated by a sense of civics or lofty goals, but just want to run a system where they can hang out with fellow hobbyists online—discussing anything from model railroading to their favorite TV shows—or perhaps provide a service to their fellow hobbyists, like keeping score for the local rotisserie baseball league. These people work regular day jobs, and run online systems as part of their "personal" lives.

Fortunately, there is plenty of room for both types of operations today. The growth of the commercial online system does not require the death of the hobby computer bulletin board. All kinds of online operations have the same access to basic telephone services, and thus the same access to callers. Groups of like-minded system operators can and do band together to form all sorts of networks, creating broad regional, national, or international access for idealis-

> **The growth of the commercial online system does not require the death of the hobby computer bulletin board.**

tic and "hobby" systems that is just as extensive as that available for commercial systems.

Currently there are no laws favoring either commercial or non-commercial systems. This low price of admission should not be taken for granted. For one thing, it doesn't apply to much of the rest of the world. For example, consider another social meeting-place: the nightclub. Before a nightclub owner can even open his doors, he or she needs to get all the legally required licenses, and pay for all of the license fees, construction work, inspections, legal fees, and so on. Only the very rich, those willing to go deeply into debt, or those fronting for well-heeled investors can afford all of the legalities. There is little room in the nightclub field for those who are not independently wealthy or exceptionally capable and motivated in business.

In contrast, a small online system can be started for a few hundred dollars today—the cost of a computer and modem (there are free bulletin board software packages). There are no forms to fill out; just set up shop and go online. You may not have all the files or services of a mega-system, but your own system may be far more interesting in its own way.

There is a dark spot on the horizon, which has been moving closer recently. The telephone companies have been pushing the government hard to deregulate their activities, and they're starting to see some results. If they manage to cut down on existing regulations, we may start to see pricing schemes for telephone service which could have the effect of pricing certain kinds of online systems out of existence. The prospect of discriminatory pricing seems especially likely when we consider the oft-heard complaint by telephone companies that they are forced to keep their business rates artificially high to subsidize the low residential telephone rates required by existing legal rules. If the chains of regulation come off, we should expect to see the telephone companies charge the most attractive rates to those companies whose business they covet or want to keep, and the worst and highest rates to captive customers, and possibly to those businesses they consider to be their competition.

We are also starting to see strong stirrings among some politicians to regulate online systems. Some regulatory agendas come from seemingly good intentions, such as proposals to make online systems set aside some of their capacity for public access, or to regulate online systems to cut down on online porn. However, such laws could strongly restrict and burden one's ability to operate an online system, especially a hobby or low-margin system.

But for now, there is little conflict between the commercial and public spheres. It's a big networked world, getting bigger all the time, and it still has plenty of room for all comers to do what they like.

The Freedom to Continue or Quit

The greatest freedom of all is the freedom to start up and take down your own online system. Every day, it is the system operator's affirmative decision to either keep the system running or call it a day and move on to other things in life. Every day, any user of online systems can swear off them forever, and leave cyberspace for the physical world of our ancestors.

For those who run a successful online system, it may not be so easy to walk away. A local online community may depend vitally on the system operator's ministrations at the keyboard. The primary constraints on the choice to continue or quit are moral and emotional, however, and not legal. If the system operator just has to quit, it may make more sense to do so by handing the reins over to another willing soul, rather than just shutting down the system.

> **The greatest freedom of all is the freedom to start up and take down your own online system.**

Significant legal obligations could arise when shutting down a pay system. If you hold significant prepayments from callers for future access, those callers should get the unused portion of their money back. Freedom to go out of business does not mean freedom to take other people's money with you. Likewise, if you made deals with other businesses, such as for advertising on your system, or "renting out" space on your system to provide their own services, you may have a set of obligations that you need to unwind properly before you can finally lay the system to rest.

Contracts and Commercial Arrangements

At the core of nearly every relationship between online systems and users lies a contract. Some may reject this view as too legalistic. However, online systems are filled with expectations and risks, for owners and users alike. We use contracts to organize what each side expects, and to settle in advance the problems that people and businesses may face online.

What do people expect from others online? The user of a system expects various services: electronic mail, public conference areas, file uploads and downloads, chat features. The list goes on. The system provider, likewise, expects certain things from users: don't abuse other users, don't try to crash the system, do follow system rules, do pay system fees and charges, and so on. Beyond these basic expectations, what problems might arise on each side of an online relationship? Users face a variety of potential injuries: defamatory remarks, accidental disclosure of an employee's private e-mail, erroneous information, fraud, and copyright infringement are only a small sample. System owners also face their share of risks, from computer crime by intrusive hackers, to viruses from uploaded files, and the possibility of system seizure where criminals like pedophiles or drug dealers are discovered in private e-mail areas by prowling online undercover agents.

These expectations and risks can be managed through the use of contracts. Contracts allow each person and business to state their wants and needs clearly, lessening problems later on based on misunderstandings. The contract can also spell out the remedies for any injuries each side may suffer in connection with online activities. This can create predictability and important legal protection in case of a lawsuit.

The user contract is a tool for making every online system a productive, stable environment. By spelling out the rules for everybody in advance, system operators and users each know what is expected of them. For system operators who choose not to set up a clear contract, legal relations with users can be reduced to a series of misadventures with unpredictable results.

System operators are often concerned that using an official contract makes the online system a less friendly place. The answer is a more friendly contract, rather than abandoning all the benefits a contract provides. For example, the sample user contract in Appendix A is designed to be user-friendly, including within it an explanation of the reasons behind each provision. It is our hope that users who read this sort of contract come away better informed about their responsibilities on the system, and feeling pretty good about a system that bothers to set things out in terms that are fair and understandable, but firm.

With increasing commercialization online, contracts are assuming many new roles beyond setting up the basic agreement between system and user. Companies are providing the public and each other with all sorts of services and deals: shopping services, daily news, virtual storefronts, professional Internet services, and so on. Contracts are the medium in which these deals are spelled out, reminding each side of its obligations and, when necessary, making sure each side can be justly compensated if the other side breaks any of its promises.

There is an irreducible element of uncertainty in legal relations, online and in the physical world. But a properly set up contract will help answer most legal questions arising between people and businesses working together online.

What Is a Contract?

A contract is an exchange of promises or other things of value between two or more people. If you and I agree that I will give you an apple in exchange for half a dollar, we have a contract: I promise to give you an apple, and you promise to give me half a dollar.

The basic contract online is nearly as simple: A system or resource provider promises to provide access to its system, services, or resources—or perhaps all three. In exchange, the other person or business agrees to pay for the things provided, and, if system access is provided, to follow system rules.

A lot of details are often added to this simple structure. By setting up your contracts properly, you can have legal relationships online that meet everybody's needs in most situations.

What Matters Do You Cover in a User Contract?

In this book we are mainly concerned with what follows, legally and socially, when people interact online. The most fundamental online contract, then, is the one that attaches to the user's entry into an online system.

In general, every system that expects anything at all from users in exchange for system access or services, even if it is only to speak with some semblance of civility, could be said to have a contract with its users. There are some systems where it's hard to say that any kind of contract applies to users, but they're a small minority. For example, it might be said that there are no contracts covering Usenet, the vast distributed public conference on the Internet. However, every user reaches Usenet

"Hey Internet Kid, Wanna Green Card?"

The Internet has been drifting gently away from its anti-commercial acceptable use policies over the past few years, making way for commercial uses and the arrival of the greater mass of society. Businesses crept in slowly and respectfully, to avoid disrupting the culture of sharing that nurtured and shaped the Internet. A couple of lawyers from Arizona changed all that.

Lawrence Canter and Martha Siegel, a married couple in legal practice together, decided the Usenet discussion groups on the Internet were a good place to scare up new clients. One day in early 1993 they sent out identical ads for their "green card" legal services for immigrants to every Usenet newsgroup they could find. This is a practice known as "spamming," and Canter & Siegel did it on a grand scale. The response was enormous. They received many leads for prospective work. They also enraged thousands, perhaps millions of Usenet readers who were repulsed when they stumbled over the same crass ad over and over in every online discussion they entered. No one before ever had the hubris to invade every discussion on Usenet with such a message. Advertisers had restricted their spamming to specific newsgroups whose participants might be interested in the message being broadcast.

Usenet users felt violated, and retaliated in kind. They showered fake pizza and magazine orders on Canter & Siegel. A Usenet user in Sweden became famous for setting up a "cancelbot" on the Internet that automatically wiped out further messages from the couple. The company providing them Internet access shut off their account, responding to pressure and rage from the rest of the Net, not to mention more hate e-mail than it could process. Canter & Siegel reveled in the initial flare of communal rage, and gleefully set about writing a book on Internet marketing. As retaliations stepped up, they played the part of victims, decrying the lack of civility among Usenet participants. The shock waves have since leveled off, though the event won't soon be forgotten: Canter & Siegel slammed home the commercial reality of the Internet so hard the online world could no longer ignore it.

During the fracas, many asked whether Canter & Siegel had done anything illegal in their spamming spree. It appears not. There are still acceptable use policies hanging around on the Internet, but they're not laws, just system rules made up by some scientists. Usenet is a very public place, more public than the city streets or county roads which are regulated by local authorities. How can Usenet even have a "local authority" when it is equally present in the computers of dozens of different countries? To the chagrin of those who hate what Canter & Siegel did, there is no law against putting ads all over Usenet.

In the aftermath, Internet users suggested a traditional Internet solution to the Canter & Siegel problem: a better articulated code of online conduct, a greater commitment to respecting others' rights to pass through the net free of obnoxious, repetitive advertising. An honor system. Another group, more jaded, doesn't believe a basic change in human nature is at hand. They would force obnoxious advertising off the net through regulation, or perhaps industry self-regulation in which the online services would agree to keep ad pollut-ers off the networks. Yet others advocate developing more sophisticated cancelbots and "bozo filters" that would keep ugly e-mail from ever reaching the user's eyes.

All these measures will likely be tried, and they should keep Canter & Siegel incidents from flaring up too often. But the cat is already out of the bag. The public Internet is not regulated, nor would it be easy to regulate, and there are some who will misuse the Internet's natural anarchy to their advantage.

through an access system, and access systems can impose limits even for Usenet activity. This was demonstrated, in one famous recent case, when Internet access provider Netcom booted lawyers Lawrence Canter and Martha Siegel off its system, in connection with their widely despised mass advertising of legal services on Usenet.

Many system operators will want to flesh out their contracts with users, so each side understands what the other expects or a number of important subjects. This may strike some as a cold way of relating to others, but for system owners, it can help create the stability in user relations necessary to keep the system running even when disagreements and difficulties arise.

Access and Services Provided to Users

The first question in each system-user relationship is: can I come in? And once I'm in the system, where can I go? User Agreements that answer these questions can be structured a number of ways.

The simplest approach is to give all users full access to the online system and all services. Under this approach, new users commonly start with limited access until they are registered with the system. Registration enables the system operator to identify the users. For commercial systems, it begins the paying relationship. The large national online services offer full access to all users, provided they can pay the prices charged to use different parts of the system.

Online systems often grant different access levels to different classes of users, each class defined by the amount of payment or other compensation they give the system owner. One way to create different access levels is to give each user class a stated amount of access time, with those who pay more getting more time on the system to browse, chat, upload and download files, or engage in other online activities. Access time can be measured by the number of minutes per day the user is permitted on the system, though the time can just as easily be measured weekly, monthly, or yearly.

Another way to differentiate access levels is not to distinguish between the time different users may be on the system, but to permit users with greater access privileges to go into additional, limited-access areas in the system. This approach can be used to set a higher fee for business users who want to use certain business-related sections, and a lower fee for hobbyist users who have no use for business areas on the online system. It is also commonly used to separate general public areas on an online system from "adult" areas where minors are not permitted.

The majority of systems now offer gateways into various networks, such as the Internet or MCI Mail. This is another kind of "access" which the online system can choose to give to all users, or only to those who pay an additional fee.

The user contract should list the kinds of access offered to users. If different amounts or types of access, or various access "packages" with different access options, are offered, then the contract might describe all of them with checkboxes for choosing options, or a separate contract might be offered for each different access option. Users should understand exactly what access privileges they have on the system.

In addition to different access levels, an online system often offers a variety of different services to users. Services commonly offered include:

- News feeds, from services such as Clarinet or NewsBytes

- Electronic databases, either searchable by the user directly on the online system, or downloadable to the user's own computer

- Private message services offered to local businesses or other groups

- Automated collection of a user's messages and delivery to the user each time he or she logs on

- Electronic newsletters available for free or by paid subscription

This is only the tip of the iceberg. Special-purpose systems already offer a great variety of other services, such as news clipping services, job placement services, coordinating baseball rotisserie leagues, posting and collating local racing results, and real-time games for play by several users at the same time.

The user contract can list the various services available on a system, or it can be silent on the exact services. If the system owner imposes special or separate fees for any services, they should at least be mentioned in the contract so users better understand what to expect when they pay money to use the system. If the system doesn't charge separately for services, and would like to keep a free hand to change services easily, then it may be better not to list system services in the contract. Whatever is promised to users in the contract becomes a legal obligation from the system to the users. It is easier to change system services if a system is not locked into specific service offerings in the contract.

Even when system services are listed in the contract, the system owner can retain the ability to freely change services simply by having the contract state that the system owner can change services as it likes. It is nice also to provide for reasonable advance notice of any changes by posting a bulletin or message to affected users. Beyond being nice, advance notice can be important for user relations. Users can grow to rely on certain system services even if the system operator doesn't hear much from them about it. For example, if users had been permitted to rummage freely through a large database on the system,

> **Even when system services are listed in the contract, the system owner can retain the ability to freely change services simply by having the contract state that the system owner can change services as it likes.**

then suddenly the system operator changes his or her mind and restricts their access, the operator may hear from a crowd of unhappy users who have suddenly become very vocal. It may or may not be a contract violation, but it could be a disaster for the online relationship.

Giving users a reasonable notice period, say two weeks or a month, prevents such unpleasant surprises, and gives them the ability to let the operator know what they think of the new plan. It also gives the system operator the chance to find out if the new plans are worth pursuing, or perhaps should be changed, postponed, or shelved based on user response.

Price and Payment

If the system charges for system access or services, it should spell out all prices in the contract, and explain how fees and charges are calculated. For instance, if users are charged monthly or yearly for system use, with additional charges based on connect time for database use, the system operator should set out the entire scheme so users know what they're in for. If they don't understand the charging method, there can be trouble when the system owner tries to collect fees.

> **A gentle way of encouraging payments is to reduce a user's access to the system until he or she brings the balance up to date.**

The contract should describe the payment methods users can use. It should specify whether checks or credit card payments are accepted. The contract should also specify when payment is due—for instance, thirty days after the user receives a bill. It is a good idea for operators to be strict about payment times, since some users will stretch payments out forever if given the opportunity. Let a user slide for a couple of months, and he or she may never catch up to the current bill. A gentle way of encouraging payments is to reduce a user's access to the system until he or she brings the balance up to date.

As a continuing theme rooted in early bulletin board culture, there are still many system operators who ask users to make voluntary contributions or donations to the online system instead of paying mandatory access fees. This accords with the hobbyist nature of many systems. In such cases, users may freely give or withhold payment, with no compulsion other than the user's own conscience.

The concept of donation sometimes becomes skewed in the online world. Some systems reduce access or services for users who do not "donate," or offer advantages to users who do donate. This is actually charging for access and services, under the guise of asking for contributions. Such misuse of the terms "donation" or "contribution" may reflect a system operator's innocent belief that he or she is only asking users who are in a generous mood to help out in supporting the system. In other cases, it can be a calculated piece of marketing, baiting users into joining the online system by falsely portraying it as an informal, noncommercial place.

To clear up such confusion, one can apply a simple rule of thumb: If all users equally have complete access and services on a system without having to pay a dime, then it is accurate to call their payments "donations" or "contributions." If it is necessary for users to pay before they can receive access, services, or other system goodies, then their basic access payments are fees or charges and not donations.

Another continuing practice is barter exchanges between systems and users, such as "upload/download ratio" requirements. Users who upload specified numbers or quantities of new computer files to the system are given the ability to download other files maintained on the system. To complicate matters, some systems offer users either the "upload/download ratio," or money payment, as alternative ways

Digital Cash: Long Green Online

Electronic payments have been with us for years, first in the form of credit cards and interbank wire transfers, and then cash machines and electronic debits with direct access to our bank accounts. One might think, then, that everything is already in place for a totally digital, paperless economy.

Almost everything. One thing we don't have yet is a digital equivalent to cash. The electronic payment schemes we use today generate trails of information leading back to the buyer and his accounts. In contrast, paper money and metal coins don't reveal the identities of their holders. When we spend cash in a store where no one knows us, no one can analyze that cash and figure out who paid it.

The ability to spend anonymously was never much of an issue for law-abiding folks up to now, but things are changing. Systems for tracking all kinds of personal data are rapidly increasing in power and coverage, latching onto electronic transactions and shunting records of them to dozens of databases. People are becoming understandably

concerned and nervous about their privacy. The ability to pay cash is one of the last refuges of the private transaction. Many will not let go of it without an equally private online payment scheme.

Such an alternative has been developed, and actually existed in prototype form since the late 1980s. It's known as "digital cash," and its principal designer and spokesman is David Chaum of Amsterdam. Digital cash enables people to draw electronic checks on their own bank accounts, but when the check comes back to the bank for payment, the bank has no way of knowing which of its depositors was responsible for the check. This way we can spend electronic money wherever we wish, but keep the full circuit of our electronic finances safe from prying eyes.

Digital cash is based on the same public key encryption system used in other new Net developments like secure e-mail and digital signatures for contracts. It is not yet deployed routinely for commercial use, but the process of acceptance takes time; it needs to be broadly sponsored by major banks and credit institutions, not known for moving at quicksilver speeds. However, commerce is finally heating up on the Net, and electronic shopkeepers are hungry for anything that can break down consumer resistance to online shopping. Since digital cash will perform a prime role in making consumers more comfortable with spending online, don't be surprised to see it rolled out within the next year or two.

---

for users to gain permission to download files. Another barter exchange, seen on some "hacker" systems, requires users to disclose new and useful information on computer and network security or other hackerish subjects to be admitted to the privileged areas of the system.

Barter exchanges qualify as payments of some sort, though the money value of the items exchanged might be impossible to measure. When an online system does not offer users the choice of paying money, only upload/download ratios, perhaps the online system does not receive anything of value at all. It could be said the users are actually bartering with each other through the online system. At any rate, if an online system imposes any barter requirements on users, that should be considered part of the basic system-user contract.

Limitation of Liability

For system operators concerned about the risk of lawsuits from users, this can be the most important part of the user contract. A strong limitation of liability clause will establish that users are responsible for their own use of the system and its contents.

Perhaps this seems an irresponsible or selfish stance for the system operator. In most cases, however, it is perfectly reasonable. If a user's computer catches a software virus from a file that passed through an online system, that does not mean the system operator put it there. In most cases, that virus was uploaded to the system by another user. If a user's copyrighted text file maintained on the system is redistributed by other users into other online systems not authorized by the copyright owner, the system operator didn't do that copying and redistribution. He or she just held the file uploaded by the copyright owner.

In other words, most of the actions that might injure users on the system are not performed by the system operator, but by other users. Why should the system operator pay the consequences when the real wrongdoers are the users? Is it right to hold the online system (and system operator) caught in the middle of an illegal file transfer just as guilty as the user who directly performed that transfer on the system? Is this the reward for providing an online service to the public? Indeed, it is almost never fair to make the online system the target of legal action based on user actions on the system. The contract clause recommended here, limiting the liability of the system operator, is simply a way for the system operator and the users to mutually recognize this fact. It permits the system operator to do the job with far less fear of being caught in the crossfire of lawsuits between users.

This does not mean system operators need not strive to provide a safe online environment for users. Many systems are able to scan program files for viruses automatically before they are made available for download. Public message areas can be sampled periodically for obscene, defamatory, or copyright-violating materials. This makes good sense for user relations, legal aspects aside.

But what if something illegal or damaging slips through despite the system operator's efforts, and a user is injured? Is it time to put the online system up for auction to pay legal defense fees? For any system operator who plans to stay in operation over the long haul, a big part of the answer is a user contract that properly limits system operator liability to users.

> **Placing a liability limitation clause in the user contract "allocates risks" (as lawyers say) between the system operator and the users.**

Placing a liability limitation clause in the user contract "allocates risks" (as lawyers say) between the system operator and the users. Who bears the cost when a downloaded virus wipes out a user's hard disk—the user or the online system? The limitation of liability provision allows the system operator to avoid being subject to a costly lawsuit when this happens, by allocating the risk of virus damage to the user. Since the system may have hundreds or thousands of users, some of whom can be pretty sloppy or naive in their use of downloaded materials, such protection can be essential.

Another way to look at the liability limitation clause is that it helps define the online system's place in the scheme of things: the system operator only provides access to certain information, files, and services. If users want to play, they're welcome to join in; but if they get hurt while playing, they're not entitled to try to squeeze huge amounts of money out of the system operator for things that are not his or her fault.

Indemnities

An indemnity agreement between system operator and user is simply this: Let's say User A gives an indemnity to System Operator, and then User A does something on the system that injures Mr. B (such as infringing Mr. B's copyrights). If Mr. B sues System Operator based on User A's actions on the system, the indemnity means User A will repay System Operator for any monetary losses due to Mr. B's misdirected lawsuit. Depending on the way the indemnity clause is worded, User A may also take on the task of defending System Operator in court. The indemnity clause is, in a way, the flip side of the limitation of liability clause discussed just above. The limitation of liability clause reduces the system operator's liability to a user when that user is injured by another user on the system; the indemnity clause obligates the user who injures others to protect the system operator if he or she is sued by the injured party.

With both a limitation of liability and an indemnity clause in place, the system operator is protected almost completely from being caught in the middle of legal problems between users. Indemnity clauses obligate users to protect the system operator from the problems they cause not only for other users, but even for outsiders who do not use the system themselves but are injured by an activity taking place on the system (such as someone whose stolen credit card number is posted on the system by one if its users).

> **With both a limitation of liability and an indemnity clause in place, the system operator is protected almost completely from being caught in the middle of legal problems between users.**

Judges will likely not recognize indemnity obligations from users to system operators, unless those obligations are expressly spelled out in the user contract. Indemnity provisions are common in many industries. They come in a variety of flavors, ranging from very broad protection of the system operator or other indemnified party, to almost useless. A good, broad indemnity provision would require the user to defend the system operator from any legal action related to that user's actions, and to pay any losses suffered by the online system in connection with that action. In contrast, a narrow indemnity might require the system operator to pay his or her own legal fees, fight a lawsuit to the end, and only if he or she loses the last possible legal appeal will the user pay the judgment. System operators should try for the broadest possible indemnity provision.

Realistically, if the system operator is ever sued and calls in the indemnity obligation, many users will not have the financial resources to protect the system operator from suffering losses. Nonetheless, it is still important to include an indemnity agreement in the user contract, as part of setting up the system operator's overall legal protection. Users who agree to indemnity obligations are apt to be a little more careful about doing legally questionable things on the system.

Privacy

The user agreement can be an important tool for setting up the proper scope of user privacy on the system. The subject of user privacy in general is discussed at length in Chapter 5.

If the system operator does not make any agreement with users about their privacy, then legally he or she would have some right to review their e-mail, but would not be permitted to show it to anyone else, with a few exceptions. By addressing privacy in the user contract, system operators can vary from this default setting toward greater or lesser privacy for users.

System operators can increase user privacy by agreeing not to monitor their e-mail, private message areas or private chats. This way, users can feel much more comfortable that no one's looking when they have private discussions with others. Some users would greatly value this approach, and it could set a system apart from many others. Special increased privacy provisions could also be especially useful in setting up private discussion areas where companies may disclose or discuss their sensitive trade secrets.

There is also some risk to the system operator in this approach. As discussed in a later chapter, a system may face some risk of seizure if its users pursue illegal activities in private areas. If the system operator agrees *never* to look at users' private activities, it is that much harder to protect the system when suspicious activities may be afoot.

A better approach, then, might be for system operators to promise not to look at users' private discussions, unless they reasonably believe that user activities occurring in private are placing the system at risk. By promising not to look at private materials unless there is a reasonable belief that something's wrong, the system operator is not free to routinely or randomly monitor private user discussions looking for illegal activities. Something suspicious needs to take place before the system operator could look into private areas to make sure nothing illegal is happening. Since the system operator who makes this promise would be prohibited by the contract from performing random monitoring, users could still gain substantial comfort and value from this approach.

At the same time, a "reasonable belief" threshold for viewing private materials means the system operator does not get into trouble under the user agreement if it turns out nothing illegal is occurring in the private e-mail reviewed. If the system operator wants to justify his or her actions in such a case, all that is necessary is to show that based on certain information, the system operator reasonably thought something suspicious might be going on in private, placing the system at risk. The system operator checked to see if this was the case, and when it turned out to be a false alarm, he or she immediately stopped looking any further at the private discussions.

The system operator might also choose to go the other direction, and tell users they have little or no privacy under the user agreement. Those who like this approach offer two main justifications.

The first justification for a "no privacy" approach is that users do not have any particular desire or need for privacy on the system in question. This might be the case, for example, in a library-type system, used purely for research and not as a social meeting place, nor for confidential business discussions. This is fine, as long as all are agreed the system is being used in this limited way. Some system operators may find their original plans for structuring the online system will need to be changed to reflect the actual desires of the users. If users ask for privacy for certain purposes, it may be foolish to deny them that option.

The second justification, perhaps more like an excuse, is the fear that private discussions create such a great risk of system seizure by the authorities that the system operator cannot afford to give users the luxury of online privacy. Those who act on such fears and eliminate user privacy on the system will never be able to give users a full array of services. This may or may not affect the system operator's ability to run a viable system; users who need privacy will migrate to systems where privacy is available. In most cases, barring user privacy for this reason is most likely an overkill approach. A fairer approach is to respect user privacy, and investigate private e-mail only if it looks like there is good reason to do so.

Regardless of their reasons, system operators who want to limit user privacy by contract can easily do so. The existence of federal or state protection for privacy does not prevent making private contracts overriding that protection. As in most other areas, the system operator and the user can make almost any agreement they want on the terms of use of the system. This is called "freedom of contract."

Editorial Control

When users log on to the system, everything they see will be under the system operator's control. The operator may choose not to exercise that power, but it is there, and can be a powerful tool. The system operator can mold the system into a social environment, a news center, a commercial product, an art project, or anything else he or she desires. The operator can delete or move messages or files, create or deny user access, offer or withdraw services, rename and restructure entire message and file areas, or move the system to different computer hardware or software, or to a different state or country.

> **The system operator can mold the system into a social environment, a news center, a commercial product, an art project, or anything else he or she desires.**

It is a good idea for the user agreement to make it clear that the system operator indeed has a great deal of control. This is probably more important for relations between operators and users than for strictly legal purposes. Users should be made aware that the system operator has the last word on the system.

There is a certain degree of self-regulation among the people who exchange messages on any given system. After an online system is in existence for a while, the veterans start feeling and acting like they own the place. If a "newbie" user steps out of line, the old-hand users set them straight. With this increasingly sedimented social structure in place, sometimes users forget whose system it is, and try pressuring the system operator into following their ideas of how the place should be run.

This effect is often illustrated when system operators remove messages they find objectionable from public message areas. There can be good reasons for removing messages, such as when a user libels another user, or when a single user takes over a discussion area and drives other users away through excessive profanity and sheer unpleasantness. But the moment the system operator tries to straighten things out and touches one of the offending messages, cries of "censorship!" are often heard. These shouts come not only from the user whose messages are being canceled, but sometimes even from the other users who are the very targets of his venom. The fact that the system operator is in charge of the system sometimes seems to be the worst sin of all in the eyes of some users.

Such user attitudes against system operator control can be softened somewhat, by making it clear at the outset in the user agreement that the system operator is the boss. Spell out the main powers of the system operator: the power to remove or move postings, or send public messages into e-mail;

> **There is a certain degree of self-regulation among the people who exchange messages on any given system.**

the power to reject uploaded files; the power to open and close file areas, and so on. If users protest when the system operator actually does any of these things, the operator can point to the contract and show the users they accepted the operator's power over the online system from the beginning.

Though users may agree under contract that the system operator has ultimate power over the system, this does not guarantee they will be happy with everything the operator does with that power. If the system operator is not sensitive to user needs, he or she may be faced with constant rebellion, and eventual user flight from the system. The lives of others can be powerfully affected by simple deletions or adjustments here or there in an online system, even if it seems to the operator that he or she is just twiddling knobs on the computer.

At the same time, it is the rare system that can keep all users happy all of the time. A few discontented souls are bound to show up. Vocal protests about unfairness may not objectively reflect on the system operator's sensitivity to user needs. Some people are driven to complain, and the online environment—semi-anonymous yet well-attended—is an appropriate place to let it all go. It is probably best for the system operator to try to understand this phenomenon, develop a tolerance for it, and get on with business.

Ownership of Messages

Ordinarily, users own the copyrights to their messages in the public discussion areas of a system. However, this too can be altered through the user agreement.

If the system operator wants to own all messages on the system, the user agreement can be written to make the users assign their ownership to the operator. A raw assignment may not go over well with users, though. They may be uncomfortable forfeiting all control over their own messages, which are often composed off the cuff. They may also be suspicious that the system operator might try to make some money or gain a reputation for himself or herself by publishing their messages in some way, but leaving the creators of the messages out of it.

Such users may find it more palatable to license the system operator to use their messages for certain stated purposes, rather than give over all ownership. Such a license can be custom tailored to the exact usage rights desired by the system operator. By specifying the licensed rights, the agreement tells users in advance what kinds of use the system operator is allowed to make of their messages.

One major reason for system operators to obtain at least a license to user postings is to gain the ability to work with message threads (a thread is a public or semi-public online discussion consisting of a series of messages from two or more users). Message threads can be used to illustrate the variety of views held on many different subjects; to convey multifaceted and densely packed information on a subject by excerpting from a discussion among experts in the field; as stories written jointly by groups of users; as new forms of poetry, based on rare and exotic forms of "topic drift"; and so on. Clearly, the ability to move message threads from one online system to another, or to distribute them electronically or in print, can be very appealing.

> **To establish a system operator's ability to move, distribute, or publish message threads, the user agreement should state that the operator is the owner of all message threads as "collective works."**

To establish a system operator's ability to move, distribute, or publish message threads, the user agreement should state that the operator is the owner of all message threads as "collective works." This confirms that the system operator owns each thread as a whole, and can prevent others from reproducing threads from the system without the operator's permission. In addition, the user agreement should contain users' permissions for the system operator to freely copy and distribute user messages as part of the threads they help comprise. Without this grant, ownership of the thread as a whole is much less effective, since each individual user with a message in a thread could stop the system operator from using his or her posting under copyright law. For users with especially valuable messages, due for instance to their celebrity or their status as experts, the desire of operators to publish or distribute their postings may provide an opportunity to get something extra in return from the system operator. If getting paid for the use doesn't make sense, such users may still be able to get other compensation, such as credit in the republished message thread, or perhaps free use or privileges on the system.

Some systems approach the message ownership question from the opposite direction. They require that all users agree in advance that their contributions to the online system will be dedicated to the public domain. If this is properly done, it can be effective in stripping message ownership rights from users. Having the user clearly agree to the public domain status of his messages in the user agreement can meet the requirement of the modern copyright law: that a copyrighted work will go into the public domain only when the owner expressly declares his or her intention to make the work public domain.

This approach could enable an online system to become a resource for absolutely free information, usable by anyone without having to seek permission. There is a question whether enough users will be interested in such experiments to make the resulting free message bases important enough to make a difference in the world. This approach is also limited to messages first placed in the public domain online system. A system operator cannot cause incoming messages from outside networked message bases, such as Usenet, Fidonet, or RIME, to go into the public domain when they reach his or her system, because the operator has no direct agreement with the users who post their messages into the network through other systems.

Contracts and Corporate Systems

Corporate systems have different relationships with their users than "private" systems. The user relationship is naturally business-oriented, contrasting with private systems that range from commercial to social to political activities. The corporate system is just one component of a larger business, and subject to overarching business goals, methods of operation, and relations with the rest of the world.

The users of a corporate system might be its employees, suppliers, customers, clients, business associates, or all of these. Its system operators work for the company in some capacity. They might have been brought in by the company especially to run the online service, or they might be company employees being weaned from in-house LAN administration to new kinds of job responsibilities. In addition, corporate online systems are commonly within the purview of the corporation's DP or MIS department, along with other corporate systems ranging from accounting and inventory systems to workflow and document management systems.

Running an online system can make for interesting cultural and organizational changes in the corporation. In traditional corporate data processing systems, humans tend to be involved mainly at the input and output ends and in system design and maintenance, while the computer operations proper

> **Running an online system can make for interesting cultural and organizational changes in the corporation.**

take place in a "black box" occupied only by computers and communication systems. MIS managers are therefore accustomed to treating the various systems under their control as machines, very sophisticated but machines nonetheless. In contrast, the new online environments, such as e-mail, workgroups, and bulletin boards, are thickly inhabited with corporate employees and other people. If an online disagreement erupts between company employees, and the MIS manager takes the traditional MIS approach of fixing the machine to get rid of the problem, the human users of the system can become incensed, and the problem will be worse than before. Even more bewildering, in-house online systems create new opportunities for employees at different levels and in different departments to interact, cutting clear across organizational lines and barriers of authority.

Since online systems bring people into environments previously reserved for the use of machines, corporations will need to bring their people management skills and personnel into that environment as well. Online systems are not a mere adjunct to corporate MIS, but a multi-functional extension of the corporation's overall business operations. This will become increasingly clear as use of e-mail and group work environments increases, and as corporations continue to hook up with their own remote offices, with each other, and with the world through the Internet and other large-scale networks.

The two major kinds of corporate systems, in-house and customer support, are discussed below.

In-House Systems

Online systems are still very new in the workplace. They have enormous potential to increase production and employee effectiveness. If a business plans to assert effective control over an in-house system, it should set out clear rules in advance. This is no mere technique to keep employees in line, but a way to express mutual expectations and avoid damaging conflicts and uncertainties.

Recently, well-publicized employee lawsuits against Epson America and Nissan for unconsented monitoring of employee e-mail showed what happens when a large company fails to formulate effective corporate system policies. Other companies can avoid the expense and embarrassment of court fights by establishing clear and reasonable corporate system rules before trouble starts.

The user "contract" in an employer-employee setting is, in a sense, just another part of the employment agreement. The fundamental rule of the workplace—that the employer is largely in control—applies to most affairs in an online corporate system. The employer has total discretion over employee access privileges and the nature of public discussions on the online system. The one area where there may be progress toward employee "rights" on corporate systems relates to privacy. This area is explored in Chapter 5.

In smaller businesses, the terms of the employer-employee agreement may not be contained in any written document, but only in the informal customary rules of the workplace. In larger businesses, printed "corporate policy manuals" prevail, spelling out the rules all employees must follow.

Businesses with existing policy manuals should consider creating a separate section in the manual just for online system policies. Businesses that survived up to now without policy manuals should seriously consider creating such a document, to cover the previously uncharted territory of in-house system policy.

Major subjects for a corporation to cover in a corporate system policy manual for employees include:

- *Permitted uses of corporate e-mail.* Employees could be told to limit their discussion to company business, but the rule is hard to enforce with any consistency unless there is e-mail monitoring by the employer. Nonetheless, without a general business-only rule biasing use of the system by employees toward productive purposes, e-mail can become a time waster instead of production enhancer.

- *Whether employees' e-mail will be monitored by the employer, and under what conditions.* If employers do plan on monitoring employee e-mail, they should have enough respect for their own workers to let them know in advance. It's hard enough on employees to know the boss is looking over their shoulder. If they're deceived into believing they have privacy, they may reveal private matters the employer has no legitimate reason to know about.

- *Any activities prohibited on the online system, such as carrying on of private business by employees, or calling the employees' own private accounts on the Internet or other outside services or networks.* It could be particularly important to prohibit employees from using an in-house system to contact outsiders on public networks, making the in-house system suddenly potentially regulated under federal privacy laws applicable to public communications systems.

- *Use of the online system to maintain personal or business software.* It is hard enough for large businesses to keep their own software licenses sufficiently in order to satisfy the Software Publishers Association in case they come around looking for infringements; uncontrolled employee stocking of online servers with strange software could greatly increase the infringement risk. And of course, software randomly brought in by employees, whether from home or by download into the in-house system directly from an outside network or online system, increases the likelihood of viruses and other dangerous code entering the corporate system.

- *The permitted uses of employees' individual storage areas on the online system or local network.* Employees could use their directory areas or folders to store all kinds of personal files and information. If the files are not part of the business in some way, it is a good idea to keep them off the business system to avoid the corporation somehow being mixed up in employees' personal affairs.

- *Procedures for working with or transmitting trade secrets of the business on the online system.* With encryption becoming increasingly usable, employers may now or in the near future require all discussions of the least sensitivity, or simply all discussions, on the online system to be encrypted to reduce the risk of interception from the outside. There may also be a prohibition against discussing any internal company affairs on any online system other than the in-house system.

- *Keeping the online system secure from outsiders and from computer viruses.* This can involve, as mentioned above, limiting the amount and manner of contact between in-house employees and external networks and online systems. It could also involve strong prohibitions against employees setting up their own modem links outside the in-house LAN facilities, or acting in ways that might compromise security firewalls set up by the employer.

- *Different access and service levels for different types of personnel.* Higher-level personnel may have broader system access than lower-level personnel, and greater access to outside networks and services. In addition, employees may be given different access areas depending on the kind of work they do.

- *Guidelines for employees' conduct in public.* When a corporate employee does communicate using the corporation's online system but outside the corporation's borders, he or she needs to operate within the company's public relations agenda. Rules could include express limits on what an employee can speak about; requirements that the employee either identify himself or herself as a company employee, or not disclose such information to others unless specifically asked; and requirements that employees must clear certain kinds of communications with their superiors before they are made in public. These may seem to bog down the corporation's ability to engage fluidly in online communications, but in practice once the employee is "with the program," he or she can operate with great facility in the public networks on behalf of their employer.

There are many other possible areas where clear rules should be established, depending on the exact nature of the business. The goal should be to cover all the major bases, even if some details are missed.

Customer Support Systems

A customer support system has a very different set of goals from an internal system meant mainly for use by employees. Businesses need to keep their customers happy to stay in business. Therefore, business efficiency considerations could take a back seat to making the customer system an inviting, comfortable place.

This marketing goal may make it difficult or impossible to impose much of an online system contract on the users. The system itself is not the "product" offered to customers, but an added service supplementing the company's real product, whatever that may be—services offered by a real estate brokerage, travel agent, career counselor, software company, and so on. Telling customers/users that they must follow a strict set of system rules goes against the grain of the relationship. The system is not a privilege for the users, but a service designed to make the company's products more attractive.

> **The major way to prevent abuse of a customer support system is to sharply limit the functions available.**

The major way to prevent abuse of a customer support system is to sharply limit the functions available. E-mail between customers and company representatives is fine; e-mail directly between customers is often neither necessary or desirable. Public message areas focused on discussions of the company's products are okay (though the company may wish to screen messages critical of its products before they become publicly accessible). Expanding those discussions to include politics and sex may create a social scene and irrelevant controversies, digressing too far from the purposes behind setting up the customer support system in the first place. It is also a good idea to completely shield the customer support system from any in-house system functions maintained by the company for use by its employees.

There are some rules that can probably be established and enforced generally for in-house systems. Anyone who makes the online system unpleasant for other customers can be gently steered in the right direction by sensitive system operators. General rules on commonly agreed "bad practices" can be posted and enforced: no obscenity, stolen information, defamatory remarks, pirated software, and so forth. Inviting customers to your store does not give them license to trash the place; a customer support system is no different.

It will not be realistic in most cases to expect customers to sign written contracts containing the support system rules. The company operating the system may be able to do no more than lead new users through a series of screens describing the system rules, and let them go from there. If a support system is part of a product maintenance arrangement, then it may be possible to add system rules to the signed maintenance contract, or at least a provision saying the customer agrees to rules posted on the support system.

Commercial Arrangements Between Online Businesses

The previous two sections of this chapter dealt with contracts covering system-user relations, both in public systems and in-house corporate systems. This is just the tip of the iceberg for online contracts. There is a large and increasing array of business arrangements being made every day between and among online businesses. Companies providing online services to the public very often acquire their data, news feeds, files, images, and other materials from other people or companies. To assure stable supplies and rights to that data, the system/data provider relationship is usually covered by some kind of contract. Increasingly, we are seeing the overall business of providing online services being broken down into separate components. Different companies specialize in the different pieces, such as providing access to the Internet or other data or user networks, managing computer equipment and systems, and maintaining bulletin board functionality (or, as is currently the fad, World Wide Web servers) for rent to other companies. A company can now become a significant online service provider largely by buying these various resources from others, tying them together in a supervisory capacity, and putting its own brand name on top. Such an online business is very much a creature of the contracts it creates with others that assure it will get the resources it needs to keep operating.

General Concerns

The goal of this section is to provide the reader with some useful ways of thinking about online business arrangements. Unfortunately, this fascinating, growing subject is too involved to explore in detail in this book. If you are going into some sort of online business and there is significant money involved, get a lawyer to help out with the contracts. That said, the information presented below is industrial-strength. It will provide a good introduction to online commercial deals for those new to the business.

What is the Model for the Online Arrangement?

It can be surprising to find out that companies making online deals often do not share the same picture of the resulting business operations. When each side expects the deal to work differently or produce different benefits, it may never work out, yielding losses and uncertainty instead of predictability and profit. This may seem fairly obvious in the abstract, but real online business deals today often have this failing. Most likely it is due to the failure to adequately visualize the online environment in which the deal will play out. Such an effort can be daunting to the uninitiated, and most of those putting together online business arrangements today are still either relatively new

Taking the Internet Private

One of the first things people hear about the Internet is its traditional culture of sharing and noncommerciality. History made it that way. The Internet started as ARPAnet, an experimental defense network well outside the bustle of commerce. Then it broadened into a place where research scientists across the world shared their work, a benign golden age that Net veterans already look back on with nostalgia. The next wave of expansion brought college kids teeming into the Internet and all its MUDs and newsgroups via their homework computers and tuition-paid online accounts. For all participants, the Internet came free; someone paid for it, but most using it never saw a bill.

Through all these phases, the Internet was populated by people outside the business realm: civil servants and soldiers, ivory tower scientists, kids on a last fling before entering the work force. The collected legacy of these groups is an abhorrence of commercial activities, and on the positive side, some really swell, and totally free, Net organizational software tools like Gopher, Archie, WAIS, World Wide Web, and the Mosaic WWW browser. The sense of freedom and purity was enshrined in the National Science Foundations's "Acceptable Use Policy," which forbade any commercial uses of the publicly funded network.

These artifacts are still very much in evidence on the Net, causing many mistakenly to think the Internet is entirely noncommercial. But in fact, the Net is now largely commercialized, and becoming increasingly so by the day.

Take those "free" software tools. The new, improved versions are starting to show up exclusively in commercially licensed form. Net providers must choose between sticking with the aging free tools, or paying for up-to-date commercial versions. Or how about that "free" access? By now, most academic sites have shut down the freebie accounts they once gave out generously to anyone who asked. As we go to press, the Commercial Internet Exchange is seeking to enforce a per-system fee for Internet access providers to remain usefully hooked up to the Internet, and the NSF is cutting off most of its funding of the backbone. The new costs will be seeping out to everyone's Internet access bills, swelling them gently over time. Likewise, businesses are swarming onto the Net like it's the next gold rush, moving through the researchers and college kids like wolves among sheep. Legal fights over the trademark rights to Internet addresses are starting to clutter the courts.

So to those contemplating starting up business operations on the Internet, take comfort—you're in plenty of good company. If anyone is still reviling doing business on the Net, it's really just a symptom of their sense of loss. They had their temporary online utopia pulled out from under them, and have lost their way to the next one. In the meantime, our society of commerce and capitalism is rapidly making the Internet into its own image, with all the good and ill that implies.

online users or people who never even went online. Nonetheless, conditions in the real online world must be properly accounted for if we want the deal to work. Companies venturing together in this new online world should always make sure they share a realistic model of how they will do business together.

Arriving at a realistic, shared model is often not as difficult as it might first appear. Many online deals today can, in fact, be modeled after familiar, traditional business arrangements in the physical world. Sometimes, both sides to a deal will intuitively realize that a specific physical world model has precisely the shape they're looking for in an online deal. At other times, when intuition is not so directly helpful, the trick is finding the right model among the many candidates. Once a good model is chosen, it can support both sides' confidence that the arrangement will prove successful for everyone. A quick look around the online world shows many online business relationships based on physical world models: rental of space in a shopping mall; selling goods through a mail or phone order catalog; management of a company's computer systems by an outside firm; bookstores and newsstands; personal advertising; text publishing; rental of a convention hall; and computer support services, to name just a few. We can think of certain online businesses not only being modeled after physical businesses, but actually marking the beginning of a migration of the analogous physical businesses into the online world. Indeed, as online transmission speeds increase, existing companies in the business of delivering information in physical form, such as bookstores, record stores, video rental stores, courier services, and so on, may largely disappear as their online equivalents take over.

> **Many online deals today can, in fact, be modeled after familiar, traditional business arrangements in the physical world.**

Once the right model is chosen, the rest of the business arrangement hopefully should follow organically, with neither side getting lost in the online ether. Each side knows the broad outline of what it is supposed to do: provide certain information, services, goods, or money to the other, in certain quantities and on a certain schedule. Often, the parties will be required to pursue parts of the project together, with the success of the deal riding on their ability to cooperate.

The details are filled in when the parties draw up a contract. If a sample contract for the kind of online arrangement they're making can be found, this part can go fairly easily as well. If no sample contracts are available from past online deals, the parties can still readily draw on contracts developed originally for analogous physical business deals. Thus, if the parties are contemplating an online retail store rental, they can draw on contracts used for physical rentals; if the parties want to enter into a deal for the supply of video clips to an online video store, the deal can mirror deals used currently in physical video stores. In each case, the parts of the physical deal that address physical contingencies, such as delivery of physical goods, warehousing, risk of damage, and so on, will need to be adjusted or eliminated altogether in the online deal. After making these adjustments, the physical world contracts can also be used as checklists by both sides, to make sure they have reached agreement on all important aspects of the deal they're about to make with each other.

There are some online business arrangements for which there may be no adequate models that can be drawn from preexisting businesses. In this case, the parties must invent a new model. In fact, it is particularly important to put together new models for unprecedented online business arrangements when preexisting models can't be found. Merely stumbling forward and seeing what happens might yield unexpected benefits, but it can also lead to disaster. Even if the companies involved can afford to lose their entire investment in the deal for the sake of exploring new ways of doing business,

The Online System as a Shopping Mall

Anyone who's ventured onto the large online services knows the shopping mall concept is in full flower on the Net. Since physical shopping malls have become the premiere public centers for much of the United States, it is not surprising to see their pulsing shadows, the electronic malls, exerting a powerful online presence.

There are dissimilarities between online and offline malls, of course. Under today's technologies, one does not walk into online stores, or hang out with one's teen friends by the online fountain and the soda shop. Instead, most online stores are little more than text catalogs with pictures of stuff you can buy with your credit card and receive through the mail. Technologies will advance, though. Within a few years, virtual malls and their various stores and common areas should present very convincing three-dimensional appearances. People will be able to walk among the various stores and see others calling in from other computers to shop at the same time. Simulating the ubiquitous food courts and their fat-laden foods may be difficult, though, unless taste stimulation user interfaces have been developed by then.

The stores in an online mall make rental deals with the system owner reminiscent of space rentals for real stores. They receive a certain amount of space in the mall, with the ability to put their own service name up in front of the store, and certain utility services from the mall owner. They also join in group or cooperative promotions organized by the mall owner. Like the stores in a physical mall, they rely on the foot traffic of mall-goers to provide for their own success; if the overall system is not sufficiently visited by online callers, the mall stores will suffer.

We mentioned above that physical shopping malls often function as public centers in the United States. If online malls serve the same function, then do they have to recognize free speech rights for online users? For now, the law seems to say they don't; online mall owners do not have to give anyone the right to speak in their systems. However, in the past few years, several states have given protesters and leafletters the right to spread their messages in or near physical malls because they are public places. These cases were decided under state constitutions, not the federal constitution, and there's no saying that the state courts would regard today's online malls as serving anywhere as vital a community gathering function as is performed today by physical malls. That could change, though, depending on how many people end up coming online in the next few years.

they may be less able to figure out how or why they succeeded or failed if they did not do the preliminary work of putting together some sort of feasible model for doing business together.

How do we make a model for a new kind of business deal? Mostly, we just use common sense. First, see if the kinds of business the parties want to do can be broken into coherent pieces; it may turn out that each of those pieces can be modeled after existing business arrangements. If that does not result in a model, then the parties should work together to build a new model for a new kind of business. They should make sure they're clear on where their resources and supplies come from, and what

> **How do we make a model for a new kind of business deal? Mostly, we just use common sense.**

they might cost; what they're making or selling; who are the buyers, and who are the sellers; and how they will be able to generate the return they need to justify the venture and, if it's an ongoing business, to keep the business going. As time goes on and the deeper potentials of online interaction are discovered, it is likely that many kinds of online businesses and deals will emerge with absolutely no counterpart in the physical world. The resulting interlocking online business environment will most likely complement, rather than reflect, the physical business world.

In every deal where a company plans on depending on another company to provide services or payments over a period of time, it is important to have a written contract (or the online equivalent of a written contract, as such things evolve). Many business people strongly prefer handshake deals, on the theory that if the person you're doing business with can't be trusted, a contract on a piece of paper is not going to save you. This may be so, but there is another consideration, at least as compelling. The person you're making the deal with today may be entirely dependable to carry out his or her side of the deal, but what if he or she is gone from his or her position in the other company tomorrow? There is no saying the next person at the other company, who is now handling your contract, will be interested in performing it at all. In fact, new blood often comes in with an agenda to make the position their own by dismantling much of what the prior person or regime put in place, and that could well include your contract. If this worst-case scenario comes to pass, of course it is not likely you will continue doing business with the other company for long, or making new deals with them. However, you may be in the middle of business operations that require the other company to honor its commitments at least for a while longer, while you find alternative arrangements. If for no other reason, this need for at least temporary support while switching to an alternative source for the things previously received from the other side to the contract should convince most of those who prefer handshakes to get their deal in writing anyway.

This is where the model for the deal reappears. Every contract covering a business deal, online or otherwise, should mirror the model used for the deal itself. Preferably, this should be done in the first few pages of the contract. If someone reading the contract does not know what the deal is by the third or fourth page, then either it is a bad contract, or there is actually no coherent deal model or concept underlying the contract. Accordingly, in online deals, especially deals with no clear preexisting models, it is no empty exercise to carefully consider and negotiate a contract both parties will sign. It is the last, best chance for both sides to agree on a clear, coherent model for how they will do business together, and to explore additional facets of that model as part of the discipline of the contract negotiation process. Once the contract is negotiated and the mutual business of the companies is underway, the contract becomes a reference, checklist, and map, reminding companies of where they are and where they plan to go in this new, still largely unfamiliar online business terrain.

Being Dependent on Others

If you engage others to help you in providing online services, you can swiftly become dependent on them for the fate of your entire business. If the other company is reliable and supportive, you can proceed with your plans, and possibly on to great success in your business. But if the supporting company is not reliable, your business can seriously flounder.

Virtual Corporations

Big companies do not dominate our economy quite as thoroughly as they did for most of this century. "Virtual corporations" are emerging to fill in the cracks, thanks to on-line communications.

The erosion of the big firms was inevitable. Rapidly changing consumer and market needs are proving difficult to serve through large-scale, inflexible business structures. At the same time, it was demonstrated in the '80s that corporate size and success often lead not to stability, but to becoming a takeover target valued most highly for its breakup potential. Affirmative conditions for change appeared as well, most notably usable high-speed communications at low cost.

People are now able to coordinate their work effectively from all over the country through the use of e-mail. It is unnecessary to gather them together physically to run a business. Businesses that leverage the newly flexible availability of geographically dispersed workers and companies can now compete effectively with businesses anchored to one spot. These new, small spread-out businesses are the "virtual corporations" we have been hearing so much about recently.

What is a virtual corporation? Definitions vary, but certain essentials stand out: It is a group (often small) of self-sustaining people and companies that work together, from wherever they are located, to pursue large-scale business projects. Typically, though not always, one or two of the participating companies take the lead and get the others under contract as suppliers or service providers to the joint effort.

For instance, to run a small book publishing operation, one might set up a small company as the lead business for the virtual corporation. It would make contracts with the other companies and coordinate their activities; be primarily responsible for obtaining and working with authors; determine promotional strategies, product lines, production runs, and other such matters; and generally be the home of the publisher's imprint. Supporting and service companies would include printers, graphic designers, editorial services, marketing consultants, sales reps, accountants, and lawyers. For some of these companies, such as the printers and designers, long-term contracts would be drawn up assuring a commitment to the virtual corporation for a number of years at a stable, affordable price.

Most participants in a given virtual corporation do not derive all of their income from it, but rather regard the virtual corporation as one of several projects sustaining them. With this kind of structure, the virtual corporation can rapidly bring in new participants with needed skills and capacities, and phase out others when their involvement is no longer required. A virtual corporation is not truly virtual, but a business as real as any other. Nor is it necessarily a corporation, though that is certainly among the legal forms which its participants may choose for their joint business.

Any group can form a virtual corporation. The most important step is assembling a group of component companies compatible enough to work together. After that, the two main organizational tools are contracts and a system for working together between remote locations. The contracts are used to create a dependable business structure among the various participants. They are especially important for assuring long-term access to supplies and services on affordable terms, in case the virtual corporation's products prove a big success. For working together remotely, the parties must settle on a mutually accessible communications system, to serve as a command and messaging system to keep the whole virtual corporation coordinated. Whether the organization is traditionally hierarchical, or run horizontally by consensus with no particular leader, effective group communication is the key to letting the whole thing blossom.

Are virtual corporations just a fad? Probably not. They are the first new business form based on the power of online communications, and already display advantages that will help them compete effectively with larger, self-contained businesses in many industries. We will, however, probably watch them evolve greatly over the coming years and decades, as working together remotely becomes the norm.

For instance, let's say you sell online news services to large institutional customers. Instead of running the entire operation yourself, you pay another company to maintain your computer-based operations and supply the news information to your customers. As you gain more customers, you become more dependent on the supporting company. If it fails to provide computer-based news services to your customers now, you would be stuck with a bushel of major contracts you can't possibly fulfill on short notice, ultimately leading to demands for reimbursement and lawsuits. Just as bad, the management of the support company may turn out not to be trustworthy. Realizing you depend entirely on them, they may try to get more money from you. If your business relationships are not properly set up, you may find yourself submitting to a stick-up by the support company, paying far more than agreed just to keep things going while you search for a way out of the mess.

Or consider this scenario: your company provides cutting-edge online services to consumers, specifically the latest in virtual reality interfaces. You depend on an outside software developer for the new features of your user interface software. You must offer new features quickly and on a regular basis to your customers, or your equally eager competitors may lure them away because they have the next great feature first. As long as your developer moves quickly, your software will be upgraded speedily enough and you will stay in the running. But what if your developer slows down? Perhaps your company is just not one of their bigger clients, and they begin allocating resources according to the size of the client, rather than the size of the client's need. Obviously, you need to move to another developer to support your need for rapid development. But if the first developer owns the software you're using, you may need their permission before you can have it modified by someone else—and that permission may not be forthcoming. Even if you're willing to pay to create new software from scratch, there may be no other available suppliers of the kinds of software and services you need, or none that could emulate your existing software quickly enough to save your business. Again, you will be stuck with unsatisfactory software support until (and unless) you put together an alternative plan enabling you to break away.

These are just two examples of dependence situations gone wrong. Such problems crop up every day. The examples above, in fact, are drawn from real-life problems the author was asked to assist in resolving, after the over-dependent basic deals were already made. If you are planning to go into an online business that will depend at least partially on outside businesses to become a success, how do you avoid problems when your supplier goes sour on you?

The first way to curb the risks of being highly dependent is to have a written contract with your service supplier. As discussed above, written contracts really come in handy if the management of the other business changes or even just remembers the deal differently than you do. A piece of paper will not prevent all bad behavior, but it can certainly help. Service suppliers will be far less likely to toy with your business needs if they know you can easily bring them to court for violating the clear terms of your contract. Of course, this requires that your contract spells out your exact business deal with the other company. Contracts specific to a given deal usually don't grow in form books; you will probably need a lawyer's help to achieve a contract fully tailored to your situation.

> **Service suppliers will be far less likely to toy with your business needs if they know you can easily bring them to court for violating the clear terms of your contract.**

Another way to reduce the dependence problem is to make sure, up front, that you will receive a timely response from your supplying company on all time-sensitive matters. When service is needed or something goes wrong, how long before the supplying company responds? Your supplier's response time can be especially critical when you must respond to the needs of your customers or business partners, and your own response time depends in turn on how quickly your supplier responds to you. Common online situations where fast response time can be important include: moving quickly to fix reported problems or errors in the system; putting the system back online if it goes down, especially if it is supposed to be continuously available to users; updating databases with new information quickly after it is delivered; resolving billing and other financial errors; and adding or changing system features to keep the system in compliance with legal or regulatory changes.

In more elaborate arrangements, service needs may be graded according to urgency, with more pressing matters invoking a faster response time commitment from the supplier. For instance, total system shutdown should receive immediate attention from the supplier's service personnel, while problems that cause inconvenience to customers but do not prevent the system from providing services can receive a less critical level of attention. Other items, like upgrading system software following a new release, may receive even slower, back-burner treatment.

Addressing the response time question properly requires fully airing the issue with the supplying company before you agree to work with them. If the supplying company shows an understanding of your particular need for speedy responses in certain situations, and makes other helpful gestures like giving you referrals to other customers who will testify to their timely responses to problem calls, it's a good sign. On the other hand, if they attempt to avoid the discussion in some manner, such as by dismissing your concerns or refusing to explore your needs in depth, you may have a real problem later on. When you do find a supplier or vendor you are ready to deal with, make sure your contract spells out their exact commitment for every situation where response time is critical. For instance, your contract

> **When you do find a supplier or vendor you are ready to deal with, make sure your contract spells out their exact commitment for every situation where response time is critical.**

may specify that the supplier will respond to a problem call within one hour, immediately begin working to fix the problem, and continue to work until the problem is resolved; if the problem persists for more than four hours after the initial problem call, the supplier will immediately develop a temporary workaround solution, then return to its efforts to fix the problem permanently. Remember, make sure all foreseeable situations where timely response is important are covered by your contract. The situation you leave out may be the one where you end up twiddling your thumbs waiting for the supplier to do his job, while you watch your business deflate like a flat tire.

Another way to reduce your dependence is to make sure you control the software used by the supplier to support your delivery of services to your own customers. If you ever plan to upgrade your services, it is best not to be forced to ask your original supplier to make the changes. If you ever need to move from your original supplier to a new one, you should have your system's software available so you can be up and running quickly on a new system. Generally, any time your supplier uses software that may become essential to your online service, such as user interface software or database or communications modules, you should arrange for a license to the source code, so you can work with the software directly in the future whenever the need comes up. For online service providers, software is a critical tool in the delivery of all services; without control over the delivery software, you will not have control over your own services. How far you can go in obtaining source code rights will vary according to the supplier. It is best to address this need at the outset of the relationship. Move on to another supplier if it looks like the one you're talking to could end up holding your business hostage to their control over the delivery software.

You should also be careful to retain control over all data used in your online service business. This is similar to the software control issue. When your supplier controls your databases, your ability to get your data when you need it, or to take that data with you when you move to another supplier, can be unclear. Usually, your right to your own data will not be open to question; what may not be certain is whether the supplier is maintaining the data in a format you can work with on your own, and whether the supplier retains some or all of the data for its own use. Your data can be very valuable, for a number of reasons. It might be a laboriously compiled database, used to provide special research services to customers; customer lists and demographic information valuable for marketing your services; or descriptions of business or development methods that qualify as trade secrets. Once again, you should secure an understanding with your supplier about your business data up front. In particular, it is good to make sure the data is portable and readily available to you without having to ask the supplier; that the supplier agrees that the data is your confidential information; and that they cannot use it except to support your own online services.

Finally, you should be confident that the supplier is willing to give you uninterrupted service, despite disagreements or even your announcement that you are moving to another supplier or your own self-supported system. There is not too much you can do about this in advance, except develop a strong sense of the supplier's trustworthiness. Will they respect your need for uninterrupted support, or will they stop supporting you without advance warning every time you have a mild disagreement with them, to force you to give in to their point of view? Talking to the supplier's customers can be very useful here. Checking their financial health can also be useful, since a desperate company will be more likely to use desperate measures in case of problems. Your contract should, of course, specify the amount of service interruption permitted, beyond which the contract will be violated. You should also try to obtain a commitment from the supplier to continue supporting you for several months after the main contract period ends, while you complete your transition to another system.

Commercial Indemnities

We described how a basic indemnity clause works in the section on user agreements above. When you run a business in a networked environment, indemnities become even more important. Companies doing business online are regularly exposed to possible lawsuits due to the actions of other companies, with whom they may or may not have direct business relationships. To handle this problem, online commercial contracts often provide for each company to indemnify the other for certain kinds of legal problems that may result from its actions. The result is chains of indemnification, where a company hit with a lawsuit based on the actions of another company should be able to bring others into the lawsuit, until the company ultimately at fault is defending the suit and holding the others

> **Companies doing business online are regularly exposed to possible lawsuits due to the actions of other companies, with whom they may or may not have direct business relationships.**

harmless. No one company is responsible to set up this chain of indemnities. If each company doing business online makes sure to get indemnities from the other companies it deals with directly, the chain forms automatically.

If this all seems a bit abstract, an example should clear it right up: Suppose a print magazine business licenses an electronic publishing company to publish a story from the magazine, and the electronic publication is in turn distributed on a computer bulletin board. Suppose further that the story contains a serious copyright infringement, such as several pages of dialogue taken verbatim from the last Godzilla movie. If the owners of Godzilla movie rights sue on the infringement, they may well start their lawsuit against the ultimate distributor: the bulletin board. If the bulletin board prepared its contracts correctly, it should have an indemnity from the electronic publisher, and it can bring the publisher into the lawsuit to defend it. The electronic publisher, in turn, should be able to bring the print magazine publisher in to defend the lawsuit under its own indemnity. The magazine publisher may have its own indemnity from the writer of the article, and use that indemnity to get the writer in to defend everyone else from the infringement suit. Now it looks like we have the actual accused copyright infringer defending everyone else who published and distributed his or her story in reliance on it being original and not some Godzilla rip-off. In reality, most of the time the buck would stop in a case like this with the magazine publisher; few writers have the money or insurance to make good on an indemnity.

Such chains of indemnities can be used to correctly allocate responsibility not only for copyright problems, but all kinds of other problems as well, ranging from libel and invasions of privacy to claims of damage due to badly transmitted data. In approaching every deal, be aware of the situations in which your business might be exposed to legal risks based on the actions of others—these are the matters you should make sure to cover with an indemnity clause.

Data Provider Agreements

If any kind of online service could be said to have a tradition, this is it. Data provider businesses are the oldest kind of online service outside of straight time-sharing, going back to the '70s. The early services include companies and services like Sabre, Dialog, BRS, Quotron, the Source, and Lexis. They are mostly still in business today, many enjoying better business prospects than ever as experienced veterans in an increasingly online society. They are being joined by newcomers in the thousands.

Data providers come in many flavors. Some are live data feeds, providing up-to-the-minute news, stock quotes, and other hot information. This same data may also be offered in delayed versions for lower prices, lukewarm data for the price-conscious. The news can also be packaged as the electronic equivalent of a daily newspaper, delivered either in the seller's standard format or a format specified by each user, and of course it can also be available as a large-scale historical database of past news stories. Directory services, such as OAG, online yellow pages, trade and professional directories, and so on are increasingly moving from big books to online services. Library-style research services are as popular as ever, both for librarians and library users. This list doesn't even scratch the surface, but perhaps it conveys some idea of the variety of services offered by different data providers. Many online services operate as hybrids, offering not only data provider services but also bulletin boards, file transfer libraries, gateways to networks, and so on.

> **Many online services operate as hybrids, offering not only data provider services but also bulletin boards, file transfer libraries, gateways to networks, and so on.**

Data providers often do not own the information they supply, but license it from the owners. In a sense, then, data providers are the publishers of the online world, bringing information (also known these days as "content") from its creator or owner to the public. We will now review some of the major concerns in license agreements between data providers and their sources. We will use "data provider" to refer to the company offering online access to data to the public or trade; the company supplying the data to the data provider is the "source."

Payment

There are many different payment schemes used today in contracts between data providers and sources. There is little by way of "standard" payment terms other than the standard terms each source may try to impose in all of its deals, except where competing source companies create a market for the same kind of data, and they are forced to offer deals that are comparable in price. So far, such data source markets with more than one or two suppliers are few and far between. For example, newspapers tend to have exclusive data turfs defined by their dominance of specific geographic areas; stock quote data is controlled largely by the exchanges; legal research data is mostly controlled by only a couple of companies able to make the enormous initial investment necessary to bring large enough chunks of legal libraries online to make the service useful. As long as robust markets in various information categories remain suppressed, price will not be set strongly with reference to market rates, but on the basis of how much the provider can afford to pay under the circumstances.

There are various methods used for calculating payments. The simplest is flat fees, payable weekly, monthly, or yearly, without regard to how much the database is used or accessed. This method has the advantage of ease of calculation, and enables both sources and providers to easily project their respective receipts and expenditures from the arrangement. The disadvantage, of course, is that the provider risks overpaying if the data is little used by its customers, while the source risks being underpaid if it receives only a modest periodic fee for data that turns out to be really popular with the provider's customers. The natural answer to this concern is another common method for calculating payments: a per-transaction fee paid by the provider to the source every time a customer enters, or retrieves data from, the database. This often achieves tight correlation between actual use of the data by the provider's customers, and the amount the source receives for such use.

In some cases, fees triggered every time a customer touches the data don't accurately reflect actual use of the data, either. In a library-style database, some customers may enter the system with detailed descriptions of the data they need, identifying and retrieving it quickly, while others may search and sift through the database for information. In such cases, the source may want to impose different charges for data access depending on type of use, such as simple retrieval of identified data versus performing searches on the system using local searching software tools. To keep its own finances straight, the provider will typically pass such differential charges on to its own customers, so that customers take responsibility for the costs generated by their own searches.

These are only a few of the available pricing models for database use and access. In each deal between provider and source, expect the source to seek the maximum price possible, except for the rare altruistic business, and not to be highly sensitive to the possibility that their data may turn out to be unpopular with the provider's customers. The provider will seek lower prices, of course, and will also seek to correlate the price of the data, as much as possible, with actual customer use of the data.

The Online System as a Toll Road

When you go out for a Sunday drive on the big, broad information superhighway, bring along some pocket change. A lot of the on-line experience is metered. All telephone calls outside one's immediate calling area are billed by the minute. Even within one's calling area the use of local dial-in packet switching networks to reach remote systems is often charged back to the user one way or another. Local access providers often charge flat fees for basic use, but premium uses or extended use over the billing period can add surcharges. If you want to do some research online, be prepared to pay hundreds of dollars per hour for some systems (such as the ones lawyers use)! When you consider the charges that pile up on many trips down the information superhighway, it starts looking more like the information super toll road.

The use of metering to charge for online use is growing in popularity. In fact, the toll road is rolling right into the heart of the personal computer. Several systems have been introduced recently allowing your use of software or data on CD-ROMs in your own computer to be metered in connection with online systems. Using encryption-based technology, these systems would keep track of your every access to the disk-based data, and shut down the metered software against further use when your prepaid credits are used up. You will need to call out on your modem to prepay more credits and unlock the software. At that time your recent accesses to the disk would be uploaded to the licenser, who could then use that information to pay royalties to its own suppliers if necessary. Whether or not this approach ultimately proves popular, it will certainly give hackers a challenge they can't resist.

Like a toll road, the endless stacked fees involved in calling through computer networks can grow tiresome. They are unlikely to go away, though. Charging users for use of the road, whether it's referred to as "access" or more euphemistically as "service," is one of the very few ways that online systems can keep themselves in business. As the Net grows more complicated, we may see some interesting developments in helping users pay the least freight, such as master online access systems that charge users a single lump-sum monthly fee for access to a large variety of different online services, or intelligent agent software that charts out and compares the costs of using different pathways through networks and services to find the lowest-cost routes.

One other similarity with physical toll roads is the stickiness of the toll charges—they're hard to escape. On a physical road, if you run through the toll booth without paying you can expect a noisy visit from the highway patrol. Online, it's much harder just to crack the system and avoid charges, though of course there are youthful adventurers who make that their highest aspiration. Most of us just pay the charges. Those who skip the virtual tollbooth can find online security and government agents on their trails. If caught, they will discover one other difference between running toll booths online and offline—online violations can result in far greater penalties.

Delivery of Data

It is important to specify how the data will be delivered from the source company to the data provider. The threshold question is whether the data will be maintained for use by the data provider's customers on its own computer system, or on a system controlled by the source. In the past, the data was almost always delivered by the source to the data provider, resulting in a database at the data provider's site mirroring all or part of the data source's originating database. This was mainly because data source outfits wanted no part of maintaining their own online operations. Now, though, with the growth of the Internet and services like the World Wide Web, data sources like universities and publishers can easily maintain their own full-time links, making it much more feasible for data providers to act merely as gateways between customers and each data source's database. At the same time, there are reasons that a given database may still be mirrored to the data provider rather than made available to customers in the source's own system—reasons such as security concerns, or the needs of some data providers to furnish uniform or special interfaces to their users. There is no standard arrangement; the parties should do what makes sense given the particulars of each deal.

Where the data is maintained on the data provider's system, it needs to be delivered by the source periodically. As recently as a couple of years ago, it was still common for data to be delivered on tapes used in mainframe computers, on a daily or weekly basis. Now, delivery online, with frequent updating, is probably the most common method—after all, what better use is there for an information superhighway than bulk transmissions of wholesale information? Delivery on diskettes is also common.

Often even more important, the parties need to specify the format in which the data will be delivered. If the source uses a custom or archaic format, the provider may end up spending extra money on conversions. Both sides should figure out early on if substantial conversion costs will be involved, and how those costs shall be shared.

Form of Presentation

If one pauses for a moment to consider the experience of the customer or user of a data provider system, it is instantly obvious that the form in which the database and the data are presented to the user is of paramount importance. We can no longer count on typical users to be specialist librarians or computer scientists quite happy to hack their way through any difficulty. These days, it is just as likely to be someone who got five free hours on America Online, CompuServe, or Prodigy thrown in when they bought a computer at the Price Club. Such users will use systems that feel comfortable and useful, and will shun alien-feeling systems, quite without regard to the theoretical wondrousness of the search, filter, or data manipulation tools available on the system. Providers of online information, both sources and data providers, are becoming increasingly aware of this. A big part of the response is taking control of the user interface to make sure it is properly presented.

> **We can no longer count on typical users to be specialist librarians or computer scientists quite happy to hack their way through any difficulty.**

There are other reasons each online service might like to take control of the user interface. One is that it is a way of building customer recognition for the data service, so that customer satisfaction with one service will encourage them to try other services from the same company that have the same look and feel. Another reason, for data providers offering data from a variety of sources, is that it is a way to give a uniform look to the system as a whole, instead of a patchwork crazy quilt of unique interfaces from each provider. Another concern, specifically for sources, is that if the data presentation is altered from their own authorized format, it may impair the reliability or usability of the data content for users.

Sometimes, between the source and the data provider only one party is strongly interested in controlling the look and feel of the user interface and the presentation of the data. That party should make sure its desired control is stated in the contract. At other times, both sides want to control the interface. In such cases, they should seek a compromise, in which each gets the kinds of control it needs to achieve its objective. For instance, both sides might get to display their brand names on the opening database screens, so customers associate the service with both providers; the formatting of the data in ASCII by the source company is transmitted untouched by the data provider; and the data provider's own search tools and Windows user interface for searches and reports are presented to the customers, so they need to learn searching and reporting techniques for all data sources available through that data provider only once. This is one possible compromise; many others are also appropriate, depending on the situation.

Exclusivity

One of the most important terms in a data provider deal is whether it is exclusive or nonexclusive. Exclusivity can apply to either party. For instance, a data provider may be appointed the exclusive conduit through which a given source's data reaches the public. In this case, the source may charge a premium for the exclusive relationship, which the data provider will gladly pay if being the exclusive provider of that data will bring it many customers, or an important competitive advantage. Think of being the exclusive online source of Walt Disney materials, or the *New York Times,* or Madonna fan materials, and it is clear that exclusivity in some cases will be very valuable and desperately sought after. The data provider holding an exclusive relationship with any source should be aware that the law will often imply a "best efforts" obligation on the provider to maximize sales or use of that source. The data provider can't just pick up an exclusive license

> **The data provider holding an exclusive relationship with any source should be aware that the law will often imply a "best efforts" obligation on the provider to maximize sales or use of that source.**

and then let the source's data go stagnant instead of bringing it to the public, unless it is clear that the data provider is paying the source a substantial amount for the right to do just that.

A data source may, similarly, be the exclusive source for certain kinds of information delivered by a given data provider to its customers. Again, there could be a price exacted for the privilege of exclusivity, this time going the other direction; the data source that wants to lock a provider out of dealing with competing sources may be forced to take less in fees to compensate the provider for lost opportunities to work with other sources. The scope of exclusivity can vary widely from deal to deal. In one case, the data provider may be the exclusive provider of any and all data content services offered by a given data provider; in another, a data source specializing in information on migration patterns of pink flamingos may get an exclusive on that precise subject, but the data provider could go to other sources for data on other long-legged aquatic birds, or perhaps even on other aspects of pink flamingos, such as their eating habits.

Many deals are nonexclusive on both sides. These deals often make sense in the current online business environment. Data sources are seeking to diversify and spread their content as broadly as possible to many audiences, so they will strike up deals with two or more competing data providers. Likewise, providers are happy if they can give their customers two or more quality databases on different angles of the same subject, so customers interested in that subject get more value from the data provider system as a whole, and come to view it as a one-stop shopping source for certain information needs.

Naturally, not getting an exclusive relationship makes the price for the data or for access to the data provider lower, possibly much lower. As the online world develops, we will probably witness a broad range of exclusive and nonexclusive relationships being tried out, with no one approach winning out as the best arrangement between all sources and all providers for delivery of data to customers. Sources and providers can experiment with various exclusivity and pricing combinations to find what works best for them.

Ownership

When a data source licenses its data to others, it is tacitly telling them that it owns all rights necessary to charge a price for that data. If the source does not own the data, why pay the source a nickel for it? The real data owner could show up any time and sue for infringement. Or perhaps there is no owner at all, and the data is public domain—in which case, why should the data source receive any money for the data? For these reasons, contracts for the supply of data should routinely contain warranties from the data source that it owns the data and that the data is noninfringing, and an indemnity where the data source agrees to defend and indemnify the data provider if the provider is sued for infringement. Those purchasing license from data sources should carefully look over the contract for these clauses, because the source companies often make them very weak, or even leave them out of their form contracts altogether, waiting for the provider wishing to receive data to spot the absence of these provisions and insist on their inclusion in the contract.

There are further ownership issues to consider in the contract. For instance, if the data provider alters, adds to, or reformats the data received from the source company, does that altered product still belong entirely to the source company, or is there now some dual ownership of the hybrid product by both companies? If someone infringes data received from the provider's system, who enforces the copyright—the source, the provider, or both?

Basic Communications Utilities

Anyone creating an online system needs to set up business relationships with various services that will enable communications with the rest of the world. Such communications resources include sufficient local telephone service, which in the case of a multiline system can involve special arrangements with the telephone company; line leasing, for systems making high-speed connections with the Internet and other systems; services providing their own networks with local dial-ins in many localities, enabling customers around the country to reach the system with a local call; and other special arrangements. Relationships with these companies are almost always utilities arrangements, like most people's relationships with local power and water companies. The communications resource provider furnishes generic services, with little or no particularized customer support. Those receiving the resource pay their money, and the resource provider supplies its particular type of data pipe.

Contracts with providers of utility resources are not highly negotiable, except by the very largest corporations that use enough of these resources to motivate the resource providers to cater to them. Certain resource providers, such as all telephone companies, have their contract terms partially controlled by government-filed tariffs, making negotiating custom contracts even more difficult. Moreover, many utilities-style contracts make it difficult to hold the resource provider responsible for bad service. For instance, it is typical in line-leasing form contracts for the resource provider to state that service interruptions, even substantial ones, do not give the resource customer the right to terminate the contract. Instead, the customer can get a modest credit against the next few payments due the resource provider, as an adjustment reflecting the temporary loss of service.

The moral here is that online service providers (except the largest) who want to cut themselves good deals should look to their business relationships with companies other than resource providers, where negotiation and compromise are more realistic. Getting the best deal from a resource provider usually means getting the best standard deal. It still could require a little research to find out the best deals they offer others; you may not find out about those deals from the resource provider's own sales representative without asking specifically about it. Also, be aware that many resource providers periodically offer special deals to certain classes of customers they want to attract, increasingly including small online services; smaller online services should keep their eyes open for such deals, especially at trade shows.

> **Getting the best deal from a resource provider usually means getting the best standard deal.**

That said, it is useful to get as much advance information as possible, and see if you might be able to squeeze out a better deal. As a threshold matter, find out not only the resource provider's current array of resources and services, but the new resources and services they plan on adding in the future. Communications facilities will be changing rapidly over the next few years, and a resource provider that looks state of the art this year could be a dinosaur next year if it is not already acting on upgrade plans. Make sure the resource provider will have the capacity to handle not only your current but also your future needs if your own online services (and those of its other customers) rapidly expand. It can be devastating if a sharp increase in message traffic on your system burdens your resource provider to the point that your online services suffer. Your service could gain an unwelcome reputation for sluggishness or unreliability along with the increased business.

> **Communications facilities will be changing rapidly over the next few years, and a resource provider that looks state of the art this year could be a dinosaur next year if it is not already acting on upgrade plans.**

Also, examine the response time commitments the resource provider is willing to make—how quickly the resource provider promises to respond to service calls. Even when your only remedy is a small credit against future payments to the resource provider, they take the commitment seriously; those credits get multiplied across all customers affected for system-level problems, resulting in a potentially large loss for the resource provider if it dallies in providing the fix. Similarly, look into the minimum uptime commitment, typically phrased as some percentage of a given time period in which the system will be up and running normally, such as 97% during normal business hours every month. Such commitments are gross indicators of overall system dependability. Some resource providers are willing to make such commitments, some aren't. Be careful when considering these figures. While 97% looks like a pretty good number at first, it is the equivalent of a full day down every month. Such downtime might be acceptable if it comes mostly during low traffic hours and in small chunks, but unacceptable if it means major interruptions during prime time use two or three times per month.

Gateway Arrangements

Online service providers that give users the ability, whether apparent or real, to leave their own systems and enter other systems can be referred to as "gateways." Some of the oldest research services, such as Dialog, have used gateways for years for at least some of the databases provided their users. Other older systems, such as Inet, were comprised entirely of gateways with a menu-based system for moving between them. New gateway-type systems have arisen in the past few years on the Internet, in the form of the gopher and World Wide Web (WWW) services now available at many Internet sites. While gopher and WWW are often referred to as navigational tools, they offer users services very much like the old gateway systems. Gopher servers provide users with a hierarchical set of menus and sub-menus, where many of the menu choices put the user into direct contact with another Internet site where the chosen information or services actually reside. WWW servers do something similar, except they are structured as a set of linked texts and files spread across the Internet, rather than a hierarchical menu system.

The concerns of an online service, when contracting with another system for which it is providing a gateway, are similar to many of those discussed for deals with data providers: how are payments calculated, whose system interface is used to present the service to the user, whether the gateway access is exclusive between the systems, whose "brand" of service the user thinks he or she is getting while in the remote system. The general considerations of response time and indemnities described above also apply, as well as the dependency considerations if your online business is highly dependent on a given gateway arrangement to a particular online service.

One subject of special concern in gateway arrangements is dividing or allocating the risk of injuries or problems between the two systems. If the user of my online service downloads virus-infected software from a different system he entered through one of my gateways, and subsequently suffers computer system damage, who should bear the responsibility in a lawsuit, my system or the system on the other side of the gateway? There are arguments for both sides. As system operator for the user's local system, I could claim the remote system is responsible because that is where the user picked up the virus. Since only the operator of the remote system can take steps to make sure there are no viruses there, it should be responsible. On the other hand, the operator of the remote system might claim I'm responsible. He or she could argue that users enter the remote system through the gateway at their own risk, and that as operator of the local system, I'm responsible to the users to make sure they understand and accept their risks. To avoid such quandaries, the two systems should use their contract to designate in advance who is responsible to the user in such cases. Further, if they agree one system is responsible to the user in a given case, they should also determine whether that responsibility internally gets divided up between them. This kind of agreement largely gets worked out as part of the indemnities section, discussed earlier in this chapter. Of course, the system that directly hosts the users should also make sure to protect both itself and the other system with appropriate limitations of liability in the user agreement, as discussed above.

Gopher and WWW server arrangements are much newer. For the most part, the systems linking together through these servers do not enter into formal agreements, as is common with most traditional Internet cooperative relationships. If a user is injured on a remote system reached through a gopher server or WWW server, and if the user's local system has limited its own liability (but not the remote system's liability) in the user contract, can the user take legal action against the remote system? This is not entirely clear right now, though it appears the user has a good chance of suing the remote system if his or her legal claim is otherwise sound. With increasing commercial use of gopher and WWW servers, it is likely all systems will act in the future to better protect themselves from user lawsuits. The easiest method is simply for each system to specify, in its own user agreements, that liability to the user will be limited not only for the local system, but also for all systems the user reaches through gateways or Internet servers from that local system. If all systems use such user agreements, they will protect each other from excessive liability to users hopping from system to system.

Online Space Rentals

Many systems look to rent out online "areas" to other businesses who wish to offer their own online services, but do not want to set up and run a whole computer system themselves to do it. In this section, the term "rental" is used to describe the overall business arrangement. However, among the deals being made today you will find such arrangements offered under many titles, from "forum management" to simply "online services." Don't get hung up on the names. If the deal resembles the kind of arrangement discussed here, then it is useful to think of it as analogous to a rental of office, storefront, or warehouse space.

The basic rental deal is that the host system provides the tenant business with its own space or area within the host system. This space has some areas for storage and provision of services to the public or trade, and one or more online addresses at which it can be reached from the outside world.

Rental customers are usually successful in some business or trade and looking to expand in online services, perhaps for the first time. Consequently, they may have pretty strong ideas of what kind of online service they wish to provide and how they will provide it, subject to the fundamentally exploratory nature of all startup online services. For such companies, a rental of online space lets them maintain strong control over the delivery of services to their own customers, while outsourcing all computer and communications support functions.

There are no standard deals for space rental in the online industry, which is still young and rapidly changing. Even the largest online services such as CompuServe, Prodigy, America Online, Delphi, and eWorld offer very different arrangements. Companies contemplating online space rental should carefully consider the kinds and amount of system resources they are being offered on a given system. Smaller online services keenly interested in the rental customer's business may make more resources available than large online systems, or available at a significantly better price. Prospective rental customers should also look at the possible benefits of working within a host system with major name recognition and significant "foot traffic," such as those just mentioned.

Resources and Services Available to the Rental Customer

Our use of the term "rental space" is metaphorical, but it can also reflect the way the online service environment feels and functions once it is set up. Physically, the "space" is made up of the set of system resources provided by the host system to the rental customer. The rental customer should make sure every resource necessary for its own planned online service is spelled out in the contract. The standard contracts of many host systems today skim over describing the resources available, but it can be dangerous to leave this matter for later, after you're already doing business. It could turn out that resources essential to the rental customer's business needs are simply not compatible with the host system's computer system (such as, for instance, highly secure communications channels, or the ability to process certain kinds of electronic payments), or that providing such resources may not be affordable to either party. At that point, the rental customer will need to either search for a new online host, or pay an unreasonable amount for required system resources because of the host system's incompatibility with its needs.

> **The standard contracts of many host systems today skim over describing the resources available, but it can be dangerous to leave this matter for later, after you're already doing business.**

Resources found on many systems available for online rental today include:

- File storage areas, both for the rental customer to distribute materials to its users, and for users to exchange files with each other.

- Database and document management areas accepting information in one or more popular formats, for special services the rental customer may want to provide its users.

- Bulletin boards or public conferencing areas, for group discussions among the rental customer's users.

- Private electronic mail.

- Dedicated system storage capacity, in an amount sufficient to enable the rental customer to store all necessary data on the host system.

- Sufficient line and user handling capacity for all reasonably anticipated rental customer needs.

Other desired or available resources may include real-time chat areas, multiuser game capability, gateways to the Internet and other networks and systems, electronic payment capability—the list is long and growing longer, as new kinds of services are developed practically by the day. It is beyond the scope of this legal book to provide guidance on the exact mix of services that online businesses should offer or seek from others. The important thing is to remember that *whatever* services are chosen, they should each be listed and briefly described in the contract covering the online rental arrangement.

> **Some host systems offer not only a rental of virtual space, but system operators who can assist the rental customer in providing its online services.**

Some host systems offer not only a rental of virtual space, but system operators who can assist the rental customer in providing its online services. This assistance can be ideal for the rental customer that wants an online presence, but really does not want to learn much about providing online services. The system operators provided by the host system can perform generic online functions, like file and message management, answering general and system questions from users, and configuring online areas and user privileges as requested by the rental customer. They will likely not be able, though, to replace the rental customer's own expertise and customer relations personnel, nor would the customer want them to. If the rental customer is a manufacturer of bows and arrows, for instance, it will have to have at least one or two of its own people going online to answer user questions about archery in general and its products in particular, deal with customer problems and complaints, and so on.

One important issue in using the host's system operators is how answerable they will be to the rental customer. Most businesses are tremendously concerned about how their online services will affect their reputation with the public and with their customers. Accordingly, the rental customer should be able to control how the host's system operators interact with customers, and instruct them not to perform intrusive system maintenance operations during prime time or important business hours for the rental customer. If the host system seems incapable of ceding partial authority over its own system operators as necessary to accommodate this simple request, it may be a warning sign that the host and rental companies will have trouble cooperating generally.

Just as important as the initial set of resources and services is the ability for the rental customer to expand its use of the host system's resources as its online services grow. The rental customer should find out at the outset whether the host system can keep up with the customer's potential growth. Likewise, the host system should structure its system so that it will not cripple its rental customers; they will leave if their resource needs are not met.

Most host systems prepare for future demand not by having the increased resources currently available, but by configuring the system so it is expandable as necessary. There are a number of potential issues that should be looked at when addressing the host system's expandability. One is whether the host system will commit to expanding when needed by an individual rental customer, or only when required by the overall needs of the entire system and all of its customers. Rental customers, of course, will always prefer that their individual needs be all that is necessary to justify expansion, but they may have to fight for this commitment from some hosts. Another question is who pays the cost of expansion. If a host system plans to pass on expansion costs, the way landlords pass on the cost of building improvements to the tenants, the rental customer should know this in advance, and negotiate a different result if desired. Finally, the rental customer should review the online host's basic system to satisfy itself about expandability. Reliance by the host system on outmoded or unpopular computer hardware or software can make future expansion difficult, costly, and time-consuming. The rental customer should make sure the agreement accounts for such limited expandability, either by making the host commit to upgrading the system on a reasonable schedule, or as the basis for negotiating better terms on other matters important to the rental customer.

Service Identity

When users call an online service, who do they think they are calling? Do they believe they are visiting a particular online store or service, unaware of the host system that supports the online operations of that store or service? Or are they fully aware of the host system as a global online service, equivalent to a shopping mall that contains a variety of stores or services they might visit?

Different host systems and rental customers make different arrangements on how they present themselves to users. Some host systems are quite content to work in the background, letting users think they are calling directly to the tenant business. These hosts consider themselves to be serving the "trade"; their only customers are the businesses who rent use of their systems and in turn provide online services to the public. Many tenant businesses require such subordination of the host system in order to properly coordinate their own customer relationships. They need total control of the presentation of their services to online customers, just as they control their physical storefronts, the way their employees dress, and the packaging of their products. Nike, for instance, would likely want to run the "Nike" brand online service, and not just be the athletic shoes component of the "Acme" online superstore.

> **Different host systems and rental customers make different arrangements on how they present themselves to users.**

Other host systems insist on being the primary focus of user attentions. There are several reasons for this. First, host systems perform a very important function in the online world: they are, by default, the landmarks and community gathering spots of cyberspace. Physical shopping malls and community centers are anchored to towns, neighborhoods, and road crossings, and derive much of their identity simply from their locations. In contrast, there are no natural geographic anchors online. Large online systems are equally reachable from any spot in the nation, or even the world; if they have a location at all, it is the location they create by being a focal point for user activities. In fact, one of the main benefits they offer their tenant business is giving them a location *within* the host system. In order to strengthen its role as one of the landmarks of the online world, a host system must forge a recognizable identity. That often requires giving the host system, rather than the tenant businesses, control of the primary user relationship.

Second, general-purpose host systems often do not want to rely too much on any particular business tenant. It is more likely that users will keep patronizing the host system despite turnovers in individual tenant businesses if users identify the various services on a host system with the system itself, rather than the specific businesses providing individual service. Consider how large shopping malls persist over a period of time despite turnover in their business tenants. The shoppers know they will always find a few bookstores and shoe stores at the mall, even if the exact stores are not the same as last year's selection.

Third, mailing lists: if all users are considered primarily to be host system customers, rather than customers of the individual online businesses they visit within the host system, then the host system controls the list of customer names. Such lists can be an immensely valuable commercial resource, subject to the limits imposed by data privacy rights of users. Keeping customer lists out of the hands of tenant businesses is also a way for host systems to reduce attrition of their user bases. If each tenant business could use the list of all their online customers to start up a competing online service on another system, the host system could find much of its user base drained away.

So while some host systems seek to create their own identities with users, others are happy to provide background technical services and remain invisible to users. Each online service needs to resolve the question of its presentation to users at the outset, and make its arrangements with other online businesses accordingly. If the agreement between host system and rental business does not make it clear which business is highlighted to users, the online tenant might be in for a rude surprise when it finds itself reduced to nothing more than an obscure, faceless service option in a shopping area with the host system's name plastered all over it.

Who Holds the User Agreement?

In the preceding section we saw that in a given case, either the host system or the tenant business might be presented as the service that users are visiting. A related question is: who has the privilege and responsibility of setting up the general legal environment for use of the service, through control of the standard user agreements (the terms of user agreements were discussed earlier)?

> **Generally, the business that controls the user relationship also controls the agreement with each user.**

Generally, the business that controls the user relationship also controls the agreement with each user. An online space rental involves at least two companies supporting user services, but in most cases only one of these companies has a direct agreement with the users. For the company without the direct user relationship, this means if it wants to establish any legal obligations on the part of users, it will need to ask the other company to put those obligations into the user agreement.

For instance, presume we have a tenant business that provides financial information used by large companies to make cost projections. The tenant business has a couple of major legal concerns regarding users of its information. One is that if it accidentally provides erroneous information, faulty cost projections could result, which might be very damaging to large companies using those projections as the basis for multimillion dollar projects. The tenant business would like these large companies to assume the risk of such problems, rather than sue the tenant business if they lose a major project because the cost projections fell through. Another legal concern is that users could download large chunks of the financial information from the tenant business, then republish that information in competition with the very business they just acquired it from. In this case, the tenant business might want to have users agree to use the downloaded information only for research purposes in preparing their cost projections, and acknowledge they have no license to republish the information in any form.

If the tenant business has a direct agreement with the users, it is simple to create these legal understandings and protections. Just write them into the standard user agreements, and make those provisions nonnegotiable. But what if the host system insists on controlling all user agreements, so that the tenant business only has a direct contract relationship with the host system? In that case, the tenant business needs to make sure the host system's standard user agreements give it the protections from users that it needs. If those protections are not in the host system's existing form agreement, the tenant business will not get them unless it can prevail upon the host system to change its standard form as necessary. If the tenant business makes this a basic requirement for working with the host system, it can often get the user agreement changed sufficiently to meet its needs, and not leave it unnecessarily exposed to user claims.

Interestingly, at the time we go to press, at least one of the major "brand name" national online services protects only itself from liability in its user agreement. If a user who is injured online wants to make a legal claim against one of the tenant businesses, the user agreement gives him or her a clear path to do so. The host system's standard agreement hangs the tenant business out to dry on all user claims, for no discernible business reason other than corporate unresponsiveness.

Other Agreements

The agreements discussed above cover only some of the kinds of arrangements that online businesses will make. Other common arrangements include:

- *System operator agreements*. When the system operator is an employee of the online business, no written agreement is usually necessary unless he or she is a key employee whose presence is necessary for the system's success, and who could seriously injure the business if he or she leaves to work for a direct competitor. In such cases, the employer may want to have an agreement giving the system operator a piece of the business in exchange for exemplary performance, and containing substantial nondisclosure and noncompetition provisions. If the system operator is an independent contractor, then a contract is advisable.

- *Advertising Agreements*. If the online business sells advertising, whether display or classified, it's a good idea to have agreements with advertisers. These should be form agreements, the terms not varying between advertisers unless a company giving the online service a lot of business and money requests a reasonable modification or two.

- *Software Development Agreements*. Online businesses often require custom software work in order to offer new system features or improve existing ones. It is prudent to document the working arrangement with a written agreement. Among other things, the online business needs to decide whether it wants to pay for the development work strictly on an hourly basis (often called "time and materials" arrangements), or establish a fixed price with the supplier for a specified custom-developed software product. Also, as discussed above, the online business should arrange to obtain the source code for the software, and obtain either ownership of the software or a license to modify it freely.

Whatever the contracting needs of an online business, it should obtain the assistance of a lawyer with some background in the area. Picking the right lawyer for an online service can be a little tricky right now. With all the fanfare surrounding the "information superhighway," lawyers with no background in online legal matters are paying someone to put up a web server with their name on it, and then proclaiming themselves instant experts. In reality, a lot of these lawyers want to learn by doing work for the first online business or two they can pick up as clients. This is perfectly fine, if the client agrees that training the lawyer is part of the project. But it

> **Picking the right lawyer for an online service can be a little tricky right now.**

also makes it very important for online businesses to inquire into the backgrounds of lawyers they are asking for help. If the business seeking legal help is new itself to the online environment, then choosing a lawyer without appropriate experience will result in the blind leading the blind.

How Do You Form a Contract?

A contract is formed when two parties have a "meeting of the minds." You can make contracts online, or using old-fashioned pen and paper.

Online User Contracts

Online systems naturally want to establish their contractual relationships with users online. That is where users first come into contact with the system, and once the contract is agreed to, the user can go right into the system and start using it. Compared to this approach, it seems complicated and slow to make users read, sign, and mail back a user contract before letting them use the system.

The basics of making an effective online user contract are simple. Before being permitted access to the online system, or to special areas or services within that system, users are led through a set of screens containing contract terms. To move beyond this area of the online system, the user must give a response that either indicates his or her consent to the contract terms, or brings him or her out of that part of the system without agreeing with anything. The online system software should save all affirmative responses, keeping an organized record of each user's agreement to the contract terms for the system.

A contract made in this fashion is complete and fully enforceable. The user is shown the terms of the contract before agreeing to them, and is given the choice to freely accept or reject the terms. It is, in fact, far more enforceable than the "shrink-wrap" license agreements found in almost all commercial software packages. The problem with shrink-wrap agreements is that software customers usually buy the software before they get a look at the license terms, and have no option to back out of the deal after they have paid for it and opened the box.

It is still early in the history of online environments. There remains some question about how you would prove the existence of a purely online contract in court. The main risk is that the question will be raised whether the user really accepted the terms of the agreement. This risk can be very low where the system operator does the following:

- Make the user go through the contract term screens before they can use the system in other than "demo" mode.

- Give the user the option to leave the contract screen sequence at any point. They cannot become registered or accepted users, though, until they do go through the whole sequence.

- Make the user show consent to the contract terms in an unambiguous way, demonstrating that he or she really agrees to terms just displayed. For instance, after showing the contract term screens, tell the user that to indicate contract acceptance, he or she must type a lengthy, unambiguous character string like: "I, _____, hereby accept the contract terms of Acme Online." (The blank line is for the user's first and last name.)

- Keep a well-organized record of user acceptances of the agreement terms. One way, conceptually simple and effective, is to keep a log of the sequence of contract screens shown to each user together with the user's acceptance response. With this approach, the online system can change standard contract terms from time to time, and show exactly which set of terms each user agreed to when they first entered the system, without having to perform any involved file management or correlations.

- If the online system wants to change its user contract terms upon occasion, there are two things it can do to make sure they are effective for all users. First, the basic agreement with each user should specify that the service provider can change terms upon some number of days notice, and if the user does not like it, he or she can terminate the agreement and leave the system before the change takes effect. Second, every time there is a change, all users should be alerted in a manner that will definitely reach them, such as a combination of e-mail and opening-screen bulletins.

- Systems especially concerned about user identities can take additional steps. One common approach is to require use of credit cards to pay for system access. Another is to call back a phone number given by each user as part of the registration process, to verify that that user is really at that number. These extra verification steps are not normally necessary, though, except in special cases such as systems containing confidential information or adult materials. For other systems, taking these extra steps to definitively determine the true identity of each user is not important for defending the system from user claims, since any user suing the system would identify him or herself as such, or could be found to be a user in the course of the litigation.

If the online system routinely follows the procedures outlined above, or equivalent procedures recommended by its attorney, there will be little risk of a user successfully claiming that he or she never agreed to the system's user agreement.

Other Online Contracts

Any business or commercial contract can be made online these days. However, many of these contracts are still negotiated and signed on paper, with use of online services confined to transmitting revised copies of contracts between the parties by e-mail or fax.

There is a good reason for this. Many contracts between businesses are not for tidily packaged consumer services, but for close working arrangements in which each business takes on certain detailed responsibilities in a combined business operation. Form contracts are rarely useful as-is for these kinds of relationships, though they may be used as a basis for negotiating contract terms. Each negotiated contract is unique to the relationship it covers, and each party needs a copy to put away against the day it might need to refer back to the written deal.

The contract-keeping techniques described above for standardized user agreements do not work very well for negotiated business contracts. In particular, a running log of all contract changes leading to final agreement may not be possible or desirable. Such a log would not show a coherent contract but a dialog leading to a contract; it might be differently kept by the two businesses involved, making the log a source of confusion rather than stability; and the businesses involved might prefer to refer only to the final, agreed document, not the interim versions showing the other kinds of deals they did not make on the way to the deal they did make.

That said, if two businesses are committed to making a deal entirely online, they can do so. They need to assure that when they're done negotiating there is a single electronic document, preferably in a commonly used format like ASCII or Word, bearing the electronic signature of each party to the deal. In

More Reliable Than Pen and Ink

If I make a deal in e-mail and the other guy breaches our digital contract, can I enforce my rights? I don't have the other guy's signature in ink on paper, so he can claim I made it up on a word processor. Should I forget about online deals and stick to paper contracts?

Not at all. Despite popular opinion, the law never generally required paper contracts and handwritten, ink signatures. For centuries ink and paper were all we had, so the symbolic act of signing a contract seemed an absolute physical requirement. However, over the past few decades new electronic means of communication arose, starting with the telegraph and Telecopier, and then fax machines. Courts have been willing to enforce contracts made with these devices once it was demonstrated the electronically conveyed signatures were authentic. Absolute certainty is not necessary, just evidence that it's very unlikely the signature is false. The same kind of evidence, in fact, that is used routinely to prove that ink signatures are authentic: a witness testifies that he or she recognizes the handwriting, or remembers when that signature was placed on the contract.

Good evidence of the authenticity of online agreements is readily available today for two common classes of online contracts: standard user agreements for online services, and the repetitive form agreements used for buying, selling, and funds transfer in electronic data interchange ("EDI") environments. For user agreements, the online system owner can keep regular logs of every new user's sign-on to the service, and the character string that user transmits to indicate his or her assent to the system's condition and rules. For EDI, the trading partners typically sign a master agreement on paper that lays out how their computer systems will transact business, and provides that all electronic deals made according to those procedures will be valid. In each case, courts will readily accept the validity of the electronically signed contract, based on the reliability of standardized, repeated forms or procedures.

But what about nonstandard contracts negotiated in e-mail? How can I prove you agreed to the exact terms in my copy of an electronic contract, and that I didn't just add them with my word processor?

In fact, there's new software now available that will let us all do just that, based on public key encryption systems. The same basic technology used for securely encrypted e-mail can be turned around and used to create "digital signatures" of unassailable authenticity. In a nutshell, each person signing an electronic document uses the digital signature software to create a smaller file uniquely correlated to that document, and encrypts it using his or her private key; the electronic document with both encrypted files attached comprises the signed contract. To prove its authenticity, all we need do is decrypt each encrypted signature file using that person's public key, and show that the information in it uniquely corresponds to the document. The fact that a given person's public key decrypts the information proves it was encrypted using that same person's private key.

Contracts signed using public key systems are, in fact, more verifiably authentic than ink on paper contracts. You can't forge a public or private key. The only weak link in the chain is making sure you really do have the other person's public key. There are several projects underway right now to set up "trusted server" public key repositories, institutions that can assure us of the linkages between real people and their public keys. When they are established, paper contracts will assume their rightful place as pretechnological relics with second-class reliability.

the past couple of years, encryption technology has emerged as the means for ensuring reliable digital signatures. The approach most likely to be used is public/private key systems, in which anybody holding the signer's public key (an encryption/decryption code given out by the signer to others) can verify a message encrypted by the signer using his private key (an encryption/decryption code which the signer keeps private from everyone else). Those relying on such encryption systems must correctly follow the instructions of the encryption tool providers if they want the resulting contracts to be authentic and reliable. At least as important, anyone who relies on someone else's public key to assure the authenticity of that person's digital signature must make sure they get that person's real public key. The best way, of course, is to have it handed to you in person.

There is an area of online contracting that is fairly well established and on the increase, known as electronic data interchange, or EDI. Currently, it is used almost exclusively for routine, bureaucratic commercial transactions that differ little from transaction to transaction. Major current uses include parts ordering in the airline, automotive, and other industries, and debits and credits between banks and other financial institutions. These transactions resemble form agreement situations much more closely than highly negotiated deals, so EDI is ideal. If the arrangements underlying EDI transactions between two large businesses require special negotiation, then those arrangements might be reached in a signed master agreement, and the ensuing EDI transactions carried out online in accordance with the terms of that agreement.

In the future, we should expect to see EDI and other online contract techniques extended further and further toward all kinds of contracts, even the most highly negotiated ones. Major developments that will help establish a fully online contract regime will be the spread of easy-to-use, encryption-based techniques for authenticating digital signatures; the establishment of universal document formats for digital contracts; and the development of easy-to-use contract negotiation software packages making it even easier to negotiate online contracts than paper ones.

While there is much more to be said about online contracts, full treatment of the subject would be a book in itself. The resources listed in the appendix are an excellent way for the reader to learn more about this subject.

Written Agreements with Users

Written agreements are starting to look a little old-fashioned in this age of electronic texts. They retain certain advantages, however.

> **The physical ritual of signing and delivering the contract, and the deep impression it can make on the signer's mind, are largely absent from many purely electronic contracts.**

One is that a signed contract is presumed authentic unless someone can show a reason to question it. Another is that people really *feel* like they're agreeing to something when they sign the contract form and send it back to you. The physical ritual of signing and delivering the contract, and the deep impression it can make on the signer's mind, are largely absent from many purely electronic contracts. With highly automated online contracts, users might just ignore the contract procedures as a one-time distraction on the way to the online activities they really want to pursue.

For systems requiring user payments, it can be fairly easy to obtain a written contract together with the first payment. All the contract terms can be printed on the payment form which the user signs and sends back with his or her payment. If such an approach seems to assault users with too much upfront verbiage, then the payment form can simply include a statement that the user agrees to all the rules of the online system, which is signed by the user. If a system uses this latter approach, it should make sure the rules are posted in an easy-to-find area on the system.

Written contracts can also be used to supplement online contracts. The standardized master agreement with each user can include a clause stating that online agreements between the system and the user will be considered fully valid contracts. With these master agreements in hand, the system provider can count on the enforceability of its subsequent online contracts with users. The master agreement can also affirm the enforceability of online rule changes, making those changes as enforceable as the original agreement.

An important contractual detail, often overlooked, is making sure the right parties sign the contract. This means the legal entity running the online system—whether an individual, a partnership, or a corporation—should sign the user agreement. For the user, this means the person or entity responsible for the user's activities signs the agreement. Someone using the system as a corporate employee should sign the agreement as an agent of the corporation, not in his or her own name. If the user is a child, the system provider should consider getting the agreement from the child's parents, since agreements by children are often voidable at will.

Owning and Using
Online Property

An online system serves as a storage and transmission area for the property of many different people and companies. Start-up systems are usually generously stocked with the owner's property: welcoming messages and announcements to incoming users, bulletins, structured file areas, message areas, discussion categories, various programs for users to run, not to mention logon banners, messages, and bulletins. Users immediately start leaving their own possessions around as well—public postings, e-mail, files, secret information, advertising materials, contracts, and the like. Soon, the online system becomes a fluid medium for the exchange of all manner of property among its owner and its users.

There is growing confusion about property rights to online materials. Large entertainment and publishing companies are now setting up online operations. Many of them are finding their own intellectual property assets already strewn among thousands of bulletin boards and ftp sites by others. Companies in other lines of business are extending their local networks to the Internet. They are becoming concerned about both company information assets that may leak out into the Net, and who owns the rights to materials their in-house users bring in from the outside and use in company business. Multimedia creators now use the networks as one of their main resources for audio, image, and video clips for inclusion in their products. They have a wide range of perceptions about how far they can take and use materials they find online without seeking the permission of the owner or creator.

Some say this new electronic medium transforms the movement of information, so that our old concepts of property ownership no longer apply. However, United States intellectual property laws, such as copyright and trademark laws, evolved, grew, and matured through many past changes of information technology. They are fully adequate for defining property boundaries in cyberspace under current communications technology. Some small adjustments will be necessary from time to time to track social, business, and technology changes, but that has been the case for intellectual property laws for well over 100 years.

Brief Introduction to Copyright Law

This section provides a background on United States copyright law useful for following the discussion of online property that follows. More in-depth treatments can be found among the law review articles and basic texts listed in the back of this book.

The moment someone creates a book, a piece of music, computer program, or other copyrightable work, it is *already* copyrighted under federal law. That's it. No notice, no registration are necessary for the creator (called an "author" in the copyright statute) to have and keep that copyright.

> **The moment someone creates a book, a piece of music, computer program, or other copyrightable work, it is *already* copyrighted under federal law.**

Notice and registration are helpful, though. When making a work publicly available, placing a copyright notice on it prohibits an infringer from claiming he or she is an "innocent infringer" in a lawsuit. This benefit, though technical, can increase the money damages available to those whose copyright is infringed. Therefore, it's a good idea to place a copyright notice on all published works. The best form of notice for United States and international use is ©*[year of publication] [name of copyright owner]*. For instance, if Mr. Software creates a user's manual for snow cone machines in 1994 (which is when his copyright starts), but only first circulates it to people outside his immediate family and closest friends in 1996 (thus "publishing" it), he should put the notice © *1996 Mr. Software* in a conspicuous place, such as the inside front cover or title page of his snow cone manual.

It is even a better idea to register the work with the Copyright Office as early as possible. If the work is registered *before* an infringement occurs, the copyright owner has a good chance of being awarded his or her attorneys' fees in a successful case, among other benefits. But if the work is registered only *after* the infringement, the copyright owner will definitely have to pay his or her own attorney fees, even if he or she wins. Such fees can outweigh the money awarded to the owner by the court for the infringement. Many times, the copyright owner's decision to sue for infringement will depend on whether attorneys' fees are available, which in turn is based on whether the copyright was registered prior to infringement.

A copyright gives certain exclusive legal rights to the owner of a work; these are listed in the copyright statute. An "exclusive right" means the copyright owner totally controls a certain use of the work; only the owner and those he or she authorizes (usually called "licensees") are legally permitted that use of the work. For online systems, the following exclusive rights are particularly important:

- The right to copy the work.
- The right to make modified versions of the work (sometimes called "derivative works").
- The right to distribute the work.
- The right to transmit the work.
- The right to perform the work publicly.
- The right to run computer programs on a computer.

All of these rights can be important in different aspects of online system activity. Every time a file is moved within or between computer systems, it results in "copying" that file, and "distributing" that file to the other systems. Every message and file maintained on an online system for online system users can be considered massively "distributed" to all those users. When a system operator deletes language contained in a user posting, he or she is "modifying" it.

Copyrights Online—Nothing New, or Vast Expansion of Rights?

The White House formed the National Information Infrastructure (NII) Task Force in 1993, and charged it with finding out what needs to be regulated on the networks. One of the first reports back was from its Working Group on Intellectual Property, a voluminous document published in 1994 and known simply as the "Green Paper." Despite the thickness of the Green Paper, the Working Group's main finding was that little needs to be changed to apply copyright law to computer networks, either now or in the foreseeable future.

One of the few changes recommended by the Working Group is to make it clear that the copyright owner's permission would be required every time a copyrighted file is sent from computer to computer on a network. Wait a minute—isn't that just common sense? Yes, but copyright has some traditions to wrestle with.

Under traditional copyright law, there are limits on how far a copyright owner can control distribution of physical copies like books, records, and tapes. The owner has the right to control initial distribution of a book, but after that, buyers can freely resell their copies to whoever they want and at any price. This right of the buyer to resell his or her copy outside the copyright owner's control is known as the "first sale doctrine."

The Working Group saw that a technical problem could arise if you applied the first sale doctrine literally to file transfers in cyberspace. If everyone who downloads a file copy to their own computer is equivalent to the buyer of a book, then the first sale doctrine could give them the right to freely redistribute those copies to everyone else on the Net, at any price or for free. This means every new online work could spread like wildfire through the Net, and the copyright owner would lose all ability to charge money for it. To prevent this loosening of copyright, the Working Group recommended that for file transfers over networks, a "first sale" that would cut off the copyright owner's control of online distribution never occurs.

For many, this is a minor but important adjustment that will help copyright function online much the same way it has in the physical world. Others, however, proclaim this move the most radical change in copyright law in the last century. They argue that existing copyright law reflects a carefully calibrated balance between the rights of creators to control their works, and the rights of the public to use and distribute those works. For example, writers of popular books must live with the fact that, thanks to the first sale doctrine, an aftermarket of used books will eventually arise to compete directly with new editions of their works. This puts a limit on the profits a copyright owner can wring out of his or her work, while the public gets the continuing ability to recirculate existing copies. If the first sale doctrine is eliminated for online transfers as the Working Group recommends, then there will be no possibility of an aftermarket in used digital copies on the Net, and no limit on the copyright owner's control of the work. The public will no longer be able to recirculate copies at prices set by the marketplace; every transfer will be made under conditions and at prices set by the copyright owner.

This author prefers the approach taken by the NII Task Force Working Group. While it is true that every file transfer would be within the copyright owner's legal control if we eliminate the first sale doctrine, there are other factors that will keep files moving on the Net. One is the implied license to redistribute files, as discussed in the text; another is the continuing use and development of shareware and other file distribution schemes that depend on widespread distribution, rather than strict control, to achieve the copyright owner's goals. Another development that could make this whole debate irrelevant is the rise of encryption-based metering software: copies of works contained in metered files could be distributed endlessly, but no copy could be accessed by a user without paying the copyright owner or its agent for the privilege, on a time or usage metered basis. In any event, there should be continuing debate on this subject over the next few years.

Most of these everyday activities are performed legally, because they are done with permission from the copyright owners. Everyone who participates in a given online system implicitly agrees that any materials he or she places in a public area on the system can be treated in the same manner as others' materials are customarily treated in that area (provided the treatment is not outrageous). This is called an implied license. On some systems, users might be required to grant a broader license than would be available under the normal implied license. For example, a system operator may seek users' advance consent to collect their public messages on the system and publish the collection in book form.

Customary uses and implied licenses help keep many of the online activities we see from being infringements, but these rights do have limits. Users who place their materials on an online system still retain many rights that are not included in implied licenses. Unfortunately, that is not always clear to others who find the materials online.

Indeed, some people believe that anything injected into the online domain is fair game for anyone else who wants to use it, as though copyrights are somehow "stripped off" the work when it is recast in electronic form. We recall a system user who insisted that collages he made using large portions of others' digitized pictures were entirely noninfringing as a matter of principle. The theory was that anyone who sends his copyrighted picture into a publicly accessible online system automatically makes that picture a public resource, and gives up all rights to stop others from using those pictures as they wish.

This certainly is an attractive way to look at things when you want to justify using others' works without permission, but is not in accord with the way intellectual property law really operates. Using substantial parts of a picture within another picture is creation of a "derivative work" which, as you may recall, is one of the copyright owner's exclusive rights. Making such a derivative work without permission will be an infringement, regardless of whether it is done with magazine cutouts on cardboard or digitized graphic images on a computer screen.

Various other, equally illegal, practices of using materials from the Net without the owner's permission have arisen over the past few years. You may be surprised at some of them. Or perhaps you may be surprised to hear that these practices are infringing:

- Taking images from online services and printing them by the thousands in large-scale corporate newsletters or newsstand magazines.

- Using image, text, and animation files from the Internet in multimedia CD-ROMs.

- Taking excerpts from various online news services to create a customized newsletter distributed to its own set of customers.

- Taking online discussions from a private service or from Usenet, and republishing them either online or in print for a fee.

All of these activities can be fully legal, as long as all the owners of the copyrights involved give their permission. However, getting those permissions requires doing some work, and some owners may not even want to permit the intended use. So we expect to continue to see such infringing uses by the lazy or dishonest, replete with ringing defenses of information freedom whenever it is suggested that they get permission when they use others' property.

Is Copyright Dead?

There's a belief in the air that copyright law as we know it will die out on the computer networks. It's at root a Utopian view: cyberspace is a vast new frontier with laws unwritten, a place where we can leave behind crude turf-based concepts of property, intellectual or otherwise, and enter into a new era of information sharing. "Information wants to be free."

This sentiment was bolstered in recent years by the revelation that individual acts of copyright infringement are impossible to prevent. You or I can easily copy any digital work and send it to many thousands of computers around the world on the Internet, with just a few keystrokes. If we take the extra step of using an anonymous remailer when sending out the mass infringement, then no one can ever trace the infringement back to us. This is seen by many as conclusive proof that copyright-based control of image, text, data, software, and other files on the networks is not only pointless, but literally impossible.

But is it? In fact, the copyright system never depended on stopping all infringement dead. Look at the entertainment industries: record and video companies flourish, despite rampant infringements on the sidewalks of all major cities and in the aisles of country flea markets. Look at the software industry: despite years of vigilant enforcement activities by the Software Publishers Association, software is copied with impunity in business offices across the country, and in entire countries on the other side of the world. This has not prevented the software business from becoming America's leading industry, with some of the biggest profit margins around.

These industries are successful because copyright law is very good at its real job: keeping major markets for copyrighted works free of infringing copies. In the physical world, we're talking about record, video, and book stores. The online equivalent is the large online services like Prodigy, America Online, and CompuServe; the hordes of smaller BBSs serving local or specialized communities; and Usenet and major ftp sites on the Internet. Some copyright owners are already beginning to clear off infringing copies in these places using their two favorite techniques: prowling around and eliminating all major displays of infringing copies, and making examples of selected infringers with vicious lawsuits.

On the prowling tip, it's been reported that the SPA has roughly 2,000 BBSs under surveillance as known or suspected infringe-

ment sites. Many individual copyright owners, including Walt Disney, Paramount, Lotus, LucasArts, and BMI, have been sighted making the rounds and sweeping infringing materials off the major sites. It should not be long now before we see these companies and others sending out intelligent agent programs to multiply their prowling effectiveness. We knew those darn critters would be good for something beyond gathering the morning news.

The symbolic copyright lawsuits started slowly, but now they're coming fast and furious. Civil suits include Playboy's action against Event Horizons BBS for copyright infringement, resulting in a well-publicized $500,000 settlement, and its subsequent lawsuit against Tech's Warehouse BBS, resulting so far in a well-publicized holding that the BBS violated Playboy's copyrights in its girlie pictures. Sega successfully shut down the Maphia BBS, which had set up a cottage industry infringing Sega and Nintendo game software. New York-based music licensing giant Harry Fox Agency is suing CompuServe as this book goes to press, trying to make CompuServe cough up millions for infringements of music files by its subscribers.

On the criminal side, MIT student David LaMacchia was indicted on wire fraud charges for promoting copyright infringement on a BBS he covertly set up on MIT's computer system (the indictment was dismissed as this book went to press), and the Davey Jones Locker BBS has been indicted for copyright infringement of hundreds of files, in what the Justice Department calls the first criminal copyright prosecution ever of an online system. Waiting in the wings, unindicted so far, are the Rusty and Edie's BBS, and five BBSs busted recently in Texas for copyright infringement.

Put the prowling and scary lawsuits together, and it's clear we won't find random infringements lying around in any of the obvious places. Those who really want to get hold of those anonymously made, illegal copies will need to go deep underground, to data black markets big enough to have the exact stuff they want. Deep, deep underground, because any organized market for infringing copies will be busted by the cops the moment it gets easy to find. This is the key to what makes copyright work: individual infringements are unstoppable, but participating in data black markets is so difficult and risky that most people will just plunk down a few bucks in the nearest legit online store for the legal version of the software, book, music, or video they seek.

So, it seems copyright isn't dead after all. To those who are disappointed, don't despair; there's a silver lining: The continuing viability of copyright-based markets will encourage more people to create valuable works for distribution online to the general public. And that's why we have copyright law in the first place.

When a copyright owner's rights are infringed, he or she has two major legal remedies. The first is to seek an injunction, which is a court order compelling the wrongdoer to stop the infringing activity. An injunction can be valuable in situations where the longer the infringement continues, the more it damages you or your business. For example, consider "pirate" online systems devoted to spreading illegal software copies. The longer the pirate activities continue, the greater the damage to the software owners through lost sales. Copyright owners can and do obtain injunctions shutting down pirate boards from time to time; see the *Playboy v. Frena* and *Sega v. Maphia* cases discussed just below. A related legal remedy, impoundment of the equipment used to perform the infringement, is also available under the copyright statute, though much more rarely authorized by courts.

> **Copyright owners can and do obtain injunctions shutting down pirate boards from time to time.**

The other major remedy for copyright owners is "damages": a specified amount of money that the court orders to be paid by the infringer to the copyright owner. Copyright damages are usually equal to the sum of two related amounts: the copyright owner's lost sales due to the sale or distribution of infringing copies, plus the infringer's profits from the sale of those copies, to the extent they don't overlap. If the copyright owner had the forethought to register before the infringement occurred, as described above, he or she might also be able to obtain a court order directing the infringer to pay his or her attorney fees, and the option of requesting the court to calculate "statutory damages." Statutory damages is a money award set by the judge in an amount he believes proper. It is a valuable alternative to normal damages in those cases where the copyright owner cannot prove how much money was lost, or how much the infringer made, even though it is clear an unauthorized infringement occurred; such situations of difficulty in calculating damages occur more frequently than one might suppose.

Two courts recently issued decisions holding BBSs liable for copyright infringement. One involved software, the other image files.

The first case was *Sega v. Maphia*, a copyright and trademark suit (ongoing as we go to press) by videogame manufacturer Sega against Maphia, a California BBS. Maphia trafficked in videogame software for the Super Nintendo and Sega Genesis, as well as many other items. How did they get the software out of ROM cartridges and onto the bulletin board? It seems there were machines made for this exact purpose, with names like Super Magic Drive and Multi Game Hunter. They were used to download game software from cartridges to standard floppy disks, and also to play game software from disks on videogame consoles.

Maphia's illicit game software business was booming. It offered all the most popular titles, even prerelease versions of games not yet in the stores. Maphia also sold the videogame copying machines needed by its customers to play the software on their home consoles. It was a tidy racket: customers who bought a copying machine from Maphia also received free download privileges on the BBS, letting them obtain game software worth more than the price they paid for the copying machine. In a stroke of twisted marketing genius, Maphia had found a way to share the cost savings created by software infringement with its customers.

Sega inevitably got wind of this arrangement and busted it, having Maphia's BBS equipment confiscated under a civil seizure warrant. The basis of Sega's copyright claim was simple: Maphia was a BBS which knowingly encouraged its users to copy, upload, and download software without permission from the copyright owners. In fact, it looked like Maphia's operation was entirely predicated on user traffic in unauthorized software files.

Surprisingly, Maphia boldly fought the seizure and injunction. It asserted that the traffic in unauthorized software, as well as its sales of cartridge copying machines, were exempt from copyright infringement as "fair use." Nonetheless, the court readily found Maphia liable for direct infringement of the software found on the system. It pointed out that Maphia directly promoted the upload and download of unauthorized files to and from the BBS, maintained the files on the BBS, and operated the BBS as one side of each upload and download transmission.

So in the Maphia case, the law was clear. If you run a pirate software BBS and you're dumb enough to get caught, then you're in trouble. This comports with basic common sense.

The second case was *Playboy v. Frena*, another copyright and trademark suit (also ongoing as we go to press), this time by Playboy Enterprises against the owner of Tech's Warehouse, a Georgia BBS. This case was not some random stab by Playboy at one of the many online systems known to carry files infringing its photographs. For over a year previously, Playboy had aggressively approached large and small online systems with files infringing its pictures, and made them clear off the infringements. One of the very first large publishing operations to take a serious look at how materials were distributed online without permission, Playboy went against the grain of an online culture where many thought it okay to scan magazine pictures and spread them across the networks. Playboy didn't accept the theory that it lost its copyrights in the online world, and pushed back hard. Its first suit was not against Tech's Warehouse, but Event Horizons, a large and very successful BBS. The suit was eventually settled for $500,000, which Playboy noisily publicized throughout the Western world.

> **One of the very first large publishing operations to take a serious look at how materials were distributed online without permission, Playboy went against the grain of an online culture where many thought it okay to scan magazine pictures and spread them across the networks.**

Playboy's job was not done, however. The settlement money was good and certainly helped fund its enforcement efforts, but Playboy still needed to show the world that a BBS could be held liable in court for infringing its photos online; it still needed to show those steeped in online culture that digitizing a copyrighted photo simply does not strip off its copyright.

It settled on Tech's Warehouse, where proving copyright infringement was as easy as shooting fish in a barrel. There were 170 files on the system that were obviously scanned from *Playboy* magazine. In fact, the system's own descriptions for these files all included the terms "Playboy" or "Playmate," putting the lie to the sysop's claims that he had no idea there were images from *Playboy* on his system. The court decided there was infringement on a summary judgment motion, a fairly rare event in copyright cases. This means there was no dispute on factual matters that could possibly make a difference in the court's legal decision, so no trial was necessary on the question of infringement. So Playboy got the example it wanted in Tech's Warehouse: moving image files through an online system without permission from the copyright owner is now officially a copyright infringement. As we go to press, there is still no decision on the damages Tech's Warehouse will be ordered to pay for the infringement.

A Special Infringement Rule for Online Systems?

The *Playboy v. Frena* case, discussed in the text, included a holding that a BBS with infringing files was liable to the copyright owner, regardless of whether the system's owner or operators were aware of the infringement. Many online systems, especially the larger ones, were disturbed by this holding. It implies that if users upload and download infringing files entirely outside the system operator's knowledge, the system owner can still be held legally responsible by the copyright owner. Running an online system under such a rule means either taking a big risk that the system could be brought down at any time due to user infringements, or closely inspecting every file for infringement and challenging any file that even remotely looks illegal.

There are several reasons not to take the *Frena* court's holding on this point too seriously. First, a different part of the case report, dealing with trademark infringement, shows that the system operator clearly *did* know there were infringing files on the system, which could easily have colored the court's opinion. If Frena had seemed genuinely to have no idea that infringing files were on his system, the judge may not have so readily laid down its blanket holding that lack of knowledge is irrelevant to infringement (a holding technically necessary for the court to give summary judgment to *Playboy*). Second, *Frena* was decided in the lowest level of federal court, in a circuit not relied on by other courts for guidance in copyright matters; it does not bind other courts, and given its questionable reasoning, it is unlikely even to be viewed as a compelling example by other courts considering similar cases. Third, and perhaps most important, the case report makes no mention of a First Amendment defense by Frena's attorney. If indeed this defense was left out, which would be an astonishing omission, then the judge was not presented with perhaps the most important reason not to hold a system owner liable for infringement without knowledge: Such liability could cause system owners to bog down message traffic on their systems while checking for possible infringements, resulting in a "chilling effect" prohibited by the First Amendment, something the courts must seek to avoid.

Even if the *Frena* court's decision is followed by other courts, it's not necessarily that bad for online systems. Copyright law works a little differently from many other laws. It is possible to be absolutely liable for copyright infringement even when you don't know you're doing it. This was established in old cases involving dance halls, where the hall owner was held liable for the playing of songs that he or she had no idea were infringing. This approach could end up applying to online systems as well. But in civil lawsuits, establishing "liability" is only half the battle. To obtain an award of money damages for the infringement, the copyright owner must still independently prove that he or she is entitled to them.

This may end up being an online system's strongest defense. Copyright law has a long tradition of courts awarding little or no damages against "innocent" infringers. This seems a perfect description of the honest system operator, who has no idea that the system's users are infringing. Accordingly, such system operators might consistently find themselves shielded from having to pay money damages for their users' sins, regardless of whether they are technically responsible under the law. What makes such a no-money approach even more likely is the First Amendment protection accorded to online systems, as described just above: The prospect of big money damages could result in a "chilling effect" on the flow of Constitutionally protected speech through online systems. This is the courts' cue to carefully consider just how much in damages can be awarded against online systems without offending First Amendment values.

The Public Domain

There is a large body of "public domain" materials online, in addition to copyrighted works. One of the recurring questions is whether a given file or work online is copyrighted, or has fallen into the public domain, becoming a public resource freely available to everybody.

As copyright law evolves through the 20th century, it becomes increasingly difficult for newly created works to fall into the public domain. Under the old Copyright Act of 1909, if the creator accidentally published his or her work without registering or putting a copyright notice on it, the work was automatically injected into the public domain, for all to copy with impunity. Many valuable books, films, and other materials inadvertently went into the public domain this way, long before their natural copyright terms would have expired. In the revised Copyright Act of 1976, a work no longer went automatically into the public domain if the creator published it without copyright notice. He or she could keep the copyright alive if they discovered the omission of notice within 5 years, and acted reasonably to correct the omission by informing those who might have received or bought copies of the work without notice.

The copyright laws underwent another major revision in 1988, as the United States joined the Berne Convention, the major international copyright treaty. Now, any work published after March 1989 in the United States cannot lose its copyright due to lack of notice. For a newly created work of any kind to become public domain, it must be clearly dedicated to the public domain by the copyright owner. This was always an option, but now it is the only way for works published March 1989 and after to lose copyright protection (other than through copyright misuse).

This means that even when one cannot find a copyright notice on a recent work, it does not imply that the work has no copyright protection. This is particularly applicable to works found online. Many files found in online systems and networks are no older than a year or two. Even most of the older files are updated every now and then, resulting in a mix of older and newer material that is protected under current copyright law despite a lack of notice. As a rule of thumb, one should treat recent files (and recently revised files) as protected by copyright, unless there is a very good reason to believe otherwise.

> **As a rule of thumb, one should treat recent files (and recently revised files) as protected by copyright, unless there is a very good reason to believe otherwise.**

It also means if it isn't clear whether someone has disclaimed their copyright in a given online work, then they probably still have the copyright. As mentioned above, omitting the notice is irrelevant to whether a recent work is copyrighted. If a creator of a set of program files states that you can use his or her program files for free, but you can't modify them, then he or she did not give up copyright at all. They only gave you a free license to use the files in unchanged form.

Despite the modern legal safeguards against newer materials falling into the public domain unless the creator deliberately wants them there, there remains an abundance of public domain material online. Perhaps the most important category is materials so old that their copyrights have expired: books, pictures, musical scores, plays, maps, and other works from ancient history through the beginning of this century. This category includes the vast bulk of what we consider the "great works" of civilization. Most of this material, today, is found in electronic form primarily in the large institutional online libraries and archives, though some has made its way onto CD-ROMs that can be made accessible through online systems. As the world becomes more wired-up, and as optical character recognition technology improves, enabling easier transfer from books to computers, works spanning the centuries will be far more common in the online world. One must be a little careful about some of the more obscure paintings, even though they're old; if they were only displayed and never reproduced in copies in centuries past, the copyrights in some of these paintings may still be active.

The other major sources of public domain materials are materials that accidentally lost copyright protection under the older copyright statutes for technical legal reasons such as publication without using notice, and materials expressly dedicated to the public domain by their copyright owners. The former category is a catch-all of all types of older works. As described above, it is now nearly impossible for recent works to similarly "fall into" the public domain by accident. As for works dedicated to the public domain by their owners, they can often be found online in the form of small utility computer programs or image files containing express declarations of their public domain status.

Copying Within the Law

Does copyright law ever permit you to copy from others' copyrighted works without their consent? The answer is a qualified yes. You can use the ideas found in others' works because copyright protection does not apply to ideas. You can also copy small parts of others' works exactly if your copying falls within the fair use exception to copyright. These conditions are sketched out below. Keep in mind that a full discussion of the exceptions to copyright protection is far beyond the scope of what we can explore here.

Giving Information Back to the Taxpayers

When United States government projects lead to the development of large, valuable databases of information, who owns those databases? It seems they are frequently controlled by large or influential companies that have close relationships with government agencies. These companies dole out the data to the rest of us, often at a hefty profit.

In 1992, the Taxpayer Assets Project (TAP), a Washington-based group led by famed consumer advocate Ralph Nader and economist Jamie Love, began probing these database deals. TAP's theory was simple and compelling: If the United States government used taxpayer money to fund the development of a database, then that database belongs to the taxpayers. If a private company somehow comes to control that data instead, then we are all being charged twice for the same information—once through our taxes used to fund development, and again in fees charged by this private company for access to the public's own data. TAP is devoted to getting the information already paid for by the public back into the public's hands, and eliminating exclusive middlemen and double charges.

What kind of data is involved? Consider the following databases identified by TAP in 1993 as the "crown jewels" of government information resources: the SEC's EDGAR system that maintains all public filings made by shareholder companies under the federal securities acts; the Justice Department's JURIS system, containing among other things all federal case reports online; the LEGIS systems used by Congress, with full text of all pending bills and other congressional information; ISIS, a superset of LEGIS containing additional research and Library of Congress materials; the Automated Patent System; SCORPIO, a system used by Library of Congress; abstracts contained in the National Technical Information Service (NTIS) system; and the Foreign Broadcast Information Service maintained by the CIA, with abstracts of foreign news from all over the world—currently available only in paper. At the time this list (far from a complete rundown of government-funded information) was first assembled, the only way we could get at the data in most of these databases was through exclusive managing companies that charged for the privilege.

However, in the past two years TAP has made substantial progress in opening public access to some of these databases. Its first triumph was creating greater public access to the EDGAR database. Mead Data Central controlled access to EDGAR in electronic form for many years, and charged handsomely for the privilege. Under the public pressure and scrutiny generated by TAP, Mead publicly backed off from its exclusive position. Arrangements are underway for various organizations to spread EDGAR information to the public through a variety of less expensive channels.

More recently, TAP persuaded the Government Printing Office (GPO) to begin providing the public with 24-hour-a-day Internet access to the "GPO Access" product line. GPO Access includes the Congressional Record, the Federal Register, all versions of all bills introduced in the current congress, a locator service, and many thousands of files from 25 federal agencies.

TAP encounters setbacks as well. When it asked the Justice Department to open public access to the JURIS database of federal case law controlled by West Publishing, West did not simply acquiesce, as Mead Data Central had with EDGAR. Instead, it came out swinging. Somehow, West convinced the Justice Department to announce that West alone owned the case law database whose creation was funded by the Justice Department using taxpayer dollars, and that the Justice Department itself was going to start paying West for access to those cases as part of West's expensive Westlaw legal research service. TAP has not finished fighting this battle, however; latest word as this book went to press was that the selfsame Justice Department is investigating possible antitrust violations by providers of online legal research services.

By the way, how can we legally be charged for this data? It's well known that the United States government does not get a copyright in anything it creates, so how can anyone charge for government data? The answer is: because they can. Those who control access to data can always impose "toll road" charges on those who wish to enter their computer systems to get that data. This commercial reality, unlikely to go away anytime soon, adds another dimension to the concept of online "property."

The broad limits of copyright protection are defined by a legal concept called the "idea/expression distinction." Copyright protects expressions of ideas, but not the ideas themselves. Anyone can copy the ideas found in someone else's text, as long as they do not copy the way the ideas are expressed in that text.

This may seem a mysterious distinction at first, but most of the time it's not very difficult to apply in practice. Think of it as a matter of detail. For instance, many books can be written that contain the same set of ideas, expressed in different words. The ideas in all of them are the same and will not be protected by copyright, while the detailed way each author expresses the ideas in words will be protected. If you can take only the ideas from one of these texts and express them in your *own* words, then there will be no copyright infringement.

For a concrete example, consider the basic "idea" of *Romeo and Juliet*: Boy and girl fall in love, are kept apart by their families, plot to escape together, but their plans end in tragedy. This idea was expressed in a Shakespeare play set in Europe hundreds of years ago involving well-to-do families.

It was retold much more recently in *West Side Story,* a play set in Manhattan, with poor youth gangs taking the place of families. The second play, although based on the same ideas and even the same general plot as the first, would not infringe the first. None of the dialog is the same, there are many significant differences in the details of the plots, the characters are largely different, and so on.

If you wish to exploit the "idea/expression distinction" on an online system by using ideas found in others' copyrighted works, stay away from copying any of the exact wording used by the first author. Put the idea entirely in your own words, and use it for your own purposes. Similarly, stay away from copying the detailed sequence of ideas found in another's work, since such a sequence might also be protected by copyright. If you respect the works and writings of others, and use their ideas only as a complement to your own ideas and way of expressing them, you will likely stay out of trouble. Consider also that while copying ideas is perfectly legal under copyright law, in some cases it could be viewed by others as plagiaristic or intellectually dishonest.

The other major exception to copyright is "fair use." This is a subject of confusion among nonlawyers, and often enough among lawyers as well. We have heard users often state that fair use means they can copy someone else's work, as long as the copying meets their personal sense of fairness. This is not the legal standard for fair use, however.

Fair use is a legal excuse (built right into the copyright law) that permits one to take quotes from others' copyrighted works and place them in one's own work without violating the copyright law. Such quotes normally would be an infringement, but fair use allows us to use them and get away with it in certain situations. The fair use exception is based on the First Amendment guarantee of freedom of speech. Its purpose is to permit certain kinds of limited copying, when it is necessary for public use and discussion of copyrighted works, as long as the copying does not seriously interfere with the copyright owner's ability to make money through controlling the work.

Such a powerful loophole in the copyright law is very tightly constrained. Otherwise it would greatly reduce copyright protection in general. Your chances for fair use treatment of quoted or copied material are greatest when:

1. you take very little of the copyrighted work.

2. you make the quoted portions a small part of your own work.

3. your own work does not interfere with the sales of the original copyrighted work.

4. you don't depend on the quoted material to sell your own work.

5. your use of the copyrighted work promotes a publicly valued objective, such as education, or public commentary.

Examples of fair use are all around: short film clips in movie reviews on television and in film documentaries; excerpts from books in book review sections of magazines and newspapers; excerpts from books in news articles and works of history; limited photocopying of articles for one-time classroom use. Such commentaries, historical accounts, and educational uses, which are valuable to the public, benefit greatly through the availability of fair use. Commentators can include examples from a book being reviewed, or quote the exact words used by a famous public figure, without the burden of extracting the right to do so from the copyright owner in each case.

All of these fair use options are fully available for online systems. Movie, music, and book reviews, political discussions, and electronic newsletters are all common online. Small excerpts from copyrighted works can be quoted exactly in these contexts under the fair use doctrine. Other types of fair use are also possible, but may require an attorney's review of the exact situation to be sure.

One thing to avoid is selling others' works under a false claim of "fair use." One example might be a thinly packaged set of copyrighted text articles by others, prefaced by a short introduction by the compiler. The packager may claim he has a fair use right to sell this collective work without permission from the authors, because he phrases his introductory material as a commentary on the articles in the collective work. In fact, such a work would infringe the copyright of each author whose article is used. Fair use cannot be used as a clever trick to divert profits rightly due to the owners of copyrighted works.

> **Fair use cannot be used as a clever trick to divert profits rightly due to the owners of copyrighted works.**

Another danger spot is the common practice of posting entire newspaper or magazine articles to a public conference, newsgroup, or mailing list. Those who do this—and many journalists are as guilty as everyone else—often do not even consider whether they're violating someone's copyright. They think they're just spreading some interesting or important news. Others defend the practice by claiming that disseminating news is a "fair use" activity, giving them total carte blanche to distribute articles written and published by others however they see fit.

In fact, posting an entire newspaper or magazine article will almost *never* qualify for fair use. The fair use law does not permit distributing more than a few copies of an entire work even in the most justified circumstances, such as education. The point here is this: If someone wants to distribute the news online, they can take a few minutes to put it in their own words. Valuable as the news of the day or moment might be, there is nothing about it that justifies mere laziness by those who prefer to spread the news by simply copying the words of others.

Public Messages from Users

Many online systems maintain areas where users can post messages for all to view. In fact, for many users this is the main attraction of online systems—a social gathering place where large groups of people can join in ongoing discussions. These discussions are usually organized into major topics or subjects, then subdivided into various facets of each topic, and finally specific conversations, or "message threads" within that facet of the general topic. The subjects for these discussions are endless, ranging from politics to comic books to astrophysics.

An individual public message can be a few words or many paragraphs long. Except for the very shortest messages, such as responding "you bet!" to a prior message, all messages qualify for copyright protection as "literary works." The term "literary" does not mean messages need be high literature to be copyrighted. It is only the name used by the Copyright Office to refer to the category of text works generally, from advertising copy to computer program source code.

The person who writes a public message is the author of that message, and under copyright law, that automatically makes him or her the owner. The only exceptions are "works made for hire" as defined in the copyright statute. For example, when an employee posts messages publicly as part of his or her job, the employer would be considered the author and owner of those messages.

> **The person who writes a public message is the author of that message, and under copyright law, that automatically makes him or her the owner.**

In a discussion made up of messages from 20 different people, there are 20 copyright owners. As explained above, there is an implied license from each of those owners, permitting their messages to be displayed on, and copied from, the online system. The messages displayed on an online system can be compared to pictures in a gallery, or poems in a book of poetry. As usually happens with pictures or poetry, each message is labeled with the name of the author, who is also the copyright owner. So in the normal course of events, it all works out neatly. The messages are posted on the online system with the owners' permission, and the owners' identities can be easily discovered within the confines of the online system.

Collections of messages comprising discussions, often known as message threads, can also be owned under copyright law. The message thread would be owned as a "collective work," the same copyright category that applies to anthologies, magazines, and newspapers. It is often believed that the system operator or owner of the online system is the owner of the collective work copyright. In fact, unless the contract between system and user clearly covers this point, it is legally unresolved just who, if anyone, owns the collection of messages in the thread, for a number of reasons.

First, on systems where the messages are collected more or less automatically as the result of user discussions, there is a question whether the system operator contributes enough of his or her own creative authorship to qualify as a copyright owner of the collective work. Second, for nearly all collective works in the physical world, such as newspapers, magazines, and anthologies, the creator of the collective work pays individual contributors to include their contributions in the collective work. In contrast, in the online world the payment situation is often reversed. The users, rather than the online system collecting their messages, pay for the privilege of contributing to the collective work. These questions do not mean online systems cannot claim collective work ownership, only that the test to be met to qualify as the owner of a message thread is not yet clear.

> **One way system operators can strengthen their claims on message threads is to actively shape the discussions between users.**

One way system operators can strengthen their claims on message threads is to actively shape the discussions between users. When topic drift occurs, the system operator should post messages steering the discussion back on track. The operator might even delete or move messages not germane to the discussion. Too much editorializing will be experienced by users as annoying meddling, so the best approach is to guide message threads with a firm but subtle hand.

So when we look at a message thread, who is the owner? Each user owns the text of each message he or she posts on the online system. At the same time, the system operator might own the collection of messages on the online system (to the extent he or she can claim such ownership at all). His or her property is the message threads as a whole, not the individual messages.

What if someone copies a message thread (or a substantial part of one) from one system to another without permission, or reproduces it in a print publication? The copyright in the thread as a collection would be infringed, because the way messages were selected and arranged by the system operator was copied. In addition, all users with messages in that thread would have copyrights in the individual messages, and those copyrights would be infringed. So the unauthorized copier would be answerable both to the system operator for infringing a collective work, and to the individual users for infringing their messages as text or literary works.

Copying only a couple of messages from a thread may not violate the system operator's collective work copyright. In this case, so little of the selection and arrangement of user messages has been taken that the copying could be legally deemed too minimal to be infringing. It is probably necessary at least to copy either several messages in a row, or small groups of messages from scattered points in the thread, to infringe the collective work copyright. At the same time, copying even a single message would infringe the copyright of the user who posted that message, even if it does not violate the system operator's copyright in the thread as a whole.

E-mail

Each user owns the e-mail he or she sends into an online system or network. As with public messages, the text of the e-mail is considered a "literary work" for copyright purposes.

Ownership rights under copyright law are separate from privacy rights, which the user may also have in his or her e-mail. For instance, an online system could declare that the system operator may freely disclose the e-mail of users to others. Such a rule reduces or eliminates the user's privacy. However, if the same system operator publishes a series of e-mail letters from a single user outside the online system, this would still be a copyright infringement. While the user in this case agreed to system rules eliminating his or her right to privacy, this does not mean the user also gave up the right, as a copyright owner, to prevent the system operator from copying or distributing his or her e-mail texts outside the system.

Files

Online systems are loaded with computer files of all kinds. Users regularly upload and download programs, texts, images, data, sounds, music, multimedia, and other works capable of being stored in digital form. Files can be sent through e-mail, maintained in dedicated file areas, and sent through distributed networks such as Usenet. System operators maintain a great many files for purposes of running the online system.

The basic rule of owning files is simple. The person who created the file is the original owner of the file under copyright law (where the creator develops the software at his or her job, the employer becomes the original owner). Of course, the file has to contain a new, copyrightable work, such as a text, picture, MIDI score, or other work. If the file is merely a computer copy of someone else's work, such as image files created by scanning pictures from magazines into the computer, then the newly created file is not a new piece of property, but an infringing copy of someone else's property.

The major types of files found on online systems are as follows.

Computer Program Files

One of the major activities on online systems is program file transfers. Programs are copyrightable, and those copyrights can be legally enforced against those who copy programs. Various parts of a program can also be separately copyrighted.

The source code of a program—the program as expressed in programming language by its human programmer—is considered the main copyrightable form of a program under copyright law, since it most resembles traditional "literary works" in that it flowed from a human hand. The object code—the form into which most modern programs are compiled after they are written, in order to

> **If someone copies the detailed structure of a program while avoiding copying the exact code line by line, he or she could still infringe the program copyright.**

run more rapidly on computers—is considered a copy of the source code for copyright purposes. At a slightly more abstract level, flow charts, pseudocode, and other detailed representations of the program are also copyrightable. Thus, if someone copies the detailed structure of a program while avoiding copying the exact code line by line, he or she could still infringe the program copyright.

Finally, programs with original screen displays may receive some legal protection against others copying the "look and feel" of their displays. This last area is still being hotly litigated by the giants of the personal computer industry, so the ultimate extent of "look and feel" copyright protection cannot be predicted with confidence at the moment.

Most computer software found in stores cannot legitimately be transferred to others through an online system, because it is prohibited by the manufacturers. Most software manufacturers require users to pay for a copy *before* they can install or run it on their computers. Obviously, this rule cannot be enforced if the software is made electronically available through public online systems or networks where people can get a copy for free, so such distribution is simply not permitted.

So when a user is found uploading a popular retail software package to an online system, there is a good chance it is not authorized, but an infringing copy. Take a close look at the file. It may actually be shareware (described below), or perhaps a special demonstration version distributed by the manufacturer itself, in which case its presence on the system is perfectly legal.

If the file still appears infringing, the system operator should remove it immediately from public access on the system. Software companies are far more irritated by widespread distribution of their software without permission than by individual infringements. Each distributor can be responsible for many individual infringements. If the system operator stops the distribution promptly, he or she will be far less likely to get into trouble over it.

Shareware, Freeware, and Public Domain Software

Shareware, freeware, and public domain software are types of computer software and other files that can move through online systems and networks without violating anyone's copyrights.

Shareware is actually a marketing method, not a kind of software. It is sometimes called "try before you buy" software, because the user is given a free trial period to test drive the software package on his or her computer before buying it. If the user wants to keep using a shareware product after the trial period, he or she must register it by paying a fee to the shareware owner, publisher, or agent. Shareware is not the same as a software product "demo." The trial use version of the shareware package is a fully functioning program, while demo packages are crippled in some way, such as by limiting the number of times they can be used, or preventing users from printing the results of the program. If the shareware program owner or publisher is a member of the Association of Shareware Professionals (ASP), this means, among other things, that shareware is certified as not crippled.

The other major, innovative feature of shareware is the way it is distributed. For years, shareware was distributed primarily through online systems, and by companies selling it on floppy disks in flea markets and by mail order. Shareware authors permitted copies of their program to be freely distributed this way, depending strictly on end user registrations for their income. Online and disk distributors, freed from having to pay for shareware programs, spread them like wildfire, and the shareware authors benefited from the free distribution. Thus, the shareware marketing method enables software authors to sell their software without making a huge investment of money in advertising, marketing, distribution, and packaging. In the past year or so, shareware has arrived in retail stores of all kinds, from airport bookstores to neighborhood pharmacies, bringing the shareware technique to those less involved in the computing scene. Shareware authors have felt compelled to charge the companies selling shareware disks in the stores some royalties, thus watering down somewhat the concept of the free distribution license. However, shareware remains a vibrant and growing part of the software business.

There are many users who do not register their shareware, either mistakenly thinking the shareware is "free," or simply because they can get away with it. This does not make the shareware copyright meaningless, however. It is quite enforceable, especially against online systems and disk vendors who distribute large quantities of shareware. Under the shareware copyright, the following activities are infringing without the shareware owner's consent: use of shareware after the trial period; modification of the shareware files; and any distribution, except that distribution permitted by the shareware owner.

> **There are many users who do not register their shareware, either mistakenly thinking the shareware is "free," or simply because they can get away with it. This does not make the shareware copyright meaningless, however.**

Most shareware packages include express license terms for online distribution. One common license condition is that the shareware package can be distributed to others *only* in the form originally assembled by the shareware author, and that it must contain all of the author's original files. You can't just distribute the executable and user manual files, and leave out the license terms, ordering information, or other vital information included by the shareware owner in the original package.

Another common license condition is that anyone who charges a fee to distribute shareware to users must contact the shareware author for permission. This does not affect online systems that charge monthly or yearly subscription fees, or fees based strictly on connect time. But if an online system charges an additional fee specifically to download shareware, the system operator may need to contact some shareware authors for permission to do so under their license terms. The Copyright Office recently set up a Shareware Registry in which shareware owners can record their license terms. If this registry proves popular with shareware owners, it may become a valuable resource for learning about the different license terms applicable to different shareware packages.

It is sometimes asked whether anyone really takes shareware copyrights seriously. If the shareware owner just lets shareware files loose on the network, how can he or she expect to control what others do with those files? The answer, as explained above in the discussion of text messages, is first to remember that no copyrighted work loses its copyright just by being placed in an online system. Users and operators get a limited license of some sort to copy and distribute the work, but the owner retains all other rights under copyright law. In the case of shareware, that limited license is spelled out expressly by the author, compared to the vague implied license that usually applies to text messages. Shareware distribution rights were enforced in at least one case several years ago in Texas, *Datastorm v. Software to Go,* in which the makers of ProComm (which was shareware before it became a best-selling retail store product) successfully sued a software distributor for selling their shareware program without permission. Aside from court decisions, shareware has been protected as a valid form of software distribution both by Congress and the Copyright Office in setting up the shareware registry mentioned above.

Freeware owners, unlike shareware owners, do not require any payments for use of their software. You occasionally see requests for "contributions," but this is not a legal obligation. Freeware authors usually consider contribution payments for their work to be a matter of conscience for those who use it, and prefer to leave the law out of it. Freeware is copyrighted, though, and there are plenty of remaining rights that the owner may choose to exercise, such as prohibiting public distribution of modified forms of the freeware, or prohibiting charging a fee for distributing the freeware to others. Related to freeware is the concept of "copyleft," invented by developers of GNU UNIX-based software, which uses copyright protection in a very unusual manner. When a program is included by its creator in the copyleft scheme, *no one* is permitted to charge others money for a license to use the program. If a copyleft-covered program is incorporated into a larger program, the developer of the larger program is permitted to charge only for his or her own original contribution, and not the free copyleft portion. Philosophically, developers who use copyleft schemes believe no one should have to pay for the basic right to use software, though they do feel free to charge for their labor in developing and maintaining such software.

Public domain software is entirely free of copyright restrictions. As explained in the section above on public domain works, software created after March, 1989 can no longer become public domain unless it is clearly dedicated to the public by the copyright owner. Since almost all software in online distribution today has been either created or massively modified since that date, it would be wise not to treat software as public domain unless there is a clear public dedication.

Public domain software is entirely free of copyright restrictions.

Most modern public domain software takes the form of small program utilities. The authors of these programs put them out with absolutely no strings attached. Sometimes they have no desire to own the programs, and sometimes they want to see what reception the programs will get. If the public domain program is well received, the next version we see from the same author may be distributed under a full claim of copyright ownership as shareware or regular commercial software.

Text Files

Text files are electronic analogues to printed documents. A text file can contain an article, a newsletter, or a whole book. E-mail messages, discussed above, are also a form of text file.

Since they are closely related to printed documents, text files in their current form don't seem to present any interesting copyrightability questions. In other words, they're clearly and fully copyrightable. The standard for infringement is the same as for printed documents. Both literal copies, and paraphrases that are very similar to the original text, are copyright infringements.

Image Files

There are many thousands of files containing digitized images on online systems and networks. Transfers of image files, often larger than any but the largest program files, account for much of the total time spent by users on computer file transfers of all kinds. As the "bandwidth" (transmission

Writers Fight for Their Electronic Rights

The National Writers Union ("NWU") filed a lawsuit in December, 1993, against the *New York Times* and several other newspapers and electronic publishers. The NWU claims newspapers and magazines routinely exceed the print publication rights they license under contract from freelance writers. Typically, these contracts specify that the publication gets "first serial rights" to a story. This bit of legalese means that the newspaper or magazine gets to be the first publication in which the article appears, while the writer retains all rights to sell the story in other markets and for secondary publication.

For decades, this arrangement worked fine. A story appeared in a single issue of a magazine or newspaper, with a shelf life somewhere between one day and two months, and then that publication of the story was off the market. In recent years, back issue archives of publications were transferred to microfiche. This was technically another printing of the story, but the microfiche market was relatively small. The format really looked like a way to have back issues around without having to rent warehouse space just to keep all the old publications.

Online databases first became popular as an even more convenient archival storage medium for back issues than microfiche.

However, when the databases moved out of strictly in-house use and became widely available on the networks, something essential changed. The databases themselves became publishing media; indeed many electronic database businesses regularly refer to themselves as publishers. Eventually it dawned on the writers that the publications that had licensed only "first serial rights" from them were now seeking to exploit a far broader right: continuous, long-term electronic publication of their articles, without paying the writers an additional cent. The NWU lawsuit followed.

The NWU case recalls a similar situation several years ago, when videocassettes became a major new medium for film distribution. Music owners claimed the licenses they granted in the past to use their music in films and TV did not permit their music to be used in the new medium of home videocassettes. Courts wrestled with licenses that failed to mention the magic word "videocassettes" and came out with conflicting decisions on whether the film-based music license automatically created videocassette rights as well. It's not a simple decision. When the standard method of distributing a work goes through an evolutionary change in midstream, whether it's films moving to videocassette or newspapers going to online delivery, should that create an additional licensing opportunity for the copyright owner? Or is there an inherent extension of the rights originally licensed by the publisher, who should not have to pay for the same rights twice?

The other thing that is not clear is whether the writers think they're going to make money with this lawsuit. The price paid by a publisher for a new article has a lot to do with the reputation of the writer, and little to do with how many legal rights the writer has in the article. It is not clear right now that the overall revenue pie for newspapers will grow when they all offer online services, especially since they will have to compete with a host of other online publishers in the new environment. Online publishing could even turn out to be no more than an unprofitable sideline, which all traditional publishers will need to offer if they want to stay in business in the electronic age. If this is the case, it would hardly be fair for writers to get more money from publishers based on having an extra right or two.

capacity) of online systems increases, much of the new capacity will immediately be taken up with even more visual images, both still and animated.

Just as text files are equivalent to printed texts for copyright purposes, image files are equivalent to paintings, photographs, graphic illustrations, and other pictorial works. These visual images are fully copyrightable upon creation. If copied without permission from other images, either physical or electronic, they will be considered copyright infringements.

Interestingly, in the online world a theory sprang up that pictorial works, when converted into easily transmitted digital form, lose much of their copyright protection. This theory is loosely associated with a subculture of people who routinely scan photographs and illustrations from magazines into computerized image files, then upload them into online systems and networks for massive distribution. However, many of these images in their print form are fully protected by copyright law, and online copying and distribution is clearly an infringement.

This was amply demonstrated in *Playboy v. Frena*, a copyright infringement case in Georgia federal court. *Playboy* magazine sued the owner of a bulletin board named Tech's Warehouse for maintaining a large stock of online copies of photos from the magazine. These photos were not placed online anywhere by Playboy, but by system users across the country who copied the magazine pictures using high resolution scanners. The evidence of infringement was so overwhelming the court saw no need for a trial on that issue, and granted summary judgment against Frena on the infringement claim. Clearly, digitized photos are "copies" just like printed photos, and when they are made without permission, they are just as much an infringement.

When users upload their own images to an online system, they are not giving up the copyright recognized for Playboy, which had found its images uploaded by others. Instead, they are giving the online system an implied license to distribute the image, and the other users of the online system implied licenses to download the image for their personal viewing. This implied license does not authorize downloaders to redistribute the image, either for free or for monetary benefit.

Because digitized images are easily manipulated in computers, some artists like to take the visual art of others, then alter and combine it in a way that creates an entirely new work. The manipulation is far beyond traditional magazine collage, since the source images can be massively altered and blended seamlessly with other images. Does this infringe the copyright in the source images?

This is a difficult question to answer, since the image technology is so new that court cases definitively settling the issue may not arrive for many years, and the outcome in each case would depend largely on the exact source and derivative images involved. As a rule of thumb, if a source image is easily recognizable within the newly created computer collage, then there is a strong probability the collage is infringing. If the image is so altered and blended that it is not readily apparent in the new work, there may not be enough similarity for an infringement.

A Picture Within a Picture

Pictures are no longer just pictures, they are also raw source materials for new pictures. Using modern graphics software tools, anyone with a computer can scan in magazine photos, cut out desired pieces, then filter, distort, and combine them into new images undreamed of by the original artist. Drawing a moustache on the Mona Lisa was yesterday's act of aesthetic daring; today, it is cutting out her famous smile and seamlessly pasting it on the mug of Sonic the Hedgehog.

How much of someone else's work can you legally copy this way and incorporate digitally into a new, composite work? Possibly the first lawsuit asking this question was filed in February 1994 in Manhattan by stock photo company FPG International against *Newsday*, a New York daily newspaper. It seems *Newsday* ran a front page story on "Virtual Reality," with a picture of a man and woman in suits and with TV sets for heads charging madly about the landscape. FPG claimed *Newsday* created the picture by scanning and combining FPG's copyrighted images, and claimed $1.4 million in damages.

The photos involved show that *Newsday* lifted the man and woman figures straight out of an FPG image. In a press release, the president of FPG said, "There is a misbelief among the new 'desktop' designers that the law has yet to catch up to the new-age technology of digital imaging. In fact, the existing copyright laws are more than adequate ..." Recent case law suggests she's right. Rapper Biz Markie was held to infringe a song when he sampled it on one of his album tracks, and in *Playboy v. Frena* (discussed in the text) a computer bulletin board infringed when it distributed digitized girlie images from the pages of *Playboy*. The law has caught up to digitized, sampled work, and declared it infringing when baldly reproduced.

Still, *Newsday* did not simply copy the FPG images. It cut out pieces of them and combined them in new ways. It turned the figures around, took wads of money out of their hands, and replaced the clock faces on their necks with TV sets. The bodies of the figures are the same, but the look and meaning of the pictures are entirely different.

Thus, what is arguably a wholesale transformation of source materials within a new picture can be fully consistent with the continuing recognizability of the source images. It is time for the copyright law to take this into account and let artists create without legal peril, though change is far more likely to come in Congress than a Manhattan trial court. When change does come to accommodate the collage method for creating new works, what form will it take? Perhaps an extension of the concept of "fair use," which would allow creators of visual works to use recognizable visual images lifted from earlier works created by others for free, as long as the amount taken from any one earlier work is small and comprises a minor part of the new work as a whole.

If you create a computer image file by simply digitizing a public domain work, can you claim copyright in that image? Probably so, though an exact, literal digitization of an image will receive very little copyright protection. In an exact copy, the digitizer submerges his or her own original contribution in order to retain fidelity to the original. While achieving accurate reproduction is a worthwhile effort in itself, the digitizer also minimizes his claim to copyright by minimizing his own original expression. Also, copyright in a reproduction can be used only to stop others from copying that reproduction. It is useless to prevent others from going to the same public domain source and making their own digitized copy of it.

Those who alter the original picture in some way while digitizing it—by stretching it, changing the color scheme, or substituting visual textures—will gain a far more substantial copyright for their own expressive contribution to the resulting image. This can still only be done with impunity where the source work is in the public domain, however. An altered digital version of a copyrighted picture may result in new copyrighted material, but it does not permit the second artist to display, copy, or distribute the altered work unless permitted by the owner of the copyright in the underlying picture.

Clip art files are increasingly popular. These are collections of image files, often organized around a common theme like "boats," "butterflies," or "landscapes," distributed for use mainly in desktop publishing. Clip art files have copyrights not only in the individual images (unless they're public domain), but also in the collection of all of the images in the clip art collection. This is the same "collective work" copyright discussed above in connection with message threads.

The owner of the collective work copyright in the clip art collection, who is likely the compiler of the images, has a copyright in the exact selection and arrangement of the images, but not in the individual images (unless he or she also owns the copyright in each image). The owners of the individual images do not lose their ownership just because someone else includes them in a collective work. In fact, if a clip art collection contains a copyrighted image used without the owner's permission, distributing that collection over online systems would infringe the copyright in that image.

Sound Files and MIDI Files

Many online systems carry an increasing amount of traffic in sound files and MIDI files, now that sound cards have become standard equipment in many personal computers. Sound files contain interesting sound effects, noises, snippets of dialog, and short musical phrases, and the larger ones now contain entire recorded songs. There is even an Internet "radio" show, distributed regularly to the online public in the form of an enormous sound file. MIDI files are more like automated musical scores. They play a musical composition when inserted into computerized music systems, like a modern version of the paper roll in a player piano. To a large extent, both sound files and MIDI files are fully protected by copyright.

> **To a large extent, both sound files and MIDI files are fully protected by copyright.**

Sound and MIDI files, like image files, do not lose copyright protection just because they are stored and transmitted in digital ones and zeros. There is no difference, for copyright purposes, between playing a cassette of a musical performance and playing those same sounds from a hard disk or CD-ROM on a computer system. There are those who maintain otherwise, saying that the computerized, digital storage and transmission medium for the sounds makes copyright inapplicable. They are mistaken, however, since copyright law

Music Files on Networks: Publishing or Broadcasting?

The broadcast music industry finds itself converging, or perhaps colliding, with the publishing industries as they move on to the networks. Since these industries operate according to very different business models, we are beginning to see major disputes over how online file transfers should be treated under the law.

In the traditional broadcast industries, namely radio and television, music is typically transmitted from broadcaster to listener in real time, and delivered as a simultaneous performance of a prerecorded work. The rights to broadcast music are considered "performance" rights under copyright law. They are administered by performing rights organizations such as ASCAP, BMI, and SESAC, who commonly issue blanket licenses to broadcasters, theaters, and others granting permission to perform music by all their members. Performance rights licensing is the main source of income for many musicians.

In the traditional publishing industry, books and software are produced in factories, stored in warehouses, shipped in trucks, and sold in stores. The rights to perform these publishing activities are considered "copying and distribution" rights under the

copyright law. They are typically administered directly by authors and their agents. The music industry also has publishing-like activities, in a variety of flavors: licensing makers of TV, film, and multimedia productions to make and distribute copies or versions of songs and music as part of their film and video productions; sales of CDs and tapes; and sales of sheet music. However, in this area of the music industry, in contrast to the broadcast and performance area, recorded artists do not get a big share of the proceeds.

Musicians and their performing rights societies expected to see performance rights licensing extended in the online realm. It seemed natural enough. In the TV industry it is already considered a "performance" of the music in a TV show when a viewer records it on a VCR and plays it back later. Isn't downloading a music file to your computer and playing it later exactly the same thing?

Perhaps so, but when they found their way into the online world, the performing rights groups discovered the publishing model had already taken hold. Transfers of music files were considered to be a publishing-style "distribution," and downloading a music file was simply making a "copy" of that file. This was unnerving, to say the least. The performance licensers had always marked off electronic distribution systems like TV and radio as their turf, another world altogether from the hard goods world dominated by the makers of videos and CDs. Now it seemed the most electronic system of all, computer networks, had been co-opted by the publishing types. Worse, since musicians and their rights societies make most of their money off performances, a shift away from performance rights in the online arena could mean substantially less money for music going into the pockets of those who make the music. It looks like things could get far worse for them. Economist and futurist George Gilder predicts that when telephone and cable lines are capable of carrying larger volumes of information to the home, we will download and store most television programming as computer files, saving simultaneous transmissions for live events like sports and political speeches.

The performing rights societies are starting to fight back. The first overt move was a flurry of activity by BMI, asserting to the large online services that all music file transfers through their systems were "performances," requiring a performing rights license. Complicating matters is the fact that the publishing-style side of the music business is, at the same time, asserting that transfers of music files must be licensed as the making of "copies" of the music. CompuServe finds itself in the middle of the industry dilemma, hearing from the performing rights groups on one side, and defending a lawsuit brought by major music publishing licenser Harry Fox Agency on the other.

How do the various music groups reconcile these conflicts? BMI has suggested that an online music file transfer is *both* a copy and a performance. This generous view gives each of the traditional music rights licensing industries their own license fee pie to divide. For the online services, this is the worst possible result. It is simply an undignified piling-on by traditional intellectual property licensers, desperately hanging onto their piece of the action as we move deeper into the digital age, and multiplying burdens on online services in the process. This author's prediction: Performance rights on the Net will turn out to be limited to live performances. If the music performing rights societies are to strongly establish themselves on the networks, it will only be by extending their coverage beyond performance licensing to some form of online use licensing.

protects musical works once they are "fixed in a tangible medium of expression." It is immaterial whether the tangible medium is a musical score on paper, a cassette tape, or a hard disk in a computer.

An interesting question is the use of sound samples taken from recordings by others, such as Tarzan's yell, James Brown's scream, or a riff from an old Turtles song. Is it okay to take snippets recorded by others, very short in duration but very distinctive or recognizable, without triggering copyright liability? This question has already prompted much expensive litigation in the music business, where distinctive samples are routinely used in best-selling hip-hop records. In one recent case, the rapper Biz Markie was successfully sued for infringement, for using a repeating riff taken from an old pop hit as the background for one of his rap songs. Note also that performers with distinctive voices, including Bette Midler and Tom Waits, have successfully sued advertisers who made commercials featuring singers who mimicked their distinctive vocal styles. This last right—to keep others from copying a famous singing style—is not part of copyright law, but the performer's right of publicity.

Even a very short excerpt or sample, if distinctive enough, takes enough from the copyright owner that it could be considered infringing. You may encounter those online who insist that short samples are free of copyright problems, and that they should be free to trade in snippets from copyrighted works, and include them in their own sound works. Recently someone told us about a so-called "eight-bar rule" in copyright law: If the copied snippet is less than eight bars long, it does not infringe copyright. This is entirely false. There is no such rule, and passages shorter than eight bars can infringe copyright. Rules of thumb can be useful while we wait for definitive answers from the courts on the use of very short sound snippets, but they are best worked out with a lawyer who reviews your exact use of the sounds, and the reason you want to be able to use them without obtaining a license from the owner.

If you see distinctive or famous sound samples passing through your system, be aware that they may be subject to a copyright or right of publicity claim. If the uploader cannot come up with convincing evidence of authority to transmit the files, it would be prudent from a legal perspective, as well as respectful of the rights of the original creators, to remove those files.

> **If you see distinctive or famous sound samples passing through your system, be aware that they may be subject to a copyright or right of publicity claim.**

In cases where the file description does not describe the sound samples it contains, it will be hard to tell if it infringes unless you play the file yourself. This will be difficult for system operators who do not have the proper equipment to play the files, which is commonly the case for sound files specifically playable only on less common platforms, such as multimedia development workstations. In this case, a risk determination needs to be made. Should the system operator permit transfers of all sorts of sound files he or she cannot personally review, or should sound file transfers be limited to those that can be run for review on his or her own equipment? This question is dealt with generally in Chapter 4.

Databases

An electronic database is any collection of information maintained in a computer. Databases commonly found in online systems include user identities and information; system usage information for that online system; network node lists and directories. Most of these databases are organized, searchable, and periodically updated, some very frequently.

In addition, online systems often maintain databases on all sorts of specialized subjects. Such databases are not new to big businesses and universities. They have been the basis for lucrative businesses like Dialog, Nexis, BRS, Saabre, and other large commercial services for many years. Big business databases include directories of travel, industry, and personal information; financial information on companies and businesses; medical and scientific information; and collections of data on many other subjects. Smaller online systems are now moving into database areas once dominated by big companies. Hobbyist and special-interest bulletin boards are appearing in ever greater numbers. Topics include everything from the physically disabled, to statistics and information for specialized sporting events, to contact and gig information for artists and musicians, to bibliographic information for specialized industry and scientific purposes, to information for environmental activists, to thousands of other areas.

As specialized online databases multiply, and as more online systems come to focus on such databases as one of the primary services they offer to the public (not to mention a major source of income), the legal status of databases grows in importance. One of the major questions is: How much of an online database can be owned under copyright law?

The answer is that a person who compiles a database will have a copyright in the original "selection, coordination, or arrangement" of that database. However, no one can own the "facts" contained in the database, no matter how much work he or she may have put into gathering those

As specialized online databases multiply, and as more online systems come to focus on such databases as one of the primary services they offer to the public (not to mention a major source of income), the legal status of databases grows in importance.

facts. This is because facts are not originated by the database developer, but are an independent part of the world apart from the developer, free to all who want to use them. In other words, a database developer does not create facts, he or she *discovers* them, and no one can copyright a discovery. While the database developer does not own the facts, he or she does own his or her selection of particular facts for his database, the way he or she correlates them with other facts, and the way he or she arranges the facts for purposes of storage, accumulation, retrieval, and display.

The database developer's contribution must be original to qualify for copyright. For example, the Supreme Court recently held, in *Feist v. Rural Telephone*, that a white pages telephone directory was not entitled to any copyright protection. Why not? Certainly, the information is "selected"—all of the people and businesses with listable telephone numbers in a given geographic area are chosen; it is "coordinated"—people's addresses and phone numbers are coordinated with their names; and it is "arranged"—the information is listed last name, first name, address, phone number, and sorted alphabetically by the first letters of the last name. However, these methods for compiling phone books are not original at all. They are time-worn, traditional ways of presenting standard telephone information. Since the information is purely factual and the compilation methods are not original, standard white pages telephone directories are not copyrightable at all. It makes no difference that the telephone company may have spent many thousands of dollars on the work required to collect the information—without originality in its selection, coordination, or arrangement, there is no copyright.

White pages are an extreme example. Most databases will qualify for some copyright protection. However, since facts cannot be owned, many databases that are minimally original in selection, coordination, or arrangement will only have "thin" copyright protection, as the Supreme Court put it in *Feist*.

For example, a database of online systems based in New York City may list the name of each online system, the system operator's name, available transmission rates, the number of lines, the brands of computer equipment and software used, file storage capacity, and phone number, and the list might be arranged in order of file storage capacities. Such a list will be copyrightable as a thinly protected database. If someone makes an exact copy of this list and distributes it without authorization, it would be a copyright infringement. However, if someone copies the factual information in the list, and significantly reorganizes it, then offers it to the public for download, the odds are good he or she will not be considered an infringer under the law.

This legal rule may not seem fair, and perhaps it is not. It appears to penalize those who work hard on compiling a valuable database, by letting freeloaders skim off the hard-earned facts and copy them with impunity in slightly altered form. Nonetheless, it reflects a major limitation on copyright law, which protects expressions of facts only, and not the facts themselves. Legal rules aside, it is up to each person whether he or she wants to take the full extent of what the law allows in a case like this, or to respect the efforts of others and give them a chance to benefit from their work.

Many online systems claim they own the information in their databases, contradicting the limits on database protection discussed above. To a certain extent, those claims are simply wrong. Anyone can take the facts publicly available on any online database and copy them to his or her heart's content, as long as he or she does not copy any original expression contained in the database. Claims by database owners that they own every fact in their databases are mere attempts to scare people away from perfectly lawful copying of public domain materials.

How can you create more legal protection for an online database? One strategy is to make your database compilation scheme more original. If you select or present information in an unusual manner, the database becomes more original and more deeply protected under copyright law. A related strategy is

> **Claims by database owners that they own every fact in their databases are mere attempts to scare people away from perfectly lawful copying of public domain materials.**

to add original text or graphic materials to the copyright information. For instance, a restaurant list consisting of names, locations, phone numbers, and one-word food style descriptions is only thinly protected, as we described above. But if you add a paragraph or two describing each restaurant, and perhaps a rating system, you will multiply the copyright protection for your database as a whole. Others can still copy the facts in your database with impunity, but now they will have to work harder to extract those facts, and they cannot copy any of your text materials.

Another way to increase database protection is to look beyond the copyright law to other forms of legal protection. The main alternative is trade secret protection. If you keep your database secret, and require all who desire access to sign a confidentiality agreement, then the courts will help you prevent others from using the information in violation of that agreement. This approach can help you protect everything in the database, including the factual data.

The trade secret approach can be very useful where the secrecy of the data makes it valuable to recipients, such as mailing lists, or financial or market data that can help businesses compete against other businesses that don't have such information. On the other hand, some online databases are valuable only if they are subject to widespread public access; these include trade directories, medical information databases, and phone directories. Thus, the trade secret strategy, while an important option, is not for everyone or for all databases.

Besides legal techniques, there is a practical way to protect valuable databases. You can turn your database into a scarce resource, making it very difficult for others to copy large amounts of data. Methods for doing this include charging high connect time rates while users are searching or retrieving database information; permitting users to use only database management software that retrieves a small amount of information with each search; and permitting users to access your system only through a special terminal program that retrieves information in a limited way.

These techniques all amount to narrowing the "pipe" through which information flows to the database user, and raising access prices. They are appropriate to online systems devoted to making money through the control of valuable information, and can generate large profits if successful. Any system operator considering this model of system operation should recognize, though, that it moves the online system far away from functioning in any sense as a community service dedicated to increasing peoples' access to information. It will not be surprising if, in the future, we find that some online systems prosper by strictly controlling valuable data, while others succeed by providing valuable services, and letting users at their data cheaply or for free.

Structure of the Online System

Many readers have likely heard of "look and feel" copyright protection for the user interfaces of popular software such as Macintosh Finder and Lotus 1-2-3. The "look and feel" of online systems, the way they

CD-ROM Jukebox Online!

Many online services, especially the smaller ones, love the idea of putting CD-ROMs on their systems for their callers' use. The attraction of CD-ROMs online is not hard to fathom. They store a vast wealth of information, entire reference works on slim silvery disks. Those who only occasionally need the information on a CD-ROM need not buy it, if they can merely dial up their local BBS or web server and do a quick search. Many regard CD-ROMs as a new kind of ready-made information service for small online services, helping them match the information resources of the larger systems and leveling the competitive playing field.

One nagging little question: Do online systems have the right to make CD-ROMs available to their callers? CD-ROMs are covered by the copyright laws and license agreements, just like computer software. This is not merely an idle observation. Many CD-ROMs are marketed by large companies with lots of legal firepower. If an online system cuts off too many potential unit sales with easy access to the information inside the disk, these companies will move quickly to stop the bleeding. To such companies, unauthorized distribution of CD-ROM ma-

terials through an online system looks no different from pirate BBSs that distribute unauthorized software copies (and which, as we know, have been shut down for doing so).

Usually, the answer is found in the user contract included with the CD-ROM. Makers of CD-ROMs virtually always cover the question of online distribution in their license agreements. Generally, CD-ROMs marketed directly to owners and operators of public online systems include full online access rights, while CD-ROMs marketed for home or in-house business use are limited to one computer or network, with no outside dial-in access. Where licenses limit or prohibit online use, the manufacturers can always be contacted for an online license. Don't be surprised, though, if many of them refuse such a license, or will only grant one on unreasonable price terms.

But are those CD-ROM contracts binding? It depends on the contract. Whenever you sign a CD-ROM contract, you will definitely be bound by its terms, up to the limits of available copyright or other legal protection for the contents of the CD-ROM. However, if it is just a shrink-wrap license, its overall enforceability is in doubt.

What are the limits of copyright protection for the information in a CD-ROM? They are the same as the limits for the same kind of information in any form, whether online, on disk, or in print, as generally discussed in the text. For instance, if a CD-ROM contains an extensive factual database, the facts themselves may be retrievable without violating the CD-ROM owner's rights, but the owner may control his or her arrangement of those facts under copyright law. So the operator of an online service can extract unprotected factual information from the CD-ROM and put it in a new database for callers to use. However, if the system operator avoids all that work, and simply makes the CD-ROM directly available to callers, they could be exposed to the copyright owner's original arrangement of materials, and their access could cause the system to violate the owner's right to control access to that arrangement.

We would need far more space than available here to analyze the extent to which a system operator can use the various kinds of materials found on CD-ROMs without violating license agreements. In any case, system operators must be aware that CD-ROMs are full-fledged bundles of intellectual property, and cannot simply be mounted for access by users of online systems without either obtaining an appropriate license, or carefully determining which materials might be useable outside of a license.

are structured, may also qualify for such protection. There are two sources for the structure of any online system: (1) the company that developed the software used to support the online system (this company is usually unrelated to the owner of the system); and (2) the system operator who sets up and runs the system. We'll focus on the second type of online system structure here.

The online system structure created by the system operator, if detailed enough, can be owned under copyright law. By "structure," we mean the layout and names of file and message areas and the arrangement of those names and areas in the online system; all of the announcements and messages on the online system; the contents and sequence of opening screens and messages; and everything else the system operator does in setting up the online system for his users.

> **The online system structure created by the system operator, if detailed enough, can be owned under copyright law.**

The more unusual and detailed the structure developed by the system operator, the greater his or her chances of owning that structure as a copyrighted expression.

If a system operator emulates someone else's highly unique online system by copying all of the structural details displayed to users, such as unusual names and subjects for different conferences and file areas, or setting up unusual screen sequences, the owner of the first online system would have a strong claim for copyright infringement. It is hard to say, at this point, how much less than a complete copy would trigger a copyright infringement. It is such a new legal area that we have not yet seen court cases on the subject, though if the number of inquiries one sees from people setting up "CompuServe-like" systems is any indicator, we may see some online "look and feel" suits in the near future.

Protection of online system structure may become more important as the graphic power of online systems grows. Online systems will be pulling users into rich, three-dimensional environments full of artistically created and assembled images. Such user environments, consisting of the images themselves and the online system structure in which they are embedded, will be strong candidates for copyright protection.

Confidential Business Information as Property

We touched on trade secret law earlier as a way for an online system to create extra legal protection for the kinds of databases that can be exploited privately. Confidential information as a kind of property on online systems goes beyond that, however. All kinds of business communications on an online system can be protected as confidential information.

Businesses are increasingly using online systems as an essential part of their communications, both within the company and with the outside world. In-house online systems routinely carry all sorts of sensitive information about internal business operations, which the company running the system would not want to disclose to the outside world. In addition, commercial online systems are now offering private areas for in-house use by businesses that do not have their own systems, and for groups of people and businesses that need to keep in frequent, private contact with each other.

If such private arrangements are made with the understanding that the online meeting areas are to be kept confidential, then it is likely that valuable business data will be flowing through those areas. System operators must be very careful in how they treat this property. Any disclosure not authorized by the client business could cause damage to that business, and could even lead to a lawsuit against the online system.

This property right in confidential business data is different from the personal right of privacy discussed elsewhere in this book. A company's property right in confidential information sent

> **Business confidentiality rights may seem prosaic, but they can be much riskier for a system operator to violate than personal privacy rights.**

through an online service is based on its contract with that service, in which the online service agrees to keep the information secret. In contrast, privacy rights are personal, and they apply only to real people and not businesses. Business confidentiality rights may seem prosaic, but they can be much riskier for a system operator to violate than personal privacy rights. Businesses are often far wealthier than individuals, and thus better able to sustain a lawsuit based on breaching confidentiality obligations.

It is not difficult to properly respect confidentiality rights in business information. Most importantly, just be aware of when such property rights exist. If the system operator has any question about such rights, he or she should review any written agreements between the online system and client businesses, and see what they say about keeping the business' information secret. Simply follow the directives in the agreement, and there will be no violation. If there are no written agreements, or the written agreements do not cover confidential information, then review any other written understandings with the business users, such as exchanges of e-mail.

In general, if people and companies are exchanging business information in private on an online system, in the belief that the system operator keeps it private, then it would not be wise for the operator to disclose that information to others. Such disclosure could lead to a lawsuit for the damaging disclosure of confidential business information.

Trademarks

Trademarks are another kind of property commonly found on online systems. Trademarks are brand names used by product suppliers to distinguish their products from those of others, like the use of "IBM" and "Apple" on computers to show they come from different companies. Customers use trademarks to identify products from the suppliers they prefer.

The most prominent trademark for an online system is the name under which it provides its services. This name acts as the repository of the system's reputation. As the system becomes more well known, its trademark becomes an increasingly valuable piece of property. People refer to online systems by their trademarks, and tell others to try out a given system by telling them its trademark.

Where online systems display unique graphic logos or screens to their users, such images, especially log-on screens, can also function as trademarks. These pictures, just like the name of the online system, can become the bearers of the online system's unique identity, and can be protected from misuse by others under trademark law.

With the further development of graphic user interfaces, online systems will be able to stake out further trademark rights. Computer artists will increasingly be able to design online systems as detailed visual (or audiovisual) environments, with distinctive three-dimensional visual images and themes for users to inhabit and move within. If the "look" of each distinctive online system environment becomes associated in the public mind with the specific online system on which it is found, it will likely be protectable under trademark law as a type of trademark known as "trade dress." This is analogous to the trademark protection that companies in the fast food business, such as McDonald's and Wendy's, successfully use to establish their ownership of the interior design schemes of their restaurants.

As the Internet becomes more commercial, many businesses are starting to press their Internet addresses and domain names into double duty as trademarks. For instance, a company that sells "Acme" brand tires might seek to obtain and use the domain name "acme.com" on the Internet. This term would serve both as the last part of the e-mail address for every user who enters the Internet through Acme's system, and as an indicator that the owner of that domain is the company that makes Acme brand tires. There is a solid legal basis for turning Internet addresses into trademarks. Companies have been using telephone numbers as trademarks for years, such as 1-800-LAWYERS, and the courts have upheld their claims. Since an Internet address is ultimately just a telephone number in a computerized telephone network, the courts' acceptance of telephone number trademark rights should carry straight over to the online realm.

> **As the Internet becomes more commercial, many businesses are starting to press their Internet addresses and domain names into double duty as trademarks.**

There are some problems with the use of domain names as trademarks. One is that while there may be several companies coexisting in the physical world with the same brand names, but in entirely different lines of business, only one of them can get the Internet domain name matching that brand name. For instance, while "Buzz" brand yo-yos, "Buzz" brand space shuttle gaskets, and "Buzz" brand wigs would not compete in the traditional commercial marketplace, only one of them could get the Internet domain name "buzz.com." The others are out of luck, unless they want to put their own "buzz" brand name one position to the left in the domain name, such as "buzz.yoyo.com" or "buzz.rug.com," an acceptable though not ideal solution. Another problem, albeit temporary, is that some disingenuous characters have been reserving famous brand names with the intent of blocking the companies that actually own those names, and receiving a payoff for giving the name up.

Besides the trademarks that online systems own, there are many other trademarks found online. These include the names of electronic publications, such as *NewsBytes* and *Computer Underground*

The Name-Blocking Game

A couple of battles over Internet domain names made the news recently. Both of them are cases where a well known company was blocked from using its own name for its home base on the Internet.

The first involves MTV, the music television cable network, and one of its former veejays, Adam Curry. While still working for MTV, Curry got hooked on the Internet, and started some online publishing services out of a domain he procured under the name mtv.com. Sources say he discussed it with his employer MTV at the time, who said his use of their name on the Internet was fine. A few months later, when Mr. Curry was no longer employed by MTV, they decided they needed a presence on the Internet and demanded their name back. Curry refused, and as this book goes to press, they are locked in a legal battle. While decision is pending, Curry began using another name: meta-verse.com. "Metaverse" is the name for a cyberspace-like region coined by science fiction writer Neal Stephenson in the cyberpunk classic *Snow Crash*. Looks like Curry is getting shrewder. Stephenson may have some renown in the world of science fiction, but he has nothing like the legal firepower of MTV.

The second case is an example of competition gone off the deep end. The Princeton Review and Stanley Kaplan are two of the leading test preparation companies in the United States, and determined competitors. One day, Stanley Kaplan inquired about reserving the domain name kaplan.com on the Internet, only to find it already registered—to Princeton Review! Asked if there was any conceivable business justification to this move beyond simply giving its competitor a hard time, the Princeton Review claimed the name was meant for an area where prospective customers could compare the merits of Princeton Review and Stanley Kaplan. On that note, the companies went into arbitration, and Princeton Review was compelled to give up the domain name. It was not forced to pay damages or attorneys' fees, however. This is probably due to some interesting evidence Princeton Review turned up at the last minute: Stanley Kaplan had itself reserved domain names with terms that it did not own, such as "LSAT."

As the use of trademarks as domain names, and vice versa, becomes more familiar to business, these silly situations should die down, and the Internet will fill to overflowing with brand names. In the meantime, if you have any designs on doing business online, reserve your own name now.

Digest; the names of shareware programs, including their filenames in some cases; the names of online systems, from old-timers like Easy Saabre to relative newcomers like Artswire; the names of entire networks, such as RIME, ILINK, or Fidonet; and the names of the many businesses (and the products of such businesses) that use online systems and networks as part of their marketing, customer service, or business communications.

Now that we've established that the online world is rife with trademarks, what does it mean? Trademarks indicate the quality and reputation of the products they're used with, and tell us who the products' suppliers are. The range of quality that can be represented by trademarks is vast—consider the chasm in reputation between the products branded with the respective trademarks "Ferrari" and "Yugo." Since the trademark used with a product can make an enormous difference on consumer perception, and consequently on how well the product sells, unscrupulous souls are sometimes tempted to steal the reputations of others' products by copying their trademarks. When a trademark is stolen, it's called "infringement."

Under the law, trademark infringement occurs when a product supplier adopts a brand name that was used first by another product supplier, and subsequently the products and brand names used by the two suppliers are so similar that customers will confuse products coming from the two suppliers. This effect is known as "free riding" or "passing off" by the second supplier, in which it unfairly benefits from the reputation of the first supplier's products. It is what the trademark laws are designed primarily to prevent. The goal of trademark law is to maintain an orderly marketplace of goods and services, where they can be accurately and clearly labeled according to their suppliers. In case of conflict, the basic rule is very simple: The first one who used the brand name wins.

> **The goal of trademark law is to maintain an orderly marketplace of goods and services, where they can be accurately and clearly labeled according to their suppliers.**

For a concrete illustration of trademark infringement, suppose "Hilda's Hut" becomes a wildly popular online system, famed for the endless tall-tale spinning of its mirthful and diverse guests. Lurker Jim Schnook notices that Hilda, the owner of Hilda's Hut, is also netting a fair profit. So he starts up his own Hilda's Hut online system in the next area code (without asking Hilda). The fame of the first Hilda's Hut has already spread that far, and some of the same users may even show up. And show up they do, whipping up such a froth of merriment at the new place that Jim's simple "yes" to their query about whether this online system is related to the other Hilda's ends their qualms. Soon, most online system users in the region come to believe there are two Hilda's Hut online systems in adjacent area codes, both run by the same people.

Naturally, the real Hilda becomes furious. Jim Schnook stole the hard-earned reputation of her joyous online system to pocket a few grubby bucks. What's worse, Jim's true nature is slowly emerging at the fake Hilda's Hut. Users start to feel badly treated by Jim, and refer to his online system as "Hilda's Witch Hat." Unfortunately, bad reputation spreads as easily as good. Soon, Hilda finds her own users referring to her as "that witch." At this point, Hilda has a legal claim that Jim Schnook is infringing her trademark. He is both confusing users about the source of online system services provided under the brand name Hilda's Hut, and giving users the false impression that the real Hilda's Hut system gives users the same abuse Jim hands out on his infringing system. Time to consider the possibility of a trademark lawsuit against Jim Schnook.

Trademark actions are usually directed first at stopping the infringement immediately. The sooner the free ride is ended, the sooner the original product supplier can restore the unique link between his or her product and the trademark. The "Hilda's Hut" example, fairly typical of actual trademark infringement scenarios, illustrates how precious and fragile the product/trademark link can be, and how important it is to restore it promptly. In some cases, the injured party proceeds further with a suit to recover money damages.

Naturally, a system operator faced with trademark infringement will explore nonlitigation options first even with the most distasteful infringers, as litigation can be expensive. Trademark owners and infringers are often able to agree that the infringer will make changes in his or her brand name, sufficient to differentiate his or her product from the trademark owner's product in the future. Remember that litigation can be just as costly for the infringer as for the trademark owner, so the threat of litigation if a settlement cannot be reached is a powerful incentive to the infringer to change his or her brand name enough to make the owner of the infringed trademark happy.

Dangers and Responsibilities in the Online World

More and more we are living parts of our lives online, making deals, connections, and friends locally and globally. New groups are forming on the Net for social, business, religious, political, and artistic purposes. Some of these groups were physically impossible to form before the communications web closed geographic gaps. With all this social and economic interaction—"interactivity" in its most personal and profound sense—comes a great potential for people to help or hurt each other. People are still people, whether on the street or in cyberspace. If I do something online to injure someone, a real person is injured somewhere. It's not just a little electron trickle, or a few words glowing on a computer screen.

The laws of society apply equally to online and physical conduct. Granted, the exact boundaries of illegal online conduct are not fully drawn. But if you injure somebody severely enough by something you do on an online system, they can sue you in a physical court. Some romantically think of computer networks as a new kind of Wild West frontier where the law gives way to exploration and survival, but in fact the online world is not free of laws or law enforcement.

The Online World as the Wild West Frontier

Howdy pardner, welcome to cyberspace. Pull up a stool. We live by our wits here, and there are fortunes to be made by those who can face the danger. There's plenty of gentle folks settlin' around these parts, but beware the mean hacker hombres. They'll shoot holes in your credit history soon as ping you.

The legend of computer networks as a wild frontier has persisted to this day. It made some sense five or ten years ago, when practically no one was online. As in the Wild West of a thousand Hollywood movies, there were few lawmen about. People relied on their ingenuity to come up with workable social systems—bulletin boards and mailing lists and online conferences—and keep the riffraff in check. The occasional malevolent hackers were referred to telephone company security and government agents, who chased them in posses all through cyberspace.

When it came time to dispense justice within the community, the law of the frontier prevailed. The local rulers acted surely and swiftly. Those who defied system rules were banished. No need for elaborate exegeses of the local law, no room for judge and jury. The people knew what was right and wrong, and they knew what to do with transgressors.

Online cultures were mainly peaceable, and unwelcome disturbances were nipped in the bud by those who ran the system.

When mainstream society started flooding into cyberspace in the early '90s, frontier justice evaporated. Invasive hackers are now indicted and thrown in real jails. When online denizens have beefs with each other, they take them to physical courts, or set up equivalent courts online, complete with due process. The online territory keeps expanding as more computing power is applied and more connections are made, but frontier time is over. The pressing issues of the day have to do with overcrowding, not sparsely settled frontiers: How do we keep our e-mail boxes from overflowing? What do we do about advertisers invading every corner of the online universe?

The laws applicable to online affairs are not fully formed yet, of course, but this does not equate to any extension of the age of frontier justice. Today's earth-bound legislators and courts have most of the online world in their grip, even if they don't know quite what to do with it. The question is whether their control will be heavy-handed, or compatible with the continuing vigorous development of online territories.

We will see further appearances of the Wild West frontier in cyberspace. But expect them to be the stuff of entertainment—interactive remakes of classic film westerns, online Wild West theme parks. And thus, the online world will go full circle, ending up back in Hollywood, maker of the Wild West romances that retain so much power over the imaginations of some of our cyberspace settlers.

It is only common sense that those injured online can bring their claims to the courts. The legal system is often said to be the peaceable alternative to self-help. If society did not provide courts to dispense justice between those who injure and their victims, then the victim is left to seek "justice" from the hide of the injuring party. Such activity would quickly devolve into an endless cycle of feuding and revenge, and Charles Bronson-style vigilantism. The court system provides an orderly alternative to this brutal cycle, in which a societally endorsed system decides the rights of the parties.

The same reasoning applies fully to online affairs. Society does not want people injured online to run after those they blame with broken bottles, real or virtual, to exact "law of the jungle" justice. Accordingly, the courts are fully available to decide online claims and disputes, and hopefully deal fairly with those wrongfully injured, and those who are to blame for the injuries.

The legal system is divided broadly into two different realms: civil and criminal. The criminal realm consists of laws enacted by state and federal governments for the general protection of the public. Criminal laws are enforced in the street by the police, and in courts by federal and state prosecutors. Those found guilty are punished with, depending on the crime, fines, confiscation of property, imprisonment, and a criminal record that can make their lives more difficult. Criminal laws are discussed in Chapter 6.

We are concerned in this chapter with the civil realm of the legal system. There are no police involved. When civil laws are violated, it means one person wrongfully injured another, and the injured person can seek compensation in court. Each party hires his or her own lawyers. If the person suing (the "plaintiff") proves that the other person (the "defendant") violated the law while injuring the plaintiff, then the court will order the defendant to pay money to the plaintiff as compensation. Less often, the court may order the defendant to cease certain wrongful activities—this is typical in copyright or trademark infringement actions, for instance.

The split between civil and criminal violations is not absolute. A person can both violate criminal laws and give rise to civil lawsuits by the same conduct in many situations. For instance, illegally posting access codes for private computer systems on an online service can violate computer crime laws, and can also make the message poster liable to anyone whose person or property was damaged due to misuse of those access codes. Similarly, a copyright violation can lead to both criminal indictment and civil lawsuits.

In this chapter, we will explore first the traditional legal categories of wrongful conduct, giving special attention to the concepts of "negligence" and the "duty of care." Next, we will review some of the common legal claims that arise when people or businesses are injured online. After that, we will look at the obligation to maintain security on online systems. Next, we will review a company's responsibility for what its employees might do when they go outside networks. This is followed by general suggestions on how system operators can reduce the risks of injury on their systems, meet their own responsibilities, and avoid being held responsible for the acts of others on their systems.

> **The split between civil and criminal violations is not absolute. A person can both violate criminal laws and give rise to civil lawsuits by the same conduct in many situations.**

Degrees of Wrongful Conduct

If a person swinging a bat hits someone and breaks his or her leg, the bat swinger is not automatically liable for the injury. First, we must examine where he was swinging the bat (in the batter's box? on a crowded city sidewalk?), how he was swinging it (wildly? carefully?), his state of mind (did he mean to hit anyone? was he swinging the bat around carelessly?), and so on. Until these kinds of questions are answered, we can have no idea if the bat swinger did anything wrong, and if he did, what the legal remedy against him should be.

Likewise, the fact that a system operator does something (or fails to do something) that results in injury to a user does not, in itself, make the system operator liable. His or her actions must be examined based on both the intent behind the actions, and the reasonableness of the actions. These distinctions can make a big difference in whether the system operator did anything illegal, and the amount of money damages a judge will award against a system operator.

Deliberately Wrongful Acts

Deliberately seeking to injure someone else is the most serious kind of offense. Neither society, the courts, nor most of your neighbors approve of deliberate injury to others. Courts will subject a deliberate wrongdoer to the maximum money damages allowable under the law. Sometimes even a money award fully compensating the injured plaintiff is not enough. Courts and juries might heap on additional damages, called punitive damages, just to make sure the defendant gets the message that he or she should never try deliberately to hurt others.

This book is not intended to help out those who intend to hurt others in any way. Anyone out there who plans to injure others online is on his or her own.

Reckless Conduct

A slightly less serious form of action is "reckless" or "grossly negligent" conduct. If you're reckless, it means you're doing something you *ought* to know will hurt somebody, even if you're not specifically trying to hurt them. Swinging a baseball bat wildly on a crowded city street is reckless, because you ought to know you are likely to seriously injure innocent passersby.

For an online example, virus-scanning software may tell the system operator that a program uploaded by a user contains a virus that will destroy the hard disk data on any computer that runs the program. Obviously, if the virus-infected program is made available for users to download, it will likely damage the data on some users' computers. If the system operator makes the program available for download nonetheless, and with no warning to users, his or her conduct would be reckless and expose the operator to serious legal claims if any users or their computer systems are injured.

The laws against reckless conduct are meant to make people act responsibly, based on their knowledge that their own actions are likely to injure others. It is no excuse to say one did not intend for the damage to occur. If a user's computer gets a virus infection from downloading a program that the system operator knew to contain a virus, he or she could be liable for money damages both compensating the victim, and penalizing the system operator for knowingly allowing that damage to occur.

Negligent Conduct

"Negligence" is the broadest area of concern for system operators and others who operate online. It extends the concept of legal fault beyond recklessness. People can be negligent under the law even when they *don't* know for sure that their actions will injure others.

The Duty of Care

Under negligence law, a person is expected to act responsibly, and not do things that might injure others. The legal standard for responsible conduct is called the "duty of care." If someone does not meet his or her legal duty of care, and if that failure causes injury to another, the injured person can take that individual to court for money damages.

How do we find out our duty of care? There is no complete list of such duties. Our responsibility not to endanger others arises anew each time we face the world, and differs according to the situation. In every case, the question is: can I reasonably foresee that my actions might injure others, and if so, what reasonable steps should I take to prevent such injury? This is often called the "reasonable man" standard—what would a reasonable person do in my situation, to prevent injuries to others?

The need to be "reasonable" in one's actions is central to negligence law. First, one is not required to guarantee the safety of others. If a person takes reasonable steps to prevent injury to a user and the user is injured anyway, that person is not negligent. Second, "reasonable" means one has to use measures that make sense. If one has a duty to warn people about a hidden deep hole in one's front yard so they don't fall in, a warning sign in back of the house is not a reasonable way to tell them about it. If someone does not see the sign because of its unreasonable placement behind the house and injures himself falling into the hole, they would have a strong legal claim against the owner for negligently failing to warn others of a dangerous condition.

> **The need to be "reasonable" in one's actions is central to negligence law.**

Examples of negligence and duties of care abound in everyday situations. If someone invites people into her house, she has a duty to make sure there are no roller skates or other unexpected slippery objects on the floor that might cause a guest to fall and injure herself. A supermarket likewise has a duty to make sure that spilled applesauce does not remain on the floor too long, because people might slip on it and hurt themselves. A car maker has a duty to design cars so they will not go out of control when driven, which would lead to traffic accidents.

Likewise, system operators have a duty of care: to take reasonable steps to prevent injuries to users and possibly others. The courts have not defined the spectrum of system operator duties yet. That effort will take years, perhaps decades. Meanwhile, we can make an educated guess about where and how far a system operator's duty to his or her users extends.

Six Important Factors for Determining the Duty of Care

Courts asked to determine exactly how far system operators must go in protecting others will have to consider and balance a number of factors in each case. We've identified six different factors that should always be considered before imposing responsibility on a system operator. Some of these factors are also reflected in the recommended strategies for reducing system operator risk at the end of this chapter.

The Online System as Supermarket

This image got its start in the notion that system operators should patrol the corridors of an online system looking for trouble spots, as if they were supermarket managers periodically patrolling the aisles of the store. In supermarkets, spilled foods and broken bottles can lead to nasty falls and cuts. In online systems, the problems are more varied—ranging from viruses to obscenity—and the injuries emotional and economic, not physical. Despite these differences, the supermarket is a good model for understanding how traditional negligence concepts can apply in an online situation. It is not practical to try to monitor all activities continuously; periodically checking for dangers is a far more reasonable way to minimize risks to guests on the system.

However, it overstates the system operator's responsibilities to say that he or she *must* patrol the aisles. Requiring constant monitoring does not take into account the First Amendment protection of user speech, as explained more fully in the first chapter. An online system attains its greatest value as a conduit for free speech when it transmits user messages smoothly and efficiently. If a system operator must slow down message traffic in the search for dangerous materials, the speech distribution function is frustrated.

Therefore, the First Amendment makes room in the law for online systems where the operator makes a point of *not* patrolling the aisles, at least in areas where user speech is paramount. The supermarket metaphor applies best to those systems where the operators act voluntarily to keep dangerous materials off the system; and to those system areas where activities other than pure user speech predominate, such as research, software file transfers, online publishing, and shopping.

Which brings us to the newer, more literal sense in which an online system can be like a supermarket: when the operator purposely designs the system to resemble one. In the upcoming, early years of interactive television, we will see many efforts to re-create supermarkets, shopping malls, clothing boutiques, toy stores, and other archetypal palaces of consumer spending as graphically and viscerally as the advancing online technology permits. Will this entail a change in the operator's legal responsibilities? Possibly. As we move away from textual interaction to "virtual reality" interfaces online, the portion of users' activity that manifests itself as "speech" will shrink to match more closely the portion of our physical world activities that are considered "speech." The First Amendment at that point may become a less predominant principle of legal protection for online activities.

1. *The system operator is not absolutely responsible for injuries on an online service.* The system operator should only be liable if he or she acts negligently. If a person in a supermarket drops a banana peel on the floor, and someone following two steps behind slips on it and

breaks her ankle, the supermarket will not be liable. The supermarket has a duty to monitor the aisles for dangerous conditions like banana peels, but only at reasonable intervals. An injury that occurs before the supermarket finds out about the dangerous condition in the exercise of ordinary care is not the supermarket's responsibility.

Similarly, system operators should only be required to exercise reasonable care to prevent or remove dangerous conditions on the online system. Once the system operator identifies the likely sources of danger on the system, and settles on reasonable, routine procedures for dealing with those dangers, he or she is exposed to very little risk of liability. Unfortunately, there are legal areas, such as copyright infringement, where there is a prospect that system operators may be held absolutely liable regardless of their knowledge of a danger or what they do about it, but the ultimate rules in these areas are still open to change. Later in this chapter we will cover an assortment of strategies for effectively discharging the duty of care, and minimizing legal risks.

2. *Is it proper in this case to hold the system operator accountable for the actions of others?* Injuries to users on an online service will almost never be caused directly by the system operator, but by other users who act dangerously or post dangerous materials on the system. The user who acts dangerously is the real wrongdoer here. The system operator is just the innocent guy or girl who provided transmission facilities to both the dangerous users and the victim.

From this point of view, it hardly seems fair to hold the system operator responsible at all for postings. However, in many cases the system operator in fact controls whether injurious materials remain posted, and whether they are moved, changed, or deleted. In addition, due to his or her control over the online service, the system operator has a far greater ability than anyone else to prevent injuries due to a posting. For this practical reason alone, courts could find it necessary to make system operators accountable to some extent for postings by others on their online services.

3. *System operators may decrease or increase their legal duty of care by their own voluntary actions.* One irony of the law is that generally, a person does not have a duty to save a dying man passed on the street. But if one stops to help him, one voluntarily assumes a duty of care toward that person, and can be held liable for negligence if one does not help him correctly.

Similarly, a system operator who scans all uploaded program files for viruses and informs users of this practice may make himself or herself, by his or her own actions, more responsible for any viruses that slip through the screening. The system operator has assumed a substantial duty of care to protect users from viruses. Indeed, users may come to rely on the system operator's proper performance of that task. In contrast, a system operator who simply posts a warning to all users, "Beware of viruses, all ye who download from here," will have a much smaller duty of care, perhaps limited to dealing only with the viruses on his or her online service that are reported by users. (The big trade-off is that the system operator who posts such a warning instead of doing a little virus screening may also have fewer users.)

4. *A system operator should be held to a higher standard of care under the law when he or she invites others to use the system, than when he or she merely tolerates the presence of others.* In the law that applies to physical places where people visit, inviting someone into a place makes the host responsible for keeping that place safe for the invited person.

This principle might apply to most online services. Users invited into an online service, such as an interactive shopping service, are entitled to a certain level of safety from the system operator of that online service. On the other hand, if someone runs an anonymous ftp site devoted to researchers in a narrow academic specialty, Net surfers who wander in to sample the goodies are not invitees, and may not merit much attention from the system operator. The system operator who really wants to lower legal exposure might be able to limit his or her own obligation with a logon announcement that reads "Enter at your own risk," though again this could discourage most users from ever entering.

5. *The system operator may be relieved of responsibility for injury to a user when the user knowingly assumes the risk of injury.* Suppose a person dashes onto a car-filled freeway in the dark of night. If one of those cars cannot avoid hitting him, the driver will not be held negligent. The injured runner assumed the risk of injury through his own reckless actions, and the driver is not legally at fault.

   A similar assumption of risk may occur at times on an online service. Suppose a system operator warns all users that a hacker intruder has broken the security of the online service, so they should not post any information they consider secret. A user sees this warning, but proceeds to use the online service to send his private credit card codes to a friend by e-mail. If the intruder intercepts the codes, the user could be held to have assumed the risk of the interception, and the system operator would not be responsible for resulting damage to the user's accounts or property in other systems.

   Showing that a user assumed the risk is clearly a way out of negligence liability for system operators in at least some cases. It remains to be seen how far it will ultimately apply to online services. For example, if users know that viruses might be found on an online service, does this automatically excuse the system operator from liability when a user downloads a virus that destroys his data? Perhaps not; many of us may think knowledge of viruses is universal, but in court the system operator will need to prove that this specific user knew about the dangers of computer viruses. In addition, a court may be reluctant to find that the user assumed the risk of viruses if the court believes the system operator, as distributor of the software, should take some responsibility for helping to prevent the spread of computer viruses.

6. *System operator liability will be limited by the First Amendment to the Constitution, which protects "freedom of speech" and "freedom of the press" against government interference.* An online service carries the speech of its users in the form of public and private messages to others. Since lawsuits are a form of "government action," the courts' authority over system operators will be limited by the First Amendment mandate that the government cannot restrict freedom of speech.

   The First Amendment prevents the burden of legal responsibility from becoming so great it would lead to a "chilling effect," discouraging system operators from running online services. When the role of the system operator as speech facilitator becomes better understood, it will hopefully become clear to all that users cannot simply shift the risks of being online from themselves to the system operators. Only this approach will guarantee that online systems can continue to carry user speech without constant interference from lawsuits. More detailed discussion of the First Amendment and online services can be found in Chapter 1.

Killers for Hire—Would You Take Their Ads?

Discussing First Amendment protection for on-line systems may seem a bit abstract at times. As it happens, the legal system has provided us with concrete examples of the precise border territory where the First Amendment gives out: when you run ads for hired killers. In several cases in the late 1980s, *Soldier of Fortune* magazine was sued for just that.

Two of these cases—*Braun v. Soldier of Fortune Magazine*, and *Eimann v. Soldier of Fortune Magazine*—were nearly identical. SOF regularly ran advertisements for adventurers willing to do any kind of job (a practice discontinued in the wake of these cases). In each case, the advertiser was offered a contract to murder someone, and he accepted the job and killed the target. Afterwards, the survivors of the murder victims sued SOF. They claimed that by running the ads, SOF negligently aided in the murders.

SOF claimed that the First Amendment shielded it, as publisher, from responsibility for what others did with the materials printed in its magazine. Its fallback position was that it could be liable only if the ad in question openly solicited criminal activity. The courts felt otherwise. In particular, the *Braun* court stated that if the ad presented a "clearly identifiable unreasonable risk" of harm to the public, SOF could be held liable.

The court believed this struck the correct balance between the need to enforce negligence laws, and First Amendment freedom of the press. By requiring that the risk from an ad be *clearly identifiable* before a publisher could be held responsible for running it, publishers would remain free to run ads that might involve criminal activity, but not clearly so. Thus, free speech would be protected up to the edge of aiding in the crime.

It is especially instructive to look at the ads involved in each case. First, the ad in *Braun*:

GUN FOR HIRE: 37 year old professional mercenary desires jobs. Vietnam Veteran. Discrete [sic] and very private. Body guard, courier, and other special skills. All jobs considered. Phone (615) 436-9785 (days) or (615) 436-4335 (nights), or write: Rt. 2, Box 682 Village Loop Road, Gatlinburg, TN 37738.

Next, the ad in *Eimann*:

EX-MARINES—67-69 'Nam Vets, Ex-DI, weapons specialist—jungle warfare, pilot, M.E., high risk assignments, U.S. or overseas. (404) 991-2684.

They look pretty similar. Yet in *Eimann*, the court let SOF off the hook for the ad, while in *Braun* SOF was held responsible for the resulting murder.

How can we square these contradictory results? Hard as you look, the two ads seem to be for the same kind of guy—an ex-soldier mercenary volunteering to do some rough work. The ad in *Braun* is for a professional mercenary who will consider all jobs, while the ad in *Eimann* is for a weapons specialist. If there is no way to tell why one of these ads was illegal and the other wasn't, what kind of guidance do these two cases provide?

In fact, these cases provide some very precise guidance for system operators. They show that the material in question—ads for killers—straddles the line so precisely between freedom of the press and the duty not to harm others that nearly identical cases get decided differently. This is an area where you cannot depend on First Amendment protection; if you want to be safe, lay off the killer for hire ads. Perhaps most interesting is the fact that it took nothing short of blaming murders on published materials to get to the limits of First Amendment protection for those materials.

Particular Dangers and Risks

Defamation

A person defames another when he or she makes a false public statement about that person that injures his or her reputation. The injured person can sue the speaker and others involved in publishing the statement. The term "defamation" includes both libel (printed injurious falsehoods) and slander (spoken injurious falsehoods).

There is great potential for defamation on online services, especially in group message and chat areas. Hundreds of people might read the postings in a single online service discussion area. The participants may know each other fairly well, and move in the same personal and business circles.

Someone whose reputation is injured in a public discussion on an online service or network can find it has consequences in the "real world" —reduced opportunities to work, to further their careers and make money, to interact with others with shared interests. This is especially true if one's circle of business and friends is well connected to the online world. These are the kinds of losses for which defamation lawsuits seek a remedy.

A statement only defames a person if it is false. Truth is an absolute defense to a defamation claim. If I say, "Bill tortures turtles," and it is false, I have defamed him. If my statement is true there is no defamation, even though Joe's reputation among animal-lovers will certainly suffer. Thus, if anyone ever claims that a public message on an online service defames him or her, the first thing to determine is whether the statement is true. If so, there is no defamation problem.

Even when a statement is defamatory, system operators still have fairly strong protection from liability.

Even when a statement is defamatory, system operators still have fairly strong protection from liability. One major defense is the public figure exception, which news publishers and reporters rely on routinely. Online services also likely qualify for this protection as both publishers and distributors of information.

The public figure exception permits the press to subject public officials and so-called "public figures" of various sorts to all kinds of public comment, even ridicule, under a series of rulings by the Supreme Court. It is important to be able to discuss the affairs of public figures candidly as part of the press' general coverage of public affairs. If famous people could successfully sue the news media every time they disagreed with a public statement about them, it would create a "chilling effect" discouraging the press from discussing anything controversial about well-known people. This would violate the public's and the news media's rights under the First Amendment to discuss public affairs freely without government interference.

Accordingly, the press, including online services, can publish all kinds of material about public figures, even defamatory statements, without liability. This exception is not absolute. The press is still liable for defamation when it prints a falsehood either maliciously, or with reckless disregard for whether the statement is true. The protection is pretty broad, though, as a quick survey of the scurrilous rumors packing our national sensationalist tabloids will readily demonstrate—if it was easy to sue for lies in the press in this country, those papers would all be out of business.

> **The press is still liable for defamation when it prints a falsehood either maliciously, or with reckless disregard for whether the statement is true.**

For system operators, this means that just about any believable-looking statement about a public figure can be published without liability. If, however, the statement is outlandish, or if someone provides proof to the system operator that the statement is false, then the system operator must look into the truth of the statement before posting or continuing to post the statement on the system.

Exactly who counts as a "public figure" for purposes of the exception from defamation liability? For starters, this term includes all public officials in the performance of their official duties, from local village councilmen to the President of the United States. It also includes everyone who is famous on the national or regional levels—the kinds of people you read about in the newspaper. These are the traditional types of public figures about whom the press may write freely. Some people are "limited-purpose" public figures, who are only famous in connection with a particular event or issue. The liability shield for press reports is somewhat narrower for these people—to be protected, their statements must concern matters of legitimate public concern in connection with the person's involvement in the event or issue.

The opposite of a public figure is a private person. The exception does not apply to them. If a false statement is published injuring a private person, he or she can take the speaker and the system operator to court. So it is very important, when reviewing potentially defamatory statements on a board, to determine whether the subject of the statements is "public" or "private."

Can the "public figure" exception from defamation liability be extended even further for online services? For instance, if a user regularly posts many messages on an online service and becomes well-known to the other users, does she become a public figure on that online service? If so, it would greatly broaden the public figure exception, so that well-known users on an online service (even if they're absolutely private offline) could not sue the service for defamatory statements posted in the online service's public forums, unless they were retained on the service recklessly or with malice. This intriguing possibility is likely the way courts will decide if asked to rule on the issue, for two reasons: (1) when someone becomes famous in an online discussion, he or she then becomes a legitimate subject of interest and discussion among the others in the discussion, and (2) someone who is well known enough to be a celebrity in an online context also likely has strong enough access to the ears of others online to contest any falsehoods that may have been said against him or her. Under such circumstances, courts may feel their help is not needed, and use the public figure doctrine as a convenient way to gracefully back out and let the defamed user fend for himself or herself.

Are the Courts Necessary to Combat Online Defamation?

The Net is creating a media field vast enough to assure everyone their 15 minutes of fame. Virtually anyone who wants a little celebrity can find his or her audience among the many thousands of online social spots. Celebrity cuts both ways, though; even the best-liked receive their share of sniping and disparagement online. Occasionally it rises to defamation: accusations detailing instances of dishonesty, disloyalty, distasteful sexual practices, and other reputation-staining events that never happened. Until recently, lawsuits over online injury to reputations were rarely worth the expense. Now money flows freely into cyberspace, and online defamation lawsuits are beginning to appear.

Are there any major differences between defamation in the traditional media and defamation in the online world? According to some, there is one big difference: defamation lawsuits don't make sense for online services, which are far more accessible than older media like newspapers and television. If someone tells terrible lies about you in a public online forum, you can go immediately into that same public forum and tell everyone the truth. That being the case, our courts should follow the Constitution's edict to make no laws abridging freedom of speech and bow out of the equation, letting accusations and defenses work themselves out on the public stage.

This view is attractive, but not compelling on a practical level. Those who feel wronged by others will continue to insist on using the power of a court of law to punish the wrong-doers, and to be declared the winner of any arguments affecting their reputation. Courts will not soon be freed from being asked to decide matters of online defamation.

There is another, weaker form of the argument for reducing the courts' role: while courts will still be asked to decide claims of defamation, their power may be limited (or perhaps self-limited) to making liars post retractions in public, particularly in the same online forum where the defamation first appeared. This approach again places a premium on the power of speech to rectify the problems caused by bad speech.

This is another attractive view of how things should work, but major practical problems remain. First, if the only penalty for making false and illegal accusations is being ordered to post a retraction, those who want to ruin the good name of others will hardly be deterred by fear of the penalty. Second, the real problem created by most defamations is the set of unpleasant associations created by the false accusation. The accusation can be retracted, but the negative image of its victim can remain in the public's mind for years. Telling everyone you're sorry for falsely accusing Jim of beating his wife recalls the image of Jim as a wife-beater even as it claims the image is a lie. For a complete remedy, the defamed person needs the impossible—the ability to erase the public's memory of the original lie about him or her. Failing that, victims will demand that courts provide the same cure-all answer they provide for injuries ranging from broken legs to betrayal of trust: money damages.

Satirical material and political commentary receive extra protection from defamation lawsuits. Satire almost always concerns public figures, so it already has the benefit of that exception to defamation liability. The satire defense goes even further—statements that might be considered malicious and illegal, even under the public figure defense, can be protected if they are shown to be part of a satire regarding the subject. A famous example is the Hustler magazine story that told of a well-known minister having his first sexual experience with his own mother in an outhouse. Hustler was sued for publishing this obviously false article, supposedly with malice toward the minister. The courts denied the claim, saying the article was clearly satire and protected from a defamation lawsuit.

Another protected category is statements of "mere opinion," such as editorials and critical reviews. The writer must keep it clear that he is, at all times, only humbly offering his personal opinion. A recent Supreme Court case pointed out that for this exception to defamation liability to apply, it must be genuinely and obviously presented as mere opinion; calling something an opinion while presenting it as fact will not qualify for protection.

For example, "I think Sam stole $100,000 from his partner," will probably not be treated as mere opinion, but as a defamatory statement if it is false. Using the words "I think" to frame the factual statement would not succeed in converting it into mere opinion. On the other hand, "Although I can't prove it, in my personal opinion Sam is a crook," is far more likely to be treated as mere opinion, not subject to a defamation claim.

Believe it or not, name-calling is also protected from defamation claims, as an extension of the opinion defense. The theory is that no one would reasonably believe that the person calling names is actually stating facts about the target of his or her attentions. For example, one court denied a defamation claim against someone who publicly called a stockbroker a "silly, stupid, senile bum."

Right of Privacy

A violation of privacy can arise from publishing messages on an online service about a person's private affairs that a "reasonable person" would find highly offensive, and that are not part of the public's "legitimate" concern (we are not talking about e-mail privacy here, but public discussion of private matters about people). These concepts are not precisely defined in the law, but a little common sense can help determine if the particular dirty laundry on display is likely to lead to a legal claim.

When a person is not a public figure, his or her right of privacy includes most of the affairs of his or her life. As a practical matter, though, only public disclosures that would cause them great pain or embarrassment will lead to legal claims, because only such injuries can support a claim for substantial money damages. A violation of privacy claim could arise, for example, from a public message revealing that a named user regularly visits a therapist for help in overcoming sexual disorders. For another example, a New York court held a few years ago that an advertisement containing a photo of a naked woman and child by a lake in a forest, taken secretly by a photographer without their knowledge, violated their right of privacy when the man who was their husband and father recognized their bare backs in a magazine ad.

Privacy claims don't apply to events that occur in public, are a matter of public record, or can be claimed to be "newsworthy." Revealing that someone failed his or her driver's test fifteen times and never obtained a license may not be a privacy violation, if

> **Privacy claims don't apply to events that occur in public, are a matter of public record, or can be claimed to be "newsworthy."**

that same information is available from publicly accessible motor vehicle records. Similarly, if publicly available divorce papers disclose that a man was divorced by his wife because he was always gnawing on the furniture, he may have no basis for legal action against the publication of this unsavory information.

Despite this exception for matters of public record, even "public figures" have an enforceable right of privacy against the pointless disclosure of private and embarrassing facts. Being famous does not make someone fair game for all manner of privacy violations, the example of Jackie Onassis notwithstanding.

There is a variation on the standard right of privacy claim called "false light" privacy. A false light claim arises when someone reports something about someone else in a misleading context that injures that person. Rather than attempt to further define this legal theory, it is better to illustrate it through a couple of examples from past court cases.

In one famous case, a woman was accidentally included in a photograph used in a broadcast news story about prostitutes (she was not herself a prostitute). The woman successfully claimed that this picture, though perfectly accurate in itself, cast her in a false light by making it look like she was also a prostitute. In another case, a picture of a couple kissing was used as an illustration for a magazine article about the superficiality of "love at first sight." This use was held to deceptively portray the couple's loving relationship as superficial, therefore casting it in a false light. False light privacy claims usually do not succeed unless the false light portrayal would be offensive to the average viewer or reader.

Another privacy-related right is the right of publicity. The right of publicity is a person's right to prevent others from exploiting his name, likeness, image, and so on for profit. It is often considered a property right rather than a personal right, because the owner of the right of publicity can exploit his or her own image for profit, often through licensing arrangements with merchandisers.

A person usually has to be a celebrity or famous personality in order to have a protectable right of publicity. Fights over the publicity rights to Elvis Presley images have been sighted in several courts around the country. These cases also deal with one of the great unresolved issues in this area of the law: does the right of publicity descend to the heirs of the famous person, or does the public get to use that person's image after he or she dies? The publicity right most often involves the use of a person's name or picture; less frequently, it has attached to such things as Bert Lahr's (the cowardly lion's) speaking style, the use of "Here's Johnny" for television personality Johnny Carson, and Tom Waits' or Bette Midler's singing voice and persona.

Is the right of publicity really of any importance on online services? If we consider marketing and advertising, the right of publicity could be an important concern.

Any advertising that uses famous characters, such as Charlie Chaplin for IBM computers or William S. Burroughs for Nike sneakers, should be fully authorized by the celebrity appearing in the ad. A video store chain got into trouble when it ran advertisements that showed a nerdy Woody Allen lookalike buying copies of Woody Allen movie videos. Similarly, any advertising on an online service that trades on a celebrity's name or image could run afoul of the right of publicity unless properly authorized by that celebrity. This kind of celebrity marketing online is becoming pretty popular now: come to our online forum where the stars hang out!

> **Any advertising on an online service that trades on a celebrity's name or image could run afoul of the right of publicity unless properly authorized by that celebrity.**

What about users who pose as famous people—does this violate the right of publicity? It depends on the circumstances. If an online service hires a bunch of people to pose as celebrities to lure star-seekers into the system without telling them about the fakery, there would seem to be a fairly straightforward violation of the real stars' right of publicity. But what if someone poses as a celebrity just to impress people? If they're not selling any products or gaining some advantage for a business, it would be hard to say they've violated the right of publicity, which is the right to control commercial exploitation of one's image and persona.

Erroneous Information

One of the major functions of online services is to provide useful information to users. Can an online service get into trouble if it gives out information that is inaccurate or wrong, and a user is injured in some way?

In a New York case a few years ago, *Daniel v. Dow Jones*, a disappointed user sued over an erroneous item carried on the Dow Jones News Retrieval Service. The user had invested in a company based on the news item, which reported certain dollar figures regarding the Husky Oil Company, but failed to state that the figures were in Canadian, not U.S., dollars.

The investor lost the case. The court said there had to be a "special relationship" between the user and Dow Jones before the news service could be liable for errors. Such a relationship did not arise from the mere fact that the user was a paying user of the Dow Jones service. The Court said the relationship between Dow Jones and the user was identical to that between a newspaper and its readers:

> The instantaneous, interactive, computerized delivery of defendant's service does not alter the facts: [the user] purchased [Dow Jones'] news reports as did thousands of others. The "special relationship" required to allow an action for negligent misstatements must be greater than that between the ordinary buyer and seller. (*Daniel v. Dow Jones*, 520 NYS2d 334, 338 (1987))

In arriving at this decision, the Court relied on prior cases that refused to hold information providers liable for errors in the following situations:

- a misstatement in the print edition of the *Wall Street Journal*
- a cookbook containing a recipe with a poisonous ingredient
- a textbook erroneously referring to the plaintiff's chemical as poisonous, when in fact it was not

The court also stated that, "The First Amendment precludes the imposition of liability for nonde-famatory, negligently untruthful news."

Are system operators entitled to the same protections as Dow Jones? Many online services provide news in much the same way that Dow Jones does. They may offer their own news reports, or they may provide news feeds obtained from services like News Bytes or ClariNet. In addition, users regularly tell each other the news and give each other information, including recipes that may prove poisonous just like in the cookbook example above.

Based on the above, it appears that online services, whether larger or smaller than Dow Jones, are no more responsible for the accuracy of the information they provide. This does not mean system operators have a license to post false information. We are talking about honest mistakes, not deliberate misinformation.

The only exceptions to the system operator's freedom from liability for errors would be where a "special relationship" arises between the system operator and users (such as a stockbroker/client or lawyer/client relationship), and any other situations in which the system operator guarantees the accuracy of the information in question (it is strongly recommended not to make such guarantees). In such special cases, the system operator could be liable for the negligently erroneous information.

If a user posts negligently false information on an online service, the system operator should not be held liable for it unless he or she is specifically aware of both the message and its probable falsity. As a matter of caution and common sense, operators should delete or correct any messages believed to be incorrect.

Copyright Infringement

We reviewed copyright ownership in some detail in Chapter 3. Here, we will discuss briefly the risks involved when infringing material is posted or transmitted on an online service.

Copyrighted materials include messages, e-mail, text files, program files, image files, and database files. Copying or distributing any of these materials without the owner's consent is a copyright infringement. If a user posts any of these infringing materials on an online service, the posting itself would be an infringement, and any downloading of these materials from the online service would also be an infringement.

If the materials are maintained on the online service and downloaded by users without the system operator's knowledge that they're copyrighted or that they infringe someone's copyright, the operator may not be at risk for more than having to remove the materials from the online service. The first and most commonly used legal weapon in the copyright owner's arsenal is the right to obtain an injunction—a court order preventing further infringement. For infringing materials posted on an online service, that just means the online service cannot transmit or copy the file any more, which is very little loss to the online service in almost any imaginable case. If a copyright owner threatens a lawsuit, it can be mostly defused simply by removing the files at issue from the online service.

Can the owner go further and sue for money damages? This is possible, but if the system operator was not aware of the infringement, it is unlikely he or she will have to pay damages for infringements committed by other users on the online service. As we discussed in Chapter 1, the online service as a distributor of others' speech is not liable for every text or file that passes through the system. The infringement is really committed by the uploading user, and the uploading user is primarily responsible to the copyright owner. Nonetheless, as we go to press, a group of music publishers is suing CompuServe to try and establish just such liability by CompuServe for music file infringements by its users. It remains to be seen whether the result will force us to change our reading on the law in this area.

> **A system operator's relative freedom from liability for infringements by users does not mean, though, that he or she can just say "I didn't know it was infringing" and go scot-free in all cases.**

A system operator's relative freedom from liability for infringements by users does not mean, though, that he or she can just say "I didn't know it was infringing" and go scot-free in all cases. One glaring example is the "pirate boards," online services that serve as distribution points for an underground market in infringing software. The system operator of a pirate board cannot believably maintain that he or she does not know the software on the board is infringing, since the entire board is devoted to encouraging infringements. If caught, he or she is likely to be fully prosecuted as a copyright infringer, and as a "contributory infringer"—one who encourages others to infringe copyrights. Some of the large software companies, most notably Novell, investigate and shut down pirate boards regularly, issuing press releases of the event to warn other software pirates. Recently, videogame maker Sega obtained a court order against a bulletin board that was trafficking in software illegally copied from videogame cartridges.

A similar risk exists for online services that maintain large libraries of graphic image files uploaded by users who scan and digitize printed magazines and other print materials. Many graphic images now found on online services and in networks such as Usenet are, in fact, infringing files created by users who just slapped a copyrighted magazine on a scanner. Some users know this is infringing; others argue that once the visual image is recast in electronic form, copyright no longer applies. This is not true. A copyrighted magazine picture does not lose its copyright in digitized form, just as a book does not lose its copyright when typed into the computer. This point was hammered home in the recent case *Playboy v. Frena*, which confirmed to all doubters that copyrights really don't get stripped off when magazine pictures are digitized.

So how should one manage the risk of infringements from user files and postings, when the goal is to run an online service that does not carry infringing files? There's no need to monitor every posting or file, but if one hears of any possibly infringing materials, it deserves investigation. If the materials look like they might be infringing, they should be removed, at least until the uploader can show that he or she has all rights necessary to copy and distribute them. In any case, don't let the uploader assert that copyright law does not really cover files in electronic form. This nonsense argument has gained some currency in the online services and networks, but it is dead wrong.

Online services that maintain a fair number of program files may come across various kinds of "patches" (programs that modify other, popular computer programs) and "hacked" programs. Many, or perhaps most, of these files are either infringing, modified versions of copyrighted programs, or programs permitting others to modify a copyrighted program without the owner's permission. Be very careful about carrying any of these files. They are just the kind of files that fill the pirate boards, and can bring the wrath of large software companies down on an online service. Those who wish to carry any such files should consult with an attorney familiar with software about the risks involved with those particular files.

Access or Security-Related Information

Another kind of information that can pass through an online service and cause injury is data related to the access or security of people, businesses, or computer networks or systems. It can show up anywhere—in public postings, e-mail, or binary files.

There is no special body of law dealing with system operator liability for holding such information on the online service. The general principles of system operator liability would apply, though: the operator will be liable for any injuries which he or she intentionally, recklessly, or negligently permits to be caused to others. The system operator has a duty of care to act reasonably to prevent foreseeable injuries to others due to the presence of security- or access-related materials on the online service.

Some of the most common data of this type found on the networks is credit card and other credit-related information. Such data is periodically put into circulation by intrusive hackers to embarrass, damage, or get revenge on somebody or some company, or simply to buy stuff on

The Long Arm of the Law

The most important single feature of the online revolution is that it brings people together from remote places in new and powerful ways. Groups are being born that were impossible before because the members live too far apart, and these new groups can leverage the power of the networks to pursue their goals more effectively. This new far-flung intimacy also has a downside. It may put U.S. citizens within reach of the legal system of every state of the union.

Of the lawsuits over online events receiving some attention over the past couple of years, several involve people and companies hauled into out-of-state courts to defend their rights. To those who start the suits, it is irrelevant whether or not the defendant ever set foot in the state where the court is located. The dark deed was done on telephone lines passing through the state, and that is enough.

Among those called into out-of-state courts were two members of the "Money Talks" discussion area of Prodigy. Each allegedly damaged the stock value of a medical device company he badmouthed to others on the system. Peter DeNigris of Babylon, New York was first, sued in Newark, New Jersey by a company named Medphone. Next was A. Karl Kipke, a resident of Kansas who worked in Kansas City, Missouri. He was sued in Portland, Oregon, by a company named Epitope. Have a nice trip, Karl—ever been to Portland before? There seems to be a pattern here: say the wrong thing about a company on a national online service, and you may be invited by some nice judge to visit another state.

You don't have to go on a large-scale national service like Prodigy to be sued out of state, however. Running your own local computer bulletin board seems to do the trick. Recently, the owners of the Amateur Action computer bulletin board, located in Milpitas, California, were convicted on obscenity charges in Tennessee. It's bad enough they were forced to defend themselves halfway across the country (over objections that the recently concluded NAFTA treaty prevented such remote jurisdiction). What was worse, the local community standards of relatively repressive Tennessee were applied to decide whether Amateur Action's online offerings were obscene. If other courts follow this lead, we could see the most repressive morality zones in the country dictating what will be legally available to those in more liberal neighborhoods.

Luckily, there is finally one court decision pointing the other way, declaring a limit to out-of-state jurisdiction over modem users. It came in *Patterson vs. CompuServe,* involving a dispute over software brand names. Following the growing custom in cases involving online affairs, CompuServe sued Richard Patterson, a Texas resident, in federal court in CompuServe's home town of Columbus, Ohio. Patterson was not too excited about commuting to Ohio. He filed an early motion to dismiss the case for lack of jurisdiction, and—surprise—it was granted by the court.

The judge recognized that using an online service with national coverage does not automatically make the user available for lawsuits in every state of the union, saying: "It appears that the customer's primary interest is in the information contained on the network, much of which may come from other CompuServe users in states other than Ohio." He even declined to simply transfer the case to a court with proper jurisdiction in Texas, although federal courts have that option. It was more important to make the point of dismissing a case in Ohio against a guy who never even set foot in that state.

Does this one case mark the beginning of a trend, limiting remote jurisdiction over modem users? Probably not. Local courts protect local citizenry and institutions, and many will continue to extend that protection against long distance interlopers. This growing problem may not be resolved until (and unless) big guns like Congress or the Supreme Court step in to fix it.

someone else's account. Other types of sensitive security and access information that one may come across include:

- information on other financial accounts held by people and businesses
- access codes and information for private computer systems and networks
- information on breaking into telephone systems and obtaining the ability to make phone calls charged to others
- trade secret information of various companies
- computer viruses and other dangerous computer code (covered in detail later in this chapter)
- classified government information

This is only a sample. Many other types of security-related information could come into an online service at any point.

Not all of this information is illegal, or damaging to anyone. It can be hard, though, for a system operator to figure out which information is harmless, and which could lead to damaging computer break-ins just by being left on the online service. The safe course, then, is to remove any such materials discovered on the online service. This way, the operator minimizes the risk that others might be hurt through misuse of the information, and by the same stroke minimizes his or her own risk of being liable for negligently allowing dangerous materials to remain on the online service.

If one is willing to take a walk on the wild side by regularly posting security- and access-related materials on an online service, bear in mind that if any mistakes are made, people could get hurt (at least financially), triggering a lawsuit, in addition to any criminal consequences. Also, if an online service looks to the outside world like it is devoted to collecting and distributing such materials, it risks being treated like a "pirate board." The operator will not be able to avoid liability by claiming he or she was not aware of a specific security-compromising file that caused damage, because the entire online service contains many such files, any of which could be misused in that way.

Maintaining System Security

In the preceding sections, we looked at a system operator's duty to keep activities on his or her system from harming others, regardless of whether the potential victims are members of that system, can be found only on other systems, or never went online in their lives. This is because online activities affect a far broader social and business sphere than the user base of the local system where the activities occur. System operators owe a general duty of care to all who might foreseeably be affected by those activities, wherever located.

There is another major, more focused area, however, where companies and their system operators need to exercise care: when they process or carry data for themselves or others, or offer online services to others. In this case, they have a direct responsibility to those whose data they are carrying or processing, or to whom they are providing services. The potential victims may be full-fledged customers of the data processing company (including, when the company is an online service, all of its users), unrelated people or companies who receive the company's services in some anonymous fashion, or it may be the company itself. The project of keeping the companies and data under one's care safe from harm is known generally as the subject of system security.

Most system operators strive to keep their systems reasonably secure from hacking, viruses, and other outside intrusions. However, users today are often suspicious of the security of online systems, and with good reason. There have been a number of highly publicized virus scares and hacker intrigues in the first part of the '90s, with no promise that they're about to end. Those who follow network happenings a little more closely may note reported hacker break-ins at various systems around the country every month or so. Finally, experts on network security assure us that for every reported security breach, several others go unreported because the victim companies wish to avoid the embarrassment of appearing easy targets for hacker attacks. The perceived insecurity of online systems and networks is largely responsible for the rising interest in using encryption software, which can make e-mail truly impregnable even on a Swiss cheese system.

> **The perceived insecurity of online systems and networks is largely responsible for the rising interest in using encryption software, which can make e-mail truly impregnable even on a Swiss cheese system.**

Beyond their own use of encryption, users are still expecting ever greater security from the providers of online channels. Large volumes of highly confidential data move out regularly through the Internet, including financial transaction data and prized company trade secrets. People are also becoming aware that network ubiquity is a two-way street. While the new connectedness lets us hook up with friends and associates all over the world, it also enables far more complete surveillance of our lives than ever before in history. Some aren't bothered by the prospect of spies and marketers surveying their lives, but others will seek systems or ways of communicating that are not so open for inspection. The popularity of demonstrably secure systems is only going to increase.

The Major Security Threats: Viruses and Intruders

Viruses

Viruses and other dangerous program code (we will refer to all such code as "Dangerous Code") have been a feature of the bulletin board landscape for many years. They are unlikely to disappear any time soon. Some examples of Dangerous Code appear to be designed only with mischief in mind, while others are purely destructive.

Indeed, the most famous virus (actually a worm) author, Robert Morris, claimed that his Dangerous Code that went amok on the Internet was intended only as an innocent tool for mapping the network by going from computer to computer. But as his program proved, most Dangerous Code is capable of great damage to computer systems, regardless of the exact motivation of the developer.

Kinds of Dangerous Code

The term "virus" is often used today to describe any kind of dangerous computer program that is passed from one computer system to another. In fact, there are several types of dangerous program code, and they have somewhat different characteristics:

- *Virus*   The best-known type of Dangerous Code. In its pure form, a virus program is a small program that attaches to a stored copy of a program file (such as an application program) kept in the computer system. When the main program is run, the virus program causes the computer to make one or more copies of the virus. This is the primary virus activity—it alone can bring a computer system to a standstill by tying the system up with endless replications of the virus program.

   Most viruses attach themselves to other program files in a way that makes them hard to detect without special analysis. When the "infected" file is passed to another computer and operated on that computer, the virus replicating process is repeated. In this way a single virus can quickly infect and distort the operations of large computer networks.

- *Trojan*   Before viruses showed up, trojans (named after the Trojan Horse) caused the most problems in computer networks. Trojans are based on deception—the distributor of a trojan disguises it as something else, often a well-known program. When the caller attempts to run the trojan program, it will do something unexpected, and sometimes very nasty, such as erasing the caller's entire hard disk. To add insult to injury, a trojan program might also flash a message like "gotcha!" on the screen display as it performs its dirty work.

   Trojans, in their pure form, differ from viruses in two ways: (1) they do not usually replicate themselves upon the operation of other programs, and (2) they do not "hitchhike" with other unrelated programs. Thus, their passage from computer to computer is not generally as rapid, and they do not dynamically find new hiding places in different programs in the computer. However, they are just as dangerous to the caller's computer when activated.

- *Worms*   A worm is a small program that hides in the computer, and begins to operate when certain events specified by the worm developer occur within the computer. A worm can be destructive, like a trojan. Worms are sometimes inserted in systems for constructive purposes, such as monitoring computer states, and performing certain necessary functions when certain pre-specified conditions occur within the computer system.

   Worms, unlike viruses, need not be attached to files for other programs. Instead,

> **Worms, unlike viruses, need not be attached to files for other programs. Instead, they are usually programmed to "hide" in the computer system so they are difficult to detect.**

they are usually programmed to "hide" in the computer system so they are difficult to detect. Unlike trojans or viruses, worms in their pure form are not automatically transferred from computer to computer, but are separately installed in each system. In some cases, like the Internet worm, the worm program might actually dial another computer system and transmit itself into the other computer.

- *Time Bombs*   A "time bomb" or "logic bomb" is not a type of program, but a specific computer program feature. A program with a time bomb will "explode" upon the occurrence of a certain event—often the occurrence of a predetermined calendar date on the system's clock. The so-called explosion can be anything the developer designs into the program, from a complete system wipe to a display of annoying little messages all over the computer screen.

   Time bombs are often not alien code like viruses, trojans, and worms, but are put into programs by their developers to discourage unauthorized use of the programs. For instance, if a software developer leases his program to his customers for limited-time use, he may include a bomb disabling that program after the authorized use period.

   In such cases, the "danger" posed by a time bomb has to do with the choices made by the developer. Does the time bomb merely cause the program not to work the next time you run it? Does it corrupt data files maintained by the program before the time bomb kicked in? Or does it go further, causing havoc in other computer operations not related to the program containing the bomb? And are there bugs in the time bomb mechanism, causing it to do things the developer didn't intend?

In the above descriptions, we carefully distinguished between different types of Dangerous Code. In fact, many of the examples of Dangerous Code in existence today have some or all of the features mentioned above. For example, a program may distribute and replicate itself like a virus, then detach itself and hide in a system like a worm, and rise to cause mischief or damage on a certain date or event like a worm or time bomb.

> **Software that is poorly designed, or not fully debugged, can play tricks on a computer system as damaging as anything a virus might do.**

There is another sense in which the definition of Dangerous Code is not exact. Software that is poorly designed, or not fully debugged, can play tricks on a computer system as damaging as anything a virus might do. This is also literally "Dangerous Code," but it is different from the programs described above because it was not designed to have any damaging effects. Such software hazards are usually viewed as a normal incident of the software business, and are not typically viewed as "computer sabotage" the way Dangerous Code usually is.

How Dangerous Is Dangerous Code?

There is a fair amount of debate on this subject. No one doubts that a virus, trojan, or similar program can cause great damage when set loose in certain system environments. When Robert Morris' virus got loose on the Internet a couple of years ago, the total damage was estimated at up to 1.2 million dollars. Computers in universities, industrial research sites, government sites, and many other applications were temporarily hobbled, as were the lives of the people who used and depended on those computers.

However, some claim that the general danger is not as great as sometimes stated by the "security experts." Screaming reports of national Dangerous Code threats, such as the fabled "October 13th" virus of 1989 or Michelangelo virus of 1992 (neither of which materialized on the predicted scale), sell plenty of newspapers and anti-virus computer programs.

It has also been suggested that anti-virus mania supports a hidden agenda of commercial software developers. If the public believes there is a great risk of downloading Dangerous Code from bulletin boards, where the bulk of shareware ("try before you buy" software) distribution takes place, then members of the public will prefer to purchase commercial software copies at retail and mail-order stores, with their aura of supposed safety. Ironically, some say, Dangerous Code turns up at least as often in shrink-wrapped, over-the-counter, big brand name software as in shareware files downloaded from the local bulletin board. A major vendor of local area networking software and a leading manufacturer of personal computers have both been known to ship out large quantities of their products infected by viruses.

So where does this leave us? Not too scared, but wary. A bulletin board with significant file uploading/downloading activity carries hundreds, perhaps thousands of different files over the course of just a few months. Some such bulletin boards may be maintaining, and making available to callers, one or more programs with Dangerous Code.

Intrusive Hackers

Those with even a passing acquaintance with online affairs know there are legions of computer-savvy youths who break into computer systems for the sake of mischief. We do not have the space in this book to go into the hacker culture or mentality, fascinating as they are. Several good books on the subject are listed in Appendix J.

What is worth mentioning here is that hackers have a wide variety of intentions. Many are kids who like to show they can get past any security scheme, just for the heck of it. Every system they break into is another notch in their belt. Even when these intruders copy secret or valuable information from a system, their purpose is relatively benign: to bring back the information as a trophy of the hunt, or to use it as a personal academic resource for learning more about the arcana of computer systems. There are also pranksters, of course, whose satisfaction comes from giving headaches to legitimate systems users. And there is a contingent of actual spies, embezzlers, and other criminals, who can spell real trouble for the company whose systems they invade.

Unless the system operator is dedicated to running a truly open system, it is a good idea to keep hackers out. Those who start out with benign intentions may not remain that way. If a hacker thinks he or she has been detected by the administrator or operator, the hacker may try to hurt the system or the data on it with little regard to how much damage is being caused. Remember, they are for the most part relatively immature and irresponsible youths. For companies who hold company trade secrets on computer systems accessible from the outside either through the networks or by dial-in, there is another, technical reason to use good security to keep hackers out: it enhances the ability to claim ownership of the trade secret information. Otherwise, if John Doe needs to sue Mary Smith one day for misusing his trade secrets, Mary Smith might defeat John

> **Unless the system operator is dedicated to running a truly open system, it is a good idea to keep hackers out. Those who start out with benign intentions may not remain that way.**

Doe's claims in court by showing that he cared so little about the claimed secret information that he kept the information on a totally insecure server in a world full of hackers.

How do hackers get into a system on which they don't belong? There are many ways, but a few general types have been cataloged. Here's a brief rundown of the most prevalent, from the highly recommended book *Firewalls and Internet Security*, by William R. Cheswick and Steven M. Bellovin (Addison Wesley, 1994):

- **Stealing passwords**—finding the file where the user passwords are kept, or logging them as they are entered, lets hackers walk in the "front door" of the system.

- **Social engineering**—an elegant name for fooling users and administrators into giving hackers the information they need to enter the system, often by posing as someone else, such as a telephone service person.

- **Bugs and backdoors**—finding holes and flaws in the system that can be exploited to yield access.

- **Authentication failures**—ways of fooling software designed to authenticate legitimate users of the systems.

- **Protocol failures**—the processes used in setting up secure communications may have holes that can be exploited.

- **Information leakage**—while security-related information may be well protected in its official storage place, there may be other clues to that same information stored in places no one thinks to secure, but hackers know to find.

- **Denial of service**—this is not an unauthorized entry into a system, but an attempt to make it cease functioning correctly through outside maneuvers, such as sending repeated messages that overload system resources; the computer equivalent not of breaking into a car, but slashing its tires.

The Duty to Maintain a Secure System

Many companies today need to be concerned about system security not only for their own information, but also because they hold, process, or carry valuable information belonging to others, under an almost endless variety of arrangements. A few such arrangements are:

- handling vital core functions for other businesses like payrolls or claims processing

- operating an online service, bulletin board system, or e-mail system open to users outside the providing company (which includes all publicly available online systems)

- using secret mailing lists belonging to others to perform direct mail campaigns

- holding the source code of software owned by others, under strict confidentiality agreements

- handling shipping and deliveries for other companies

- selling supplies and services to other companies under long-term, needs-based relationships

- supplying customer service, where the service company learns about much of its customers' operations in the course of servicing its own products

Some of these business operations start out as online activities. Many others start offline, but eventually develop an online aspect when the companies involved set up e-mail systems to coordinate their operations, either privately or through the Internet.

What is the responsibility of a company handling the data or messages of others? The first part of the answer is easy: if there is a contract covering the relationship in question, look for the answer in that contract.

When There Is a Contract

When people and businesses make a contract, they are in effect setting up their own private law of responsibilities. If the parties agree the service provider will meet certain precautionary standards in maintaining system security, then those standards become the measure of the provider's responsibility. Possible security standards range from merely requiring that the service provider be "reasonable" in its security procedures, to mandating that the service provider use the most effective securities techniques as soon as they become available and are proven reliable. The parties may even specify certain procedures that the provider must follow on a stated schedule, or it will be in breach of the agreement.

Conversely, the parties may agree that the service provider takes on little or no security obligation, in which event the customer takes a far greater security risk itself. The customer who accepts this approach hopefully is prepared to meet the security risk, such as by using secure encryption for its own messages, or by using the service provider's systems only for data or communications whose security is not critical. Most subscribers to paid bulletin boards and large online services find themselves in this situation.

The big advantage of contracts is that they enable the parties to define security standards that both meet the customer's needs, and are achievable by the service provider. There is no need to bother in these deals with the system operators' nebulous "duty of care" to the world at large; through an express agreement, the parties can adjust the service provider's security commitments to be as specific or loose as they please. An additional advantage is that an agreement makes it easier for the parties to set a fair price for the security levels desired by the customer (the justification for charging a price for greater security is that it entails a greater liability risk for the service provider, and requires extra manpower devoted to security matters). Since most systems operate at a single level of security against intrusions and viruses, customers usually end up paying for the security they want by using the service provider that meets their particular security standards. Everything else being equal, a service provider with substantially better security should be more expensive. Expect to see a niche market develop for highly secure systems, charging a premium to protect customer data using state-of-the-art security measures.

> **The big advantage of contracts is that they enable the parties to define security standards that both meet the customer's needs, and are achievable by the service provider.**

When There Is No Contract, but a Direct Relationship

There remain plenty of situations where there will be no express contract between the service provider and the person or company being served. This might be due to a distant business relationship between the parties, or because all sides prefer not to set things down in a formal agreement. Examples include service provider companies that:

- act as mere intermediaries, passing messages of strangers between sending and receiving nodes.

- operate anonymous ftp, gopher, or WWW sites, or other Internet services open to the public, which can be freely entered by anyone on the Internet.

- run customer support BBSs, which exchange e-mail with public callers and permit all callers to download materials from the system.

- open their in-house LANs and other systems to the Internet, permitting free exchange of e-mail and files with outsiders who may or may not have formal arrangements with the company.

- operate an electronic store within a larger online system, where only the owner of the larger system has a contract with the customer.

This is only a small sample of the direct but informal relationships that are common online. Those who run in-house systems can readily come up with their own lists of situations where their company handles the data or communications of outsiders, without any formal arrangements covering the relationship.

In all of these direct relationships without formal contracts, the service provider's obligations often will simply revert to the general negligence standard discussed earlier: the service provider must act reasonably to prevent foreseeable dangers to others, subject to the limits discussed in that section.

Remember, however, that we're talking in this section about security dangers to those whose data is *directly* involved in the service provider's system (and *not* about random strangers completely outside the system, who happen to libeled by some user or have their copyrights infringed on the system). For directly involved relationships, there are additional factors bearing on the service provider's responsibility. Three in particular bear a closer look.

Is There a "Special Relationship"?

You may recall from the *Daniel v. Dow Jones* case, discussed earlier, that Dow Jones was not responsible for a data error after the court decided it had no "special relationship" with the injured person. In contrast, in the situations we are now looking at there is *always* a direct relationship between the service provider and the injured party, even if it is anonymous in some cases. Is this direct relationship the same as a "special relationship," so that service providers will be held highly responsible for data errors, security breaches, and other injuries to those whose data or messages they are handling?

Not exactly, though some direct relationships between service providers and other companies are indeed "special" relationships in the *Dow Jones* sense, making its limitation of liability inapplicable. For instance, there is a class of relationships referred to in the law as "fiduciary relationships." These are relations of special trust, such as between partners, joint ventures, authors and publishers, attorneys and clients, employers and employees, and businesses and trusted advisors, among others. Fiduciaries must act honorably towards each other. They must protect each other in their mutual business, and advance their mutual interests. They are not permitted to treat each other as badly as the law otherwise permits businessmen to treat each other. If the relation between the service provider and an injured company qualifies as a fiduciary relationship, then it will most likely also be considered a special relationship in the *Dow Jones* sense, and the service provider must exercise extra care in providing services to its fiduciary.

For instance, the service provider might be a company that finds investors for small businesses. It encourages its small business clients to leave their confidential business plans in a special storage area in its online system, for perusal only by prospective investors who sign nondisclosure agreements. Unfortunately, it turns out the system is highly insecure, easily allowing outsiders to hack in. A hacker makes off with copies of the secret business plans and reveals their contents to competitors of the small business clients of the finder company, resulting in serious business setbacks for one of those clients. The injured client sues the finder company, claiming it did

> **If the relation between the service provider and an injured company qualifies as a fiduciary relationship, then it will most likely also be considered a special relationship in the *Dow Jones* sense, and the service provider must exercise extra care in providing services to its fiduciary.**

not use adequate security measures to protect the business plans. The finder will undoubtedly raise the *Dow Jones* case in its defense, asking to be absolved of all responsibility. However, it is likely in this case that the court would find a fiduciary relationship existed between the finder company and its clients. In addition, the finder company encouraged its clients to rely on the security of its system by depositing their confidential information in it. This is more than enough to show a "special relationship" which would make *Dow Jones* inapplicable. The finder company would likely be required to meet a higher standard of care towards its clients than simply to use "reasonable" security measures.

In other situations, though, the *Dow Jones* limit will remain fully applicable, even though there is a direct relationship between service company and injured party. For instance, say a company downloads a nifty new WWW browser from an anonymous ftp site, and it turns out the browser file is infested with a mean virus that blows out computer monitors and wipes network server files. The company that operates the ftp site performed reasonable virus screening, but did not actually try out every program before making it available for download; the virus in question was so new that the latest version of the virus software used by the provider company did not catch it. Can the downloading company successfully sue the company operating the ftp site for inadequate virus screening procedures? Not likely, because in this case, while the relationship between the companies is direct—one company went into the other company's system and downloaded a file from it—there is absolutely nothing "special" about an anonymous ftp download. In addition, the provider company's use of the latest virus screening software would likely be found reasonable. Going the extra step of actually trying out each piece of software in advance of making it available for download is exactly the kind of burdensome obligation that the *Dow Jones* court refused to impose on First Amendment grounds. It is an extra level of effort that can only be justified, if at all, by a special relationship between providing and receiving companies, which is conspicuously absent in this anonymous ftp situation.

Hopefully, the above examples demonstrate that some direct relationships between companies are also "special" relationships in which a higher duty of care may apply, while other direct relationships are not special at all, and only require the exercise of reasonable care. The easiest way to identify a "special" relationship between provider and user is to see if it also qualifies as a fiduciary relationship under the law (see the examples listed above). Even if it doesn't, there still may be good reason to treat the relationship as special and requiring a higher standard of care. For instance, if a system encourages people to use its e-mail services on the basis that they are more secure than other services, there may be a special relationship even though the system and its users are not fiduciaries pursuing common goals.

Consumer Protection and Statutory Duties

As the masses move online, consumer protection will become an increasingly important factor in setting standards for the security of online systems. "Consumer protection" is both a constant theme in business matters involving consumers, and the driving force behind a number of laws on all sorts of subjects and in all sorts of industries. Even when there is no law in sight to protect consumers, courts will sometimes bend other laws to create such protection, supporting their approach with a vague citation to public policy.

We should expect to see consumer protection concerns appear first online in the same areas where they have been predominant in the past. One is financial transactions. There are plenty of consumer protection laws in this area already, but they apply mainly to traditional money lenders and banks. As other kinds of companies offer online financial services, we should expect to see strict security standards eventually applied to them as well, to help make sure consumers do not lose their money from easily preventable system intrusion. Another area is information identifying the consumer. Wherever the law may end up on the right of a company to use identity information obtained from its own customers (see Chapter 5 for more information on privacy issues), we can at least expect a strong trend in the law to require that all systems containing customer identity information must keep that information highly secure from outside intruders.

> **There are few particulars at this stage in the development of online consumer protection law, but the public policy of protecting consumers is clear enough.**

There are few particulars at this stage in the development of online consumer protection law, but the public policy of protecting consumers is clear enough. You can't get consumers online without also getting consumer protection. Systems serving consumers have a choice today on how to meet this issue. They can identify consumer security needs now and set up security procedures to meet those needs. Or they can wait until the law in this area starts to develop. The first successful lawsuit for inadequate protection of a consumer transaction or the first enactment of a law specifically aimed at protecting consumer security online will serve as their wake-up call.

A related area is laws setting special security standards for certain industries. For instance, firms involved in international dealings may need to comply with the Foreign Corrupt Practices Act. Firms that maintain or transmit health records may need to conform to the requirements of a number of laws governing health record confidentiality. It is beyond the scope of this book to comb through all the special system security rules that might apply to particular industries and practices at the state and federal level. If a service provider is operating within a certain industry niche, or moving specialized information, it should consult with an attorney to determine if there are any special security requirements for that industry or information.

Use of the Latest Security Technologies

At the time this book is being revised, one of the hot product categories in computer networking is firewall software, with new products being announced every week. The industry obsession with firewalls and other security measures is keeping pace with the current national push to get businesses more fully online. As the Information Superhighway drumbeat accelerated, companies from older industries looked over the online landscape and found a lot lacking in terms of security, especially each time a hacker break-in was reported in the papers. When they expressed their reluctance to open their doors to the online world to the high-tech companies trying to entice them into that world, the lack of adequate online security quickly became seen as one of the chief obstacles to establishing a full-fledged commercial environment on the Net. Hence, the flurry of new development of system security products. They are the online industry's engraved invitation to offline businesses to join the party of computer communications.

The pace of new development of online security products may eventually ease up as the networks prove sufficiently safe for prime-time business, but it will never lose its urgency. The online environment contains a natural factor stimulating the continuing improvement of security—namely, the wily computer hacker. Every new security measure is a challenge to the hackers and virus writers, most of them young, who have nothing better to do than prove that no security system can keep them out. Sometimes the hacking is a real problem, as when someone seeks to embezzle funds, or engage in corporate or government espionage. Most often, though, it is a function of sheer bravado, equivalent to the guy who flew an airplane from Russia into Germany just to show it could be done. Harmless as such acts might be, online businesses do not want young hackers showing off how smart they are on systems used for business, any more than the folks in charge of German state security were pleased to see a little plane sailing in from out of nowhere. So we can expect to see a continuing spiral of increasingly powerful security products and techniques, and increasingly sophisticated means of cracking new security measures.

> **The continuing development of new security products has an impact on the system operator's duty to maintain a secure system.**

The continuing development of new security products has an impact on the system operator's duty to maintain a secure system. At the time a system operator formulates security standards, there will be a certain range of security products available, and a certain set of security techniques. These products and techniques will vary in their particular purposes, in their effectiveness and reliability, in how capable they are of repelling intrusions, and in their cost of purchase or implementation. The system operator must evaluate these factors, in light of the kind of system being operated (e.g., a low security standard for a public information site with no e-mail and a high security standard for a private corporate site holding customers' trade secrets), and come up with an overall security program that meets the needs of the system.

Let's assume the system operator did his or her homework, and came up with an appropriate security system for the kind of online service being offered to users, customers, or the public. It's fine today, but what about next year, after a whole raft of new products and techniques have come out? Does the system operator need to revamp security to take advantage of the new security tools? What about the other online systems—does it make a difference whether or not they have moved to adopt new tools as they come out? If everyone else has decided to stand pat and use settled security procedures for at least a couple of years before reviewing them, can the system operator take their lead, and similarly ignore new security products and techniques for a while before revisiting the issue?

A famous legal case suggests it would be dangerous for system operators with security responsibilities to ignore new, effective security products as they come out. The case, named *T.J. Hooper*, was a lawsuit in the early 1930s against a tugboat company for letting a coal barge pulled by one of its boats sink in a storm at sea. It was proved that if the tugboat had a modern radio, it would have received weather forecasts that would have enabled it to avoid the storm. The tugboat company's defense was that there was no duty to have such a radio on board, because it was not an established, standard safety practice in the tugboat industry. The judge in the case rejected this defense and held the tugboat owner liable, observing, "there are precautions so imperative even their universal disregard will not excuse their omission." This language in *T.J. Hooper* is a little strong, but it is easy to understand why it's there. Only a lost coal barge was at issue in that case, but the next time a storm was encountered at sea because the boat had no weather radio, lives could be lost. It was important to send a loud, clear message to the entire nautical industry about keeping up with modern safety trends. All the same, the holding was addressed directly to the security measures necessary to prevent a business loss, and not lost lives.

What does *T.J. Hooper* mean for online system security? First, it means that system operators charged with security responsibility cannot ignore new security developments. They must keep up with the industry, and when new security tools come along that appear appropriate to the security risks and needs of the system, look into them. This does not mean that the system operator should become a leader in testing out every possible new security tool. New tools of any kind are often unreliable or ineffective, and the system operator could actually decrease security if he or she implements new, unproven tools too quickly. But when new reliable tools appear, and seem appropriate to the type of system being operated, it would be a good idea to seriously consider adding them to the system.

Second, while it is instructive to keep up with the security procedures used by other system operators, it is dangerous to ignore an effective security tool just because others are ignoring it. Other system operators may not be using a particular security tool because it is too new and unproven (a generally valid reason if they're right), because it does not make sense for the kind of system they

> **System operators charged with security responsibility cannot ignore new security developments. They must keep up with the industry, and when new security tools come along that appear appropriate to the security risks and needs of the system, look into them.**

run (perhaps valid for their particular systems, but not necessarily valid for all), or simply because they're not in the mood to add new security measures to their systems very often (not highly valid). In surveying existing industry practices and the failure or refusal to adopt new security tools, it is important for each system operator to separate valid from invalid reasons for trying or using that new security tool himself or herself.

These concerns are heightened when we consider the dynamic nature of changing computer security needs. In the field of seaworthiness considered in the *Hooper* case, the challenges posed by rough weather have remained constant over the centuries. New safety devices, such as weather radios, mark a series of advances toward greater control of the environment. Once the weather radio was adopted, a certain amount of progress was made against the ravages of sea storms, and it will never be taken back. The radio will never become less effective; the question for boat owners is always whether they need to adopt the next new development to make seafaring even safer than before, and cut down even further the risks of losing ships in storms.

In contrast, in the online arena, the challenges faced by security systems do not remain constant at all. Hackers start work immediately on breaking down each new system as it is introduced. As time passes, previously adopted security systems do not even retain their original effectiveness. System operators need to keep up with new developments just to keep security from slipping behind last year's security levels; *improving* system security over time is an extra responsibility. Under these circumstances, it seems the system operator's need to keep up with security procedures, for systems with sensitive security concerns, is even *greater* than that of the tugboat owner in *Hooper*.

The Responsibility of Managers and Other Employees

We have discussed the responsibilities of companies and lone individuals for negligence, but what about individuals who work at companies? Do system operators who work for others have any personal responsibility to be careful in their online actions, and not negligently harm others?

Indeed they do. Acting as an agent or employee of another does *not* absolve a person of personal responsibility for his or her negligent conduct. This is a general legal rule, well established. There are a couple of limiting factors, however.

First, if handling a dangerous situation would require an employee to take action *outside* the restrictions placed on his or her authority by the employer, then the employee will not be responsible for refusing to act due to those restrictions—even if the result is that the dangerous situation is permitted to continue. For instance, say a company runs a customer support BBS, with a public posting area for its customers. It instructs its system operator, an employee, that under no circumstances can any message posted by a customer be erased, because the employer does not want to anger any of its customers. If one such customer ends up posting a series of messages criticizing another customer, possibly defaming the second customer, the employee sysop is under no personal responsibility to defy the boss' orders and remove the offending messages. If the boss is unavailable when the problem is discovered, and the problem lasts for a long period while the defamed customer complains, then perhaps the employer company would be held responsible to the defamed customer for permitting the defamatory material to remain on the BBS for an extended period. But the employee would not share that responsibility. Some other problems, such as physical dangers to others, might be so grave that the employee is justified in defying the employer's wishes and addressing the problem. But these situations are very rare online.

The other limiting factor: an employee is not responsible for injuries caused by dangerous tools or systems placed in the employee's hands by the employer, unless the employee knows they are dangerous to others. For example, a company may give its employee a file demonstrating the capabilities of its great new software package, and instruct that employee to upload the file to the download areas of many bulletin boards and large online services, so the public can try out the demonstration. Unbeknownst to the employee, but known to the employer, the file contains a dangerous bug that can damage the data of those who use it on certain computers. If a member of the public experiences serious computer damage and data loss from using the demo software, and sues the software company for negligently making the dangerous software available with a known bug, the company may be liable, but not the employee, who was ignorant of the dangerous condition. On the other hand, if the employee knows that tools or materials placed in his or her hands by the employer are dangerous to others, then the employee has a responsibility not to harm others with those tools or materials.

So much for limits on employee responsibility. There is also a situation where an employee's responsibility to others increases: when the employing company places him or her in charge of an area used by others. In such cases, the employee manager is just as responsible for the safety of that area as the employing company. This rule was established for physical premises like restaurants and hotels, but there is no reason that it will not transfer right over to the virtual premises of the online world. Therefore, we should expect that the main system operator or administrator for an employer's online system used by others will be legally held directly responsible for keeping that system safe for use and clear of dangers. For system managers facing this level of personal risk as employees, it would be a good idea to seek an indemnity agreement from the employer, so if a legal problem does arise, the employer (or its insurer) will pick up the tab.

Can the employee be liable to the employer for negligence in performing his or her duties for the employer? Yes, though it is relatively rare in practice for employees to be sued for such negligence. Usually, they're just fired. But suits are a possibility, and likely scenarios are easily imaginable in the online sphere. For example, if an employee in charge of in-house system security fails to perform routine security procedures, and the failure permits outside hackers to invade the system and steal valuable company trade secrets, the company would have a strong claim against that employee for damages. Or if an employee is given the job of acting as a cheerleader for the company's products on the Internet, and inadvertently blurts out the company's secret marketing plans in front of an audience of thousands, the company again would have a substantial legal claim against that employee. In such cases, a company will sometimes start up a lawsuit against the employee, in order to make a point to other employees: some mistakes are so serious that you can be sued over them, so care is advised.

Finally, what about employees who supervise other employees? Are managers responsible for the negligence of their staff? Generally not—each employee of a company is responsible for his or her own negligence and not the negligence of others, even others generally under his or her supervision. Managers are responsible, however, for proper selection, training, and supervision of their staff. They are also responsible for their own instructions to their staff which, when faithfully followed, result in negligence toward others. For instance, let's look back at the example of the company support BBS where one customer defames another, and the defamatory messages remain on display for far longer than they should have because the company's system operator was not given the authority to remove the messages. While the system operator may not be responsible for negligence because his or her authority was so limited he or she could not prevent the injury, the manager may be personally responsible for negligence in setting such limits. A court could find that the manager should have foreseen situations where a customer's messages must be removed to avoid

> **For example, if an employee in charge of in-house system security fails to perform routine security procedures, and the failure permits outside hackers to invade the system and steal valuable company trade secrets, the company would have a strong claim against that employee for damages.**

injury to others, even at the risk of offending that customer, and rule that the manager should have acted to prevent injury in such situations by giving the system operator emergency authority to remove messages that appear harmful to others.

Company Responsibility for Its Agents and Employees

In the last section, we saw that negligent employees are sometimes personally responsible to those in the outside world who are injured by their actions. Does this let the employer off the hook?

Not by a long shot. There is a long-established legal principle called *respondeat superior:* those who use employees or other agents to do their bidding are answerable for the injuries those agents might cause to others. It's largely a matter of symmetry. Every company has the privilege of acting through agents to secure contracts, receive money, pay its debts, and receive a great many other important benefits. The flip side of this privilege is that every company also has to take responsiblity for the damage its agents might cause to others as they carry out their tasks for the company. The result is that when a company employee injures somebody while performing his or her job, the employee and the company *each* could be liable to the injured person.

How does *respondeat superior* play out in concrete terms, online and on the networks? Let's look first at system security situations, discussed at length above. If a company handles the data of its customers on an online system and its manager in charge of security messes up, permitting intruders to enter the system and damage the data, then the company will be directly responsible to the customers for its manager's negligence under *respondeat superior.* There is no way the company can escape this obligation by pointing its finger at the manager. Maintaining security is a prime responsibility for the company, and it chose to meet this responsibility by hiring the manager in question. When the manager failed at his task, his negligence was imputed to the company that chose him and acted through him, making it liable for any injuries caused. Even if the company can prove the manager was entirely derelict in his duty to maintain security, such as by routinely ignoring intrusion alarms or user suspicions of the presence of outsiders, all it accomplishes is to add the manager personally as another party who is answerable to those who were injured. The most the company can do in response to this bad situation, aside from paying compensation to those injured, is fire the manager and sue him if he has any money to pay a judgment.

Keep in mind, we are still talking about negligent and other wrongful activities. The mere fact of a computer break-in does not imply the company or the security manager were negligent. Negligence only occurs where the manager did not act reasonably to prevent foreseeable dangers to the system. If the manager performs his or her duties properly and generally pays attention to performing the job well, negligence is unlikely. It is still possible, when the company is under contract with its customers, for it to be liable to those customers for a security breach even if there was no negligence at all. But that is purely a contract matter, in which

> **If the manager performs his or her duties properly and generally pays attention to performing the job well, negligence is unlikely.**

responsibilities are privately set by the parties, and many of the normal concepts of fault and negligence do not apply.

Another increasingly common situation for *respondeat superior* is the company that gives its employees access to outside computer networks, or perhaps the Internet itself, through links with its local area network. Let's imagine this company instructs some of its sales employees to go into public Internet areas from the employer's in-house system and act as cheerleaders for the company's products. Some of these sales people get overzealous, and begin spreading terrible lies about the company's competitors, their products, and their employees. The Net begins buzzing with rumors, and soon the company finds itself served with a defamation lawsuit based on its sales peoples' actions. Again, the company is stuck with full responsiblity for the employees it sent out on the networks. Or suppose the employees choose to send complete copies of newspaper and magazine articles published by others out on the Internet, perhaps to illustrate the business problems the company's products are supposed to solve. The company is now ripe to be held responsible for copyright infringement by its employees. These, of course, are only two examples of the many legal problems that might be created by employees on the Net, only to be eventually laid on the employer's doorstep.

When a company is blamed for its employees' actions, sometimes it may still be able to escape liability if it can show that the employees' illegal actions were performed outside the "scope of employment"—in other words, that the wrong in question was neither a failure by the employee to perform properly an obligation owed by the employer to someone else, nor did it occur while the employee was performing some other task requested by the employer. How do you show that agents or employees are acting outside the scope of employment? There is no exact test, just a lot of factors to consider: whether the wrong was committed while the employee was engaged in the process of performing his or her tasks for the employer, or on the employee's free time; whether or not the employee used company facilities in connection with the wrong; whether or not the employee held himself or herself out to others as representing the company while committing the wrongful acts; and so on. It is useful to remember that not all activities by employees during the workday are necessarily within the "scope of employment." The question for wrongful acts committed by an employee during normal working hours is: was the employee actively engaged in working for the employer at the time he or she performed the act, or was he or she off on a "detour and frolic" at the time, temporarily abandoning his or her work for the employer to pursue personal needs or desires? If the answer is detour and frolic, then the employer is off the hook (unless, again, the employee's irresponsibility caused the employer not to meet its own obligations to another person or business).

What counts as a detour and frolic on an online system? Abandoning one's security monitoring obligations to take the company van into town to buy some beers; spending all of one's hours working as a system operator lurking in a hot chat area to trade obscene messages instead of attending to user needs, complaints, and inquiries; using one's company account as a customer service representative on a public online service to engage in arguments about investment strategies in forums unrelated to the company's business. Wrongful or negligent acts committed by erstwhile employees at these times will generally not be imputed to the company. The company should make sure to discourage employees from such activities whenever they are caught; if not, it might be argued that the company expanded its scope of employment to include such behavior.

Managing Risks

This is the part many readers are most interested in. With all of these different legal risks, how does the system operator steer clear of trouble?

Described below is a set of practical strategies that will greatly reduce a person's risks of liability for negligent conduct. Some of these measures will operate automatically to protect one after they are set up. However, if problems occur, the best protection for one's self and one's online service is taking an active role in dealing with them.

Avoiding Self-Created Problems

Most of the discussion in this chapter presumes that the problems on online services are being created for system operators by the users. This may not always be the case, however. Readers who have traveled the networks and online services may have come across system operators who cavalierly mistreat users, due to some dispute, or perhaps just because they are generally curmudgeonly.

Clearly, the system operator himself or herself should not be the source of any problems. This book

> **Part of one's responsibility as a system operator is to conduct one's self properly, and not misuse control of an online service to injure others in any way.**

is not intended to help system operators injure others with impunity. The protection strategies here are to protect system operators from liability when users injure other users, or when users injure people not even on the online service. Part of one's responsibility as a system operator is to conduct one's self properly, and not misuse control of an online service to injure others in any way.

Contracts

Well-drafted contracts go a long way toward protecting a system from problems caused by users and other businesses. By using a contract, the system operator takes control of how much legal risk he or she is willing to be exposed to through his or her relationship with others. A contract can cover many, if not all, of the potential liabilities.

The contract with users or other businesses allows the operator to spell out exactly what kind of conduct is not tolerated on the online service. The operator can also make it clear that he or she will immediately eject from the online service anyone who misuses it. Setting clear and reasonable ground rules will encourage behavior conforming to those rules. The language of the contract should explain that these rules are necessary to protect both the system and other users, so everyone can receive maximum use and enjoyment from the online service.

For purposes of controlling the operator's legal risks, the most important provisions of the contract are the "limitation of liability" and "indemnity" clauses. The limitation of liability clause sharply limits the operator's maximum liability to any user for negligent failure to prevent injury on the online service. The indemnity clause makes the actual wrongdoer reimburse the operator, and "hold the operator harmless," for all problems he or she causes to other users (and to people not on the online service) through his or her actions on the online service. In other words, these two provisions work together to reduce the operator's liability to users, customers, and other business associates, and to make them responsible to the operator for any injuries they cause to others that force the injured parties to sue the operator.

These provisions and others are discussed in greater detail in Chapter 2.

Security Measures

Before setting about securing a computer system tight as a drum, the operator should become familiar with the sources of that system's security obligations. Why maintain security on this particular system? Who or what is being protected, and from what? Knowing this will help determine just what security measures to explore and deploy.

If the need for security is based on a company's own secret data contained within the system, then the operator should learn about the kinds of data on the system, and how sensitive each type is. A large part of the security task may be fulfilled simply by designating different systems for holding and processing certain data, with the most sensitive data held on internal systems not closely coupled with the outside world. In this situation, the security need is entirely generated by the company's internal agendas and priorities. If the company is negligent in protecting its data, it is only negligent to itself. It would be a good idea to involve others in the business in determining security needs, to make sure one has an accurate sense of the company's priorities regarding its information systems.

> **If the contract says the company will use "reasonable measures" to protect the other company's secret data, then a reasonably alert approach to security will suffice. If the contract says the company will do "everything necessary" to keep the data secure, anything less than diligent, ongoing security procedures may be inadequate.**

If the company's system carries the data or messages of customers or other outsiders, there is an entirely different security need. Now, if the company screws up its data security it won't only shoot itself in the foot, it could seriously damage other companies or people whose secrets are revealed or data is destroyed. The first place to look for system security obligations is in any contracts that may exist with the outsiders whose data is on the system; the standards in the contract are the measure of the necessary security. If the contract says the company will use "reasonable measures" to protect the other company's secret data, then a reasonably alert approach to security will suffice. If the contract says the company will do "everything necessary" to keep the data secure, anything less than diligent, ongoing security procedures may be inadequate. What if there is no contract? Then it will be necessary to look into what the system users and customers expect, and double-check to see if the company made any wild promises to others about system security that are now the operator's to keep.

Once the operator determines the type and depth of the company's security needs, he or she must develop a complete set of security procedures meeting those needs. The procedures should be clear, organized, and understandable by others. Even if the operator is the only one charged with security at the company, he or she must make sure that others have meaningful access to the procedures. It's impossible to predict when one will be laid low for a month by some disease, requiring that someone else fill in to make sure security is maintained. Follow the procedures regularly, as a matter of routine. If there is a hacker break-in or virus outbreak on the system during one's watch, one can still prove the duty to maintain security was observed, by showing that a reasonable set of security procedures was faithfully followed. The law does not require us to be perfect (unless we promise perfection to someone else in a contract), but it does require those charged with the duty of protecting others to make a serious effort at providing that protection.

It is very important to keep up with new developments, and to change security procedures from time to time to keep them up to date. As pointed out earlier in this chapter, security requirements change dynamically, as intruders and virus writers rise to the challenge of each new development in computer security with new system-hacking techniques. There is no sense in which a system attains more and more complete security, unless it is unplugged from every communications line. The best one can do is periodically upgrade security to keep out the latest wave of intruders.

Explore "security over insecure networks"—essentially, the use of cryptography for sensitive information. Training company personnel to encrypt certain classes of communications, and maintaining encrypted databases, can make up for a lot of holes elsewhere in the system. Encryption won't keep intruders out, but it can keep them from taking valuable information. Fortunately, the use of encryption is spreading rapidly, especially in corporate environments. These days, one can even find fairly powerful encryption capabilities built into popular workgroup and e-mail software.

One popular class of security techniques involves leaving the system relatively open to outsiders, so that intruders can more easily be tracked in their comings and goings on various systems by coordinated teams of security people, and ultimately located or identified. This unfortunately leads to a conundrum—while leaving the system open to intruders as a way to catch them, one may also be imperiling users on the system. There seems to be a technological fix on the way: sophisticated "trapping" software that feels like a real operational system, but is actually an illusory system that keeps the outsider from causing any damage while sending out a security alarm.

Last, but far from least, are the security techniques themselves. For these, read books by the experts and go to their lectures.

Warnings and Bulletins

Bulletins can be posted at significant junctures in the online service, such as sign-on and entry into message areas, file download areas, and e-mail areas. They can provide protection in several ways.

First, bulletins can form part of the contract with users. The main contract may not specify all proper and improper user conduct, but state instead that users will follow all system rules, including the rules posted throughout the online service by the system operator. The operator can tell users that defamation is prohibited, for example, by using a bulletin leading into the public message area to inform users that they may not make any false or damaging statements about other users. If a user makes such statements anyway, he or she is not only acting unpleasantly, but directly violating the contract with the system operator. It would be a good idea either to post such messages at appropriate places in the system, or to gather them together into a set of system rules. For any risks that the operator is feeling especially cautious about, messages can be posted both in the public posting or file areas and in the system rules area.

Second, even where the user contract does incorporate online bulletins as part of the contract, they are still useful for establishing that users voluntarily assumed the risk of certain online activities. A bulletin that tells users about to sample Usenet that they may find files with viruses, or obscene materials on some remote server, effectively warns them that they proceed at their own risk. In a case like this, it probably helps to inform them further that Usenet is a common public resource, and not an in-house facility under local control.

There's a Sucker Logging on Every Minute . . .

There are a lot of con men online; when the tickets to cyberspace were handed out, they grabbed their share. There are also a lot of people online who should know better than to trust strangers, but magically lose their faculties of judgment when presented with a deal too good to be true. The simple question for con men online, as always, was how to separate these trusting souls from their money. It didn't take long to figure out a few schemes: pyramid schemes, stock scams, chain letters, and so on. Look around for them in cyberspace, and you may turn up a few.

In 1994, state and federal consumer protection agencies started waking up to online scams. After a little digging, they found out the online arena is buzzing with organized ripoffs, and becoming busier all the time. The scam operators figured out how to harness the power of computer communications to increase vastly the number of people they could expose to their schemes.

For instance, in a traditional "boiler room" operation, the victims are sold on fake investments by fast-talking phone salesmen. It is labor-intensive, requiring several people working full time on the phone, and reaches at most one or two hundred people per day. In contrast, in an online discussion a single con artist can post a series of manipulative messages for a dollar or two. Those messages will be seen by thousands, and lead the ones who are totally snowed to send money straight into the con artist's hands. A thief's dream come true.

Finally, government is starting to act. In July, 1994, New Jersey and Missouri securities regulators announced their first regulatory orders directed at online ripoffs, which they readily refer to as "cyberscams." The New Jersey agency went after the propagators of a pyramid chain e-mail letter. This is one of those schemes where each recipient is supposed to send $5.00 to five people higher on a list of recipients, and everyone is supposed to end up with thousands of dollars. In reality, a lot of people end up losing small amounts of money, and the originators of the letter can make off with a bundle. The Missouri regulators went after a guy who talked up a public company's stock on Prodigy using terms like "$1 million in profit" and "primed for breakout!" What the guy failed to disclose in Prodigy was that he did public relations for the company, and was the president's son. Typically in schemes of this sort, after the gullible buy the stock and drive up its price, the promoters sell their shares at the inflated price, leaving the suckers holding nearly worthless shares.

The Federal Trade Commission pursued its first online scam case in September 1994. The con job this time was an ad circulated on America Online for a credit repair program, "100% legal and 200% guaranteed," for "only" $99.99. People who sent in money received three whole pages of instructions sketching out how to obtain and use deceptive taxpayer identification numbers, change their addresses, and do other things necessary to fool credit agencies about your identity. The FTC asserted these activities were not legal, so the claim of legal credit repair was false advertising. Just before this book went to press, the target of the investigation, Chase Consulting, agreed with the FTC to reimburse customers who paid the $99. The FTC stated, "The commission wants to make it clear that advertisers on the information superhighway will be held to the same standards as advertisers in other media."

These actions are the tip of the iceberg. Scam operations are thriving online, and regulators are also online everywhere, trying to hunt them down. The next person you meet in a public area online could be a con man, so keep your hand on your virtual wallet.

Third, bulletins can serve a valuable role just by reminding users about local online service rules. Some users frequent many systems. If a user regularly visits other online services where the system operators encourage wild, irresponsible behavior, he or she might mistakenly think such behavior is also tolerated on every online service, unless the operators provides a reminder to the contrary. Some users will simply not be aware of the legal standards for online behavior, being very new to the whole online experience. Bulletins can help to educate them.

Fourth, by posting bulletins on the online service urging proper and legal conduct, the operator is showing government agents and other outsiders that he or she is concerned that users behave properly on the online service. This can be especially helpful where the operator does not monitor user activities. The bulletins are the operator's main influence on users' day-to-day activities in these areas.

Some system operators act like this is the Big Loophole: just by posting bulletins telling users to behave themselves, the system operator is absolutely free from any liability. This is not so. If an operator hears from a credible source that users are posting sensitive credit card information in a public area, he or she is obliged to look into it, and take whatever measures are necessary to remove that information. The operator cannot just sit back and think everything's covered because he or she plastered signs all over the place telling people what they can't do.

Before flooding the online service with legalistic user bulletins, remember that these bulletins will be experienced by users as part of the online service. Users should not encounter them too often, or they may feel too constricted to relax and enjoy using the online service. For the same reason, bulletins should all be worded in a friendly way, explaining not only what the rules are, but also why they exist. From a user relations perspective, it may be best to place all system rules in a separate area set aside for that purpose, and post special bulletins relating to those rules only at a few key points in the online service where it is important to make sure users know what they can and cannot do.

Incorporating

For any system owner or independent system operator, this is one of the best possible ways to protect against expensive lawsuits. If a person incorporates the business under which the online service operates, then anyone who sues the online service can only proceed against the corporation, and not against the individual. The only exceptions are where one is held personally liable for his or her own actions as an employee of the corporation, or if he or she does not properly treat the corporation as a separate legal entity, such as by failing to properly handle corporate income and payments through a separate corporate bank account.

Since only the corporation would be liable for any damages, the shareholders' personal accounts and property would not be threatened by a lawsuit. It is still unpleasant to contemplate a lawsuit that shuts down one's online service and exposes one's corporate assets to possible loss. Such a result is far better, however, than having that same lawsuit cause the loss of much or all of someone's personal property and force one into personal bankruptcy.

A basic incorporation costs a few hundred dollars, the exact amount varying with the state and the particular lawyer used. A lawyer is recommended here, by the way. A "civilian" can do it, but unless thoroughly educated, might mess up either the basic setup of the corporation, or the way affairs are conducted afterwards. This could lead to a court ignoring the corporation if one's online service is sued, and holding the individual personally liable for any injuries—entirely defeating the purpose of incorporating. The proper procedures for operating a corporation are not difficult or complicated, but it is far better to hear about them from a lawyer who knows from experience and training exactly where the danger areas are, than to guess at the dangers. One does not need an online law specialist to incorporate—any good local lawyer can do the job. Beware, however, the incorporation services run or administered by nonlawyers; they may operate in such ignorance of legal requirements that the corporate shield will never be properly erected.

> **The proper procedures for operating a corporation are not difficult or complicated, but it is far better to hear about them from a lawyer who knows from experience and training exactly where the danger areas are, than to guess at the dangers.**

Unfortunately, not all system operators and online services can afford to incorporate. Small hobby boards are often run on a shoestring. The cost of incorporating could exceed the cost of the entire online service setup. There are also minimum taxes to pay on corporations in many states, often on the order of a few hundred dollars a year. Online services generating revenues that comfortably exceed such amounts and online service owners who personally have deep pockets can pay such taxes, but smaller online service operations could have trouble making such payments. In such cases where incorporation is not an option, it becomes much more important to put an effective user contract in place to limit system operator liability, and to deal quickly and effectively with any user problems that come to the system operator's attention on a daily basis.

Some public interest-oriented online services may desire to incorporate as not-for-profit corporations. This is attractive both for shielding liability in legal actions, and also because it can shelter online service revenues from taxation. To qualify for tax-exempt treatment, your online service has to be pursuing a proper not-for-profit purpose. It would be rather easy to qualify many online services in this manner, since online services usually facilitate education and distribution of information, which is a valid non-profit purpose.

A ground rule is that one can't be in business to make a profit. Not-for-profit treatment is appropriate only if one has some altruistic or community-benefiting purpose to an online service. One can be paid a salary as an employee of the corporation, but that salary will be taxable, so the not-for-profit approach can't be used just to beat taxes.

Not-for-profit incorporations, even more than regular incorporations, should be done with lawyer guidance. In many states, such as New York, the process of incorporating a not-for-profit organization is much more involved than a regular incorporation. Also, applying for tax-exempt status afterward with state and federal tax authorities can be tricky, and a lawyer's help, at least in the background, can be very useful.

Insurance

Insurance is a standard way for people and businesses to reduce their exposure to losses that are not common, but very large when they occur.

Special insurance is not easily available for online services, though persistent hunting may locate some. One standard kind of insurance, called "errors and omissions" or E&O insurance, would cover at least some of the risks faced in operating an online service. But anyone looking into E&O insurance should be aware of the following.

First, it is fairly expensive—probably affordable only by those operating lucrative commercial online services. Second, insurers may or may not make E&O insurance available for online services. Online services are a fairly new kind of operation. Insurers usually like to watch the ups and downs of a new kind of business for a while before they are confident enough of the risk levels to set premiums, coverages, exclusions, and so on.

Third, if an insurer does make a policy available, it should be inspected very carefully to determine exactly what kinds of risks are covered. The insurance agent's word alone is not enough. If one ever has to collect on the policy, the agent will be nowhere in sight, and one will be left with the exact language and limitations of the policy. One way to figure out how well the policy covers risks is to compare its coverage to the various kinds of legal risks covered in this book.

Other kinds of insurance that might fit a given online service are advertising insurance and publisher's insurance.

Deal Effectively with All Known Risk Situations

There will probably be times when the operator must actively respond to risky or threatening situations on an online service. If an operator permits known risks to develop and continue without intervention, his or her online service can get into very serious trouble. We are not talking here about "patrolling the aisles" of one's online service looking for legal problems, but dealing with problems once they are discovered.

> **If an operator permits known risks to develop and continue without intervention, his or her online service can get into very serious trouble.**

What is a known risk? There are various ways to learn about troublesome activities on one's online service, including:

- one or more users tell the operator about trouble or problems occurring on the online service

- a device set up to monitor security breaches goes off

- someone who is injured by activities on the online service contacts the operator to do something about it

- the operator notices something suspicious about the patterns of file uploads or downloads on the online service

- the operator notices something suspicious while looking through a public discussion area

Once the trouble and, hopefully, the troublemakers, are discovered, the operator must first assess the nature of the problem. Are users creating problems for other users? Are they creating legal risks for the operator or the system? Are they violating their contract with the system?

> **After acting to secure the online service against further risk, one can look into the situation in greater depth.**

If the problem does not create any personal or business legal risks (such as a user who posts messages most other users find unpleasant), then the operator's response should be based on the kind of atmosphere he or she wishes to promote for the online service. If a friendly, conciliatory mood is desired, it may be wise to engage the users involved in the problem, and work towards an amicable resolution, slowly if necessary. If, on the other hand, the philosophy is simply that adults should behave like adults, the operator may just give the users involved a firm warning to shape up or ship out.

Where it appears there is a risk to the operator or other users, he or she must act swiftly to reduce the risk. For example, if there is a dangerous posting or file, such as a defamatory remark or a copyright infringement, that posting or file should be removed from public access immediately. If a specific user is posting or uploading illegal files or messages, the user's ability to make such transmissions should be suspended.

After acting to secure the online service against further risk, one can look into the situation in greater depth. If the materials or the user appears to pose little problem, they can be restored to the online service. If it turns out they really are bad news, then they're off the online service where they belong.

To affirm to users that the operator runs a "clean" online service, and to educate them about what that means, it might be wise to post a message or bulletin to all users after a problem posting or user is taken care of. It is better not to mention the users involved by name. If they harbor bad feelings toward the operator, they may try retaliating by accusing the operator of libel in this message to the users.

Such a message to users might go like this:

> *Last Sunday, we heard that two of the graphic files in library 12, POP.EYE and OLIVES.OYL, might be illegal infringements. We removed the files from public access immediately and examined them. It appeared to us that they infringe trademarks and copyrights held by the owners of the Popeye and Olive Oyl characters. We asked the user who uploaded these files to provide proof of her rights to distribute them, and she could not provide any.*

> *Accordingly, the two files will remain off this online service. We believe they are infringing. It would be illegal for us to keep them on the online service now that we know of their existence. If any of you downloaded these files, please do not copy them or distribute them any further. We have no wish to violate the property or rights of others, and hope that you feel the same way.*

Monitoring User Activity

This is the most controversial aspect of online service risk control. System operators have widely varying opinions on this subject. Some believe monitoring online services is absolutely necessary. The only way to effectively contain risks is to personally look at all materials on the online service, and make sure none of the users are making trouble.

Other system operators see monitoring of online service activities as both intrusive and a great waste of time and energy. They believe their role as system operators is mainly to provide a way for users to connect with each other. System operators should not be hovering over users, and they especially should not be reviewing e-mail. In addition, system operator responsibility for user activities should be strictly limited, just as a telephone company is almost never responsible for the activities of people using the phone lines.

The truth probably lies somewhere between these extreme views. Most online services are a mix of unmonitored user-to-user messages, and areas supervised by system operators.

There is very little case law on the question of monitoring by system operators. The most important case by far, *Cubby v. CompuServe*, held that CompuServe was not responsible for monitoring materials carried by a subcontractor distributing an online electronic newsletter through the CompuServe system. This is an encouraging result. Hopefully, it signals a trend in which system operators will be permitted to carry materials uploaded or posted by others without being legally required to review everything.

We believe that system operators do not have a fundamental responsibility to monitor users' activities. If an operator wants to run a "hands-off" online service, he or she is free to do so, and should not be

> **One must be careful with the hands-off approach. It does not shield the operator from all responsibility.**

liable for user activities that could only be discovered by routinely patrolling all online service areas. In this approach to online service management, users interact entirely with each other, and the system operator only tends the machinery supporting this interaction.

Blame the User, Not the Messenger

A few years ago, a group of policy consultants and attorneys in Washington, D.C. tried to put together a proposed law that would let system operators do their jobs without worrying about the law so much. Tentatively called the Electronic Communications Forwarding Act ("ECFA"), it would have shielded system operators from responsibility for any illegal or dangerous activities by their users. The goal was simple and laud-

able: since system operators perform a valuable role by creating meeting places where millions of people can exchange ideas, their value to society will be maximized if they can freely carry user messages without being scapegoated every time one of their users does something illegal.

This concept already underlies existing First Amendment protection for system operators. So what's new? The ECFA would hardwire that existing vague protection into a specific law, a commandment from Congress, expressly protecting system operators. The new law would avoid much of the legal confusion that can be sown by lawsuit-happy companies who want to hold system operators liable for everything on their system, no matter who the actual culprit is.

Unfortunately, the group never arrived at a proposed law to present for Congressional consideration. It wasn't a question of access to the corridors of power; that they had in abundance. They were just unable to agree on exactly what a system operator would need to do to qualify for the proposed act's protection.

One issue was whether the system operator must be entirely "hands off" toward the content of user messages to qualify for legal immunity. At first glance, this might seem a reasonable trade-off: if the system operator wants to be free of responsibility to allow him or her to concentrate on moving user messages, those messages should be given safe passage through the system no matter what they contain. What about obviously dangerous or clearly illegal messages? If dipping into content disqualifies a system operator from immunity, such a rule would discourage operators from removing such messages. A hands-off rule would also discourage system operators from performing one of their most valuable functions: shaping the unique character and community of each online place.

The other, larger controversy was over anonymity. Some in the ECFA group felt that legislators would never agree to give operators legal immunity, unless someone remained who could be held responsible for wrongful acts on the system. They insisted on an additional condition for system opera-

tor immunity: preserving all identity information for all users on the system, so individual wrongdoers could be tracked down by the authorities. This agenda ran up against an equally strong belief held by others in the group: that all users have a sovereign right to act anonymously in the online environment. This privacy-based view is admirable as a matter of principle. If it was followed, though, consider the result if a user anonymously injured others online by defaming them or posting their credit card numbers. The system operator would assert immunity from legal action, while the person posting the illegal messages would get away scot-free because he or she acted entirely anonymously.

In the battle between privacy advocates and those who believed someone has to be responsible for wrongful online activities, the ECFA ground to a halt. In the meantime, lawsuits against system operators have been starting up in a number of areas, promising to begin weaving the crazy-quilt of varying legal responsibilities for system operators that the ECFA could have avoided. Will the ECFA be revived? Perhaps, though the difficult issues mentioned here are alive and kicking, and will need to be resolved before any meaningful law protecting system operators can be passed.

But one must be careful with the hands-off approach. It does not shield the operator from all responsibility. If any specific problems or illegal activities are discovered, they must be dealt with. Further, if one's online service is known to support illegal activities, such as trafficking in infringing files or credit information, one does not have the luxury of escaping liability by claiming a philosophy of not monitoring user activities. The hands-off approach is a way to avoid routine monitoring of user activities, not a way to avoid all responsibility for one's online service.

On the other hand, many system operators choose to participate actively in much of the doings on their online services. Indeed, system operators often start up online services as a way to interact regularly with other people. One common type of system operator interaction is supervising public message areas—moving and retitling messages to improve the discussion, deleting messages that are felt to be offensive, commenting, and participating in discussions themselves. System operators do this for entertainment, as part of keeping their online services operating smoothly, and as a way to support their claims of having a collective work copyright on the contents of their public message areas.

Another common system operator activity is screening uploaded program files for viruses or other dangerous program code. System operators do this both as a service for their users and to protect themselves from claims of spreading viruses. Less commonly, system operators may review e-mail between users to make sure nothing illegal is taking place.

In all of these cases, system operators actively monitor at least some of the areas of their online services for various purposes. More than likely, such system operators will also be held legally responsible for some level of checking for problem files or postings in the monitored areas.

The responsibility imposed on system operators is similar to that imposed on supermarkets. When a jar of applesauce spills on the floor, the supermarket is not required to have its employee there instantly. It is expected, however, to have people checking the aisles every now and then, and

"You Own Your Own Words"

This aphorism, also known by the acronym YOYOW, became famous on the Well bulletin board as a terse directive for sorting out how users should treat their words and the words of others online. Its peculiar power derives from the dual meaning of the first occurrence of the word "own." Read one way, YOYOW means your messages on the bulletin board are your personal property, and that others cannot copy or distribute them against your wishes. Read the other way, YOYOW means if your messages harm anyone, such as a libel, you are responsible for the injury as the owner of those words. In the abstract, it's a fairly clear assignment of decentralized power and responsibility to every user of the system. In practice, arguments over the meaning of YOYOW in everyday situations became legendary as the longest running, fiercest flames on the Well. Perfectly typical for what might be the archetype of "First Amendment" bulletin boards.

While permissive toward eccentric users and colorful language, the Well is not entirely a hands-off operation. For instance, when the first version of the Pretty Good Privacy encryption program was released online for free in 1990, an outfit named Public Key Partners told the major online services that PGP infringed their patent, and all systems distributing the program could be liable. PGP disappeared from almost all commercial services immediately, and the Well was no exception. Moving the program offline might have been a blow to the ideal of letting everything flow through the system, but Well management realized if PGP was kept online, the Well might find itself flowing into court over a patent it really had nothing to do with. By letting practical concerns override the idealism of letting all speech flow in this special case, the Well made sure it could continue its role of supporting the free speech of others.

to discover and clean up the mess in that period of time. If a customer slips on the applesauce before a supermarket employee reasonably discovers it, the supermarket will probably not be liable; if they slip on applesauce that has been on the floor all day, the supermarket is in trouble.

It is difficult to say, at this time, exactly how frequently or how closely system operators should monitor their online services for problem materials. If a system operator participates in public discussions and creates a monitoring responsibility for himself, but the public discussion areas are so huge the system operator cannot possibly monitor them all, we would expect the legal standard for monitoring to take that into account. The system operator might discharge his or her duty in this case by skimming a volume of messages once or twice a day, but only in certain message areas, and rotating the message areas reviewed regularly.

We do not expect that any online monitoring obligation that may arise in the law will call for reviewing user activities more than once every day or two, unless the system operator already visits the areas he spends time in more frequently. If a system operator checks a public message area twice a day to perform maintenance functions, make sure users follow proper etiquette and so on, then he or she might legally be expected to keep an eye open for any problem postings in that area with the same frequency. If a system operator screens all files before making them available for download, then there would be no legal requirement to check them with any particular frequency; but when the system operator gets around to reviewing the files, he or she should keep an eye open not just for viruses, but anything else that appears suspicious from a brief look at the file.

We wish more exact guidance on monitoring was available, but online service negligence law is only partially formed at this point. The principles are easy enough to discuss, but the all-important practical application of those principles has not been definitively set down. For now we must use common sense, and be prudent in avoiding undue risk to ourselves and our online services.

As we discussed earlier in this chapter, the most valuable way to limit system operator liability is through contracts with users, customers, and other business associates. This advice is especially useful here. The user contract greatly reduces the system operator's risks if he or she guesses wrong on how far to monitor user activity on the online service. If a user is injured due to another user's posting, and the court feels the system operator should have patrolled the area containing the posting more often, the limitation of liability clause in a properly drafted contract will still limit the amount the injured user can recover in a lawsuit against the system operator (remember, the user's primary legal claim is against the other user). So even though the question of how much monitoring system operators must do remains somewhat mysterious, effective ways to minimize system operator risk are available today.

Privacy

Privacy is one of the most discussed, and most confused, subjects in the online world. We can discern at least five common positions on privacy. Look further into the subject and you may come up with more:

- *Strong privacy is a basic civil right:* Digital privacy is a necessary measure of basic decency and respect for others. It defines the boundary between state and individual, past which the state must refrain from prying.

- *Strong privacy protects criminals:* People may misuse private messages for illegal purposes. We must have regulations that would prevent absolute privacy from the state.

- *Strong privacy contradicts community:* While privacy is certainly a good thing, we don't go online for privacy, but to engage in new forms of community. Wrapping ourselves in too much privacy may defeat attempts to create online community.

- *Strong privacy limits business opportunities:* To remain financially healthy in the information age, businesses must be able to create markets in lists of customer names and develop demographic data. If this entails a compromise in personal privacy, it is necessary for our economy.

- *Strong privacy is necessary for online commerce:* Businesses demand airtight network security, to make sure no one can steal their trade secrets or tamper with internal databases. Without such protection of corporate privacy, companies will be unwilling to open their computer systems to online commerce.

Nothing to Fear but the System Operator Himself

The greatest threat to privacy in online systems may not be any anti-privacy law enacted by government, but stark reductions in user privacy by system operators. Many operators are spooked by the possibility that their systems might be raided by government agents in pursuit of online felons. To calm themselves, they reduce or eliminate user privacy on the system. Users may not like having their privacy taken away, but the system operator can sleep at night. This approach has been extended recently to the refusal by some operators to permit unreadable encrypted messages to pass through their systems.

Here's a typical message declaring a policy of no user privacy:

Pursuant to the Electronic Communications Privacy Act of 1986 (18 U.S.C. 2510 et seq.), notice is hereby given that there are no facilities provided by this system for sending or receiving private or confidential electronic communications.

The operators of this online system can, and usually do, read all messages left on this system, including "Private" messages addressed to persons other than the system operators.

The system operators reserve the right to delete any message, regardless of whether such message has been received by its intended recipient.

The system operators also reserve the right to change the status of a message designated "Private" so that such message is public and available to all users. The status of a message may be changed whenever, in the sole discretion of the system operators, it is believed appropriate to do so. Your continued use of this online system constitutes acceptance of the system operators' discretion in this regard.

This is the complete remedy for the privacy paranoid. Users never need worry that they have even a modicum of privacy on such systems.

The highly cautious approach exemplified above has taken hold in certain parts of the online world, especially bulletin board systems. However, system operators need *not* eliminate user privacy based on their fears. They can give users a meaningful degree of privacy without being exposed to fears of instant seizure of their systems. (In fact, eliminating user privacy *removes* important protection for online systems, as explained later in this chapter.)

Giving users the privacy they deserve takes a little more effort from the system operator than depriving them of the privacy option altogether. The operator must actively strike the proper balance between letting users conduct their affairs in private, and dealing effectively and promptly with any illicit activities that may come to light on the system. This kind of balancing effort is indeed what much of this book is about.

The system operator's decision on how much privacy users will receive is the dominant factor in determining privacy levels on online systems. There are also a number of laws giving users certain rights of privacy in certain situations. The rest of this chapter covers the laws of user privacy, strategies for achieving the privacy one wants online, and setting appropriate privacy levels on online systems.

Electronic Communications Privacy Act ("ECPA")

The ECPA started out as the "anti-wiretapping" act, enacted in response to the eavesdropping excesses of the Watergate scandal in the late '60s. In its original form, the federal statute targeted government eavesdropping on telephone discussions without consent of the parties to the discussion. It required government agents to obtain a judicial warrant before they could intercept discussions.

In late 1986, Congress greatly expanded the coverage of the anti-wiretapping laws to track the broadening scope of electronic communication, resulting in the ECPA. The law was revised and extended in several different directions:

- It now covers not only voice communications on the telephone, but also all forms of digital communications, including transmissions of text and digitized visual images.

- The law now prohibits unauthorized eavesdropping by *all* persons and businesses, not just the government.

- The ECPA prohibits not just unauthorized *interception* of messages in transmission, but also unauthorized access to messages in *storage* on a computer system.

How much privacy does the ECPA create for users? It depends on the circumstances. The ECPA is a complicated statute, riddled with exceptions and giving different privacy treatment depending on the form or medium of the message, the kind of system where the message is found, and whether the message is moving or standing still. We cannot possibly discuss every situation here. Instead, we will go over the most important general concepts for operators and users, and ways that providers can simplify the situation from the complications provided by the ECPA. Those with further questions should consult the ECPA—a copy of which is provided in Appendix B—and a lawyer who can help them read it.

> **The ECPA is a complicated statute, riddled with exceptions and giving different privacy treatment depending on the form or medium of the message, the kind of system where the message is found, and whether the message is moving or standing still.**

Voice Messages

The ECPA gives the strongest protection for *voice* messages on public communication systems. These cannot be intercepted deliberately by providers during a discussion between users, nor can the provider review the contents of such discussions while in storage on the system. Providers cannot review voice messages even if they fear users may be planning a crime. Such protection of voice messages would include voice mail, although those who leave voice mail messages for corporate employees should be aware that the corporation will likely consider itself the intended recipient of the message, and the particular employee merely its agent. There are two exceptions worth noting in connection with government agents: (a) if, while performing routine system operations, the provider accidentally comes across voice communications seemingly related to a crime, it can reveal the contents of those communications to the police or similar government authorities; and (b) the provider may cooperate with government agents, acting under proper orders, by giving those agents the ability to intercept public voice communications.

> **The ECPA gives the strongest protection for *voice* messages on public communication systems.**

Note that all this protection for voice messages is available in *public* systems only. On a *private* system, the provider *can* eavesdrop and intercept voice messages, under the "business extension rule" (for those situations in which the provider supplies the telephone of other voice message equipment used by the user), and/or the rationale that it is protecting its "rights or property." This is an exception given to employers and other property owners, letting them retain their ability to control the workplace and other private property when they deploy private telephone, telecom, and other voice systems for on-site communications. However, even this exception does not give private providers unlimited eavesdropping rights. The statute specifically provides that they cannot "utilize service observing or random monitoring except for mechanical or service quality control checks." In other words, they can't eavesdrop at all unless they have a specific reason, and they can't randomly eavesdrop, except as necessary to keep the system running.

Non-Voice Messages

What about *non-voice* messages, such as e-mail, non-voice file transmissions, and other texts or images? If there is no agreement on privacy between operator and user, the ECPA prohibits operators from intercepting non-voice messages in live or real-time transmission between users.* However, operators generally *can* review non-voice messages (such as e-mail) between users that are *stored* in the system. Such stored messages would include messages in the addressee's mailbox waiting to be picked up by the addressee, and records of private discussions between users.

In other words, the ECPA does not give online system users an automatic right of privacy from system operators for stored messages. Since a system can easily be configured to store all messages that pass through it, the ability to review stored messages effectively gives the operator the ability to review all messages passing through the system. Remember, though, that real-time transmissions can only be reviewed later from storage, rather than through simultaneous interception.

---

* In *Syslaw* we previously stated, "[The ECPA] does not prohibit owners or operators of online systems from viewing non-voice messages in the system (such as e-mail), whether stored on the computer or in transit between users." Our interpretation of the statute has changed. Non-voice messages may not be viewed during live transmission on a system without consent, such as in live chat areas or private, realtime MUDs. However, if the operator obtains consent from users, such as in a properly drafted subscriber agreement, then he or she can intercept such messages.

This exception allows *only* the system operators to look, though. Operators can look for themselves, but they can't show the stored private messages of users to anyone else under the ECPA. It is surprising how often system operators mistakenly violate this prohibition. It is illegal to show private messages to anyone other than the owner of the system or an employee of the owner, unless the message is to the system operator himself (the sender or recipient of a message is always allowed to publicize it), or the disclosure is permitted in one of the specific exceptions in the ECPA.

The Online System as a Postal Service

In the 1960s novel *The Crying of Lot 49*, Thomas Pynchon imagined an alternative postal system riding on the back of intracorporate mail operations, outside the monopoly reserved for the United States Post Office. In the last twenty years, such alternative postal systems have become a reality, in the form of e-mail on computer networks and online systems. Instead of just one such system, however, there are many thousands, each a vital strand in the communications web. And unlike paper-based postal systems, they are a legal alternative to the offering from the United States government.

There are many similarities between online systems and the United States Postal System. Both systems deliver mail: one electronic mail or "e-mail," the other paper mail or "snail mail." Both systems support powerful one-to-one communications. Both encourage their users to develop the fine art of writing, better to express their thoughts to others in print. Both feature private mailboxes, controlled by the person receiving the mail.

There are also important differences. Perhaps the greatest is speed. E--mail is far faster than paper mail, often transmitted instantaneously across entire continents. It is usually cheaper than paper mail, and far more easily sent directly from one's computer, instead of printed out and dropped in the mail box. Due to such overwhelming advantages, e-mail systems are quickly supplanting paper mail systems in many organizations.

E-mail has further possibilities, which are only beginning to be explored. Workflow systems automatically check on the delivery of expected e-mail to specified places, and generate their own e-mail as necessary to keep corporate processes on time. Programmable e-mail, related to software agents, can be directed by the sender to observe or perform various actions on computer networks.

Legally, the United States Postal System is a regulated monopoly. It is required to accept and deliver all mail properly stamped, addressed, and deposited, except for mail carrying illegal materials. In contrast, most e-mail systems can be far more selective, rejecting messages at the system provider's discretion. There is a price to pay for such selectivity, however: e-mail providers have no formal immunity from legal action. At the same time, e-mail providers who do not look at the messages they forward and do not knowingly carry illegal message traffic operate at fairly low risk of criminal liability, because virtually all crimes require *knowing* involvement.

The ECPA and Government Authorities

One of those exceptions is that system operators are permitted to reveal users' private messages to legal authorities, but only where such messages were accidentally obtained, and they believe legally questionable activities are taking place. The authorities can review these messages to the extent necessary to confirm the system operator's suspicions. However, if government agents wish to intercept or review messages on their own, they need to prove to a judge or magistrate their need to eavesdrop, and obtain an appropriate warrant.

The ECPA gives messages stored on an online system for under 180 days somewhat greater protection from seizure by government agents than messages stored for a longer period. A government agent must get a warrant to obtain any message less than 180 days old. For older messages, the agent may obtain an administrative subpoena instead of having to go to court for an order.

System operators who cooperate with law enforcement agents who produce proper warrants and court orders to seize their online system or system files are not subject to legal action by users whose private messages are taken as part of the seizure. However, in such a seizure situation, it is not always possible to tell if the search and seizure documents brandished by the agents are proper. A lawyer can advise an operator or user on how much to cooperate with the agents.

The Information SnooperHighway

Is the United States using the power of the computer networks systematically to build a surveillance state, giving government agents far more effective power to monitor the minutiae of our daily lives? So charges EPIC, a privacy advocacy group based in Washington, D.C.

In this view, there is an ongoing program on the part of various federal agencies to build a Big Brother in cyberspace. We can see various pieces falling into place. The most famous is Clipper, the government-backed public key encryption scheme designed to enable federal agents to decode secret messages when urgently necessary. This is accomplished by giving all Clipper users two-part encryption keys which are separately placed in escrow with two government-approved escrow facilities. Armed with a court order, an agent who needs to decode a Clipper-encrypted message can retrieve the key parts from the two services, construct the key and read the message. The point is that ultimately, no message encrypted by Clipper is safe from the government.

At present, there are other encryption methods, not similarly compromised, available to the public. However, the head of the FBI and others have indicated publicly that if the use of such alternative schemes frustrates law enforcement officers in performing their duties, then he and others would ask Congress to pass a law mandating key escrow requirements, like the one now used for Clipper, for *all* encryption schemes. Aside from Clipper and mandatory key escrow, there are other laws designed to inhibit private use of strong encryption, such as the long-standing prohibition against export of strong encryption software out of the United States without a proper license, which can be costly, slow, and difficult or impossible to obtain.

Another piece of the surveillance state puzzle is a law popularly known as "Digital Telephony." This new law requires all phone companies to install and maintain special facilities making it easy for government agents to eavesdrop on electronic communications. As communications systems become more sophisticated, the government wants to make sure it does not miss a wiretap opportunity because its agents couldn't properly splice a fiber optic cable. While under the ECPA (discussed in this chapter), agents still need a warrant to perform a wiretap, our telephone systems will stand wiretap-ready at all times.

Other possibilities for further surveillance have surfaced from time to time, such as a possible law imposing some form of national I.D. card, more tightly coordinated to United States citizens than Social Security numbers.

So, is a surveillance system being constructed, or are these the rambling delusions of privacy fanatics? It is natural to expect the FBI and others to set up surveillance measures in cyberspace, and that they are in fact doing so. A vast new online territory is opening up, and those charged with guarding the public's safety are scrambling to make sure they can gain access to any place they need to in order to prevent harm. Thus, one should expect surveillance-oriented measures, for purely benign reasons. The problem arises when those measures fail to properly respect the privacy of people in their online activities, or when they are misused by those with governmental power to pursue agendas, such as in the Watergate affair, that have nothing to do with the legitimate purpose of protecting people from crime. Sadly, these misuses are still all too likely in today's society.

Violating the ECPA

If a system operator manages to violate a user's privacy rights under the ECPA, such as by publicly posting private e-mail for all to see, the ECPA gives the user the right to sue the system operator. This includes the right to have the public posting removed, and the right to recover money damages representing the user's injury due to the privacy violation. These rights are important, but in many cases they would be meaningless for users. A posting may be long gone by the time a lawsuit is underway, or it may be impossible for a user to prove the dollar amount of any injuries he or she may suffer from a compromise in privacy.

However, the ECPA also allows recovery of attorneys fees. This means if a user's rights are clearly violated by the system operator, and he or she wants to maintain a lawsuit as a matter of principle, the user will less likely be deterred by the prospect of legal costs. If the user wins, the system operator pays the attorney fees.

There are also criminal penalties for violating the ECPA. Of course, the risk of criminal prosecution depends on what the government prosecutors are seeking to establish in each case. It is hard to say whether they will ever be much interested in private disputes between system operators and users, especially since users do have the right to bring a civil action. For instance, where employers accuse ex-employees of stealing trade secrets in starting their own business, one rarely sees the ex-employees arrested for stealing. The employers and ex-employees are usually left to sort it out between themselves in a non-criminal legal action over claims of breach of contract and trade secret misuse. Nonetheless, a system operator should never be too smug about whose secrets he or she may be violating. If the user is "connected" with the authorities, or if pursuing a case may help some prosecutor's or politician's career, criminal prosecution of a system operator under the ECPA for violating a user's privacy remains a distinct possibility.

For these reasons, even system operators who do not strongly believe in users' privacy rights must take the ECPA very seriously, and keep private user e-mail from public view.

Negotiating Privacy Under the ECPA

All of the above privacy protections are what we may consider the "default" setting of the ECPA: the privacy users should expect when there are no agreements on the subject. However, the ECPA carefully carves out the ability for online services to obtain consent from users, cutting back on the default ECPA protections.

In other words, for both voice and non-voice messages, whether on public or private communications systems:

- The provider can intercept messages during transmission, *with prior user consent.*

- The provider can disclose user messages to anyone it chooses, *with prior user consent.*

> **The ECPA carefully carves out the ability for online services to obtain consent from users, cutting back on the default ECPA protections.**

Thus, operators and users can arrange between themselves for any level and kind of privacy they want.

Operators and users who want strong privacy can agree to run strongly private systems. In fact, if they want, the operator can prohibit himself or herself by contract from viewing non-voice messages in storage, even though the ECPA normally permits such viewing (although they cannot limit the ability of law enforcement agents to obtain private messages under proper legal orders). If the operator wants to give users a substantial amount of privacy, but retain the ability to review or disclose private messages whenever he or she feels they may pose or reveal a threat to the system, they can agree on such a scheme. Or if the operator wants no privacy on the system at all, that can be established as well.

Such an ability to establish different bundles of negotiated privacy rights on different systems may contribute in the future to the pricing of online services to the public. No-privacy or low-privacy systems may be less expensive, while high-privacy systems may charge a premium for that service. Part of the premium could relate simply to the high value placed by users on their personal privacy, but much of it would also be justified by the additional security procedures necessary to operate a system secure enough to make good on privacy promises to the user.

Piggybacking on User Privacy

Many operators of smaller online systems readily succumb to fear of their own users, and declare there will be no private e-mail on the system. It's a simple strategy. If users feel they are being scrutinized under a bright light they'll refrain from illegal activities, or at least pursue those activities on other systems more congenial to e-mail privacy. Ironically, such a strategy could backfire, making no-privacy online systems among those most vulnerable to seizure by eager government agents.

There is a symbiotic relationship between user privacy and the rights of online systems to be free of government search and seizure. It is rooted in the Electronic Communications Privacy Act (ECPA), described at length elsewhere in this chapter and reproduced in the back of the book. Section 2701 of the ECPA makes it illegal for anyone, including government agents, to seize stored messages without proper authority. If a law officer seizes a computer containing stored private messages, or even browses the messages without seizing the computer, there is a violation of multiple privacy rights—the privacy rights of the participants in every one of those messages—unless he or she has a warrant. This was made abundantly clear in

Steve Jackson Games v. U.S., which held that the United States government had violated the privacy rights of several computer bulletin board users when Secret Service agents seized the bulletin board and read through its contents. The government's misdeed was in searching and seizing the messages without proper authority and without a warrant.

A strategy for increasing the protection of online systems from unwarranted government intrusions readily emerges from this scenario: let users send all the private messages they want, let the system fill up with private messages, making it nearly impossible for government agents to rummage freely through the system without a warrant. Even when they do get a warrant, one that is properly drawn will not compromise the privacy rights of all system users, but force the agents to narrow their search to messages between specified users. This does not mean users should take measures to frustrate legitimate law enforcement activities. The point is that a legitimate search is one that is narrowly drawn to cover specific messages on a system enumerated in a properly issued warrant, and that it will be extremely rare for agents to make any credible case for disrupting an online system and searching messages generally.

But what if there are no private messages on the system? Then by definition, *everyone* equally has authority to look at the messages on the system, including law enforcement agents. So if agents can lawfully get their hands on the computer used to run an online system, there is no further legal barrier stopping them from going on a fishing expedition through the entire system, or at least none based on user privacy. In this way the very system operators so paranoid about wrongful system seizures that they eradicate user privacy make their systems more vulnerable to the seizures they seek to avoid.

For all system operators contemplating a no-private-message policy, please consider this: the privacy rights of the system are based largely on the privacy rights of its users. For a system to be legally protected from government prying, the operator should give users that same basic protection from prying.

Care must be used to make it clear *which systems* are being altered from default ECPA privacy treatment when operators and users make special deals on privacy. For instance, take a system provider who wants the right to eavesdrop on live, private chat sessions if he or she feels apprehensive or suspicious about what is being said between users (ordinarily not permitted under the ECPA). If the system in question is a simple bulletin board, run by a single person and with no network connections, then a subscriber agreement on the subject will readily give the system provider that right.

But what if the system provider rents out space on the system to other companies who also provide live chat areas, but the user only signs one agreement, and that agreement is with the main provider? If that single agreement is not properly drafted to include sub-providers, then the main provider may have the contractual right to eavesdrop on live chat, but not the sub-providers, even if the chat session is occurring in an area supposedly under their own control. This, of course, is only one example. The point is that when a service provider wants to alter the ECPA's privacy protections by contract, that contract should include all people and companies who are being released or partially released from the ECPA's protections by the user.

> **When a service provider wants to alter the ECPA's privacy protections by contract, that contract should include all people and companies who are being released or partially released from the ECPA's protections by the user.**

By the same token, users participating in a private discussion, either one-to-one or in a group, should be aware that *any* of the other users in that discussion can contractually compromise ECPA protection for the entire discussion. For instance, among the thousands of Internet mailing lists now in operation, there are many that are considered highly private. However, the nature of mailing lists is that messages originate from, and are distributed to, the e-mail boxes of users spread across hundreds or thousands of different online systems, all connected in some fashion to the Internet. This seriously compromises the privacy possible for such lists. If just one user, in the most private mailing list in existence, has a contract with his or her system provider allowing that provider to disclose freely all of that user's messages in storage, then all the most private messages on that list can be publicized by that provider at any time, perfectly legally.

How, then, can users keep their discussions private? One answer is simply to encrypt all messages on the system. This can work fine for one-to-one discussions, but for group discussions, privately implemented encryption-based security permitting all group members but no one else to read the messages may be difficult and time-consuming to achieve. Another, more easily manageable answer for group discussions may lie in the development of a market for highly secure systems, briefly discussed above. For discussions and meetings demanding true privacy, participants may be required to call in from certain online systems known to give users the kind and level of privacy necessary for such a discussion.

Other Privacy Laws

The ECPA is a major federal law, but it does not rule out other legal rules covering electronic privacy. There are several other legal rules relating to privacy on both the federal and state levels.

There is a federal right of personal privacy from government interference, not spelled out in any statute enacted by Congress, but in Supreme Court and other federal rulings. This has been called a "penumbra right" of the Constitution. Neither the Constitution nor the Bill of Rights expressly states that United States citizens have any right of privacy. Yet the Supreme Court has recognized the right of privacy as implied by the Bill of Rights. Examples include the right of women to privacy against government intrusion in their decision to obtain an abortion, and the right to possess obscene materials in the privacy of one's home.

> **There is a federal right of personal privacy from government interference, not spelled out in any statute enacted by Congress, but in Supreme Court and other federal rulings.**

This Constitutional approach has also been invoked to carve out a broad right to privacy in the use of the public telephone system. The general test is whether the person claiming a privacy right has a "reasonable expectation of privacy" under the circumstances. People speaking on the phone in their own homes or privately in a public telephone booth have a reasonable expectation of privacy; people yelling to each other across a table in a noisy public cafeteria, on the other hand, could not reasonably expect their discussion to be private from eavesdropping. As in situations covered by the ECPA, any eavesdropping by government agents on discussions reasonably expected by their participants to be private would require a warrant.

Is it possible the Constitutional privacy right may expand online system user rights against the government beyond the rights given by the ECPA in some situations? For instance, if a system operator tells users their e-mail discussions are entirely private from the entire world, could this increase the users' reasonable expectation of privacy, and their rights against government intrusion into that privacy? If so, law enforcement agents may not be able to take advantage of the relaxed procedures under the ECPA for obtaining messages stored over 180 days, but may have to obtain a warrant. This possibility is entirely speculative, but it is one of the possible outcomes as Constitutional privacy rights on online systems and networks are tested in the courts in the coming years.

Another Constitutional privacy right that may be directly useful to system operators resisting government intrusions is the First Amendment right to peaceable assembly. This right was used in the past in *NAACP v. Alabama* to prevent the state of Alabama from obtaining NAACP's membership

The Online Service as Private Home

Many system operators treat online systems as if they were homes, and user discussions as if they were taking place indoors. Here, it is not the "rules of the road" that prevail, but the rules of socializing in intimate settings. Acceptable conduct comes in many flavors according to the place: from graceful good manners suitable to a drawing room tea, to the rough camaraderie of a rec room football party.

Another kind of "home" online is a user's home account or home directory. In UNIX-based systems, this can be a literal space in the system storage directory allocated to each user, in which operator and user both store information. If I want to share certain texts or information with others, I can upload them to my home directory, set the permissions to general access, and invite others to partake.

In the near future we will see the "home" and "room" metaphors visually literalized in a variety of ways. Users may be able to let rooms in stately online mansions, share virtual beer and pretzels in the family rooms of online suburban split levels, huddle together over fat-fed fires in igloos (virtual cold optional). People will be able to build, dwell in, and even host parties at their next home online, years before they obtain a corresponding physical dwelling. Or perhaps for those of lesser means, their online home will be the nicest one they will ever have. In the information age, "let them eat cake" may translate into "let them live in online dream homes."

The undeniably private nature of online dwellings holds interesting possibilities for the development of online law. One is that configuring a system space as a "home" may bar unauthorized entry by government investigators. Ordinarily, investigators can roam online systems silently and freely, holding them under regular surveillance. But setting out a sign on your online door saying "Private Home—Invited Guests Only" can stop them cold. If you also follow a strict policy of identifying all who enter according to their digital signatures, the agents will be turned away at the door, and would be forced to return with a warrant if they want any kind of entry at all.

Another, more intriguing possibility is that spaces defined as private online homes could be freed of regulations generally. Then, even if government agents did enter, their outside laws could not be enforced inside the home. This possibility is suggested in particular by the Supreme Court case *Stanley v. Georgia*, in which the First Amendment prevented state law from regulating what a person reads inside his or her home. Taking this reasoning further, we can easily imagine an online home acting as a place for all manner of discussions which might be illegal in the outside world, but are nonetheless protected from prosecution by the First Amendment. Here might be the start of the separate, sovereign online legal regime some are looking to build in the online world: government that begins at home.

list. The court permitted the NAACP to keep its member list private, for the reason that revealing the members' names could severely injure the organization by giving those opposed to it the ability to intimidate individual members.

The same right to keep member names secret could be asserted by system operators against law enforcement agents who seek to obtain a list of users of the system, especially where the online system serves as a focal point for a user group organized for social, political, or other purposes. If revealing the names of those users damages the organization's ability to pursue its lawful goals (even if those goals are no more than to meet in private away from the glare of public attention), then the Constitutional right of peaceable assembly is violated. Again, this is not yet a court-tested proposition for online systems, but it can be strongly advanced if the government seeks to pry into the membership information on private online systems.

Many states also recognize another kind of right of privacy, under both statute and case law. For instance, New York Civil Rights law sections 50 and 51 expressly recognize a right of privacy for New York state citizens. Unlike the ECPA, these state rights are not automatically violated by any compromise of a person's privacy. The New York law, for example, is violated when someone's "name, portrait, or picture" is used without consent for purposes of "advertising" or "trade." This narrows down the privacy right, but it can still be violated in certain situations that may take us by surprise if we are not aware of it.

For instance, an online system wishing to attract new users may advertise that various famous or prominent individuals participate in the discussion sections. Suppose one of those famous individuals greatly values her privacy, and never publicly posted a message but only used the e-mail facilities. The advertisement could be held a violation of the user's privacy under the New York law, and the user could sue the online system both to stop using her name, and for an award of punitive damages to punish the system operator for brazenly violating her privacy.

Such privacy rights differ greatly from state to state. If one is interested in the limits on such rights, there are compendiums of privacy law available that list applicable privacy laws on the state and federal levels (one such book is listed in Appendix J).

User privacy rights can also be greatly affected by any contracts between the online system and the user. When a privacy question comes up, it is important to review the understanding between the online system and its users regarding privacy. If such an understanding exists, it could turn out to be more

> **Privacy rights differ greatly from state to state.**

important than the privacy laws discussed above for determining the rights of privacy on the online system. The contract may grant users more expansive privacy rights than they are given by state or federal law, or it may cut back on those rights or deny privacy altogether. User privacy agreements are explored further in the section of this book on user contracts.

A closely related subject, though not always discussed as a "privacy" matter, is trade secrets and other secret business information. Trade secrets are legally protected from disclosure because they give the business owning them an advantage over competing businesses. Companies often consider their trade secrets to be among their most valuable assets. A well-known example is the secret formula for the flavoring used in Coca-Cola (now "Classic Coke"), jealously guarded by the Coca-Cola company for most of this century. Other kinds of trade secrets include computer program source code, technical product information, customer lists, and marketing plans.

Trade secrets are routinely exchanged on online systems with direct ties to businesses, such as in-house online systems or outside online systems that provide communication services to businesses under special arrangements. They are also often exchanged in e-mail on private online systems without special business contracts. Trade secrets are most strongly protected by the courts when the owner company makes sure, usually through a contract, all those with access to the information agree to keep it secret. If the information becomes public knowledge, the company cannot sue anyone who learns about it afterward for further disclosing the information. Indeed, the information loses its status as a trade secret. Trade secrets are further discussed in Chapter 3.

The Market Defeat of Lotus Marketplace

People dislike having their names on mailing lists, yet we have few laws in this country against the sale and use of mailing lists and demographic databases. It's such a big business that all the popular sentiment against it has barely made a dent. At the same time, there is a potent force keeping corporate incursions on privacy from becoming too bold—the power of public outcry.

In 1991, Lotus Development Corporation and Equifax Corporation teamed up on a new software product for the retail market called *Lotus Marketplace: Households*. It contained specific demographic information about 120 million Americans, including names, addresses, buying habits, and estimated incomes. The product would have sold for roughly $700 at computer stores with a few thousand names, with more names of the customer's choice available for a few pennies each. It was designed to give cheaply to small businesses the same kinds of information to which marketing departments of larger companies have had access for decades.

If Lotus Marketplace was such a great product, where is it? Lotus never got it out the door. Shortly before the planned release of Marketplace, privacy advocates decried it as a tremendous blow against the privacy of United States citizens. They started a letter-writing campaign among users of the computer networks. Before long, Lotus received over 30,000 letters telling them to call the product off, and it decided to do just that. In public statements at the time, Lotus said Marketplace was not really a core product for them, and not worth a huge public battle over privacy. In other words, Marketplace did not have either the profit potential or strategic importance to Lotus to risk the public black eye it was likely to receive if it released the product. So it retreated, and looked halfway like a hero instead. Shortly afterwards, Lotus sold Marketplace to another company, which brought it to the market under a different name, and with a very low profile.

This was not the first or last time public outcry caused a privacy-invasive product or operation to be withdrawn. During the writing of this book, the sale of mailing lists by America Online was singled out for public attack by some privacy advocates, more as a symbol than because America Online did anything differently than its competitors.

But how effective is this approach in the end, even with the leverage of Internet letter-writing campaigns? The name and marketer of Marketplace were changed and it went out into the market anyway, privacy invasions and all. Other privacy-invasive databases and operations are handled in a low-profile manner from the start, so the public is never alerted to the problem, such as the commercial sale of names and addresses by the United States Postal Service. Are letter-writing campaigns really an affirmation of public decency? Or are they nothing more than occasional tests of public opinion on the question of whether such trading can be done openly or must continue to occur largely out of consumers' view?

Privacy in the Workplace

Personal privacy concerns are especially sensitive for in-house company e-mail, groupware, and other online systems. As we saw above, employers and other private system providers are not permitted routinely to eavesdrop on or intercept employee voice discussions. They may only eavesdrop when they have a good reason, such as when they think certain communications may relate to damage or injury to the employer's property or business. However, employers are *not* similarly prohibited from intercepting e-mail and other non-voice messages. The ECPA does not prevent employers from looking through employee e-mail at their leisure.

ECPA aside, many workers believe that personal e-mail on the company online system should be just as private as a personal voice telephone call. In contrast, their employers often believe that workers have no privacy rights on the company online system, since the employer owns the system.

This sharp difference of opinion has led to litigation over online privacy rights under state laws, including two well-publicized cases. In *Shoars v. Epson*, an employee of Epson America was fired for vehemently refusing to participate in her supervisors' surreptitious monitoring of employee e-mail. She sued the company for violating a California law that prohibits electronic surveillance of employees.

While this seemed to be a convincing argument, the court saw the statute as applying only to employer surveillance of *voice* conversations, not text e-mail. It denied her claim, saying it was up to the state legislature to extend employee anti-surveillance rights to their non-voice communications. This kind of result can be expected to surface with some regularity in litigation regarding online rights. Courts asked to apply older laws to new technology will sometimes be afraid to make that leap, throwing the ball back to the legislature to confirm that the same rights indeed apply to new technologies.

In *Bourke v. Nissan Motors Corp.*, another California case, a company fired an employee based on certain personal messages she transmitted through the in-house system, including some with sexual content. She sued for wrongful termination, claiming the company had illegitimately read the e-mail that led to her getting fired, and for invasion of privacy. This employee claim was also denied. The court pointed out that the company made all employees sign an agreement that all use of the company's computer systems would be restricted to "company business," and also that she and other employees had become aware months earlier that the company did monitor messages. The employee contended that she and others were given passwords and told to keep their accounts secret, but this did not give rise to any reasonable expectation of privacy in the court's view. Such security measures are fully consistent with the company wanting to keep the in-house system secure from outsiders, and do not imply any personal privacy right of the in-house employee against the company on whose system the account is maintained.

> **Most lawyers agree that under current laws, workers do not have privacy rights on in-house company systems unless their employers give them those rights.**

Most lawyers agree that under current laws, workers do not have privacy rights on in-house company systems unless their employers give them those rights. This can happen in two ways. First, if an employer knowingly allows private employee messages to grow and flourish on the company online system without opposing it, then an implied agreement can be established, under which employees have a right to expect their private transmissions to remain private. The employer may be able to negate the employees' privacy rights by declaring that messages are not private, but this would likely affect only future messages, and not messages transmitted before the announcement.

Second, an employer can affirmatively create employee message privacy rights by an express agreement with its employees, which will normally take the form of inclusion of such rights in its policy manual. This is the more generous approach, especially where employers choose to give their workers express, well-defined message privacy rights.

For instance, an employer may tell its workers that private messages are permitted only in certain designated areas of the system. The employer may further agree that it will not randomly or routinely monitor messages, but may look at specific messages if the employer reasonably believes that activities damaging to the employer or others are taking place in connection with those messages. The employer will notify the parties to the discussion of any such review. The employer may also set out its policy on whether or not encrypted messaging is permitted on any part of the in-house system, and if so, what encryption methods and keys may be used. For example, the employer may require all messages to be encrypted so outside intruders cannot intercept them, but may forbid employees to decrypt messages in any manner not readily readable by the employer using the decryption keys in its possession.

The above is only one of many possible approaches. The Electronic Mail Association publishes a guide that gives employers a "Chinese menu" of policy manual options to mix and match in fashioning an e-mail privacy program they (and hopefully their employees) will find comfortable. Information on this manual is contained in Appendix J.

There is movement in the direction of establishing more privacy rights in the workplace in connection with new electronic technologies. In 1993, for example, legislation was proposed in Congress entitled the "Privacy for Consumers and Workers Act," which would have forced disclosure of employer monitoring of workers, and limited that monitoring in certain cases. The bill was not passed at that time, but similar legislation is likely to be put forward again, as workers find themselves increasingly immersed in automated systems.

Self-Help Privacy: Encryption

Encryption is a way for users to insure their own privacy against all who would invade it. Users can transmit their messages as encrypted files without giving anyone but the intended recipient the decryption key, thus assuring that no one else can find out the contents of the message.

Encryption options are growing, as the self-help approach to privacy is proving very appealing to those who dislike eavesdropping of any kind. The most popular and useful method of encryption for general messaging is public key cryptography. In this scheme, each person uses a cryptography program to generate two paired, standard keys (a key is a long string of arbitrary characters) for use in the encryption process. One is that user's "private key," and the user keeps it secret from everyone else. The other is that user's "public key," which the user gives to everyone with whom he or she wishes to have private, encrypted discussions. The relation of the keys is this: messages encrypted with a given user's public key can only be decrypted with that user's private key, and vice versa. Analyzing one of the keys will not enable you to figure out the other key. So if I want to send Joe a secret encrypted message, I use the public key Joe gave me to encrypt it. Only Joe himself can decrypt that message now, by using his private key. In fact, after I encrypt a message with Joe's public key, even I cannot decrypt it, in spite of the fact that I created it.

The major security gap for public key schemes is that one must be sure one actually has the public key of the person to whom one is sending an encrypted message. For instance, if I receive an e-mail message on a large online system from my friend containing his public key, can I be certain that really is his public key? Of course not. It could be an impostor making it seem as if the message came from my friend. If I use that key to generate encrypted messages, we might end up with a situation where the impostor can read every message, but my friend cannot, because it was encrypted with a public key from the impostor.

> **The major security gap for public key schemes is that one must be sure one actually has the public key of the person to whom one is sending an encrypted message.**

There are various methods for avoiding this problem. One is to receive public keys in person. Another is for each message to include a section with each message where a group of people endorse the sender's public key contained in that message with messages encrypted using their private keys, so that if I know that one or more of those endorsing messages is genuine, I can consider trusting that the endorsed public key is genuine as well. While imperfect, this approach, combined with adequate detection of impostors, can help create informal networks of trust among senders of encrypted messages. Finally, "trusted" key keepers can be established. These administrative organizations would have stringent procedures for verifying the identities of the owners of the public keys they hold, and would be accepted as trustworthy by the user communities that depend on them.

There are several major products enabling public key encryption now, and many more are on the way. Popular groupware and e-mail packages from companies like Lotus and Novell contain public key encryption functions, though they are deliberately made weaker than they might be in order to meet United States export regulations regarding encryption software. There is also a program called "PGP" (for Pretty Good Privacy"), which started off the popular trend toward public key encryption when it was released by programmer Phil Zimmerman in 1990. There have been legal questions surrounding past versions of PGP, but current versions of both the "commercial" and "non-commercial" form of the software (the latter known as "Viacrypt PGP") seem to be circulating within the United States without much problem at this point. In addition to PGP, there are other public key encryption packages coming on the market, offering "privacy-enhanced mail," or PEM.

Finally, there is the United States government's controversial array of public key encryption products known generally by the name "Clipper," although the non-voice version is also referred to as "Tesserae." The controversy surrounding these products comes from the government's requirement that all private keys must be held in escrow with specified government agencies. This way, law enforcement agents can obtain the keys to decrypt messages in emergencies, regardless of whether the owner of the private key wants the message decrypted. In effect, the government is saying, "trust us," and a lot of people don't. Fortunately, there are several readily available encryption options aside from Clipper, such as those mentioned above, and the keys in those schemes are not required to be held in escrow. Various government officials have been heard to say that if they find the use of non-Clipper encryption schemes seriously obstructs their efforts to investigate crimes, they may then push for a law banning the use of *any* public key encryption scheme, unless its private key is escrowed with the government as the Clipper keys are. But this is only speculation at this point; if the government ever does push for such a law, it will be important to let one's voice be heard on the issue.

> **Encryption is basically an indication of users' distrust—of the security of the system, the owner or operator of the system, or law enforcement authorities.**

What does encryption mean for those who operate the systems on which the encrypted messages are transmitted? Encryption is basically an indication of users' distrust—of the security of the system, the owner or operator of the system, or law enforcement authorities. Indeed, encryption is often referred to as a way of achieving "security over insecure systems." This distrust may or may not be justified, but it is the driving force behind the use of encryption. The system operator's reaction to encryption thus depends on how he or she feels about the underlying distrust.

One common system operator response is simply to permit users to transmit encrypted files as they wish, without being able to read them—to trust users even though the users may not trust the operator. If the operator is concerned about the possibility that users might be using the system's e-mail facilities for illegal acts, such users are then barred from figuring it out on their own. Of course, since the operator cannot know if criminal activities are occurring, then he or she cannot be considered to be participating in any crimes being conducted through encrypted messaging. However, if a small system where encrypted messages originate or are received becomes vulnerable to seizure as evidence or instrumentality of a crime due to activities in encrypted e-mail, the operator will probably not find out about it until he or she sees the system being hauled out the door by government agents.

Pleased to Meet You, You Can't Guess My Name

"On the Internet, no one knows you're a dog," goes the famous caption of a cartoon from *New Yorker* magazine, depicting a discussion between two dogs. Anonymous and pseudonymous messaging have always been standard features of the online landscape. Most online systems, including the large national services like America Online and Prodigy, accept the use of "handles" in the CB sense rather than proper names if their users so choose. Some systems even require the use of handles, to make the system feel more special to users and take them outside the pedestrian concerns of everyday life.

Using fictitious names allows users to experiment with different behaviors, roles, and personas, freed from having to present an integrated account of their conduct to others. Online systems are, at times, grand costumed balls, where many may not be who at first they seem. For instance, many people present themselves as members of the opposite sex, to experience the gender gap from the other side. Users who are young see if they can fool adults into thinking they're old, and vice versa. Those who are bedridden may show up online as grand world explorers and adventurers; those with conservative politics may hang out incognito with a group on the radical left to find out what really makes them tick. The results of these experiments and many others are not all in, but the clear trend is toward an increase of social understanding among all who play this game online, a deepened appreciation of the perspectives and experiences of others.

Advances in cryptography have recently upped the ante on anonymity. Now, through an online software device known as the anonymous remailer, users can send messages via Internet e-mail and into Usenet newsgroups that are untraceable to the sender. Most people are using these bulletproof systems for the innocent and playful purposes described above, deriving extra comfort from knowing that now they can't be "outed" under any circumstances.

But anonymous remailers have other uses as well. Some are socially productive, or at least benevolent. For example, anonymous remailers permit whistleblowers to expose corruption and dishonesty at far lower risk of being discovered. They also permit persecuted groups to meet online without risk of others discovering their identities and using that information to harass or intimidate individual members.

Other uses of anonymous remailers, some of which can be found readily on the Net today, present problems. People can anonymously transmit all sorts of illegal and injurious materials into public areas: copyright infringements, obscenity, stolen credit information, lies and slander, and so on. Individuals with a bone to pick against anyone else can get their licks in without fear of reprisal. Anonymous remailers are great for cowards. People who want to spread messages of hate and misunderstanding, but are unwilling to stand behind their views in public, can operate behind a wall of complete anonymity and inject a strong dose of thought pollution into the public arena.

There are now entire conference areas devoted to anonymous messages, forums of outspoken and at times irresponsible opinion. What if someone sues an anonymous conference for an illegal posting, such as a serious libel that injures his or her reputation? The court would be faced with an entire discussion forum full of people, none of whom can be identified, and a wrong that needs to be righted.

Some have suggested that in such a case the libeled person would have to go without a remedy, because the First Amendment would protect the anonymous conference as an arena of truly free speech. This does not seem realistic. Most courts do not let clear wrongs go unremedied. If it looks like an anonymous messenger is using the anonymity function to commit illegal acts but avoid enforcement, courts could order the entire forum where the libel appeared to be shut down, unless the wrongdoer is identified. In such a case, there could be a compelling state interest in favor of disclosure—making a wrongdoer responsible for clearly illegal actions—that would override the public desire for anonymity.

Another response is to meet user distrust with operator distrust, and bar all encrypted files from the system. If one is barred from reading the message by encryption, it doesn't go through one's system. This need not be done in a hostile way. The operator can tell users that he or she respects their need for privacy, but users cannot expect the operator to expose the system to seizure by being absolutely barred from reading messages. If users wish to transmit encrypted messages, they should use public systems like the Internet.

If these two reactions seem extreme, there is a third approach—permit users to use the system to pass encrypted messages only if they give the system operator the decryption key. This tells users they need to trust the operator if they use his or her system, while giving them some measure of protection against government intrusion. The protection, admittedly, is not absolute—it is not clear at this time whether the government could demand the decryption key from a system operator. In addition, if a user gives one a key, how does one know if it works, except by using it on the actual encrypted files? It's impossible to know for sure until one needs to use the key. The other drawbacks of this approach are that it requires more work on the part of the system operator, and that the system operator has some potential liability if he or she accidentally or negligently permits the decryption key to fall into unauthorized hands.

Thus, the third approach has problems as well. But at least it requires trust on both sides of the relationship while enabling users to have some genuine privacy, instead of the unbalanced situation where users pass encrypted messages with no system operator ability to read them in emergency situations.

Strategies Regarding User Privacy

There is a debate among system operators about how much privacy should be permitted to online system users. Those interested in avoiding all legal risk advocate simply banning private messages. Though this remains an option, it is not recommended here. Private messaging is a valuable function for users. Eliminating it on an online system promotes an uncomfortable and distrustful atmosphere. It may also severely reduce user interest in using the online system. Also, as explained elsewhere in this chapter, eliminating user privacy can severely reduce the systems' legal protection from wrongful government search and seizure.

The most important strategy is to communicate the system policy on message privacy to all users, through both well-placed bulletins and the user agreement. A balanced approach is to tell users that their messages are private, but the operator may need to review them on rare occasions to protect himself or herself, other users, or the online system from trouble. As discussed at the beginning of this chapter, the user agreement should specifically set the privacy agreed to by operator and user in light of the privacy protections of the Electronic Communications Privacy Act.

> **The most important strategy is to communicate the system policy on message privacy to all users, through both well-placed bulletins and the user agreement.**

Under such a policy, the operator should only look at private messages when he or she hears of suspicious activity on the online system. This could happen by being tipped off by someone else, by noticing unusual or suspicious file activity on one's system, by seeing mysterious references to e-mail activity in public postings, and so on. It is impossible to predict all the ways in which one may see something suspicious going on. But usually, the alert system operator will know it when he or she sees it.

Even when suspicions arise, the operator need not actually look at the e-mail in question if it's not an emergency. The operator can copy and safely store the questionable messages, then contact the users involved and tell them his or her concerns. Depending on the response, the operator may or may not choose to look at the messages. If the user stonewalls the operator, then the operator can look at the messages, or simply hold the messages unseen and kick the uncooperative user off the system. In the latter case, if the authorities come by later, the operator can give them the messages without ever having looked at them himself or herself, provided the law enforcement agents are properly authorized to receive the private messages. In this way, the operator can protect himself or herself and the system, and personally respect user privacy at the same time.

Crime and the Online System 6

Crime on the networks is a subject of great public fear and excitement. In the past few years, events that have set the online world buzzing include the following.

- The Internet crash caused a few years ago by Robert Morris' worm showed the public how widespread and important computer networks have become, and how disastrous it can be if they are tampered with.

- In the best-seller *The Cuckoo's Egg*, astronomer Clifford Stoll told how he traced and helped apprehend West German youths who broke into U.S. computer systems under an arrangement with the KGB.

- Robert Riggs and Craig Neidorf were prosecuted for obtaining, and publishing in an electronic newsletter distributed through the networks, telephone company information relating to its 911 emergency system.

- In the summer of 1990, federal and state agents cooperated in Operation Sundevil, a nationwide crackdown on alleged computer criminals, mostly youths, resulting in dozens of arrests and the seizures of many computer systems.

- A bulletin board operated as a customer support board by Steve Jackson Games was seized by federal agents pursuing an alleged "evil hacker group" known as the Legion of Doom, which the agents believed was using the bulletin board system as a meeting place.

There's more where those came from. Anyone not familiar with the field might scan the above list of events, all from the last five years, and conclude that computer crime is rampant in the networks. However, celebrated computer crimes are not always what they seem. Exploring a bit further each of the events described above, we see they do not raise as much cause for alarm as may first appear:

- The Internet crash was not purposely caused by Robert Morris. He designed a benign worm program to explore the boundaries of the Internet and report the results to him. Unfortu-

187

nately, a bug in the program made it crash computer systems instead. Robert Morris was not a fearsome computer criminal, though his creation was indeed dangerous due to its flaws.

- The West German hackers pursued by Clifford Stoll were indeed selling information to the KGB, but apparently never obtained any classified information from U.S. computers. The worst they did was rummage around in unclassified materials on various computers connected to the networks.

- In his trial, Neidorf was accused of complicity in a scheme to steal telephone company information on its 911 system. This information was valued at many thousands of dollars by the telephone company. Neidorf's defense learned, however, that the same information was published by the telephone company itself in a book readily available for about $14. The prosecution had to stop the trial in midstride.

- Operation Sundevil, at the time of this writing, happened over four years ago. Very few convictions resulted. It is generally viewed today as a monument to law enforcement naiveté about the Net and its inhabitants.

- After retaining several of Steve Jackson Games' computers for several months, the agents who seized them returned them with no charges against the company, or anyone else. In the meantime, Steve Jackson Games suffered serious business losses. It sued the U.S. government for wrongful search and seizure, and won.

In other words, many of the sensational headlines of computer crime tell less than half the story. That does not mean there isn't any illegal activity. There are plenty of hackers out there, amateur and expert alike, continuously probing the defenses of online systems to see if they can get in without permission. A top security officer for DEC recently stated that its systems must repel several intrusion attempts every day using highly secure firewalls. Thousands of other, less secure systems have their defenses breached regularly, though publicity about such events is minimal. How many large corporations and government agencies want it known that their computer defenses were cracked by 12-year-olds?

> **When hackers are caught they are routinely vilified, but often they are guilty of no greater crime than getting a little extra use out of their phone service, or looking around in a computer in which they don't belong.**

In most cases, the intruders cause little or no damage. Their goal is usually to prove they can get in, and perhaps learn something about different kinds of computer systems. Intruding hackers may also set up impromptu discussion areas inside hacked corporate systems, copy off some information that is meaningless to them except for its value as a trophy of a system conquest, use the systems as jumping-off points to hide their tracks in further travels, or gain free telephone service.

When hackers are caught they are routinely vilified, but often they are guilty of no greater crime than getting a little extra use out of their phone service, or looking around in a computer in which they don't belong. These things are defined as crimes, nonetheless, and so examples are made of the hackers, and they are sent off to jail. It makes for exciting reading, but there is often little real danger to most users and operators of online systems. There is no crime epidemic on the networks, or at least no greater level of crime than we see out in the streets.

Confusion or Convictions?

In cyberspace, it can be hard to tell when you're guilty of a crime. There is no murder or bodily harm (at least in the current state of technology). Most of what looks like "stealing" is really just making another copy of some information while the original remains in the owner's possession, or getting more use out of a communications system than the owner authorizes. Most of what looks like "trespass" is really just punching in an access code belonging to someone else, and using the resulting computer services that flow out. What's going to count as the online equivalent of jaywalking, in a new world where crimes and their traditional physical embodiments have been blasted apart?

The current confusion over online crime is strikingly illustrated in recent prosecutions and investigations. Consider the 1990 trial of Craig Neidorf for helping distribute some supposedly secret information purloined from a Bell South in-house computer system. Midway through trial, it was discovered that the information in question, alleged to be worth thousands of dollars, was being sold by Bell South itself for a mere $14 through an obscure technical publishing service. The prosecution dropped the case in a flush of acute embarrassment, having lost its way on the fundamental question of whether Neidorf had done anything wrong, morally or legally.

More recently, and still ongoing as we go to press, is the investigation and official government harassment of Phil Zimmerman, the program developer who created the Pretty Good Privacy (PGP) encryption program. When he finished the first version of the program, Phil uploaded it to a few Internet ftp sites maintained on computers located in the United States. Almost immediately, Internet users from overseas downloaded copies of PGP to their own countries, causing the program to be spread worldwide. Since then, U.S. Customs has pursued an open-ended investigation into whether Zimmerman criminally violated U.S. export laws (which prohibit unlicensed export of cryptography software) by putting PGP on the Internet. However, there is little indication at this time whether the government will move forward. Could it be that in cyberspace there is no line defining the U.S. border, making the concept of "export" meaningless?

There will likely be continuing missteps by the authorities in chasing computer crime over the next few years. A prosecutor's gut sense of right and wrong is simply not enough. Society as a whole has to redefine the contours of criminality for the online world. To do so it needs to come to a greater consensus on the moral component of online activities, and a better shared answer to exactly what constitutes harming people online, and what constitutes online "property."

Regardless of the reality of threats posed by computer criminals, government officials have been busy beefing up laws aimed directly or indirectly at computer crime. These include the recent Digital Telephony bill, which mandates easy physical wiretap access to phone lines by government agents; changes to the Computer Fraud and Abuse Act, making it harder for accused hackers and virus developers to slip through loopholes in existing laws; increased criminal provisions in the Copyright Act; and changes to the computer crime laws of several states.

Computer crime will never go away. In fact, it is likely to increase, as a greater part of the traditional underworld goes online and learns to use computer networks to its own advantage. Generally, as society reconstitutes itself online, we should expect to see roughly the same spectrum of law abiders and lawbreakers we see offline.

Crimes Against the Online System and the Operator

An online system is a valuable piece of property. If someone seriously attacks or misuses it, it is a crime just as surely as the theft of a car or burglary of a home. While most illegal hacker activity is fairly harmless, more malicious types have been encountered on the networks as well. Some of the potential crimes that might be committed against an online system include:

- users uploading viruses or other dangerous code into the online system.

- users trespassing into non-public areas of the online system, or taking system-level privileges for themselves and using them against other users.

- users crashing the system.

- theft of copyrighted, secret, or other proprietary files from the online system.

These activities and many others may violate both federal and state criminal laws. We will review two of the most important federal criminal laws, the Computer Fraud and Abuse Act and the Electronic Communications Privacy Act, and as an example of state legislation, the New York computer crime law.

The Computer Fraud and Abuse Act ("CFAA")

The CFAA was first enacted in 1984 to combat so-called "computer crime." It was revised in 1994 under the "Computer Abuse Amendments Act." The following activities are considered criminal under the CFAA, provided certain conditions discussed below are met:

- trespass (unauthorized entry) by users into the online system;

- users exceeding their authorized access to the online system; and

- users exchanging information on how to gain unauthorized access to computers.

"Trespassing" and "exceeding authorized access" are viewed similarly under the CFAA. In each case, the user intentionally goes into places he or she is not authorized to visit. Therefore, a user who commits a crime against the operator or the online system is not necessarily protected from the CFAA just because he or she is a registered user and has authorized access to the online system. If the user knowingly exceeds that authorization in any way and certain other statutory conditions are met, then he or she is treated the same as a trespasser.

The CFAA does not apply to all attacks against online systems; it has certain limiting conditions. Let's examine it a little more closely.

It takes more than a simple trespass into the online system to trigger a CFAA violation. Three different kinds of trespasses are covered by the CFAA:

1. A trespass made with "an intent to defraud," that results in both "furthering the fraud" and the trespasser obtaining something of value in the process (we'll call this "fraudulent trespass");

2. A trespass coupled with actions that intentionally cause damage to a "computer, computer system, network, information, data, or program," or result in withholding or denial of the use of a "computer, computer services, system or network, information, data, or program," and cause at least $1,000 total loss in the course of a year (we'll call this "intentional destructive trespass"); and

3. A trespass coupled with reckless actions which, though not necessarily deliberately harmful, still cause damage to a "computer, computer system, network, information, data, or program," or result in withholding or denial of the use of a "computer, computer services, system or network, information, data, or program, and cause at least $1,000 total loss in the course of a year (we'll call this "reckless destructive trespass").

Fraudulent trespass is aimed primarily at telephone fraud committed through a computer system, such as "phone phreaking"—using a telephone company switching computer to obtain free telephone service. It can also apply in some cases to activities within an online system. For instance, two users of a system who are working together to develop computer software may be sending source code back and forth through private e-mail on the system. If another user intercepts that e-mail and obtains a copy of the source code, he or she has obtained something of value, and has violated the CFAA.

The prohibition against intentional destructive trespass is more valuable to online systems. It can be used against a variety of criminal activities. One is deliberate attacks against the online system, such as attempts to make the online system crash. Such things do happen once in a while. The culprit is usually some computer-capable youth who, whether out of a need to prove him or herself or a need for revenge, deliberately seeks ways to bring innocent online systems down. The CFAA applies to such attacks, provided that the user causes at least $1,000 worth of damage. Perhaps it is most important to try to understand people who do such things, but while that effort is underway it is good to have criminal laws to hinder their destructive activities.

> **The intentional destructive trespass provision also covers those who would propagate viruses or other dangerous programs through the online system.**

The intentional destructive trespass provision also covers those who would propagate viruses or other dangerous programs through the online system. A virus certainly may "damage, alter, or destroy" information on the online system, and prevent proper use of the online system while they're on the loose. Further, it can also do all these things to the computer of any hapless user who downloads it from the online system. The CFAA would apply to such damage both to your own online system and to the computers of your users, again provided the $1,000 loss condition is met.

The crime of reckless destructive trespass was newly added in 1994. It is nearly identical with intentional destructive trespass, except that it is more easily triggered: the crime is committed when the intruder does something reckless that causes damage in a computer, whether or not he or she meant to cause the damage. The penalty is also lighter. The maximum jail sentence for reckless destructive trespass is one year, while the maximum jail sentence for intentional destructive trespass is five years. This new section creates an official government recognition that sometimes computer system intruders are just explorers who don't mean to cause any damage at all. While they will still be punished if caught going into systems where they don't belong, they will not be exposed to the same jail terms that apply to those who intentionally damage the online systems of others.

If two or more users violate the CFAA by trafficking in computer access codes on the online system, it is not so much a crime against the online system as the commission of a crime against others within the online system. This will be discussed a little later in this chapter.

There are some other crimes defined in the CFAA, but they have little to do with many online systems—crimes involving classified information, financial records, and medical records. If the online system is somehow involved in any of these areas, the CFAA may provide the operator with additional protection against criminal activity.

Hackers and the Law

Adventurous souls have been exploring computer networks for decades. The first big fad was phone phreaking, including use of the infamous "blue boxes" in the '60s and '70s that emitted tones causing phone company switches to give up long distance access. The phreaks were pursued by the cops throughout the '70s, and many were caught and put behind bars. Perhaps the most fa- mous was John Draper, the infamous "Captain Crunch" who could, as legend has it, get free long distance access using a whistle from a Cap'n Crunch cereal box. The main legal tool used by the feds was the wire fraud law, a catch-all statute that made it illegal to do anything deceptive or dishonest over interstate telephone lines.

In the '80s the hacker underground grew, exploring both the newly computerizing telephone networks and the new computer networks. The major prosecutions of this era occurred at the end of the decade. First, Robert Riggs and Craig Neidorf were prosecuted in Chicago for a scheme to steal and publish secret information, specifically a Bell South document relating to its 911 emergency phone number system. Riggs, who actually broke into the Bell South computer system, was convicted, but Neidorf as publisher escaped penalty when it came to light that the information was not secret in the first place. The other major case involved Robert Morris, who was sent to jail for releasing a "worm" program that brought the Internet to a screeching halt for a few days in 1990. The laws asserted against Riggs and Neidorf were the same wire fraud laws used previously against the phone phreaks, plus a law prohibiting interstate transportation of stolen property. The Morris case was perhaps the first use of the then-new Computer Fraud and Abuse Act outside of an embezzlement context.

In 1990 Operation Sundevil, with searches and seizures of hackers across the country, was more of a bust for the feds than for most of the hackers who were its targets. Announced with a lot of fanfare, it was attended by confusion and delay in the following years, and ended with a trial or two, and no triumphant press release from the forces of law and order. The post-mortem is still to come.

The most recent major hacker prosecution occurred in 1992, when five members of the Masters of Deception were indicted, including Phiber Optik, Acid Phreak, and Corrupt. The Computer Fraud and Abuse Act was again the main legal tool used by the prosecutors. There was no trial, however—all five defendants pleaded guilty, and most went to jail.

This is not a complete history, just a tiny sketch of some of the better-known events in the ongoing battle between the forces of law and order, and the young network explorers who don't feel the law applies to them. In case the above account gives the wrong impression, many of the hackers have never been caught.

The Secret Service is expressly authorized to investigate and enforce violations of the CFAA. Penalties for violating the CFAA include fines and prison sentences of up to ten years. For those further interested in the details of the CFAA, it is reproduced in an appendix in the back of this book. The fraudulent trespass discussed here is found at paragraph (a)(4); the destructive trespass provisions are at (a)(5); and the provision prohibiting trafficking in access codes is (a)(6). Also reproduced is the related statute prohibiting credit card fraud, 18 U.S.C 1029.

Electronic Communications Privacy Act ("ECPA")

This statute was discussed in Chapter 5, and it is mostly concerned with the privacy of electronic transmissions. However, part of the ECPA is worded in a way that appears to make it apply to certain attacks against online systems.

Specifically, Section 2701 of the ECPA makes it a crime to trespass into an online system, and "obtain, alter, or prevent authorized access to" any message while it is being stored on the online system. Like the CFAA, the ECPA concept of trespasser includes both unauthorized users, and authorized users who exceed their authorized access to the online system. However, unlike the CFAA, the ECPA does not require the trespasser to have an intent to defraud, or to cause a certain dollar amount of damage, before the crime is committed. The statutory provisions are triggered by any unauthorized access to private communications.

> **The ECPA makes it illegal for users to look at private messages between others that are maintained on the online system, or to tamper with those messages. It also makes it illegal for any user to prevent others from getting access to their own messages.**

ECPA makes it illegal for users to look at private messages between others that are maintained on the online system, or to tamper with those messages. It also makes it illegal for any user to prevent others from getting access to their own messages. Preventing access can be specific, such as barring the intended recipient from receiving a particular message. It can also be accomplished by disrupting the online system's entire operations to the point that most or all users cannot retrieve their messages. It appears, then, that the ECPA prohibits outsiders from crashing an online system, or sending in a virus that crashes an online system, as much as the CFAA does. In essence, the ECPA's protection of communication privacy extends to protecting the computer system that supports the communications.

This seems almost too good to be true. The CFAA, as described above, has several conditions that must be met before it kicks in to make crashing an online system illegal, but the ECPA seems to cover the same situations automatically. Perhaps the courts will try to limit the ECPA if it is used in this way, on the grounds that it is really directed at privacy, not at damage to computer systems. It appears, nonetheless, that the plain language of the ECPA makes it apply to crimes against the online system in the way we describe here, and it is available to redress criminal damage to the online system.

> **In essence, the ECPA's protection of communication privacy extends to protecting the computer system that supports the communications.**

The penalties for violating Section 2701 of the ECPA are up to a year in prison and $250,000 in fines if the offense is committed for personal or commercial gain, or maliciously; up to six months in prison and a $5,000 fine if committed for any other reason. The entire text of the ECPA, including Section 2701, is reproduced in Appendix B for further examination.

New York State Computer Crime Statute

Most states in the U.S. have laws dealing with computer crime. It would require a book several times the size of this one to analyze the computer crime laws of all fifty states. By way of example, this book will restrict itself to reviewing the New York State law, which is fairly typical. Readers interested in their own state's computer crime laws will find a list of references in Appendix I. (Keep in mind that the laws change and the list included in this book may not be completely current at the time you read it).

The New York State computer crime statute, section 156 of the Penal Law, became effective in 1986, and was amended in 1992. It applies to "computers," "computer programs," "computer data," "computer material," and "computer services." An online system is likely to be considered a "computer service" under the New York law.

The statute describes several different kinds of prohibited computer crime activity. We will look at each briefly.

Unauthorized Use

The least serious crime under the New York law is simple "unauthorized use" of an online system or other computer service. If the owner of an online system describes the scope of authorized use of the system to all users, and employs any coding or access level scheme to make the system provide to each user only the access to which that user is entitled, then anyone using the online system outside the permitted scope is committing a crime. The law is intended to protect against the casual cracker, the user who breaks in or exceeds his or her authorization without necessarily intending to do anything harmful. Since it does not require a strong showing that any harm occurred, the unauthorized use offense is a misdemeanor.

Like the federal statutes, the New York law treats users exceeding the scope of their authorized use of the system the same as users with no right to use the system at all. Operators who want maximum protection for private areas of their systems under this provision should consider posting a notice in those private areas, telling users they should not be there unless the operator gave them specific permission in advance. If there is a violation, the operator will also need to show in court that the online system is equipped or programmed with a device, coding system, or other feature designed to prevent unauthorized use. In other words, for the crime of unauthorized use, system operators should presume that the law only helps those who help themselves, by setting up some kind of security protection for their online systems.

Computer Trespass

Where someone uses an online system without permission in connection with committing another crime, the New York law establishes the crime of "computer trespass." A user is guilty of computer trespass if he or she knowingly uses an online system without authorization, and either:

1. commits (or attempts to commit, or furthers the commission of) any felony during unauthorized use, or

2. knowingly obtains or sees computer material during his unauthorized use.

Alternative (1) is straightforward. If a user uses the online system without authorization to run a bookmaking operation, or drug ring, or to transmit illegal inside information for stock trading, or for any of hundreds of other possible crimes, he or she is guilty of computer trespass against the online system.

Alternative (2) turns simple unauthorized access (the misdemeanor discussed above) into the more serious crime of computer trespass if the user takes "computer material" in the process. "Computer material," as used in this statute, has a higher order of legal protection than ordinary computer data under the New York law. For the information on the online

> **For the information on the online system to qualify as computer material it must be valuable commercial data kept on the online system and properly available only to the owner of the information and others authorized by the owner.**

system to qualify as computer material it must be valuable commercial data kept on the online system and properly available only to the owner of the information and others authorized by the owner. Typical computer materials include a great deal of the information transmitted through in-house online systems, and private areas of other online systems dedicated to confidential use by a company or group, including all trade secrets; business databases and lists held on the online system for the exclusive use of its registered users; and computer programs on customer support online systems available only to registered users.

There are certain limits on what can qualify as computer material. Public domain and shareware programs probably would not qualify because they are commonly available, with little or no restrictions to access. Similarly, databases and files would have to be something more than mere compilations of commonly available facts, in order to have significant commercial value. Information on the online system, whether it belongs to the system operator or a user storing it on the online system, has the best chance of qualifying as "computer material" if the system operator or user has exclusive rights to the materials, and they are not legally available outside the online system.

For example, if an unauthorized user downloads a program from an online system that he or she could have obtained by mail order from the program author for $22.50, he or she may have engaged in theft of services or computer data, but it may not be computer trespass under the New York Penal Law because the material is easily available outside the online system.

Computer Tampering

The original New York law created a new crime called "computer tampering," with two levels of severity, and the 1992 revision has four levels. Fourth-degree tampering, the least serious level, is a misdemeanor. It consists of deliberately altering or destroying another person's computer program or data, though it does not apply if "computer materials," as described above, are affected..

The fourth-degree tampering offense protects the system operator against users who might mischievously reformat the online system hard drive, or knowingly upload a Trojan program that writes over the data on the hard disk. Can users turn around and accuse the operator of "computer tampering" for deleting their data from the online system's storage area? They can try, but the system operator should have the solid defense that he or she is authorized to delete data on the system.

In contrast, first-, second-, and third-degree computer tampering are serious felonies. Third-degree tampering occurs when a user commits second-degree tampering (as described just above), and any one of the following elements is also present:

1. the user commits the tampering in the course of committing (or attempting to commit, or furthering) a felony-level crime; or

2. the user was previously convicted of any computer crime as defined in the New York law; or

3. the user intentionally alters or destroys "computer material" (discussed just above in connection under computer trespass); or

4. the user intentionally alters or destroys computer data or a computer program in an amount exceeding $1,000.

Thus, the third-degree tampering provision penalizes repeat offenders more heavily than first time tamperers, and creates greater protection for computer materials by making any attack on such materials automatically a felony-level crime. First- and second-degree tampering are basically third-degree tampering involving alteration or destruction of progressively more valuable computer data: $3,000 worth of computer programs or data for second-degree tampering, and $50,000 worth of computer programs or data for first-degree tampering. As the severity of the crime goes up, so does the severity of the felony and the associated sentencing.

Duplication of Computer-Related Material

Another new felony created by the New York law is called "Unlawful duplication of computer-related material." This provision makes it criminal to:

1. copy any computer data or program without permission, and knowingly gain an economic benefit of at least $2,500 from doing so; or

2. copy any computer data or program while committing (or attempting to commit, or furthering) a felony-level crime.

This provision may not be enforceable due to a conflict with federal law. Specifically, the U.S. Copyright Act forbids the states from passing any laws that make "copying" illegal. This is because

---

Next Time, Use a Collection Agency . . .

Michael Lafaro, a Long Island computer consultant, was not pleased when Forecast Installations paid him only $1,200 for a $3,600 custom software system. Lafaro sent a technician to Forecast's site on the pretext of software maintenance. Instead, he modified the system to shut down at a specified time. When Forecast found out, it trumped Lafaro by filing charges leading to his arrest in November 1993. Lafaro and his technician face sentences of up to seven years in prison and $10,000 in fines if convicted.

Lafaro was arrested under the "computer tampering" provisions of New York State's computer crime laws, which have nothing to do with computer consultants, payment disputes, or software time bombs. Instead, they are directed at uninvited intruders into computers on networks, and were recently beefed up to scare "dark side" computer hackers and plain old embezzlers into thinking twice before their next uninvited computer foray. But by casting the net wide, the computer tampering laws became available for use against a small businessman, and an everyday commercial dispute that does not belong in the criminal courts.

Forecast's attorney characterized Lafaro's system-disabling software as a "virus," a wildly inaccurate label that whipped up real hysteria by recalling the computer virus scares of the past few years. He claimed Lafaro's time bomb function could have caused over half a million dollars in damage (in fact, the system was never even shut down). Lafaro's attorney said the computer crime law was badly misapplied in this case, pointing out that the Class C felony charge against Lafaro is equivalent to rape or sodomy in the second degree under NY law. The case is still unresolved as this book goes to press.

Congress wanted to be sure that copyright laws would be the same throughout the country without state-by-state variations, and chose to achieve this goal by making the federal copyright laws the only ones that can apply to wrongful copying.

Criminal Possession of Computer-Related Material

Another provision of the New York law makes it unlawful to possess programs or data that were unlawfully copied, provided the possessor knows that they're illegitimate copies. If a dishonest user illegally downloads more than $2,500 worth of proprietary data from the online system and passes it to someone else, both the user and the recipient can be prosecuted. This provision may be subject to the same infirmity as the unlawful duplication provision discussed earlier: if unlawful duplication is preempted by federal copyright law and thus not capable of being a crime under state law, then possessing materials that violate only the preempted law might not be a crime, either.

Finally, the New York law establishes a defense of "reasonable belief" to the various crimes described above. If the defendant user can prove that he or she reasonably believed he or she had authorization to use the online system, or the right to copy, alter, or destroy others' data, the user may go free. This is not an easy defense, though; an honest belief is not enough. It is also necessary to prove, to the satisfaction of judge and jury, that it was *reasonable* to believe the conduct was authorized.

For example, suppose an online system contains a bulletin in the opening screen stating that only registered users can go to certain areas of the system. The user does not register, and hacks his or her way into the area for registered users only. There, the intruder finds some newly developed software owned by other users who are storing it temporarily on the system, downloads a copy, and then distributes it and collects money from the public for use of the program. If the intruder is found and charged with a crime, he or she might profess an honest belief that these things were permitted, and that there were no laws against it. But under these facts, it is clear that even if we think the intruder honestly believed everything he or she did was okay (perhaps because he or she looks very reasonable while making excuses), it would still not be reasonable for the intruder, or anyone else, to believe that breaking into the online system and stealing others' program code is okay.

New York's law defines quite a number of different "computer crime" offenses covering different kinds of wrongful acts that could occur on the online system. For system operators in New York, it fills in significant gaps in the federal law. Among other things, it makes simple trespass (unauthorized access) a crime, unlike federal law, though the crime is not very serious unless it is coupled with other wrongful acts, such as stealing property.

What to Do About Criminal Activity Against a System

First, one must gather all evidence of the crime. This could include system records of user login times, other records of user access to various areas or uploads or downloads, messages to or from the users involved, files uploaded, downloaded, or looked at by the users involved, and any available personal information on the users. There could also be other kinds of evidence in a given case. Just be sure to gather it all, preferably without letting the suspect users know it is being done. If the information is on a hard disk, back up the entire hard disk to a tape or set of disks and stash the backup away somewhere safe. If the information is spread throughout the system, it would also be good to make another file or set of files, containing just the information relating to the criminal activities.

This is not to advocate that system operators routinely keep files on their users against the day the stored data might come in handy, as if they were the KGB or FBI. Gathering evidence is called for only when it is strongly suspected that crimes are actually being committed. But when the suspicion is there, it is very important to gather evidence for two reasons: first, to preserve the evidence in its original state so it will not get lost, and defense attorneys will have a harder time trying to discredit it; second, to convince the state or federal authorities to prosecute, in the event the operator wants to file criminal charges.

After securing the evidence, the operator should decide whether to contact the authorities. As explained in Chapter 7, there is a possibility that the legal authorities, if they hear that the problem is on a small online system, will mistakenly make seizure of the online system their first priority. This would be a mistake, of course, but one that might happen. Try to develop a sense, perhaps with the aid of an attorney familiar with the local police and federal agents, of whether the authorities will be more likely to help or hurt the online system once they take an active interest in the case. If the problem does not seem serious, it may be advisable to refrain from contacting the police, and see if the problem fades away by itself. If it becomes significant, the police can always be contacted then, but in that case, it will be best if evidence of the suspicious activity has been set aside and collected from the beginning, as suggested here.

> **Gathering evidence is called for only when it is strongly suspected that crimes are actually being committed.**

If it seems necessary to contact the authorities, go to the local police station or agency office in person, and fill out all the proper forms for reporting the problem. It is important to do this personally, and not just call them by phone and complain about computer crime. A formal filing puts the report into the case disposition process, and will be more likely to be investigated and acted upon. Next, find a police officer or agent, and tell him or her about the problem. Be prepared to explain all sorts of things about computers and online systems to them. Computer literacy is not a prerequisite for being an police investigator or government agent. Ask if the local precinct or agency has anyone who specializes in computer crime. If they don't, ask if they can contact any such specialists elsewhere for consulting backup.

It will also be necessary to deal with the ongoing criminal activity itself. If the suspicious user is very active, and seriously threatens the security of the online system, then the operator may personally have to take steps to save the online system, even though the authorities have become involved. For instance, the operator may attempt to cut off all avenues for the user to get into the online system.

Otherwise, just gather evidence and let the suspected criminals continue their activities until it is clear they are committing or planning to commit a crime against the operator or the online system. If the authorities are involved, they will decide if the evidence you already have is sufficient to prove a crime.

> **If the suspicious user is very active, and seriously threatens the security of the online system, then the operator may personally have to take steps to save the online system, even though the authorities have become involved.**

If there is not enough evidence, they will work with the operator to plan ways to get additional evidence. At that point, the investigation is in their hands. There is nothing more to do except cooperate in the investigation, and watch to make sure the investigators themselves do not damage the online system.

Of course, it is also possible the authorities will not be interested in looking into the complaint. One common scenario is that federal agents refuse to investigate because they feel it's really a local matter. Then, the state police must be convinced to investigate. As mentioned above, at every turn there may be a lot of work involved explaining to them what an online system is, and also how the problems being encountered break laws and seriously injure the operator. There are a few computer-literate, even online system-literate law enforcement agents around, but currently they are the exception rather than the rule.

One important option is to seek a lawyer with a criminal law background, and familiarity with local law enforcement officials. The lawyer can help determine if the problems really support criminal charges, and can give valuable advice on both the other steps discussed earlier and others not even mentioned here. He or she can also help present charges to law enforcement authorities in a manner that will increase the chances they will pursue the matter.

Use of the Online System to Commit Crimes

Since the online system is a place where people meet and interact, some people might use it to commit a crime, or as the scene of a crime. This can create serious risks for the operator and the online system if not properly handled.

There are two entirely different ways that criminal activity on the online system can create serious problems for the operator. It is very important to keep the following distinction in mind, in order to make the best decision on how to deal with any criminal problems that may arise.

First, if it becomes clear that the online system is being used for criminal activities, there is a potential for the operator to be regarded as a criminal too. It depends largely on what the operator does after discovering the crime. If the operator handles it properly, he or she will be under no suspicion at all. On the other hand, in the worst case the operator could be suspected of being one of the criminals. But the worst case almost never happens, unless the operator pursues a very questionable or reckless course—for example, promoting the online system to the public as a place for maintaining and transmitting clearly obscene materials.

The second kind of problem arises when the online system is used for criminal activities without the operator's knowledge, such as when users exchange stolen credit card codes through private e-mail. The operator is certainly not a criminal; he or she doesn't even know that illegal acts are taking place. However, the online system is being used as the scene or instrument of a crime, so there is some risk that it could be seized by state or federal agents. The seizure would not be to penalize the operator, but to prevent others from committing crimes and to gather evidence. Nonetheless, it can be devastating if the online system is seized, both for the operator and for other users.

We will explore these two problems in a little more depth after briefly looking at the kinds of crimes that might be committed on or through online systems. In the following chapter, we will discuss what to do if the online system is searched or seized by law enforcement agents.

The Evil Some System Operators Do . . .

As online systems grow in popularity, so does fear on the part of those who do not understand the online world. What are those nerds doing on their computer networks, far from the light of day? Who are my children talking to? These fears are expertly stoked into leaping flames by politicians, religious leaders, and others who profit from designating new enemies for the raging herd.

In the past few years, we have been treated to newspaper stories and television exposes about bulletin boards devoted to every evil or social monster imaginable, including Satanists, Nazis, and skinheads. A system operator in Connecticut made the news for supposedly running a "bomb factory" on his bulletin board, while mothers around the nation point accusing fingers at system operators corrupting their children with filthy pictures. A major television news feature claimed that some old men used a bulletin board system to organize the production of a snuff film involving an unsuspecting young boy.

Police officers around the nation are not immune to the hysteria. Many seem fixated on a supposed equation between bulletin boards and pedophilia, as if old men seeking to seduce young children were the main users of bulletin boards. The truth is that some pedophiles have indeed been found on online systems, but they are few and far between—just like in the physical world.

The result of all this fear-mongering is increasingly urgent calls to regulate online services, especially the smaller ones. This process is particularly far along in other countries, such as Australia, Canada, and England. In the U.S., as we go to press there is a strong movement in California to impose some sort of regulatory regime on those who dare to operate online systems in that state.

The hysteria hopefully will subside over time. After all, online is becoming mainstream, as the nation continues to be inundated with the Democratic vision of an "Information Superhighway" and the new Republican vision of the "Third Wave" telecommuting economy. When the dust clears, will online systems continue to be free of most regulations, or will the fear-mongers have succeeded in throwing a heavy yoke over their activities?

Kinds of Crimes That Can Be Committed on Online Systems

Broadly speaking, there are two kinds of crimes that can be committed on or through an online system.

The first is "computer crime": acts defined as criminal by federal or state computer crime statutes, and that necessarily involve the use of a computer or computer information. The CFAA, credit card fraud statute, ECPA, and the New York law discussed above are all examples of computer crime laws. Typical computer crimes include breaking into computer systems, thefts of data, altering or destroying sensitive medical or financial data, spreading viruses, and misusing credit and other personal and business information.

The other category is much larger: all crimes other than computer crime. An online system is a powerful communications medium, and enables groups of people to coordinate and synchronize their activities in relative privacy. It has the same general purpose usefulness as a telephone, and can be used for all the same purposes, much more effectively in many cases. Thus, the online system can be used in the planning or execution of almost any imaginable crime: drug dealing; pornography operations; robberies and burglaries; illegal transfer of inside information on stocks; bribery and graft; gambling; fraud; embezzlement; violating export regulations; the list goes on and on.

Most of these criminal situations are pretty clear-cut to the ordinary observer. There might be times when it's unclear if a given activity is criminal, or whether an activity being observed crosses the line of illegality. At such times, it would be a good idea to get a quick read on the situation from a lawyer.

Ways That System Operators Might Be Criminally Liable

As a Primary Perpetrator

If a system operator runs a system in pursuit of criminal activities, naturally the operator will be a criminal. Reports occasionally surface of various kinds of online systems used for illegal activities: pirate online systems for infringing software copies, online systems for exchanging information on breaking into computer systems without authorization, or online systems for coordinating the activities of drug rings or child pornography rings.

Any system operator knowingly involved in committing crimes should be aware he or she is taking a huge risk. If caught, the operator is entitled to the same procedural and Constitutional protections as everyone else. But this book is not intended to help deliberate criminals in any manner.

Where the Online System Is Knowingly Operated Near the Edge of Legality

Some system operators work in areas where it is difficult to tell if the activity happening on the online system is criminal or not. Here are three examples:

- **Example One**   Sexually oriented materials are found on many online systems, mostly in the form of text and graphic images. They are also found extensively on the Internet, such as the "alt.sex" newsgroups on Usenet, and there are even whole networks devoted to such materials, such as Throbnet. Since transmission of pornographic materials is so widespread, observers may form the impression there's nothing illegal about them.

  However, as explained in the chapter on adult materials, pornographic images and other works certainly can be illegal if they are obscene under state law, and meet the Constitutional tests for obscenity. There is also an additional federal statute which imposes heavy penalties for engaging in child pornography. Most system operators who transmit pornographic materials are at least marginally aware of this, yet they continue their operations. Many of them consciously choose to operate at the edge of the law, proclaiming that they do not permit any truly obscene materials on their system. However, because they are operating at the edge of legality, obscene file may regularly slip through these online systems and networks, except where operators vigilantly monitor their systems.

- **Example Two**   There are online systems and networks that feature ongoing group discussions about how to break into various kinds of computer and telephone systems. The system operators who run these systems claim these discussions are perfectly legal under the First Amendment's protection of freedom of speech.

  The great bulk of these discussions are indeed perfectly legal. But can the system operator eliminate the possibility that one of these ongoing discussions could veer from mere theoretical exploration of system faults to planning an actual system break-in? If this happens, that discussion is no longer protected First Amendment speech, but part of a potentially criminal act or attempt, and the online system could be part of that criminal activity.

- **Example Three**   Utility and patch (bug-fixing) programs that originate with the large software companies, and are designed for use with their commercial software sold at retail, are increasingly finding their way online. Often, these programs are placed in the online environment by the software companies themselves, who distribute them to their customers through online customer support systems. The owners do not always consider these programs public domain, however, and often include notices that electronic redistribution outside of the company-run system is restricted. In other words, users are told they can download the programs, but can distribute them no further.

  Nonetheless, these program files often end up on other online systems and networks. Many users and system operators are aware of the software companies' restrictions on these files. Some operators take the position that once the owners put the program files out electronically, they forfeit all rights to keep others from redistributing them. This question has not been tested in court, but since copyrights in programs created after 1989 are nearly impossible to abandon by accident, it's unlikely copyright owners would lose their basic copyright protection against redistribution based on that forfeiture argument. (Other system operators try to honor the manufacturers' intent as to whether the files can be redistributed, but sometimes they simply can't figure out what that intent is by looking at the file in question; they are not included in this example).

In all three examples, the system operators are aware of the activities in question, and they know they are close to being illegal, but believe they have not crossed the line. What is a system operator's responsibility if he or she is wrong about the precise point at which legal activities become illegal?

Such system operators, attempting to skirt the edge of illegality, run a significant risk of being found criminally liable for knowingly facilitating the criminal activities of others, especially where, as in the above situations, the system operators actively encourage the questionable activity. The law does not distinguish between "performing an act that you know violates the law," and "knowingly performing an act that turns out to violate the law, even if you did not think it did," at least when determining guilt. Knowledge of criminality could be important afterward, in determining the severity of sentencing.

A system operator certainly is entitled to perform acts that are almost illegal, as long as they don't cross the line. He or she can carry almost-obscene files on the online system, and can carry discussions on computer break-in theory that do not directly lead to a break-in. But by setting up the almost-illegal situation, the operator also places a great responsibility on himself or herself to control the

The Online System as Casino

The spread of gambling in America is not limited to Indian reservations, riverboats, church bingos, office football pools, and a few opportunistic states. It's heading this way, up the old virtual turnpike.

Online systems are a natural for gambling. In fact, they enable gambling on a broad scale to be operated with an efficiency previously unimagined. Players can call in bets and receive their winnings online with a few clicks of a mouse. The games of chance themselves can all be computerized, as can registering bets, calculating odds, and determining winners and losers. Compared to physical casinos, online systems can avoid the enormous overhead of paying hundreds of workers and maintaining monumental, garishly lit edifices to house the game playing. The online house and the players can split the new cost savings, in the form of slightly better odds for the players, and a bigger net take for the house.

There are a number of obstacles to the spread of online gambling, however. Gambling is still illegal in quite a few states, and even the states that permit gambling tightly control the exact locations where it is permitted. There are also federal criminal laws prohibiting the use of the interstate telephone system to conduct gambling activities. Those who wish to set up private online gambling

operations will need to be very clever to skirt the application of the state and federal laws.

New online operators will also have to consider competition from the states themselves. Many states not only permit gambling in licensed casinos, they run their own gambling operations in the form of state lotteries, horse racing, and the like, raking in millions to supplement starved state budgets. These states could view privately operated online gambling as a major threat, sending the precious gambling money of the state's own citizens out across state borders into someone else's pockets. Similarly, the private physical casinos licensed by the states, especially in such prime locations as Reno, Las Vegas, and Atlantic City and on the Indian reservations, could find their hard-won state licenses and exclusive rights to run gambling businesses rendered meaningless by easily accessible online gambling parlors.

How might the states and their licensed casinos fight back? One way might be with very restrictive new laws, expressly criminalizing participation in online gambling by the state's citizens. Another way, possibly combined with the first, is to set up state operated or licensed online gambling operations as the only online gambling permitted within the state. Thus the states and their licensees could try to retain the gambling franchises for themselves, locking out newcomers trying to break open a new market on the computer networks.

The profits in running gambling operations are so great that such laws may not discourage new private operators from setting up shop anyway. For instance, online gambling parlors may be able to run their operations from offshore in some country friendly to their activities. They could make it easy for U.S. citizens in gambling-restricted states to participate entirely undercover and with no clue as to their real identities, using strong encryption techniques. Even if federal and state law enforcement agents find out about such operations, what can they do about them if the foreign country hosting them will not extradite, and they can't even figure out which U.S. citizens are involved due to the identity-cloaking encryption?

There is also the question of how winnings will be taxed, if the winners cannot be identified.

We don't have any answers yet, but it is clear that online systems raise difficult new questions about government control over gambling. How it will turn out is anyone's bet.

situation *closely*. There's little margin for error. If one is operating at the edge of criminality to begin with, a transmission that is only slightly excessive can easily be a criminal message. The system operator of such an online system takes on a strong responsibility to prevent all such transmissions.

It is easy enough to avoid such results: one should simply not run an online system devoted to skirting the edge of illegality, unless one is willing to become

> **If one is operating at the edge of criminality to begin with, a transmission that is only slightly excessive can easily be a criminal message.**

a trailblazer and personally test the exact scope of criminal laws in the online world. If so, then at the very least one should learn about the criminal laws that may apply to one's situation, from such sources as this book, some of the other references listed in Appendix J, and from an attorney if necessary. If the online system regularly hosts activities that are regulated under state or federal law, such as investment advice, brokerage, or degree-granting educational activities, make sure that the users involved in these activities are not skating too close to violating the regulations.

Where the System Operator Has No Knowledge of a Crime on the System

Can a system operator be guilty of a crime he or she does not know about? There is a simple answer to this one: no. This presumes, though, that the system operator is absolutely unaware that a crime is taking place on his or her system.

Crimes consist of two elements: a wrongful "act," and a criminal "intent." Without a criminal intent, such as intending to harm somebody or steal property, there is no crime. If a system operator does not know that a user is committing a crime on his or her online system, then he or she cannot possibly form an intent to further that crime, and will not be considered a criminal (we are not talking here about the situation in the preceding section, where system operators know about and even encourage the risky or dangerous nature of their online systems).

> **To remain safe from criminal prosecution as an accessory or facilitator of a crime, the operator should act affirmatively whenever suspicious activities appear to be taking place on your system.**

Unfortunately, real-life situations are a little more complicated. It's not always easy to tell what a system operator "knows" or "intends" for purposes of criminal liability. For example, a system operator may notice a certain user regularly exchanging files with several other users, and leaving public messages advertising racy materials available for other users. The system operator permits this user to continue these suspicious activities without doing anything about it, or even looking into it. If it turns out the user is regularly transmitting criminally obscene files, does the system operator "know" enough about this activity to be liable also? By not doing anything to prevent the criminal activity, has the system operator intentionally furthered that activity?

Such borderline situations—where the system operator sees enough to suspect that a user is involved in something illegal, but not enough to know for sure a crime is being committed—can be very risky for system operators. If it turns out that a crime really was committed, a judge or jury may feel that since the operator saw clearly suspicious events unfolding on the online system as the crime occurred, he or she should have done something to prevent it. To remain safe from criminal prosecution as an accessory or facilitator of a crime, the operator should act affirmatively whenever suspicious activities appear to be taking place on the system.

One approach is to confront users gently when they are observed performing suspicious acts on the system. The operator can be entirely straightforward, telling the user that certain activities have been observed that cause concern for the safety of the online system, other users, and the operator. Ask the user to explain what he or she is doing, and to agree to let his or her activities be monitored for a while. If the user satisfactorily explains away the problem, that is great (though it would not hurt if the operator kept a record of all communications with the user). If the user stonewalls, or gives weak excuses, or opposes the request to monitor his or her activities for a while, then in the name of self-protection the operator should consider booting the user off the system, and contacting the authorities about possible criminal activity.

Some might feel this approach too aggressive, that system operators should not lock out suspicious-looking users without definite evidence of a crime. This objection sounds good in principle, but it fails to take full account of the system operator's criminal exposure in these situations. If a user refuses to explain to the system operator exactly what the suspicious-looking activity is, it only makes it seem the user has something to hide. At that point, the system operator has a choice: permit the belligerent user to continue mysterious and possibly highly criminal activities on the online system without further question, or eliminate the risk by refusing further contact with the user. We would dump the belligerent user every time—what right does he or she have to insist on not cooperating with the system operator, leaving the operator wondering whether there is illegal activity on the system?

> **There are users who may be so sensitive about their privacy rights that they simply refuse to recognize reasonable system operator concerns as a matter of principle—they feel they are dealing with Big Brother instead of their friendly neighborhood system operator.**

There are users who may be so sensitive about their privacy rights that they simply refuse to recognize reasonable system operator concerns as a matter of principle—they feel they are dealing with Big Brother instead of their friendly neighborhood system operator. But honest dealings between system operators and users is one of the things that will encourage system operators to extend meaningful privacy to users. If users act trustworthy, system operators will feel more comfortable with keeping highly private e-mail on the system. On the other hand, paranoia only breeds more paranoia, and users paranoid about privacy invasions will breed system operator paranoia about what's being hidden. It is better to have frank discussion of questionable matters when they come up, and cooperation on both sides to make sure the system continues to operate comfortably. The system operator can start off right by approaching the user frankly with his or her concerns; the user can continue the process productively by responding honestly to the system operator's concerns, rather than taking sharp stands on users' privacy rights.

Another useful approach when suspicious activities occur is, once again, to consult a lawyer. This is one of the things lawyers are best for: analyzing complex legal situations, and helping one take steps that will best protect against any risks. A little money spent on a legal consultation at this point can save a lot of needless worry if it turns out a supposed problem creates little or no actual risk. It can also avoid serious trouble later if it turns out the user activities the operator observed were part of a major crime.

What if there appear to be no suspicious activities at all? We know that users might try anything, legal or illegal, while the operator is not looking. We know that other online systems have had their criminal problems. Perhaps it is just a matter of time until one's online system has its own criminal user episode. Does this general awareness that any online system theoretically can be used for a crime at any time, count as "knowledge" or "intent" for criminal law purposes? Can one's general knowledge that criminal activity is possible make one liable, even when criminal user activity occurs entirely without one's knowledge?

If the operator is prone to such thoughts, it is best to relax. Knowing that other online systems have had their problems does not mean one knows that one's own online system has problems. There is virtually no chance of system operator criminal liability without some kind of knowledge that specific criminal activity may be taking place on the online system. Unless the operator at least sees something suspicious taking place on the online system or hears about the possibility of specific illegal activities from others, he or she cannot possibly be held criminally liable. And if the operator does follow up on all possibly illegal activities that are discovered as recommended in this chapter, the risk will be close to nil.

Online System Seizure Where the System Operator Is Not a Suspect

In the preceding section, we discussed ways that system operators might be considered criminals in their own right if they don't act affirmatively against known suspicious activities on their online systems. Unfortunately, system operators face yet another major risk related to criminal activities: their online systems might be searched or seized by law enforcement agents pursuing online criminals.

The system operator is not charged with any crime in such cases, nor is the online system seized by agents as any kind of penalty against the system operator. They seize the online system to gather evidence against others thought to be criminals, or because they view the online system as a weapon or tool used by others to commit a crime. Nonetheless, a seizure of online system equipment will stop most system operators and their online system operations dead in their tracks. Mistaken law enforcement agents pursuing computer criminals can wreak damage on online systems far worse than any caused by the supposed criminals they seek.

It is unfortunate and unfair that system operators have to face this kind of risk to their online systems. Regardless of the "official" excuse for such seizures that might be issued by the authorities, seizing the online system of a system operator who is only a bystander to the alleged crime amounts to punishing the system operator for the crimes of another. Seizure also violates online system rights of freedom of speech and freedom of the press under the First Amendment. Somehow this can be overlooked by law enforcement officials in the heat of the moment. We imagine, though, that even when law enforcement agents are sure crimes are being committed, they would be far less likely to seize one of Prodigy's, CompuServe's, or America Online's host computers than the entire computer system used by a small online system operation.

> **Regardless of the "official" excuse for such seizures that might be issued by the authorities, seizing the online system of a system operator who is only a bystander to the alleged crime amounts to punishing the system operator for the crimes of another.**

This is not mere hypothesis. A few years ago, the customer support online system used by Steve Jackson Games, a major producer of role-playing adventure game systems, was seized by federal agents. They did not charge the online system owner with any crimes. They were after an "evil hacker" group called the Legion of Doom, and decided the group used this online system as a meeting place. As a result of their raid, the federal agents took several computers and computer equipment necessary for running the Steve Jackson Games business. The business floundered for almost a year afterward from being deprived of its own computer systems and records.

Steve Jackson Games eventually got most of its equipment back, and the business got back on its feet. It also brought a lawsuit against the U.S. government and the individual agents involved in seizing his equipment, which ended in a judgment that the government agents had violated the law, and partial reimbursement for the business losses. As bad as this event was for Steve Jackson Games, at least it ended in a case that will help create recognition that online systems are not just computer boxes that can be seized without thought, but sophisticated communications environments and electronic presses that should not be subject to arbitrary disruption by agents who don't understand online systems.

How can system operators guard against the risk of system seizure due to others' activities? Well, the most complete method is to turn the online system into the equivalent of a well-lit and heavily guarded prison camp. The operator can look through every single message, private and public alike, and every file, to make sure that nothing happens on the online system at any time without the operator's knowledge. While this approach might be complete, it will also scare off just about all potential system users. Few people like to conduct their affairs under a magnifying glass.

A better solution is to compromise with the unknown. Accept that part of the current online system environment is a small risk that the online system might be seized without warning. Keep a close enough eye on online system activities so that blatant misuse of the system will not escape attention, but do not monitor everything. Back up data regularly, so if the online system is seized, it can be set up again if necessary on a replacement system. And become familiar with the search and seizure rules, discussed in Chapter 7. If the operator and his or her attorney can handle the arrival of agents properly, it is possible to minimize the amount of equipment or materials they take away with them.

Searches and Seizures

All online systems face some risk of being seized by law enforcement officials investigating or prosecuting a crime. The chances of an innocent system being hit are rather small. It has happened, though, as in the notorious case of the seizure of the Steve Jackson Games BBS. It can happen again.

Sometimes it's not so clear whether a system is indeed "innocent." There are many system operators who deliberately run their systems close to the edge of illegality. Some do it for the principle of free speech. Their systems are pure forums for the free exchange of ideas, and many would sooner quit the business than act as censors. When the users of such a system indulge in illegal or suspicious activities, they put the entire system at risk.

Other system operators do not promote free speech per se, but employ it in practice by running systems devoted to unpopular or potentially illegal pursuits. It is perfectly legal to operate such systems, focused perhaps on theories about overthrowing the government, or discussions of user experiences with illegal drugs. Any sane operator of such a system, though, must be aware that it is operating at high risk. What if the treason or drug aficionados shift from idle discussion to criminal activities, and use the system as a communications resource for the group endeavor? The system could rapidly become evidence or instrument of a crime and be taken by the police, never to be returned. If the operator cares to keep the system running, then he or she must keep a watchful eye on the participants, at least in the common discussion areas.

Another class of system operators skirts the edges of legality in the pursuit of profits. There is money to be made online in hard-core pornography and bootlegged software. Apparently, quite a few operators are willing to provide trading posts to all comers, for a fee. Some rationalize this by saying they will stop carrying the risky stuff when they get their systems off the ground financially. Technically, the shrewd system operator may be able to slip out of responsibility for such illegal materials by turning a blind eye to user actions, and posting superficial notices that users may only upload files that are legally permitted on the system. But though operators may occasionally manage through this ruse to reap profits from others' illegal activities while avoiding personal responsibility, the system itself will not similarly be protected from search or seizure. When such systems are seized, the operator can certainly raise the defenses mentioned later in this chapter, though pressing technically available civil rights in such cases is no righteous appeal to grand principle, but mere loophole diving.

Searches and seizures are not entirely a chaotic matter. The police are supposed to follow certain rules. They (usually) don't just kick down the door and take your system on suspicion of a crime. This chapter gives a brief description and analysis of those rules. It also discusses the possibility of online systems being seized in noncriminal matters, such as noncriminal copyright infringement.

What Are the Rules?

The rights of system operators and owners against improper seizure of their online systems derive mainly from the Fourth Amendment to the U.S. Constitution. It states:

> *The right of the people to be secure in their persons, houses, papers and effects, against unreasonable searches and seizures, shall not be violated, and no Warrants shall issue, but upon probable cause, supported by oath or affirmation, and particularly describing the place to be searched, and the person or things to be seized.*

To this the Fifth Amendment adds that U.S. citizens will not be deprived of "life, liberty or property, without due process of law." While "due process" is not an intuitively obvious term, its meaning is simple: the authorities cannot act against you without giving you advance warning of their plans, and an opportunity to defend yourself.

Both principles are important protections against unjustified government intrusions, but they can also contradict each other. When police temporarily suspend your rights without warning in a Fourth Amendment search or seizure, you have received neither advance notice nor an opportunity to head off the seizure, as supposedly required by the due process clause of the Fifth Amendment. This contradiction is born of the practical need to catch criminals, since giving suspected lawbreakers

LambdaMOO, Mr. Bungle, and the Rebirth of Due Process

"Due process" is a central legal right in the United States. This requires notice of every legal action against a person, and an opportunity to defend oneself. Where did it come from? Don't bother picking up a history book. We can watch due process sprout online within virtual communities, as their desire for reliable online justice pushes back the anarchy and uncertainty of the untamed Net.

One striking example of this process was examined in 1993 by *Village Voice* writer Julian Dibbell. The article, titled "A Rape in Cyberspace," related some dramatic events that took place that year in a MUD called

LambdaMOO. "MUD" means "multi-user dungeon," real-time multi-user places that can be found at various Internet nodes. A "MOO" is an object-oriented MUD, enabling greater power in constructing imaginary worlds. LambdaMOO is a particularly advanced MOO maintained in a computer at Xerox PARC, the same research outfit that cooked up icons, desktop metaphors, and other familiar features found in almost all personal computers today.

From LambdaMOO's inception it had few formal social structures. Hanging out in LamdbaMOO was like being at a party, sustained in large part by the extensive leisure time available to the college students comprising much of its membership. One day a new participant showed up, a grotesque clown named Mr. Bungle. Soon after, Mr. Bungle went on a spree of virtual "rapes," using a "voodoo doll" program that enabled him to replace the self-descriptions of other MOO members' actions. The substitute descriptions appeared to others as if they were the genuine actions of the targeted members, with the targets helpless to correct the misimpression. Mr. Bungle put several members through descriptions of highly embarrassing sexual conduct in front of the other members, and kept going until someone came by with a program capable of forcing him out of the system temporarily.

Immediately afterwards, MOO members filled with rage and shame called passionately for Mr. Bungle to be "toaded" (terminating access privileges for Mr. Bungle—in other words, killing the character), the equivalent of an online lynch mob. There was a little problem with toading, though. The power to terminate member accounts was reserved for the system "wizards," who had declared before the Mr. Bungle event that they would not toad anyone unless it was clearly the collective will of the LambdaMOO membership.

However, there was no existing organized structure for expressing the will of LambdaMOO's members. This meant the members had to self-organize a government just to eject the shameful Mr. Bungle, and they started on this process. As it happened, Mr. Bungle received his wizardly toading before the process was finished. But a few weeks later, a democratic system was begun on LambdaMOO, and members began holding votes on important group issues and rules.

While building their online government, the members of LambdaMOO confronted the question of how it would treat the citizens. It was easy to respond like an angry, vengeful mob to the transgressions of Mr. Bungle, but now there was a government with its own fearful power. How could that power be properly applied, and mistakes and misuse avoided? The only acceptable answer was to build in due process, even for the lowly likes of Mr. Bungle. Thus, Mr. Bungle ended up getting a chance to defend himself and his actions, after being formally accused of violating LambdaMOO's rules. Like land-based governments, the Lambda-MOO government persisted after the precipitating cause of its existence was disposed of. It become a general instrument for self-governance of the LambdaMOO populace, for better or ill.

advance notice of every bust would assure that virtually none are ever apprehended. Nonetheless, police do sometimes mistakenly grab the wrong guy. That is why the Fourth Amendment requires that the police act reasonably, and that search or seizure warrants be issued only on probable cause.

Computers did not yet exist when the Constitution was drafted. Our Constitutional rights are not based on any specific technology, though. A person's computers and online accounts are the modern day versions of the "papers and effects" protected from unreasonable searches and seizures under the Constitution, and are fully entitled to the same protection. A police search of one's house, with the goal of seizing one's computer, is also indisputably a search covered by the rules of the Fourth and Fifth Amendments.

The law requires that when a seizure invokes First Amendment concerns, as when printers and sellers of books and newspapers are involved, law enforcement agents must be even more careful than when they perform normal searches and seizures.

There is additional Constitutional protection for online systems under the First Amendment guarantees of "freedom of the press" and "freedom of speech." The law requires that when a seizure invokes First Amendment concerns, as when printers and sellers of books and newspapers are involved, law enforcement agents must be even more careful than when they perform normal searches and seizures. An online system is no mere computer, but a publishing and distribution operation. While all searches and seizures of computers are subject to the limits of the Fourth and Fifth Amendments, using a computer to run an online system entitles it to the extra precautions guaranteed by the First Amendment.

Why would the government want to seize an online system or its contents? The motivations fall into two broad categories. The first is where the system owner or operator is suspected of personally committing a crime. The second is where the authorities are after someone else, and believe either that evidence of the suspect's crime can be found on the online system, or that the suspect used the online system to commit the crime. By the way, while these reasons may help us understand the government's motivation, they are not necessarily valid legal grounds for seizing an online system.

The Constitution, as described earlier, was designed to safeguard us from unjustified government intrusions in both of these situations. A policeman or other law enforcement agent wishing to search or seize an online system must first observe these basic rules:

- They must appear before a neutral magistrate. This is typically a state or federal judge. The job of the magistrate is to consider both the government's need to search the online system and the operator's need to have the search be as limited as possible, even in his or her absence.

- They must convince this magistrate, through the testimony of believable witnesses or informants, that there is "probable cause" to believe a crime has been committed, and that evidence relating to that crime is located on the online system they wish to search. This is not an easy task. Most magistrates are fully aware of the problems a search and seizure can cause to the subject, and will not authorize one unless they are strongly convinced that important evidence can be found on the online system.

- They must establish that the particular evidence they seek is likely to be located in the online system, and they must describe the particular place the evidence is believed to be located, and the particular evidence they wish to seize.

- If the magistrate is satisfied with the agents' proof on all of these points, then he or she will issue a search warrant. In deciding whether to issue the warrant, the magistrate must balance the importance of the government's need to intrude on a private system against the rights of system users to privacy and protection from such searches. The magistrate should consider whether the evidence claimed to be on the online system is important, and whether there is a less invasive means for the government to obtain the desired evidence.

The government is not permitted to invade a person's house merely to start a fishing expedition for incriminating evidence. Indeed, the Fourth Amendment was enacted precisely to prevent such practices, which had been commonly used by the British to suppress and harass colonial publishers and pamphleteers who spread views unpopular with the ruling class. The Fourth Amendment expressly requires that the warrant "particularly describ[e] the place to be searched, and the person or things to be seized." The affidavit submitted by the agents supporting their request for a search warrant should state that the person giving the affidavit (either a law officer or an informant) logged onto the online system and personally observed illegal material or necessary evidence on the system. Further, since an online system is full of information of all kinds involving many different users, the agents must describe the particular files and messages they seek in as much detail as possible, such as specifying all messages and files sent or uploaded by certain named individuals.

> **The government is not permitted to invade a person's house merely to start a fishing expedition for incriminating evidence.**

Police officers can conduct a search without a warrant only in "exigent circumstances." For example, suppose someone waves a gun around in public and runs into a house, and when the police follow him in the gun cannot be seen. They are permitted to hold the gunman and look for the gun. In contrast, it is hard to imagine what kind of exigency would similarly permit a warrantless search of a computer situated in one's living room. Always ask to see the warrant.

Though the police need a warrant before they can put their hands on a privately owned computer without permission, this does not prevent them from logging into the public areas of one's online system undercover. As in other social spheres, agents can go undercover online to gather evidence on potentially criminal activities. They may need internal clearance within their agencies, but there are no external legal requirements against an agent posing as a civilian to gather information, aside from the rule against entrapment. In addition, agents can even go into the most private areas of a system if the operator or others with authority to give such access invite them in. The Fourth and Fifth Amendments come into play only when the agents move from merely investigating to seizing evidence, or when they choose to go into systems or private system areas into which they have not been invited.

Sometimes it is suggested that asking a new user if he is a policeman, or posting signs stating that policemen are not authorized to use the online system, will create some kind of legal protection against undercover agents entering an online system. This is simply not so. Agents are not required to tell the truth about their identities—they will readily lie. If it was otherwise, law enforcement would be incapable of ever infiltrating criminal operations or running "sting" operations, and truly criminal operations could effectively resist all investigations.

Caution—FBI at Work

Cyberspace is crawling with cops today. The Software Publishers Association in 1994 stated they had about 2,000 bulletin boards under surveillance for software piracy, and that they believed 17% of all bulletin boards harbor illegal pirating operations. And the FBI (according to a formerly classified document from 1990 obtained by Computer Professionals for Social Responsiblity, in Washington, D.C.) is perfectly willing to eavesdrop on any online discussion where they don't believe the people in the discussion have a "legitimate expectation of privacy." To these groups we must add a number of other government agencies and private operators who are snooping around without boasting about it to the public.

Speaking of boasting, the most colorful media appearance by an online cop so far was made by "Phrakr Trakr" and his interstate Hi-Tech Crime Network. Phrakr Trakr cruises through hacker bulletin boards posing as a cyberpunk with attitude, fishing around for those who would readily trade illegal information such as active credit card numbers and telephone access codes. In a *New York Times* article in early 1993, he claimed to be studying nine different bulletin boards and working on cases with law officers in three states. His plans at the time were to build several cases and arrest a bunch of suspected criminals at once, because arresting just one online suspect would warn the others he was a cop instead of a cool dude. His musical warning to hackers, supposedly uploaded onto some hacker boards a couple of years ago, was, "Every move you make, Every breath you take, We'll be watching you."(Originally sung by a pop star named "Sting," of course.) Pretty impressive stuff, but to date there have been no announced arrests resulting from the great Trakr's efforts.

Are these cops dangerous? Some of them may be, but it doesn't pay to waste much effort worrying about them. Law enforcement agencies and police departments are realizing that this online thing is not a fad but a growing social movement. For the next several years they will be familiarizing themselves with the new landscape. They need to learn about both legal and illegal online systems, and how to tell them apart—which will ultimately benefit everyone who tries to run a clean system. So if cops are found or suspected to be on the system, the operator should not panic (unless he or she is knowingly hosting criminal activities there). They could very well just be stopping off to visit a pleasant, law-abiding watering hole for the online community, before heading out again to do battle with online criminals in the wilds of cyberspace.

Does the possibility that undercover agents might occasionally cruise through an online system put the operator personally at great risk? Not really, unless one is knowingly hosting illegal activities. If an operator follows up on all suspicious activities discovered, as recommended in this book, he or she cannot truthfully be charged with knowing involvement in criminal activities.

An agent may indeed see something happening publicly or privately on an online system of which its operator is not aware. In such cases, hopefully the agent would alert the operator about the problem instead of taking matters into his or her own hands by attempting to search or seize the system, thus respecting the operator's privacy, free speech, and property rights and those of the users. As a practical matter, most suspicious activities take place in private areas and e-mail rather than in public. Agents are barred from looking at most such materials without a warrant under the ECPA, although they might be able to get themselves invited into private discussion areas by posing as normal users.

In addition to the broad Fourth, Fifth, and First Amendment protections against searches and seizures, there are two federal statutes that give system operators and online systems added protection against police activities—the Electronic Communications Privacy Act ("ECPA") and the Privacy Protection Act ("PPA").

Special Restrictions Against Police Activity Under the ECPA

We pointed out that police need no special authority to enter the public areas of an online system, or other areas into which they may fool the operator into giving them entry, provided the operator has the authority to give them such access. Securely private areas and e-mail, however, are an entirely different story.

Ever since the Watergate scandal, the public has demanded a guarantee of the privacy of telephone discussions. This resulted in anti-wiretapping laws enacted in the 1970s, which were expanded in the late 1980s into the ECPA as we now know it. The ECPA

> **The ECPA protects personal privacy by treating government interceptions of private electronic communications as "searches and seizures" in the Fourth Amendment sense.**

protects personal privacy by treating government interceptions of private electronic communications as "searches and seizures" in the Fourth Amendment sense.

Three different kinds of online system privacy are protected:

1. *Intercepting Transmissions.* First, the ECPA prohibits government agents from freely intercepting private transmissions, such as messages sent between users while both are online, and real-time chat discussions in private areas. Before they can do so, they need to apply for special permission from a magistrate, and meet requirements much more stringent than for an ordinary warrant, as set forth in Section 2518. They have to specify exactly what they suspect the criminal activities to be, describe their sources, and describe exactly which system they wish to eavesdrop on, among other things. They also have to show that the

information they desire cannot be obtained through means less intrusive than eavesdropping on private discussions. The only exception is "emergency" situations, which are very narrowly defined in the statute.

2. *Stored Messages.* Second, the ECPA requires that agents must obtain a warrant to search or seize stored electronic communications that are less than 180 days old. It is not as difficult for them to obtain as the "super-warrant" necessary for interceptions, but the normal warrant requirements of specificity and probable cause must still be met. E-mail and other private communications can thus be stored in an online system for up to half a year with strong legal ECPA protection against official prying.

After a stored communication is more than 180 days old, it is easier for law enforcement agents to obtain. All they need is to obtain an administrative subpoena for such disclosure, which is not subject to stringent warrant requirements, and give advance warning to the parties involved in the communication, except in special circumstances. This still provides a level of protection, but it is reduced enough that system operators should consider keeping all communications older than 180 days off their system, such as in disk or tape archives stored outside the computer system, for maximum legal protection. Callers can be notified that if they wish to keep any messages older than 180 days, they should store them in their own computer systems.

Private e-mail may be stored on an online system for weeks before it is picked up by the recipient from his or her electronic mail box. Which set of rules controls government access to e-mail: the "super-warrant" privacy rules for government interceptions of communications, or the less stringent rules covering access to stored communications? On the one hand, e-mail could be said to be "in transmission" for the entire period between sending and receipt. On the other hand, it is stored on the online system for most of that period. This question was considered in only one case so far, *Steve Jackson Games vs. the U.S.* (discussed later in this chapter), and the federal appeals court held that unread e-mail in storage is not a transmission, but only a stored communication. Thus, the milder restrictions covering stored communications apply. As long as the unread message is in storage less than 180 days, the government still at least must obtain a normal warrant based on probable cause before gaining access to it; but stored messages over 180 days old are accessible under mere judicially ordered subpoenas.

> **If an operator announces to all users that access to all or part of an online system is private, and if he or she enforces the privacy rules, then government agents will need a warrant or super-warrant to eavesdrop on its activities.**

Can an entire section of an online system, or even a whole online system, be considered "private" for purposes of the ECPA controls on government electronic searches? It is likely they can be. If an operator announces to all users that access to all or part of an online system is private, and if he or she enforces the privacy rules, then government agents will need a warrant or super-warrant to eavesdrop on its activities. Remember, this does not prohibit undercover investigations. If a government agent fools a system operator into permitting him or her into a private area and becomes one of the participants, the agent can freely use whatever they see or receive in the shared private area without worrying about the ECPA.

The agent is an "authorized" recipient, even if he or she tricked the operator into giving authorization. Do not confuse this with entrapment, where government agents illegally induce suspects to commit crimes. Lying about one's identity for purposes of gaining entry does not entrap the unsuspecting operator into performing a crime, it just gains the agent entry into the area he or she wishes to investigate.

3. *User Information.* The third kind of ECPA protection, described in Section 2703, limits the ability of law enforcement agents to obtain information about the activities of users of online services. Certain basic information about a system user is readily obtainable by the government: user name, billing address, how long the user has used the service, and which features of the service were used. However, if an agent wants to know anything else about a user's activities on the system, he or she will have to present the system operator with a warrant meeting special requirements described in the ECPA. To get such a warrant, the agent must offer the judge "specific and articulable facts," showing that the desired user information is "relevant and material to an ongoing criminal investigation." In other words, the government can't just go on a fishing expedition survey of user activities, looking for suspicious patterns of service usage. While the warrant requirements of Section 2703 are not as stringent as what was described earlier as the "super warrant" necessary for intercepting transmissions, they are still more demanding than requirements for routine search and seizure warrants.

A very important point about the ECPA is that it protects the privacy of everyone who uses an online system. If government agents violate the ECPA, they violate not only the rights of the system owners and operators, but the rights of all users whose e-mail or private communications they come across. If agents wrongfully take the entire computer system used to run an online system and rummage through the contents, this is as gross a privacy violation as if they wrongfully raided an apartment building and seized the contents of everyone's mailbox.

How are your ECPA rights enforced? First, any materials seized in violation of the ECPA cannot be used by the government as evidence in court against you or anyone else. This is an application of the "exclusionary rule," used by courts to discourage government agents from performing wrongful activities when gathering evidence. The reasoning is if they can't use the wrongfully seized materials as evidence, agents will be more likely to follow proper procedures in their investigations.

Second, anyone whose property is seized in violation of the ECPA can sue the government for money damages. This can be a significant amount if, for instance, agents seize one or more computer systems, and prevent the victim of the wrongful search from operating his or her business.

Special Restrictions Against Police Activity Under the Privacy Protection Act

The PPA was enacted in 1980 to protect publishers' First Amendment right to freedom of the press. Its goal is to enable publishers and journalists to investigate and develop sensitive news stories without having their publishing activities "chilled" by fear of government interference. It is especially valuable for publishers who produce articles or books questioning the policies or activities of those in government or with strong influence in the government.

The PPA prohibits agents from searching or seizing certain publishing materials unless they have "probable cause" to believe the person possessing the materials is involved in a crime, and that the materials sought are also involved in that crime. This is an extension of the usual warrant require-

The PPA prohibits agents from searching or seizing certain publishing materials unless they have "probable cause" to believe the person possessing the materials is involved in a crime, and that the materials sought are also involved in that crime.

ments. Normally, a government agent seeking a warrant need only show the magistrate he or she has probable cause to believe the materials sought are necessary for investigating or proving a crime. This is not enough to support a warrant to search or seize publishing materials under the PPA, however. There has to be good reason to believe that both the publisher or journalist holding the materials, and the materials themselves, are involved in the commission of a crime (the same crime), or the agent is prohibited from performing the search. In addition, the agent has to show that the suspected crime is more than merely the crime of possessing the materials sought.

Protected materials are divided by the statute into two categories: "work product" and "documentary materials." Work product is material produced by the journalist or publisher in preparation for a story—notes, outlines, unfinished articles, and so on. Documentary materials are any records of facts or events—interview transcripts, photographs, notes of conversations—again, in connection with a planned publication of some sort.

Both online systems and their users are protected by the PPA to the extent they act as publishers and maintain publishing-related materials on the system. Some online systems act as electronic publishers of news and newsletters, both posted locally within the online system and transmitted to other online systems. Others publish by offering users access to various kinds of databases maintained on their systems.

Most or all such publisher online systems certainly maintain materials relating to their publishing activities on the system. Users also perform publishing-related activities on online systems, such as development and distribution of electronic newsletters, e-mail, files for distribution to others, and World Wide Web entries. Indeed, anything normally contained in computer directories devoted to World Wide Web pages, editing, or services has a good chance of being protected under the PPA. Journalists use online systems to gather information, and may keep e-mail stored on the online system for use as a resource when writing their stories. Much of the information in this book was obtained on online systems, and often stored in those online systems for a period, as well as in my home computer system. All of these items, whether owned by system operators or users, would be entitled to PPA protection.

Government agents will also trigger PPA protection if they try to seize an entire online system containing publishing-related materials anywhere on the system. In any such case, agents would have to produce a warrant indicating they reasonably suspect the possessor of the materials him or herself of a crime in connection with the materials.

The victim of a search that violates the PPA can start a private legal action for money damages against both the government and the individual agents who perform the wrongful search or seizure. The only defense available to such agents is a "reasonable good faith belief" that their conduct was lawful. Normally, such a test assumes that the agents are aware of the PPA as a law restraining their powers to intrude on publishing-related operations. However, agents who violate the PPA by searching online systems or materials may try to defend their actions by saying, "I didn't know the law applied to online systems." In the only online PPA case decided so far, *Steve Jackson Games vs.*

U.S., the court gave this ignorance-based test of reasonableness some credence, as discussed later. Hopefully, as public familiarity with computer networks and the "Information Superhighway" grows, courts will not follow the lead of the *Steve Jackson Games* case on this score. Indeed, the courts should *never* excuse agents from responsibility for injuring others on the basis of the agents' total bewilderment about the application of the law. Government agents can disrupt thoroughly the lives of others. It is not too much to ask that those agents be completely familiar with the limits on their conduct imposed by the very government for which they work.

> **The victim of a search that violates the PPA can start a private legal action for money damages against both the government and the individual agents who perform the wrongful search or seizure.**

The PPA, unlike the ECPA, is not enforced through the exclusionary rule. Evidence seized in violation of the PPA may be used in any legal action by the government.

The ECPA and PPA Compared

There is a fair degree of overlap between the protections of the PPA and the ECPA. There are also significant differences, which means having the benefits of both the ECPA and PPA gives system operators and users broader protection against searches and seizures.

- The ECPA covers only "communications" and user-related information, while the PPA protects *all* publishing-related work product and documentary material, even if they are privately kept by the author/owner and not communicated to anyone else.

- All private online system communications and user information are covered by the ECPA regardless of their subject matter, while only publishing-related materials are covered by the PPA.

- The ECPA requires a "super-warrant" for intercepting real-time transmissions, a special warrant for obtaining most user information, a regular warrant for access to stored communications less than 180 days old, and some lesser form of government authorization for stored communications over 180 days old. The PPA requires that the agent show probable cause to believe the possessor of the materials sought is personally involved with a crime, regardless of the age of the materials.

- Agents searching and seizing online system materials are legally required to keep the differing ECPA and PPA requirements absolutely straight. A warrant sufficient to seize certain online system materials under the ECPA may not be sufficient to permit those agents to seize those same materials if they are also covered by the PPA, and vice versa.

- The ECPA is enforced both through making the materials obtained by violating the ECPA inadmissible in any government prosecutions (the "exclusionary rule"), and by giving injured persons the right to sue the government for violations. The PPA is not enforced through the exclusionary rule, but it does give victims of wrongful seizures the right to sue not only the government, but also individual government agents who violate the PPA in seizing publishing-related materials.

When the Police Knock on the Door

If police or other government agents show up at the door one day to search an online system, we suggest the following:

- Find out the names of the agents, and the government agency, office or department they represent. Write this information down. Otherwise, if they disappear with one's system or other materials, a lot of time could be wasted tracking them down.

- Ask to see the warrant. Look at it closely. Is it signed? Does it name your house or premises? Does it specify the exact files, equipment, or messages the agents are authorized to search or seize?

- In the heat of the moment, and the agents' likely desire to move quickly, one may not be able to study the warrant at length before letting them in. Remember that the warrant is supposed to spell out the scope of the search they are permitted to conduct. If they don't have a warrant, they probably don't have a right to enter the house. The operator should ask calmly the authority for their search, and if he or she does not want them in the house or office, should tell them they are not welcome without a warrant. They will likely leave, possibly to get a warrant and come back again in a little while. Call an attorney immediately.

- If they have a warrant, be courteous and allow them into the house. Call an attorney immediately. It would be best, if at all possible, to have a lawyer present while the search is being conducted. The police are not required to wait for one's lawyer to arrive, but courteous or nervous policemen may comply with a request that they do so.

- Once the agents show their warrants and enter one's home or place of business, they may move swiftly to "secure the area," and may even have their guns out. This does not mean they're planning to shoot anyone—they're just making sure they're adequately protected in the face of the unknown. After all, they're conducting the search because they believe criminal activity is occurring.

- This phase should be over rapidly, and the agents should begin performing the search authorized by the warrant. If the warrant authorizes them to seize certain files on a computer, then properly they should only copy those files onto their own disk, or take the original disk and permit the owner to keep a copy, possibly minus the specific files named in the warrant. If the warrant authorizes them to take the computer system used for communications, then properly they will take that computer, and leave all other equipment on the premises. Make sure to get a complete receipt showing everything seized.

- Courteously, and upon consultation with an attorney, one should suggest to the agents less invasive means of completing their search. Ask to talk to the person in charge of the search. Point out that:

    - the computers are needed for daily work, and the police can obtain whatever they need merely by copying from the hard disks;

    - even if they are authorized to take the computers, they do not need to take the monitors, external modems, printers, or other equipment or peripherals;

- there are stored messages less than 180 days old on the system, which are strongly protected by the Electronic Communications Privacy Act;

- there are publishing-related work product and documentary materials on the system, which are protected by the First Amendment and Privacy Protection Act (if applicable);

- they need not seize any computer equipment or data other than that used to operate the online system, at most; and

- the online system computer is protected not only by the Fourth and Fifth Amendments, but also by the First Amendment, just like books and newspapers. This means the agents have to be especially careful to take only those items validly listed in the warrant, and not affect any First Amendment publishing and speech activities of the online system.

These tactics are all worth a try, though their effectiveness will vary from case to case. The goal is to make sure the agents are fully informed of the nature of the materials or systems they seek, and are encouraged to respect the legal limits on their authority.

- Don't answer questions or volunteer any information without legal consultation. The police are not required to read rights before seizing a system, unless they are also about to make an arrest, but any statements made can still be used against a person if he or she is arrested later. It is often said that the innocent are the ones most likely to get in trouble by volunteering statements to the police.

> **The police are not required to read rights before seizing a system, unless they are also about to make an arrest, but any statements made can still be used against a person if he or she is arrested later.**

- One important piece of information worth learning is whether they are seizing equipment or data based on the operator's own activities or those of others. Finding this out early can help the operator and attorney formulate the best way to approach the police precinct, agency, or judge later in seeking to recover the seized materials. Again, remember it is best not to volunteer any information when trying to find this out.

- If it's discovered that there are no charges against the operator personally, the operator should suggest very strongly that if the police seize the system in pursuit of someone else who used it, they will be gravely injuring the operator both as an innocent bystander and as a publisher. The agents should understand that the online system is not a weapon or tool for committing crimes, but a publishing operation.

Remember that not all "searches" involve physically entering one's house. As we discussed above, agents can peruse the public areas of an online system, and any private areas they might infiltrate undercover, without any need for a warrant. In addition, if agents obtain a warrant under the ECPA to wiretap an online system, they will not announce their presence. They will just listen in on the transmissions to and from the online system as authorized by the warrant.

The Show Biz Cops of Oklahoma City

In 1993, local police investigated the Oklahoma Information Exchange BBS in Oklahoma City, on suspicion that it was selling obscene material. After two purchases from BBS owner Tony Davis, they returned in force and seized several adult CD-ROMs from the stock he maintained for his CD-ROM retail business. They did not stop there, however. They also grabbed his BBS computer equipment and arrested Davis.

The event had little chance of passing unnoticed. The police brought along a professional video camera and videotaped the whole affair. Afterwards, they turned it into a weekly installment of a local reality television program called "You're Busted," broadcast throughout the Oklahoma City area four days after the raid. For that extra dose of reality, the episode was narrated by one of the policemen who searched Davis' place and arrested him.

As the police burst in on Davis, the voice-over informed TV viewers they were witnessing the headquarters for Davis' "international pornographic network." The police confiscated roughly 57 of 2,000 CD-ROMs on hand for Davis' CD-ROM retail business, under 3% of his total stock. Later in the show, the video camera focused on a computer screen showing user names as they downloaded files from CD-ROMs mounted on Davis' BBS. The narrating officer knowingly explained to the TV audience that they were seeing BBS users "viewing the smut" right then and there. At the end of the show, the narrator belted out the show's theme: "Tony Davis, you're busted!"

Federal protections for online systems and their operators and sysops were ignored wholesale in the Davis raid. The Electronic Communications Privacy Act was ignored when messages stored on the system were seized without a proper warrant, and when the names of users downloading from CD-ROMs were not only viewed by the police, but broadcast to thousands of viewers of "You're Busted." Since Davis' business activities included publishing his own "Magnum" series of CD-ROMs, none of which the police found obscene, the Privacy Protection Act was violated when they seized computers containing the materials used for publishing those CD-ROMs.

Why did the police pick on Davis, and with so little regard for his rights and the rights of system users? It certainly wasn't due to their keen law enforcement instincts. Despite the screaming headlines about online porn merchants, Davis was a well-known and respected businessman. It was also far from clear that the CD-ROMs they seized were obscene. The same titles were advertised regularly in *PC Magazine*, a national publication with over one million circulation.

Local sources blame his troubles on the creepy little deal between the local police and the makers of the "You're Busted" television program. The TV station gave the police a professional video camera and the opportunity to shoot, script, and narrate a TV program. The police officers got to feel like TV stars. In return, the station received a hugely popular "reality television" show, an exclusive relationship with the police not enjoyed by other local stations, and low production costs.

A great business deal for the police and the television station, but terrible news for due process in Oklahoma City. The police pay less attention to protecting the community and more to show biz. On-the-scene arrests make the best TV, so the police are more motivated to search and arrest, less concerned about whether the intrusion on people's lives is justified. In fact, the more individuals they intrude on, the better the "You're Busted" episode. They hit the jackpot on the Oklahoma Information Exchange BBS. Hundreds of users trusted that they had rights of privacy from the government, and the Oklahoma City police betrayed that trust. In the end, Tony Davis was sentenced to ten years in prison, under appeal as this book goes to press. That's show biz.

After the Search or Seizure

If government agents have seized an operator's computer or data files, naturally he or she will want to try and get them back.

The first thing to do is contact a local attorney, if this has not already been done. Ideally, this should be a criminal defense attorney specifically familiar with the search and seizure rules applicable to electronic communications services or publishers. If no one with these credentials is available in the local area, find a mainstream criminal defense attorney, and provide him or her with the references in this book to the ECPA and PPA.

Other good contacts include the Electronic Frontier Foundation, or any attorney who is genuinely familiar with the law of online systems. The EFF's contact information at the time of publication is listed in Appendix J. The EFF's lawyers or the other lawyers may be interested in helping directly, or they may be able to make a referral to an attorney or to someone who can assist in the computer-related aspects of the case.

There is no cut-and-dried approach to dealing with the authorities at this point. The government has the equipment, and the operator wants it back. Since the agents already took the trouble to take it to their office, they will most likely want to look at the contents of the hard disk before giving it back. It can become difficult to communicate with government agents about an investigation after they withdraw to their offices.

One's strategy really should be formulated with the attorney. Efforts to recover the equipment might be directed at first to the agency or police station itself, and afterwards to a judge with jurisdiction over the matter, possibly the same judge who issued the warrant or authorized the seizure. Some tactics to consider include:

- Attack the validity and execution of the search warrant. If federal agents seized the equipment, the operator can move for return of the seized materials under Rule 41(e) of the Federal Rules of Criminal Procedure due to violation of the warrant particularity requirements, and for suppression of any evidence that was seized. Some of the following arguments may be worthwhile:

- There was no probable cause for the search. For example, the affidavit or other materials submitted in support of the warrant request may be defective. Call to the judge's attention misstatements or omissions in the affidavit or other materials.

- The warrant was defective because it did not describe the items to be searched and seized with particularity, nor the place they would be found. If the information supporting the warrant is that messages involving a single individual might be involved in criminal activities, then the scope of the authorized search should be strictly limited to copying messages addressed to or from that individual from the online system to the agents' own disks; all other messages or materials should not be looked at or seized by the agents.

- The agents applied for and obtained the wrong kind of warrant. The protections of the ECPA and/or the PPA likely apply to one's online system, and they require special kinds of warrants for lawful searches or seizures of the system.

- The search was unnecessary. For example, the agents may have already downloaded the information they sought from one's system. The seizure therefore added no new evidence to their case.

- The actual search as executed was overly broad. For example, the police not only took the computer and disk on which the online system was installed, they took the monitor, printer, and modem and the kid's video game machine as well.

Since law enforcement officials in most jurisdictions are not very familiar with computer (let alone online system) technology, chances are pretty good they will make one or more substantial errors in obtaining the warrant or executing the search. If one can prevail in this effort early, the seized materials may be returned quickly.

- Try to impress the agents or judge with the urgent need to recover the equipment to run the business or prevent injury to oneself and others. Try to convince them to review first the material most desperately needed to resume operations, and to release the materials.

- Law enforcement officials may respond better if one only asks permission to make copies of certain files from the materials being held, and let them keep the originals. This way they know they're not letting any potential evidence slip out of their grasp. It's a judgment call whether it is better to ask for everything back at once, or only for copies of certain files while they keep everything seized.

- Consider publicizing the search and seizure, and any improper retention of materials. This is a delicate matter. Sometimes letting the light of day shine on questionable law enforcement activities encourages the agents to make an extra effort to conform to the limits on their search and seizure powers. It is equally possible, though, that publicizing the affair will make the agents react by declaring that they caught a craven criminal in the nick of time, and increase their unwillingness to return any materials.

- If the materials were not seized as a weapon or tool used by the operator for a crime charged to him or her, but in the course of pursuing others who happened to use the operator's online system as a communications medium, this should be continually emphasized to the judge and other authorities. Alert all users and others who may have communications or publishing-related materials stored on one's online system that they have been seized by the authorities. Their rights might well be violated, and they deserve to make their voices heard to the seizing authority and to the judge. One can definitely make a stronger impression on the authorities when accompanied by a group of injured citizens.

- If the agents say that they need to keep the original files as evidence necessary for trial, the operator (or more properly, the attorney) should respond that under the Federal Rules of Evidence, Rule 1001, the agents can use computer copies of the hard disk as original evidence for trial purposes. Therefore, the operator is entitled to have original disks and files back, and the agents can make any copies from those disks for the purpose of preserving evidence.

What Really Happens?

We've had a look at the rules in place for government agents to follow, and strategies to encourage them to comply with those rules. Now let's look at some of the situations that have actually occurred in the online system and network world.

Steve Jackson Games

The most important, and perhaps most dramatic, online system search and seizure so far was performed by federal agents on the Steve Jackson Games online system on March 1, 1990. The

We Took Your Computers, But Forgot the Charges . . .

"Rusty and Edie's" was one of the largest and most lucrative bulletin board systems in the United States, with roughly 14,000 subscribers. There weren't many rules on the system, which made it extremely popular with those

who were tired of rules, but also led to grumbling among other system operators that the Rusty and Edie's system was full of illegal materials. Over 120 personal computers were networked together to run the system, overcrowding and overheating the home of owners Rusty and Edie Hardenbaugh. They were having a separate structure built in the backyard, just to contain the hot pile of metal and circuitry running their system.

In January 1993, the FBI raided Rusty and Edie's, with the Software Publishers Association tagging along, and took all 120 computers running the system. The raid was based on accusations that the system contained infringing copies of many major software packages. Rusty and Edie reportedly brought it on themselves when they refused to accommodate a small software developer, who had asked them to remove an infringing copy of his program from the system. The developer called the FBI, who in turn brought in the SPA, and they found a number of suspected infringements.

Unfortunately for Rusty and Edie, this happened at a time when both the FBI and the SPA were itching to bust an online copyright infringer. Just two months earlier, in November 1992, the SPA had succeeded in having the copyright law changed to make its criminal provisions much more easily triggered. Now, it is a felony to possess ten or more infringing copies with a value of $2500 or over—a threshold easily surpassed by any computer system with a few copies of pirated software. But it was not enough just to pass the law. To deter infringement, the law had to be demonstrated to the public. In addition, the SPA felt something dramatic had to be done to combat the growing volume of software infringement online. Rusty and Edie's made the perfect example. The SPA could demonstrate the new criminal copyright provisions and give warning to the online community in one fell swoop, by taking down one of the best-known and most successful bulletin board systems in existence.

The raid was conducted in the fashion perfected by SPA in its "don't copy that floppy" campaign against large corporations: strike fast and grab everything. While it is hard to say for sure whether all applicable warrant requirements were met, the fact that all the computers were grabbed potentially invokes nearly every provision of the ECPA and PPA. For instance, if any real-time messages were in transit on the system and retained at the time it was seized, the ECPA's prohibition against interception may have

been violated. Stored messages between system users, and nearly all user information, would also be protected by the ECPA, especially from any police browsing after the raid. And if there were any materials being retained or prepared for publishing purposes on the system, which was very likely on a system as large and varied as Rusty and Edie's, the narrowly defined warrant requirements of the PPA would have to be met before the parts of the system holding those materials could be seized. Conceivably, the FBI could have obtained warrants meeting all applicable requirements, but it seems unlikely.

The latest and most bewildering development is that as we go to press, almost two years after the raid, Rusty and Edie still have not been indicted. They are convinced it is because the FBI and SPA did not find anything wrong. More likely, it is due to two other factors. First, as mentioned above, there may have been a lot of gaps in the warrants under which the system was seized.

Second, the SPA seems to be engaged in a larger plan to frighten the public about the dire consequences of getting caught being an online infringer. A few months before the Rusty and Edie's raid, a smaller bulletin board, Davy Jones Locker, had been seized for copyright infringement under the old copyright law, which had milder criminal copyright provisions. An indictment was announced in that case in Fall 1994, almost two years after the raid, with much fanfare from the Justice Department about it being the first indictment ever of a computer bulletin board for a criminal copyright infringement (funny how law enforcement types like to crow about finding new kinds of criminals). The SPA's plan thus may be to get the Davey Jones Locker prosecution under way, and when it is resolved, announce the Rusty and Edie's indictment. This would have a one-two punch effect on the public. First, a bulletin board is busted and sentenced for criminal copyright infringement; then, just when the risks of online infringement based on that case seemed clear, another indictment follows under the new, more easily triggered criminal copyright provisions, which can make a felon out of even casual infringers. The SPA's strategy seems to be that by keeping would-be infringers guessing about the risks of infringement, infringement will be reduced.

agents were hot on the trail of a youthful hacker group known as the "Legion of Doom," and thought it could be found at Steve Jackson Games. The evidence of the company's involvement was pretty thin—one of the suspected members of LOD worked a daytime job at the company.

The fact was, Steve Jackson Games had nothing to do with hackers invading telephone and computer networks. It was a small company that designed and published role-playing games, and otherwise minded its own business. It did run a computer bulletin board, but for nothing more sinister than customer support. The government agents, if they considered the company's actual involvement in LOD activities at all, may have just written it off as a front for LOD. And if they had any doubts, they didn't let that stop their dramatic raid.

When the agents appeared at the company's headquarters, they nearly broke down the door before agreeing to use a key offered by an employee. They produced a search warrant, but apparently only an unsigned photocopy—in other words, there was no evidence at the time that they really had obtained a search warrant. The agents cut locks with bolt-cutters and ripped open cardboard boxes. Eventually, they took not only the online system computer, but a large quantity of computer parts on a repair bench, a laser printer, and other items that don't have much to do with the daily operation of an online system or storage of its files.

The most illustrative aspect of the seizure was their confiscation of all copies of a book then under development at Steve Jackson Games: "GURPS Cyberpunk," a role-playing game to be published in book form ("GURPS" stands for "Generic Universal Role-Playing System"). The book described, among other things, various exotic ways to break into computer and security systems in an imaginary future world. When the agents leafed through it they thought they hit the jackpot, calling the book a handbook for computer crime and taking all copies of it with them.

The only problem was that all of the security-cracking techniques in GURPS Cyberpunk were entirely fictional, and would have been quickly seen as such by anyone familiar with the field. The agents, unfortunately, did not have anyone with such knowledge on the search team—symptomatic of the utter lack of knowledge and judgment with which the search and seizure were conducted as a whole.

The problems did not end there for Steve Jackson Games. Their computer equipment and data files were retained for a very long period, despite repeated attempts by their lawyer to recover them for the business. The disruption and loss of data and equipment caused great losses to the business and forced it to let employees go. Eventually, the GURPS Cyberpunk game was completed and released to the public, and Steve Jackson Games restored its business more or less back to normal. Neither Steve Jackson nor his company were ever charged with any crime, nor were any crimes charged against others as a result of the wrongful raid.

The matter did not end there. After pausing to catch its breath, Steve Jackson Games took the offensive and sued the U.S. government for the wrongful raid of its business. It sought compensation for injury to its business, and just as important, to establish in the law books that government agents cannot violate laws created to curb their conduct when investigating online systems. It was aided in this effort by, among others, the Electronic Frontier Foundation.

Steve Jackson Games sued both the U.S. government and the individual agents responsible for the illegal raid. It made claims under the ECPA because the seized online system computers contained stored private communications, and under the PPA because the raid affected materials being prepared for publication (such as the GURPS Cyberpunk materials). Eventually, it had to drop the claims against the individual agents, potent as they were, because pending objections to those particular claims could have delayed the trial by a year or more.

After trial, the judge held in favor of Steve Jackson Games. The government had indeed violated its own laws, causing needless injury to a private, innocent business. Taking the company's computers and holding them for weeks, browsing through e-mail from the online system, was held a complete violation of the ECPA—especially the rights of the *users* of the Steve Jackson Games system. Several users who joined with Steve Jackson Games as plaintiffs were awarded relatively small amounts of $1000 each. In addition, the company's rights as a publisher under the PPA were violated. The court awarded Steve Jackson Games $51,000, a significant amount, though far less than the company asked for.

Overall, it was an impressive step forward for online civil rights, forcing the government and its agents to acknowledge limits on their powers in the online arena. There were, though, a couple of disappointing aspects to the decision.

First, the judge gave some credence to the agents' argument that their raid was not illegal because they had no idea there was a law covering raids on online communications and publishing systems. This resulted in holding that the initial seizure of the computers by the ignorant agents was not illegal. According to the court, the ECPA and the PPA were only violated afterwards, when the agents found out about the laws and did not promptly return the seized computers. It is hard to accept this ruling as reasonable. The agents had ample opportunity to review the nature of the system and consult with knowledgeable government attorneys *before* the raid, which would have made them fully informed about the ECPA, PPA, and the applicable warrant requirements. By excusing an ill-conceived raid based on ignorance, the judge handed the government a ready excuse for future disruptive raids: just give the assignment to agents who don't know about the applicable laws.

> **By excusing an ill-conceived raid based on ignorance, the judge handed the government a ready excuse for future disruptive raids: just give the assignment to agents who don't know about the applicable laws.**

The other disappointment was the judge's ruling that e-mail sent, but not yet received, is not an "intercepted transmission" for purposes of the ECPA, but only a stored communication. Although the message is covered by the ECPA either way, the rules against interception are stronger than the rules against obtaining stored messages. In addition, for stored messages there is the loophole in which messages older than 180 days are available for search or seizure without even a warrant. This particular holding was appealed by Steve Jackson Games, but it was affirmed by the appellate court.

These disappointments show there is further work to do in securing the civil rights of online operators and users. Nonetheless, the Steve Jackson Games case, bad as it was for the victim of the illegal raid, marks a good start in the development of the law protecting all of us (in the United States, at least) from intrusive government activities.

The Smaller They Are, the Harder They Fall

In this chapter we see many tales of *Sturm und Drang*, jolting accounts of online systems both guilty and innocent ripped from homes and offices by the agents of law and order. Well, guess what? Searches and seizures are mainly for the little guys.

Larger online systems, such as America Online, CompuServe, and Prodigy, have not had any of their computers raided lately. When there's a problem with users of the system, the legal authorities work with the owners and managers of the system. They cooperate to set traps to catch the problem users in illegal activities, identify and track down users suspected of crimes, and shut down any criminal operations that may have set themselves up on the system.

Why the disparity in official treatment of large and small online systems? In the case of large, institutional company systems with their own buildings or corporate compounds, law enforcement officials understand perfectly the difference between the

company running the system and the users of that system. Agents also have good reason to move cautiously against large companies. If they make any mistakes or overstep their bounds, they are likely to get in trouble at their jobs. The larger companies with online systems cultivate relationships with local police and government agents, strengthening the sense that private company and public law officials are cooperating to curb illegal use of the system.

It is harder for law enforcement agents to tell whether the operator of a small online system is attempting to run a clean system, or is in cahoots with people illegally using it. In contrast with a small storefront business, with which a small online system otherwise has many similarities, the online system is not out on the street but tucked away in some small office, attic, or basement, lending a secretive and potentially suspicious air to the operation. In addition, the operators of small online systems may not have much sophistication in dealing with either the authorities or with criminal behavior on the system. Under these circumstances, law enforcement agents can wrongly jump to the conclusion that if there is a crime on a small system, then the system itself is a criminal operation.

How can smaller systems protect themselves from being confused with criminals who choose to take up residence in their systems? First, of course, make sure all criminal users and operations that come to their attention are quickly moved off the system. Second, consider educating the local authorities, perhaps as part of a group of local system operators. Offer to inform the local police and government agents about the system, how it works and what it does; illustrate the stark difference between the operator of a system, and the misguided users who might try to misuse it for some illegal or improper purpose; offer to cooperate in any investigations involving users suspected of criminal activities; and enlist their help in keeping the system free of illegal users and activities. Third, try to maintain an organization of local system operators with relationships with the local police and government agents. To a certain extent, such a group with its own local presence can act as a counterpart to the institutional aura surrounding larger corporations, and help achieve the proper recognition from the authorities that smaller systems deserve as much respect as larger ones.

Other Seizures

Steve Jackson Games was far from the only bulletin board system or user treated to a government raid, though it may be the most starkly clear case of an entirely innocent system and system operator seriously injured by official bumbling. Some of the other notable searches and seizures in the past few years include:

- *Operation Sundevil.* On May 8, 1990, the U.S. Secret Service used 150 agents, aided by local law enforcement, to execute 28 search warrants in 13 cities across the country in Operation Sundevil, a nationwide offensive against computer "hackers" directed mainly at the bulletin boards thought to be their hangouts. This carefully planned strike was dramatic and fear-inspiring at the inception, but ended up a fiasco by most accounts, resulting in few arrests, indictments, or sentences. This affair is, rightly, the source of much of the perception that while law enforcement agents have a lot to learn in their pursuit of crime online, that does not stop them from creating online disasters right and left as they blunder after supposed wrongdoers.

- *Operation Longarm.* On March 5, 1993, U.S. Customs used 300 agents, aided by local law enforcement, to execute 31 search warrants in 15 states and 30 cities across the country in Operation Longarm, a nationwide offensive against child pornography on computer networks. More on this in Chapter 8.

- *Oklahoma Information Exchange.* See "The Show Biz Cops of Oklahoma City" in this chapter.

- *Rusty and Edie's.* See "We Took Your Computers, But We Forgot the Charges . . ." in this chapter.

- *Ware House BBS.* See "The Connecticut Bomb Factory" in this chapter.

- *Akron Anomaly.* In June 1992, local police in Akron, Ohio grabbed the Akron Anomaly bulletin board system on vague child pornography charges. The system operator eventually pleaded guilty to one count of "attempted possession of a criminal tool" (meaning the computer), and encountered great difficulties trying to regain possession of the system from the local police.

- *Copyright Raids in Texas.* On August 23, 1994, the FBI reportedly raided 5 or more bulletin board systems in Texas on suspicion of software copyright infringement. In at least two of the raids, against the User-to-User and Agents of Fortune bulletin boards, it appears the agents did not take down the systems but only copied files. Perhaps they are starting to learn.

- *Offworld BBS.* In January 1993, the FBI seized the Offworld BBS bulletin board system in St. Louis, consisting of $40,000 worth of equipment with 4,300 users, on pornography charges. The operator maintained that he routinely eliminated all pornographic materials he discovered, and kicked the users responsible for the postings off the system.

- *Tom Tcimpidis.* This was the first well-publicized bust of an innocent system operator. Tom Tcimpidis ran a bulletin board in L.A. While he was on vacation, his online system was seized and taken apart by the state police because stolen credit card numbers posted by a user were discovered on it. He was charged with criminally publishing credit card numbers, but the charges were ultimately dropped, apparently because the prosecution realized Mr. Tcimpidis did not have any idea the stolen numbers were on his system. It is nice that the officials figured out this system operator was not a criminal, but their "seize first, ask questions later" approach caused him great loss.

- *Alcor Life Extension.* An unusual case involved Alcor Life Extension Foundation, a reputable cryogenics group based on the West Coast whose entire online system files were seized in the course of a local investigation of a missing human head. A group of online system users whose private mail was on the online system sued the agents who performed the seizure for damages based on violation of their rights under the ECPA, and after a year obtained a payment in settlement.

Why Do These Problems Occur?

Law enforcement agents disregarded Constitutional rules in many of the searches and seizures described above, causing undeserved injury to innocent bystanders. The damage most likely was not intended. After all, government agents are not out to injure the public, but to protect us from wrongdoers. So why do computer raids sometimes go so wrong?

This question has been debated widely in the networks and online systems over the past few years, in discussions that include government agents and prosecutors who specialize in computer crime. Four likely reasons have emerged for the seeming lack of regard for the rules in publicized computer system seizures by many government agents.

First, many law enforcement agents are not familiar with either online culture or the laws that apply to networks and online systems. When a government agent tosses a seized online system computer in the

> **Most agents and police officers have not been taught that properly executing a search warrant for online system files means interfering as little as possible with the daily operations of the online system.**

back seat of his car, he or she may not realize it contains private messages between many people who called from their homes and businesses to the online system operated on that computer; it's just a box full of circuitry in the back seat. To date, most agents and police officers have not been taught that properly executing a search warrant for online system files means interfering as little as possible with the daily operations of the online system.

This educational gap is widespread, will take a lot of effort to correct, and will remain a factor for a decade or more. Making this project far more difficult are the moralistic and misinformed views that spread readily among law enforcement agents, including beliefs that online systems are no more than hideouts for a motley crew that includes hackers who invade computer systems and ruin people's credit ratings, pedophiles, pornography merchants, copyright infringers, and other misfits and malcontents. Examples of all these types can be found online, strengthening these views. What the police officers and agents need to learn is a sense of perspective. People who use online systems are just like people anywhere—there are problem cases scattered about, but most people are not out to harm others. Taking down an online system based on a few troublemakers injures all the rest of the users who are perfectly innocent, and those injuries can be fairly blamed on the agents who caused the damage.

> **Taking down an online system based on a few troublemakers injures all the rest of the users who are perfectly innocent, and those injuries can be fairly blamed on the agents who caused the damage.**

On a national level, Constitutional scholar Lawrence Tribe has proposed a 28th amendment to the Constitution (it was originally proposed as the 27th, but a Congressional term-limiting amendment took that honor instead). His proposed amendment would make it clear that all of the protections we have come to expect in American society, such as freedom of the press and rights against unreasonable searches and seizures, apply equally to all new technologies and communications media. The debate over the proposal may help speed up the process by which law enforcement officials learn to respect people's basic Constitutional rights in new technological settings such as online systems.

Second, some of the agents assigned to online systems also deal regularly with major computer crimes involving huge sums of money, such as insider embezzlement, fraudulent funds transfers made to "launder" illegally obtained money, drug cartels, and large-scale telephone fraud. When one of these agents gets wind of an online system suspected of involvement in foul play, he or she can easily fall into giving it the same "standard" computer criminal treatment used for high-rolling international embezzlers.

Third, it seems government agents often see hackers, online system operators, and other network dwellers as "evil geniuses," with endlessly clever technological ways to thwart the workings of justice, such as by creating electronic booby traps to destroy all incriminating files if an improper access code is used. These agents often are not themselves conversant with the technicalities of computers. As a result, agents conducting online system searches may try to compensate for their lack of technical knowledge by searching every imaginable place in which the information they seek may be hidden. This can result in general searches and seizures that are far broader than what is legally authorized against the computer owner, but give the agents a certain comfort level that they've cast a wide enough net to capture the materials they seek notwithstanding the computer owner's trickiness.

For example, some government agents will not feel confident they can get all the files they seek by backing up an online system hard disk to their own tape or disk drive. They suspect that the owner of the computer knows some tricky way to fool their backup program, and leave critical files uncopied. Therefore, they take the whole computer for leisurely inspection back at their office.

Fourth, prosecutors sometimes mention "forfeiture" as a reason both for seizing a lot of equipment at the outset, and also for refusing to return much of it to the owner until the investigation is over and yields either indictments or no charges. Under federal and state laws, materials used by a criminal in committing a crime are often forfeited to the government if the crime is proven at trial. A common example is forfeiture of a gun used in a shooting or robbery, or a getaway car used in committing a crime.

Some agents may believe the forfeiture rationale for taking and retaining online system equipment is legitimate. Unfortunately, in practice it can work as a smoke screen obscuring gross government violations of the equipment owner's rights. By refusing to return equipment while the investigation is in progress, prosecutors are saying, in essence, that the computers have already become government property, though no one is even charged with a crime yet. This amounts to an illegal seizure, and should be attacked in court by the owner of the withheld equipment.

The Online System as a Dangerous Gadget

Many law enforcement officers today look at online systems as mere collections of electronic boxes and wires. At the least sign of trouble these boxes can be readily removed from their owners, for safekeeping at the station house. However, when cops shut down an online system it affects not only the system operator, but hundreds or thousands of other people who use the system both locally and from afar. Unfortunately, nearly every online system search or seizure reported in the press in the past few years is also a case of law enforcement officers blindly stomping all over the rights of innocent system users.

There are a number of legal pretexts under which the authorities may seize an online system as if it was just a pile of transistors and pretty lights. The first is treating the system and its contents as *evidence of a crime*, as if it was a letter opener covered with telltale fingerprints or a few drops of a suspected criminal's blood. Police are trained to secure all evidence before it is rendered useless by subsequent handling, so naturally they just grab the entire system to make sure any evidence on it is not disturbed.

Another pretext for grabbing the computer is to view it as a weapon or *instrumentality of a crime*. This would place it in the same category as guns, and baseball bats used by loan sharks to break people's legs. All suspected weapons can be seized and retained indefinitely, and ultimately forfeited to the state if the underlying crime is proved or admitted.

A third pretext for grabbing the entire system is to treat it as *property subject to forfeiture*. Certain laws, such as those for prosecutions of drug dealing and tax evasion, have particularly draconian provisions permitting the government to seize all kinds of property associated with the crime, possibly never to return it. If an online system is somehow related to any aspect of such suspected crimes, it could easily be pulled in by the cops as part of the haul.

Taking an entire system down under any of these theories is more than a little crude, like shutting down an entire hotel just because a crime was committed in one of its rooms. Currently, though, it seems the police are often incapable of making the easy distinctions between user accounts, files, and messages that would enable them to seize particular materials on an online system without destroying the whole system. Seizing the system is also grossly unfair to the system operator, whenever it is based (as it usually is) on activities by remote users on the system, neither endorsed nor even known about by the operator. Nonetheless, grossly overreaching system seizures are likely to continue until most law officers revise their metaphors, and come to understand that computers are becoming gateways and hosts to entire communities and societies.

After law enforcement agents have had the equipment long enough to know for certain that they have copied all possibly relevant files (which cannot realistically take more than a week or two, even moving at a snail's pace), there is simply no reason they should keep the online system equipment from its owner any longer. It would be even more unreasonable where the owner of the equipment is not under suspicion, but his or her equipment is seized because someone else is suspected to have used it in committing a crime. In this case, the "forfeiture" excuse is entirely irrelevant—it is merely an excuse to hold someone's equipment illegally.

Avoiding Trouble Before It Starts

To sum up much of the discussion in this chapter so far: there are Constitutional and legal rules designed to protect the system operator when the government conducts a search or seizure of an online system or materials, though government agents today do not always follow those rules. The risk of an online system or materials being seized is not limited to situations where the owner is personally being investigated as a criminal. It can also arise from investigations of others, if they are suspected of using the online system to commit a crime or store evidence of a crime.

There is some chance that anyone's online system or materials can be wrongfully searched or seized, no matter how vigilantly or carefully the system operator works to keep it clean. This is no reason to avoid running or using an online system, though. Risks are everywhere in life. Every time you drive a car, no matter how carefully, there is a risk of being hit by another driver. Every time you park the car, there is a risk someone might steal it. We live with serious risks all the time. It should come as no surprise that online systems come with their own set of baseline risks.

An online system is connected to the whole world through the telephone lines, and thus exposed to all kinds of possibilities and problems. And as in other areas of our lives, we can reduce our risks to an acceptable level by conducting our online affairs in an informed and prudent manner.

Know Your Users

The odds of an online system being misused by users is directly related to the kind of clientele the operator cultivates. It may be impossible to know every user personally, even on a small online system, but it is easy to know what *kinds* of users are on the system. For example, in an online system where users openly discuss techniques for breaking into secure computer systems or breaking software copy protection schemes, it would not be surprising to find out one or more of them is using the system itself for illegal ends. Sure, users have First Amendment rights to hold such discussions on the system, but the kind of users this system attracts will be much more likely to cause trouble for other users or the system operator. In contrast, if the online system is primarily for artists or bird lovers, it is common sense that the general run of users will be less inclined to run criminal schemes through that system.

> **It may be impossible to know every user personally, even on a small online system, but it is easy to know what kinds of users are using the system.**

Another way for the operator to "know" system users is to set up registration procedures for maintaining their names and addresses. Users' knowledge that this data is on file will naturally deter most illegal activity. If an illegal act takes place, there is a far better chance of identifying the perpetrator and turning his or her name over to the authorities or the injured parties, if one wishes.

Many system operators require preregistration of all users via voice telephone call or by mail, with a verifiable phone number and return address. Others allow users to register on the first call to the online system, but require that they provide certain identifying information, including telephone number. Some online system software even has a utility program that rejects certain phone numbers as obviously bogus (the online system's own number, 555 or 800 numbers, and so on), and drops the user. Some online systems have a no-pseudonym policy, but make no attempt to verify the name given by the user.

The stricter the procedures for obtaining accurate user identity information, the greater the system's protection against illegal user activities and from legal problems arising from such activities. The less done to identify users—no preregistration required; allowing users to use handles only, instead of their real names—the greater the possibility the online system will attract users performing illegal activities.

A system operator who does not wish to set up preregistration procedures should at least follow the next rule carefully, and make absolutely clear to users that illegal material will not be permitted on the online system.

Bulletins and Other Public Statements

The operator should make it clear in public on the online system that illegal activity will not be tolerated. This will cause users with illegal acts in mind to look elsewhere for online systems more hospitable to their mischief. It will show any agents perusing the system that it is not providing a hangout for shady characters. And if the operator ever faces criminal charges for activities on the system, his or her public statements and actions against criminal behavior will be important to help prove he or she never encouraged or tolerated any criminal activities on the system.

The operator should consider posting statements of policy in bulletins placed at various points in the online system, or perhaps in a special "house rules" area. Such bulletins must be firm, but they should also not make users feel the operator runs an overly strict or inhospitable system. This can be accomplished by explaining that the rules are necessary for protection of both the system and its operators, and of all user materials and messages on the system.

For example, a new user bulletin might read:

As you may know, sometimes people misuse online systems for illegal purposes. If the authorities find illegal activities taking place on our system, it could be seized as evidence or "instrumentality of the crime," possibly never to be returned.

You could be directly affected by a government seizure. All of your private files and mail on this online system, and any other valuable information you keep on this online system, would be seized by the authorities along with our computer equipment. This is a risk faced by all online systems and their users.

To protect us all from this risk, we strictly forbid any illegal activities on this online system. We do not permit any trading of pirated software, credit card codes, access numbers, or the like. We will warn or lock out first-time offenders, depending on the seriousness of their activities. We will also cooperate with state or federal authorities investigating violations of the law, and with any individuals or companies injured by such acts.

If any user violates such announced rules on illegal activity, the operator should deal with him or her swiftly. The operator should also consider making the matter public on the system, so other users realize that the system policy is meant to be respected and not merely for show. If the operator is afraid the user involved may try to retaliate in some way, it might be better just to tell the authorities about the problem.

> **In making any public announcements about disciplinary steps taken toward users who seriously misbehave, the operator should remember that public statements of fact about other people, if false, can lead to claims of libel.**

In making any public announcements about disciplinary steps taken toward users who seriously misbehave, the operator should remember that public statements of fact about other people, if false, can lead to claims of libel. This problem can be minimized by talking about the situation without identifying the individual involved; limiting the public message to facts known to be true; talking only about the exact event or activity that violated the rules, instead of telling the whole story of the violator's presence on the system; and avoiding any statements about the violator's character, or what he or she does in everyday life.

For instance, to announce that a user was locked out of an online system:

On Thursday, we locked a user out of our system for violating the rules against illegal activity. We regret taking such action, but it was necessary. The user uploaded pirated software to the file areas and boasted to others here of his collection of thousands of cracked programs. As you know, we need to prohibit all illegal activities to protect our system and to protect your own e-mail and files on our system.

Remember, don't mention the user's name in the general message to the public. This way, if there is any factual mistake in the announcement, it is harder for the user in question to claim his or her reputation was wrongly injured, since no name was given. In addition, if the violating user had acted under an innocent user's name, leaving the name out avoids accidentally injuring that user with the announcement.

Keep printed transcripts of all messages left to and about violating users, and of all bulletins and messages publicly stating system policy. If the operator is sued or charged with permitting illegal materials or activities on the online system, he or she will then be able to show a consistent policy of discouraging and acting against illegal activities. This helps counter accusations that the operator deliberately encouraged or permitted illegalities on the system.

Public announcements are useful for showing that the operator does not encourage illegal activity on the system, but no one should try using them to cover up illegal actions. One pirate board included in its logon message the following: "All software is believed to be public domain." Another bulletin on the same board some weeks later said: "People are saying this is a pirate board. Please help us kill this rumor." But in fact, the board contained a restricted file area with scores of pirated programs, most uploaded by the system operator himself. The online system was eventually sued by a software publisher. The presence of the system operator's own illegal uploads and the messages the system operator himself left about them showed his intention to commit and promote copyright infringement on his online system, despite the self-serving bulletins.

Act Immediately on All Suspicious Materials or Activities

Rely mainly on instinct and common sense. For example, when an operator reviews information on recently uploaded files, does he or she know the users who uploaded the files? Are they trustworthy? Are the files familiar? Does the file description give the show away? (such as "Great game, cracked by the Midnight Rambler," or "You'll know this Playmate when you see her"). If not, does the file sound like a commercial product? Business and utility programs with numerous features or great power might arouse suspicion if they're not well known as shareware or public domain programs.

If the operator strives to investigate suspicious activities but someone slips an illegal credit card number by him or her anyway, then the operator hasn't committed any crime. Prosecutors want to bring cases that will stick. It's been said that if the police had been more familiar with computer technology, the Tcimpidis case (involving the credit card numbers illegally posted on his system by a user) would not have been brought. The charges were, in fact, later dismissed for lack of proof. If the authorities want to prosecute computer crime there are enough pirate and phone phreak boards out there to satisfy them, and the operator who acts reasonably will probably be left alone.

Dealing with the Problem User

The first question for the system operator is whether to deal directly with the user causing the problem, or go immediately to law enforcement authorities. How far should the operator go in disclosing illegal activity on the online system to the authorities or to other users?

The Connecticut Bomb Factory

In 1993, a 21-year-old system operator named Michael Elansky was jailed on $500,000 bail in West Haven, Connecticut. The crime? The police found a text file on his bulletin board system describing how to build a bomb.

Elansky's bulletin board system, the Ware House BBS, was about three years old, with two lines, 1.2 gigabytes of storage and a CD-ROM drive. His specialty was utility software, but the file that led to his incarceration was a user-uploaded anarchist text named ANARC2. It preached chaos and disorder for society, and contained the bomb-making recipe.

Elansky was arrested when a 14-year-old user downloaded ANARC2, then contacted the police. Two charges were filed against Elansky. The first was inciting injury to persons and property, based on the mere fact that the ANARC2 file was on Elansky's BBS. The second charge was creating risk of injury to a minor, covering the download of the bomb recipe by the 14-year-old.

Elansky was held on $500,000 bail, far more than he or his parents could afford, so he went straight into jail to await further proceedings. On an unsuccessful hearing to reduce bail, the judge was none too sympathetic. He said Elansky ran a bomb-making factory using his BBS, and was just as dangerous as the bomber who blew up the World Trade Center. He also appeared to hold Elansky personally accountable for creating the ANARC2 file. In fact, ANARC2 was written by a stranger and uploaded by a user, and is widely available across the various computer networks. The bomb-making recipe was taken straight out of the Anarchist's Cookbook, an aboveground publication available from Paladin Press to anyone with the price of purchase.

If this seems far too much fuss over a little chunk of text, indeed it was. There was another side to this story. Elansky and the West Haven police played a game of cat and mouse for the previous few years, with bomber accusations against Elansky the constant theme. Elansky says it started in 1988, when the police found him with explosives. He said they were for a fireworks show at his high school, the police said they were bombs. They let him go for lack of strong evidence. Since then he was picked up a couple more times with explosives in his possession, but always placed on probation and let go again. Elansky maintained the explosives were always for fireworks displays, a hobby of his. Regardless of the truth, we can see that the police were eager enough to put Elansky away that the bomb-making recipe made a convenient excuse.

Nonetheless, they made a big mistake in arresting him for a text file on his BBS. The First Amendment prohibits government officials from acting against anyone for distributing material containing political content. Even if Elansky made bombs all those years, this does not justify jailing him based on a text file. There was absolutely no clear and present danger from the bomb-making file on the Ware House BBS. The text was in circulation for years in print form and is now common all over the nets, just another wild-eyed political leaflet strewn along the electronic highway.

True to the long-term tension between Elansky and the cops, Elansky eventually pleaded guilty to charges relating to real explosives, and the BBS-related charges were not pursued. What this bizarre tale demonstrates is that the rules of search and seizure are sometimes merely rules of a game, which can be discarded by the authorities at any time given sufficient provocation.

At this stage in the lawmakers' education process, it is recommended that whenever possible, operators of smaller online systems deal directly with the violating user without contacting the authorities. It is unfortunate to have to make such a recommendation, though. In an ideal world, it would be better to get the government's assistance in dealing with lawbreakers. But as we have seen, the authorities still fumble the ball too much to be trusted to deal sensitively with online system situations. If an operator tells a government agent of a suspected illegal gambling ring running on his or her system, they may immediately seize the system as evidence of the illegal activity without bothering to think about how the seizure might damage the operator.

Fortunately, there is no law that says the authorities must be notified merely because illegal materials or activities were discovered on an online system. If the operator finds any illegal materials and is not aware that they relate to any criminal investigation or case, he or she can delete them all immediately, reprimand or lock out the user, and do nothing else. Here is a sample reprimand message a system operator might send privately to a user who uploads a pirated program:

> *On Friday, September 16, you uploaded a program called "Star Blaster" to File Area Seven. I deleted this program, since it appeared to be an unauthorized copy of a copyrighted game by Innervision Software. I could not tell from the available information whether you knew this was a pirated program. Therefore I am giving you the benefit of the doubt, and will not revoke your privilege to use this online system. Please understand that I do not and cannot tolerate the uploading of pirated software to this online system. If this happens again, I will be forced to lock you out.*

There may be times where the only reasonable course is for the system operator to contact the authorities. The main reasons for contacting the authorities are: (a) the operator may be afraid of confronting a user on his or her criminal activity because the user may try to injure the operator or the system; (b) a user persists in illegal conduct on the system after the operator gives a warning or tries locking the user out; or (c) the user's activities already pose such a threat to the operator or the system that the operator needs help against the user, even with the risk the authorities will mistakenly seize the system. In the case of pirated software, the operator may also consider contacting affected private parties: the software publisher or the Software Publishers' Association in Washington, D.C. (this organization has from time to time offered a reward for information on software piracy).

Before contacting the authorities, the operator should prepare all of the records and materials he or she would use to back up statements or charges beforehand. It would also be a very good idea to consult beforehand, at least briefly, a lawyer or the Electronic Frontier Foundation. It is hard to predict what kind of reaction the operator will get from contacting the police, the local prosecutor's office,

> **Before contacting the authorities, the operator should prepare all of the records and materials he or she would use to back up statements or charges beforehand.**

or the F.B.I. They may not understand what you are talking about, or not take much of an interest. Or they may overreact and try to put the online system under lock and key, using a warrant based on the operator's own testimony.

The system operator should present himself or herself properly and in person to the authorities when obtaining their help. He or she should describe the system, repeatedly if necessary, as the carrier of private electronic mail and public messages, and as an electronic publisher. When telling the authorities about a problem, the operator must make them understand that he or she wants to continue to run the system, free of the illegal activities complained of; that the operator cannot afford for the authorities to seize the system itself; and (gently) that seizure, unless carefully made, might be illegal under the Electronic Communications Privacy Act, the Privacy Protection Act, and generally under the First and Fourth Amendments to the Constitution. The operator should make it clear he or she wants to work with the authorities, but did not approach them just so they could shut the system down while chasing down the troublemaker.

The operator should also file a written report setting out the above matters clearly. If the identity of the user pursuing illegal activities on your online system is not certain, the operator should point out that the user's name being provided to the authorities is the name he or she used on the online system, but it may not be the user's real name. If the operator notifies the authorities (or a software company about pirated software on his or her online system) prior to reprimanding or locking out the user, he or she may be asked to assist in a sting operation to catch the errant user or force the user to reveal his or her true identity.

If the authorities do not act on the operator's information or charges fairly quickly, even after contacting them again a couple of times, the operator should keep good, reliable records of the attempt to obtain law enforcement assistance and their failure to respond. Then, the operator should go ahead and take whatever steps are necessary to halt the illegal activities on the online system. These moves will counter any claims that might be made later, asserting that the operator assisted the criminal activities by permitting them to continue on the system. It would be a good idea for the operator to obtain attorney or EFF help in doing these things in a manner best suited for his or her exact situation. Pay close attention to their advice. The operator should always listen most closely to the experts assisting in his or her own case, even if it seems at odds with the general advice given in this book.

Civil (Non-Criminal) Seizures

There are two entirely different kinds of lawsuits. Up to now in this chapter, we have discussed searches and seizures in *criminal* actions—legal proceedings by the government to decide whether someone is innocent or guilty of a crime, with potential punishments including fines, community service, forfeiture of property, and jail time. In this last section we will discuss *civil* actions. These are lawsuits in which the main goal of the person or company who started the suit (known as the "plaintiff") is usually to obtain a court award of money from the person or company being sued (the "defendant").

It may be surprising to learn that plaintiffs in civil lawsuits can sometimes get the court to order a seizure of online system equipment *without* the safeguards built into the criminal search warrant process. The legal standards for a civil seizure order against an online system are in most ways less protective than the standards that apply to a criminal search warrant. However, the protection of private messages under the ECPA and the protection of publishing-related materials under the PPA still apply. The interactions between these Constitutional limits on

> **It may be surprising to learn that plaintiffs in civil lawsuits can sometimes get the court to order a seizure of online system equipment *without* the safeguards built into the criminal search warrant process.**

government power, and the power of civil seizure, can become complicated. For instance, the authorities may be permitted to take certain equipment in a civil seizure, but not be allowed to view stored messages or user information on the system without a warrant, due to the ECPA. What if there are publishing-related materials on the system, and the authorities meet the standards for a civil seizure, but not the warrant requirements of the PPA? We do not believe this question has been answered yet. The courts' legitimate answers could range from disallowing the seizure altogether, to permitting the seizure to proceed only after the publishing-related materials have been transferred to tapes or disks remaining in the publisher's possession.

It is only possible to obtain seizure orders in certain types of civil lawsuits, such as those involving violations of copyrights, trademarks, or trade secrets. Courts have granted seizure orders in the past against such goods as counterfeit watches and illegal copies of phonograph records, as well as the equipment used to make the counterfeits. Judges have also granted orders for the seizure of computer equipment in cases of software piracy and disputes over software rights.

Do You Get Advance Warning of the Civil Search or Seizure?

The plaintiff may ask for a seizure order when he or she begins the lawsuit, before the defending system operator even learns the lawsuit has begun. Federal judges prefer not to grant such drastic orders unless the defendant is notified about the request for the seizure order in advance, and given the chance to argue against it in court. However, the plaintiff might try to convince the judge that letting the defendant know about the seizure in advance would be dangerous. For example, he or she may tell the judge that if notified, the defendant will wipe the system computer's hard disk clean of any evidence of wrongdoing. The plaintiff must support such arguments with affidavits and other evidence showing that if the claimed facts are true, a serious infringement has occurred and a seizure is necessary to protect his or her rights.

If the court decides the defending operator should get advance notice of the seizure request, then he or she will receive a telephone call or letter saying that

> **If the court decides the defending operator should get advance notice of the seizure request, then he or she will receive a telephone call or letter saying that the plaintiff will be applying for a seizure order on a certain date, usually no more than a couple of days off.**

the plaintiff will be applying for a seizure order on a certain date, usually no more than a couple of days off. Those who receive such a notice should not ignore it. They should call an attorney immediately and arrange to be in court to oppose the order. Typical arguments to the court against a seizure order are that it would interfere with or destroy the operator's ability to conduct business, and that seizing the entire online system is a far more drastic measure than is needed to satisfy the plaintiff's legitimate needs. The operator should offer to supply a backup of the hard disk, or the files legitimately sought, in lieu of a seizure. If the court is convinced not to seize the online system, then the plaintiff's case will revert to a normal, slow-paced civil action.

If, on the other hand, the plaintiff managed to convince the court that the defending operator should not get advance notice of the seizure, then he or she will likely first learn about the seizure order when the plaintiff's attorney arrives to conduct the seizure, accompanied by a federal marshall or state sheriff. If this happens, the operator can employ the same strategies we suggested above in dealing with criminal searches and seizures. The operator should call a lawyer, ask to see a copy of the order, and then, with the lawyer's advice, seek to limit the seizure if possible.

After a Civil Seizure

A judge does not make a final decision in the case when he or she grants a seizure order to the plaintiff at the outset. The purpose of an early seizure of the online system is to obtain and preserve evidence that might otherwise be destroyed, dissipated, or hidden.

Within a short time after the seizure (ten days is typical), there will be a judicial hearing where the defendant will have an opportunity to challenge the seizure. Depending on the judge, the hearing may consist of anything from a half-hour of argument by the attorneys to a mini-trial lasting for a day or more. At this stage, the judge may reconsider the prior order and order the equipment released. He or she is especially likely to do so if the defendant appears to be honest, not deliberately engaging in illegal behavior, and not likely to destroy the evidence. One major reason seizure orders are often reversed is if the judge feels, after hearing the defendant's side of the story, that the plaintiff misled him or her in the initial motion seeking the seizure order. If the judge appears likely nonetheless to affirm the earlier seizure order, the defendant should once again propose less restrictive solutions. For example, the defendant might offer to let the plaintiff keep a backup of the hard disk (or the disk itself, if it is removable), while the defendant gets the computer back to continue operating his or her business.

If the judge affirms the seizure at this hearing, the seized equipment will continue to be held pending the trial of the case. The case is still not over, but the affirmation does mean that at this early stage the judge thinks the plaintiff has a good chance of proving his or her case if it goes all the way to trial. Despite winning the hearing, though, the plaintiff still has the burden of proving the defendant's liability at trial. Also, the formal rules of evidence, which are not fully applied in initial seizure hearings, may protect the defendant at trial by keeping certain evidence used in the first hearing from entering the trial record. On the other hand, losing the confirmation hearing may persuade the defendant that his or her case is not strong, and may give the defendant an incentive to settle with the other party.

If the defendant wins the case or settles it, he or she will finally get the equipment back, since the official purpose of a seizure is to preserve evidence or stop ongoing infringement, not to punish. Of course, with the rapid rate of obsolescence in the computer industry, a belatedly returned computer system may be good for little more than scrap.

The rules that apply to federal court proceedings give the defendant a secret weapon that may be very useful in a seizure case. This is Rule 11, the sanctions rule. It provides that an attorney and his or her client may be fined by the court for making frivolous requests to the court. If the plaintiff sought a seizure merely to give the defending operator a hard time or gain a tactical advantage, and not based on an honest legal claim or because there was a real threat to the evidence, then the defendant can ask the court to direct the plaintiff to pay the defendant's legal costs. Some states have their own court rules similar to Federal Rule 11.

Civil seizures, like criminal searches, are unlikely to occur when a system operator is careful in dealing with illegal material. If the operator runs a clean online system, the judge should not find a threat to the evidence sufficient to justify a seizure. Seizures are usually only granted in extreme cases, such as piracy or counterfeiting.

Adult Materials and Themes

Adult materials, and pornography in particular, are among the most controversial subjects in American society. Federal funding for sexually adventurous artistic projects has practically disappeared. Rock music recordings and computer games bear sex and violence warning labels, under continuing political pressure for industry self-regulation. Lurid tales of child pornography and pedophilia, both real and imagined, show up weekly in supermarket tabloids.

Online systems and networks receive their share of attention from the authorities. It started around 1985, when Congressional hearings in connection with the Meese Commission singled out computer bulletin boards as a major medium for producing and distributing child pornography. Official concern about online adult materials grew slowly for several years, then suddenly took off in 1993 as part of the "Information Superhighway" groundswell. The idea was, if we were going to put our nation online, it had better be safe for the kids. In just 1993 and 1994, actions against adult materials online included:

- The federal government and several states ran "Operation Longarm," a full-blown attack against U.S. citizens who downloaded adult materials, reportedly including child pornography, from three bulletin boards in Denmark.

- The operator of the Oklahoma Information Exchange was sentenced to 10 years in jail for selling and making available online a few adult CD-ROMs.

- Operators of the Amateur Action bulletin board in California were given a jail sentence in Tennessee for distributing obscene pictures from their home base in California.

- Two employees of Lawrence Livermore Laboratories were fired, and then indicted, on claims that they stored adult images on laboratory computers accessible through the Internet.

- Two bulletin boards in Pensacola, Florida were reportedly raided for pornography as this book went to press.

- Colleges and universities across the country, which pioneered the Internet as a free-ranging social environment, are responding to growing parental qualms about the adult materials

245

available on the Internet by cutting off sex-related Usenet discussions from their Internet sites. As we go to press, students at Carnegie Mellon University are contesting the university's claim that it needs to censor sex-related newsgroups to avoid potential criminal charges.

In *Syslaw* we predicted that "pornography will be surfacing as a major BBS legal issue in the future—at least for those BBSs that carry such materials." That future is now. Adult materials online have become a major legal, moral, and social battleground.

The Online System as Adult Bookstore

This metaphor is almost too apt for some of the online systems out there, whose business consists largely of distributing adult materials. Like a true adult bookstore, their offerings are not confined to one medium, but span texts, still images, animated loops, and sound files. Many of these businesses even extend beyond the online realm, also offering to send floppies, CD-ROMs, and other items by mail to customers who want more products than they can currently download through their modems.

Adult bookstores in the physical world are entrenched in a well-defined war with the local forces of morality everywhere. Civic and religious groups often try to eliminate these businesses within city or county limits, but the bookstores have the First Amendment on their side. The First Amendment's protection of freedom of the press is historically strongest for printed works, and adult bookstores are loaded with books that would never be found obscene in court. This means that local community groups can push them around, but they can't crush them out of existence. The battle lines are typically drawn at local community restrictions on the location and appearance of adult bookstores, which is Constitutionally permitted as long as the restrictions do not deprive such bookstores and their customers of the opportunity to do business.

Do online services equivalent to adult bookstores face the same situation? Not exactly, although both kinds of operations are similarly immersed in the information business. On the one hand, law officers and prosecutors will be less likely to concede that the First Amendment protects the activities of an adult online system, because it doesn't have actual printed books. Text files are the functional equivalent of books, but they are nonetheless a computer-age medium whose character as protected speech has not yet been broadly recognized in the courts. On the other hand, adult online systems are not located within physical communities, but occupy locations all by themselves, which only their customers will ever enter. There is no storefront blaring "XXX" which all members of the community must pass by, wincing, on the street. In addition, adult systems that verify the age of their customers may be viewed as trying to act as responsible as those in their line of business can be.

This combination of factors, pointing toward both greater and lesser risk for adult online systems than for adult bookstores, will fall into a new balance eventually. There is no doubt that owners and patrons of these systems are taking some legal risks today. Over time, the question is: Will civic groups successfully drive adult systems to remote corners of the online realm, or will online adult systems divorced from particular communities flourish far more openly and vigorously than their grounded bookstore counterparts?

Hard-core adult materials are thriving in the online arena. Despite the obvious legal risks, many system operators are happy to provide them in mass quantities to their users. These operators are not all porn merchants in the ordinary sense. Many are eager, even desperate just to get a system going that will pay the rent. They see pornographic materials, including image files and animations, as the cash cow that will sustain their systems while they piece together the services they really want to offer. Others are in it only for the money, and will feature hard-core materials until the heat gets turned up too high. For all operators, the warning call has been sounded: anyone still carrying hard-core materials online today takes a big risk of being caught and prosecuted.

There are also a lot of milder adult materials moving through online systems featuring *Playboy* or *Penthouse* style nudity. Like the hard-core materials, they generate a lot of money for online systems. However, the milder materials are not clearly illegal, even though they may still be very much for adults only.

In this chapter, then, we will explore the major kinds of adult materials found on online systems, and the current laws relating to such materials. We will also give suggestions on how to reduce the risks of distributing adult materials.

Sell Porn for Instant Online Success!

One of the truisms heard often on the Net is that a new medium is headed for big success if it becomes a major channel for distribution of adult materials shortly after its introduction. This theory is supported by early developments in photography, home video, and "900" telephone numbers, all of which were immediately integrated into the adult materials marketplace and became society-changing technologies (though not every successful medium starts out doing big business in the adult market—look at television, radio, and phonograph records, in which adult materials barely make an appearance). Among today's computer technologies, both CD-ROMs and online systems are at the center of a rapidly growing market in high-tech adult materials. According to the popular theory, this indicates that online systems are headed for huge success, and there will always be a thriving online market for adult materials.

What about the converse proposition? Does a system operator need to become a dealer in adult materials to succeed at this early stage in the online industry? Many system operators think so. Some of the biggest success stories so far in online services cater mainly to the adult market. As more people flock to start up their own online systems, many focus on distributing adult materials as the way to achieve a financially self-supporting system in the shortest possible time. At some point the market will become saturated, though it's probably a long way off, as a steady supply of new customers will be entering the online world for years to come.

The fact that so many online systems today distribute adult materials has created a dangerous illusion: that it is legal, or at least safe, to distribute adult materials of all kinds online. System operators look around and see others raking in thousands, even millions of dollars by offering some of the most hardcore images and other materials imaginable for their users' pleasure. Their question is: if it's illegal to distribute obscene materials,

why are some system operators permitted to make enormous amounts of money at it?

The answer may be disappointing to those who see online adult materials as the quick ticket to material success: the major online systems distributing hard-core adult materials today have profited only because their opposition—the moralists and the law enforcers—were not familiar enough with the online world to understand what they were doing, much less go after them. However, things have changed. Law enforcers are becoming Net surfers. The online obscenity and child pornography prosecutions are starting to roll in. The window of opportunity for starting new online systems to distribute extreme adult materials at low risk is closed.

The new systems starting up will have to dust off strategies used for years by mail-order houses for adult materials, such as careful selection of the exact materials sold or distributed, avoidance of that which is potentially obscene, customer identity verification, and blocking out transmissions to known repressive communities. Those who believe the online world is some vast electronic frontier where lawmen will never catch up to those operators smart enough to cash in on a business opportunity while it's hot, may be heading for trouble.

Which Laws Apply?

Pornography is regulated at both the state and federal levels. State pornography laws are many and varied, and differ from state to state. They all flow from the same constitutional basis—the states' police power to regulate in the name of the public's health, safety and general welfare. A laundry list of the exact pornography laws in each state cannot be given here, but the following sampling should give an idea of some of the regulatory approaches taken:

- "Promoting" any obscene materials (applied to sale of videotapes at a video store).
- Obscene "material or performance" (applied to sale of magazines at adult bookstore).

- Declaring any place "where lewd films are publicly distributed" to be a "moral nuisance."

- "Sending into the state . . . any obscene matter" (applied to magazines delivered by mail).

If a state desires to extend pornography enforcement to online systems, it might attempt to do so under the wording of existing laws. Sometimes, however, those laws are very specific to certain media in which the targeted materials may be contained, such as books or videotapes. In that case, the same adult content contained in a digital file may not be covered by the law. System operators should be careful before exploiting any such gap in coverage. Pornography statutes are frequently reworked in many states to reflect new media, as well as slight shifts in community values and Supreme Court pronouncements. The law on the books in the library may not cover use of a new medium for adult materials, but changes to cover that medium may have been made by the state legislature so recently that they have not yet been distributed to the libraries.

> **Pornography statutes are frequently reworked in many states to reflect new media, as well as slight shifts in community values and Supreme Court pronouncements.**

There is also a growing body of federal anti-pornography laws. One of the oldest is the law against interstate mailing of obscene materials. This was the basis for Operation Postporn, an early '90s initiative that led to multiple prosecutions of mail-order porn houses in several morally conservative states at the same time. More recent regulations prohibit pornographic materials on broadcast media such as television and radio. In *FCC v. Pacifica*, the famous "seven dirty words" case, the Supreme Court first held that the Federal Communication Commission has the right to regulate broadcasts if necessary to keep indecent materials away from minors.

Of most interest to system operators and users are the following federal laws:

1. *Federal regulation of "telephone facilities" to deliver pornographic messages*, found in section 223(b) of the Federal Communications Act and related FCC regulations (a copy is in the appendix). This law is mainly targeted at the voice "dial-a-porn" industry. However, the wording of the statute is broad enough that it could conceivably be used to prosecute online systems as "telephone facilities." This law will be discussed further in the section on indecent materials

2. *Federal child pornography law*. This law is targeted at adult materials containing visual images of minors. It is aimed at preventing the use of children in the production of adult materials, on the assumption that sexual abuse is likely to occur in such situations. It is discussed in more detail below.

All anti-obscenity laws, both state and federal, are subject to limits created by the Supreme Court under the First Amendment. The Court's role is to define how far our government can restrict pornography before it treads too hard on our Constitutional right to free speech. The balance struck by the Supreme Court and Congress is this: sexually oriented material is protected by the First Amendment from government interference, unless it is deemed to be obscene or child pornography. Once material is deemed obscene, it loses all First Amendment protection.

How Is "Obscenity" Defined?

Once every generation or so, the Supreme Court gives us a different answer to this question. The prevailing test was formulated in 1973 by the Supreme Court in *Miller v. California*, which sets the standard for obscenity laws today. *Miller* announced a three-part test for determining if the materials in question can considered "obscene." All three parts must be satisfied before the government can prosecute someone for handling such materials:

1. *Whether "the average person, applying contemporary community standards," would find that the work, taken as a whole, appeals primarily to the prurient interest.* The trickiest part of this standard is figuring out "contemporary community standards." This concept is separately discussed in the next section. Also, the work must be "taken as a whole." This means when you have a 90-minute movie with a steamy section in the middle 2 minutes long, you don't focus just on the steamy section to decide if it's obscene. The movie must be viewed as a whole to decide if it appeals *primarily* to the "prurient interest."

   What is "prurient interest"? The Supreme Court calls it "sexual responses over and above those that would be characterized as normal." Normal for whom? Under this vaguely worded test, just about any strongly sexual material might be found to appeal to the prurient interest, especially in highly conservative communities.

2. *Whether the work depicts or describes, in a patently offensive way, sexual conduct specifically defined by the applicable state law.* This is the simplest requirement. The law usually either does or does not apply to the materials in question. For example, a law against public display of obscene materials will not apply to materials secretly distributed within encrypted files. Ironically, in order to meet this requirement, some states have enacted laws containing descriptions of prohibited sexual display so graphic that the laws themselves are not fit to be shown to children.

3. *Whether the work, taken as a whole, lacks serious literary, artistic, political, or scientific value.* This part of the test is the saving grace for works which might otherwise be forbidden by the anti-pornography forces. Note how it is phrased: those who seek to declare a work obscene must prove that it has no serious value. In other words, the work is deemed valuable until proven valueless, which adds greatly to the job that law officers take on when prosecuting under obscenity laws.

   This formula is fairly flexible. There is no objective standard for measuring the "value" of a work, much less its "serious value." But at least it will make judges and juries stop to think for a moment about whether the material at hand is pure smut, or a work of art, science, literature, or political commentary that happens to be expressed in sexually explicit terms.

Which Community's Standards Apply?

Different communities across the U.S. have different standards for whether sexually oriented material is "normal" or too extreme. One area's hard-core porn might be another's ribald bestseller. When applying the first of the three *Miller* obscenity tests—whether the material appeals to the "prurient interest" according to community standards—it therefore becomes important to nail down the exact community whose standards will be used.

Most online systems do not strictly serve a single geographic community. Whether it's around the world or just around the corner, an online system is never more than a phone call away. The growing popularity of the Internet makes long-distance discussions and file transfers cheap and routine. The ease of remote access makes an online system different from a bookstore or a video store, which serve only local customers. Online systems are more analogous to mail-order or 900-number services, which reach widely distributed audiences or customers.

This means a nationally accessible BBS with adult materials is subject to lawsuits in all states to which those materials are delivered or transmitted. It is well established, for instance, that if pornographic material is mailed from California to Florida, the sender of the material can be sued in Florida. Similarly, a BBS that transmits a pornographic graphic image file from California to Florida would probably be subject to a lawsuit in Florida. And the Supreme Court recently affirmed that the local standards in the *recipient's* community are used to determine whether the material is prurient, even where the material or activities are prosecuted under nationwide federal pornography laws. This precise scenario (as we described in *Syslaw* in 1992) was played out in 1994, in the case of the Amateur Action bulletin board system: while the system was located in Milpitas, California, it was sued in Tennessee for transmitting obscene materials. Local Tennessee community standards were used to decide whether the materials appealed "primarily to the prurient interest" as required by the *Miller* test.

> **Most online systems do not strictly serve a single geographic community. Whether it's around the world or just around the corner, an online system is never more than a phone call away.**

The government can abuse the local community standards concept even beyond suing a seller of adult materials in a morally conservative community. How about suing the seller in several morally conservative communities *at the same time?* This was the approach used in 1990 in Operation Postporn. The federal government embarked on a program of "forum shopping" (trying to bring a case in the court most sympathetic to its own views) by sending in orders from several morally repressive states to a seller of mail-order pornographic materials in several states, and then suing the seller in all of them. The result was that the simultaneous lawsuits bankrupted or wore out many of the target companies. The prosecutors were chastised by several judges in the process, but this does not assure they will not try something like this again in the future, possibly against online services next time.

The time may be near for a major revision of the concept of community standards for online activities. Up to now, "community" always meant neighborhoods, counties, or states—in other words, geographically defined communities. But the growing online world is already filled with thousands of new virtual, *online* communities. If an online system provides adult materials to online users from all over the world, why should the standards of geographically based communities govern its activities? The Supreme Court made its *Miller* test depend in part on local community standards because it recognized that different communities have different moral standards, and it wanted to let like-minded people living together in communities choose rules that suit them best. This same reasoning, if applied to the online world, could easily lead to a new rule: when considering whether adult materials distributed online beyond the bounds of local geographic communities are obscene, we should appeal to standards of the online community. After all, those who live part of their lives in cyberspace ought to be able to live in a community where they feel comfortable. At this time, there is no such law, but it is an idea sure to be pushed in future litigation and legislative efforts. Of course, if online community is accepted for purposes of deciding obscenity issues, a major question immediately arises: who comprises the community—the entire populace of the online world, or some smaller segment, such as users of adult online services? Clearly, definition of the proper community, even if online communities are recognized, will be pivotal in determining how online materials will be treated.

The Online System as Singles Bar

Online systems are the newest arena for the oldest of human activities—the mating dance. This became apparent early on, such as when France's national Minitel system became most popular for its so-called "pink" areas, where users flirted and indulged in dirty talk. The social/sexual aspect of going online is still one of the greatest driving forces and sources for money in online systems, both for bulletin boards like the Garbage Dump and the large national systems. The flirting and gossip occur largely in real-time chat, just like spoken conversation in singles bars and other social scenes.

A related phenomenon is the use of online systems for people to get together and discuss sex-related subjects, without coming on to each other. It can be quite an enlightening experience, especially for those who first encountered sex in their own communities and families as a subject of superstition and fear, rather than accurate information. The anonymity available in the online medium lets people talk about their conditions and experiences, and ask the dumbest of questions about sexual matters, without being embarrassed. National online systems allow people who engage privately in practices frowned on by moralistic communities to congregate with others of like mind across the country. A recent book about dominance and submission relationships, entitled "Different Loving," resulted from interactions among dominance and submission devotees who meet regularly in a private area on one of the large online services.

What is the legal status of these discussions? Technically, they are subject to the same prohibitions on obscenity and indecency that apply to prerecorded and canned sex-related materials. However, they also resemble spoken discussions, which rarely if ever lead to any legal trouble if conducted in private (and if confined to words, and don't devolve into group sex, prostitution, or the like). The line-straddling is exemplified by "hot chat" sessions popular on many bulletin boards. Explicitly sexual discussions, full of overt sexual references, are conducted in real time, but they are expressed in text that scrolls up your computer screen, and can easily be recorded in a printed file.

As a practical matter, the way law officers end up treating sex-oriented online meeting places will depend on which physical-world metaphors apply best to the situation. Heavy flirting and singles scenes that want to minimize legal risk should be set up in age-restricted areas resembling bars and require genuine proof of age. On the other hand, frank discussion of sexual topics should be done in private, member-only areas that resemble group counseling settings. If the discussion is among minors, such as teenagers learning about safe sex and sharing their experiences, the safest way to do this may be in an area moderated by an adult qualified to counsel minors in such matters. Keep in mind that these moves do not create *legal* shields, but legitimate cultural and social contexts in which law officers will be less interested in interfering.

One more note on local community standards. They only apply to one part of the three-part *Miller* obscenity test: whether the material in question appeals primarily to the prurient interest. Community standards are *not* used to decide whether the material has serious value, which is a separate part of the *Miller* test. The test for serious value is whether a "reasonable man" (or woman) would find the material valuable, considering reasonableness on a national basis, and not whether a specific local community would find it valuable. This broad-based part of the obscenity test is necessary to fight the tendency of local repressive communities to blur the differences between sexual content and the value of the work as a whole, such as by saying, "This stuff is dirty, so it can't possibly have any redeeming value." It also allows works of serious value to circulate throughout the country unimpeded by local restrictive standards. If the rule was otherwise—if the local community was also entitled to use its local standards of taste to decide if an adult work had serious value—then the most restrictive communities could make it so difficult to sell adult works that publishers might be unwilling to sell them, even if they would be perfectly acceptable in most of the country.

Obscene, or Merely Indecent?

In struggling with the "obscenity" question over the last few decades, the Supreme Court eventually developed a second category of adult materials: "indecent" materials. Think of this as all sexually explicit materials which are not extreme, clinical, or kinky enough to qualify as "obscene" materials. Obviously, there is a borderline area where it will not be clear if certain pictures are obscene or merely indecent.

Distribution of indecent materials is protected as free speech by the First Amendment, unlike obscene materials, which have no First Amendment protection. However, legal controls over indecent materials are still permitted where they are necessary for the protection of minors.

The most famous use of the indecent materials concept was in *FCC v. Pacifica*, the "seven dirty words"

Distribution of indecent materials is protected as free speech by the First Amendment, unlike obscene materials, which have no First Amendment protection.

case involving comedian George Carlin, where the FCC was permitted to ban the use of certain "naughty" words on broadcast television. The words were not considered obscene, but the public policy of protecting children from hearing them justified the ban. The Supreme Court emphasized that broadcast television is a highly accessible medium. By doing nothing more than pushing the "on" button, a child has access to all that is being broadcast. The Court believed that only a total ban could effectively keep undesirable language on television from the ears of America's children.

Fortunately, a total ban on indecent material will probably not be carried over into the online media. The FCC tried it a few years ago and was promptly challenged in *Sable Communications v. FCC*. In *Sable*, a dial-a-porn company opposed a federal regulation prohibiting all telephone transmissions of obscene or indecent messages. The Supreme Court upheld the part of the prohibition covering obscene messages (remember, obscene messages are not protected under the First Amendment), but struck down the attempted prohibition of indecent messages. It held that "less restrictive means" than a total ban were available to limit children's access to dial-a-porn while preserving adult access, and that the FCC would need to explore them. An important factor in this decision was that a total ban would have denied adults their Constitutional right of access to indecent messages. The court also emphasized that the telephone medium is less accessible than television. The user must perform much more of an affirmative act to receive the message, and access is much more easily regulable.

Exon Amendment—Good or Bad?

The "Exon amendment" was a proposal to increase federal regulation of online services carrying adult materials. It was tacked onto a bill called the Communications Act of 1994, mainly directed at promoting competition between telephone companies and cable operators. The bill died in the last days of Congress' 1994 session, but there is a good chance the Exon amendment or another proposal like it will surface again in the near future.

If enacted, the Exon amendment would have added new rules to Section 223 of the Federal Communications Act, which regulates phone sex services. As discussed in the text, Section 223 currently prohibits obscene materials over the telephone system, but permits "indecent" materials as long as certain steps are taken to keep them from minors. The proposed amendment would have expressly extended Section 223 to cover *all* online service providers, digital and analog. It would also have given definite assurances that system operators who follow the FCC's age verification rules will not get in trouble for carrying indecent materials.

The problem was that another part of the Exon amendment went much further. It also would have been illegal for an online system to "make obscene or indecent materials available" to users, regardless of the system owner's knowledge or intent to provide such materials. Under this rule, every online system letting users call the Internet (which includes adult materials along with all its other information riches) would have to verify the ages of all users, even systems that contain only the most wholesome materials. Such a rule would be absurd. It's like making a bus driver check the ages of all passengers and refuse to take any children, because once they get off the bus they could head for an adult bookstore.

This problematic "access" provision was created through an odd skewing of one of the existing provisions of Section 223. That particular provision does not currently address online services, but an entirely different subject: harassing voice telephone calls. With a few added words, the Exon amendment would have expanded 223 to include e-mail harassment, and it would also expand the prohibited activities from deliberate, active harassment to merely running a system that makes indecent or obscene materials available to others, even if the materials reside on another system. It's hard to say whether this was a deliberate misuse of the harassment provision to extend its reach to all electronic access services, or simply the result of overbroad, sloppy drafting designed to cover future technological forms of active harassment. In any case, it was a big mistake and an unjustifiable burden on information flow, which would have effectively denied Internet access to anyone under 18.

The major online services, as well as the Electronic Frontier Foundation, greeted the Exon amendment with profound distaste. Much of their reaction was to the absurd provision that would harshly regulate online services simply because they provide access to the Internet. But there was also reaction against the very idea of extending FCC jurisdiction to online services. Such an extension of authority was seen as bad in itself, regardless of the basis—simply, "regulation is bad."

However, the Exon amendment could also be viewed as an effort to simplify and unify the law of indecent materials online on a national level (while not explicitly drafted to preempt individual state laws, it could have been treated as preemptive in practice, and possibly in consequent case law). The choice faced by online services today is either to suffer passively through piece-meal regulation of adult materials under a crazy quilt of local and state laws, or work to achieve a uniform national standard permitting them to adopt a consistent strategy for managing adult materials. The Exon amendment could have been a major part of such a national standard.

If another national-level proposal like the Exon amendment shows up, how should online systems respond? First, everyone should acknowledge that morally driven attempts to suppress adult materials in the online world will never go away. The realistic goal is not to avoid all regulation, but to assure that regulation is simple, uniform, and reasonable. That said, any future attempts at holding online systems responsible for the contents of other systems on the Internet should be opposed, as they contradict the very essence of the Internet as a general means for systems to connect to other systems. At the same time, online providers should consider how proposed regulations of adult materials could be leveraged to help define their legal exposure nationally for carrying such materials. Ideally, such a law would set reasonable standards for carrying adult materials, such as the age verification schemes in the current version of Section 223, and would expressly preempt all local geographic regulations of online adult materials, creating uniform standards across the country.

The *Sable* matter carries a couple of implications for system operators. First, the language of the telephone regulation asserted against dial-a-porn in that case can also be interpreted to apply to online systems. The FCC has not promoted this interpretation to date, but the possibility is always there. Second, the higher threshold of children's access to telephone communications recognized in *Sable* would apply equally to online systems, making a blanket ban on indecent messages very unlikely.

The FCC revised the regulation attacked in *Sable* a couple of times in the following years, and each revision was opposed in court by dial-a-porn companies. The latest revision was accepted in 1992 by the Second and Ninth Circuit appellate courts, possibly the two most influential federal courts in this country outside of the Supreme Court, and it appears it will not be successfully challenged. It continues to outlaw obscene messages, and permits indecent messages only if the service provider takes certain steps to verify the ages of the users. (The current version of the regulation, Section 223 of the Federal Communications Act, is reproduced in Appendix H, along with clarifying FCC regulations.)

Child Pornography

Child pornography is the politically sensational cousin of obscenity. It is different from the obscene materials we discussed above. As we saw, adult materials are obscene under the *Miller* test if their contents exceed certain moral bounds: highly sexual or violent images, sounds, or words with no serious merit outside their appeal to the viewer's lust are considered obscene.

In contrast, child pornography is illegal because lawmakers believe the process of *producing* it leads to sexual abuse of the children depicted. Children are presumed not to have the maturity or judgment for dealing with sexual situations, especially relating to pornography. As a result, a picture of a child that is merely suggestive of sex may qualify as child pornography, even if its content falls far short of the lewd content necessary to brand the picture "obscene" as well.

Child pornography is outlawed under Title 18 of the U.S. Code, Section 2251. The part most important to online systems is in Section 2252, which is reproduced in Appendix G. As you can see, it covers a lot of ground. Most of Section 2252 boils down to the following:

- It is illegal for a BBS (or system operator) to knowingly:

  - receive child pornography

  - distribute child pornography, or

  - possess more than three copies of any child pornography materials (each image file containing a child pornography image would likely be considered a separate copy for the "three copy" provision).

- Child pornography is defined as any visual depiction of "sexually explicit conduct." This includes sexual acts, as well as "lascivious exhibition of the genitals or pubic area of any person." For example, a photograph of a child sleeping with exposed genitals has been held to be child pornography.

- A "minor" for purposes of the child pornography laws is anyone under 18. This standard overrides any state laws that may define people as "adults" at an earlier age, such as 16.

- Just to make sure system operators get the point, the law specifically refers to the use of "computers" to traffic in child pornography.

Notice the use of the word "knowingly". This is the key for avoiding trouble under the child pornography laws. As long as system operators do not knowingly participate in child pornography-related activities online or permit them on their systems, they will not get in trouble under this law.

If a system operator hears even the faintest rumor of such activities, however, he or she should rush to find out what's going on, and stop any suspicious activities immediately. Child pornography is taken very seriously these days, and even the First Amendment shield is no protection unless the operator is absolutely firm about banning all known or suspected child pornography from the system.

> **Child pornography is taken very seriously these days, and even the First Amendment shield is no protection unless the operator is absolutely firm about banning all known or suspected child pornography from the system.**

What Can Government Authorities Do to an Online System?

As with other online conduct that might be labeled criminal by the authorities, they can seize the online system and arrest the system operator. Possible penalties include fines, jail, and confiscation of property if the system operator is found guilty. This subject is discussed more fully in Chapter 7. Notable prosecutions in which the system operator was given a jail sentence at trial include the prosecution of the Oklahoma Information Exchange in a local Oklahoma City court, and prosecution of the Amateur Action system of Milpitas, California in a court in Tennessee.

The Video Guy Down the Street Does It . . .

How does the typical system operator decide how risky it is to distribute adult materials online? It's pretty straightforward,

actually. If the operator sees video stores in the neighborhood selling "XXX" videotapes, he or she concludes that online systems in the neighborhood ought to be able to distribute equivalently racy materials, without getting nailed by the cops. There are at least three major problems with this reasoning.

First, videotapes are very well protected from legal obscenity problems, due to their ability to embed the adult content in full-length stories with plots, characterization, and so on. This makes it very difficult for any court to conclude that the video, taken as a whole, lacks serious artistic value—especially in a criminal obscenity prosecution, where lack of serious value must be shown beyond a reasonable doubt. Thus, most prosecutors would founder against the requirements of the *Miller* test, discussed in the text, and so they just leave videos alone. In contrast, adult online systems make most of their money distributing graphic still images. Isolated shots of highly charged sexual materials do not, by themselves, come off as part of any story, but are readily seen as a reduction of focus to the sex act itself—a much easier case for obscenity prosecutions. In a broader-bandwidth future where users can readily download full-length porn epics, the "serious value" defense will be readily available for online adult systems.

Second, an online system physically located in a given neighborhood is not necessarily a neighborhood system. Users typically call online systems from all over the state, and larger systems routinely get calls from all over the country and around the world. If the local police are tolerant of adult materials being sold in neighborhood video stores, all this implies, at best, is that the local police will let online systems distribute equivalent materials. But what about the federal agents who roam the networks nationally, and local police in other counties and states where users call into the system? Local tolerance of adult materials at the system's home base means nothing to these other cops. Look at what happened to the Amateur Action system of relatively permissive Mil-

pitas, California, which was hauled into court in Tennessee.

Third, even the local cops might treat online adult services differently from local video stores due to differences in the presentation of the two kinds of businesses, apart from the legal status of the materials they sell. Video stores are storefront businesses integrated into the fabric of the community, patronized by the very policemen and women who walk the beat. Most do not have signs in the window announcing that they sell hard-core pornography. They present themselves as family entertainment centers, and keep the adult materials in segregated, age-restricted sections in the back of the store. In contrast, most adult online systems make it very well known that they specialize in adult materials, to attract users looking for that sort of thing. They are usually not integrated at all into the local neighborhood community. Under these circumstances, it is not surprising that local police frequently bust adult online systems for distributing materials that are, in fact, not as wild sexually as what can be found in the video store around the corner.

What all this means is simple. Those who choose to offer adult materials on their online systems are taking a risk not easily comparable to running a video store. They need to become aware of the risks unique to the online environment, and to be highly familiar with the laws covering pornography, if they want to run a business with any longevity.

How to Avoid or Reduce the Risks

There are several techniques for reducing the risks of pornography on an online system. The basic situation is easily summed up: making obscenity or child pornography available on an online system can expose a system operator to serious criminal penalties, while making indecent messages available is not especially risky as long as they are effectively denied to minors.

System operators who don't need the headache of worrying whether they will be busted as pornographers should use the stronger control measures described below. Those who believe in open systems may want to use only the mildest measures, for the bare minimum protection from criminal liability.

- "Red Light Districts." Pretty much what it sounds like. The system operator sets up a special "adults only" area, with restricted entry policies and little or no policing by the operator. Shift the responsibility for users' behavior entirely onto the users themselves, who proceed at their own risk once they pass through the threshold.

  This approach does not give the operator a license to carry obscene materials or child pornography. Remember, there is no First Amendment protection for such materials, so the system operator cannot claim a media privilege to maintain obscene material on the board. This approach will work far better if the system operator limits the materials in the red light district to "indecent materials" which are barred to minors, but legally accessible to adults. The operator may well escape liability if occasional obscene or child pornography materials slip through despite genuine prohibitions, but if the general character of the red light district is that it is full of highly illegal materials, the operator will likely be held responsible for knowing about that general character, and be held accountable.

- Require all users of the system to register, with verifiable proof of age. The operator can then control access to certain areas of the system by underage users (this is a less formalized version of the red light district).

- The FCC's age-verification procedures for the dial-a-porn telephone services are the safest course to follow for system operators interested in verifying age for access to the entire system or for just the "red light districts" discussed above. These procedures were forged by over ten years of constitutional litigation, and are likely to set the standard for online systems as well. In brief, the system operator has to use reasonable efforts to determine that each permitted user is at least 18 years old, and then either:

  - require payment by credit card for the BBS services; or

  - obtain a written application from each user certifying he or she is over 18, mail a special access code to each such user, require entry of that code before making the service available, and have a procedure for immediately canceling access under that code if it is lost or stolen, or the user no longer wishes access; or

  - scramble or encrypt all indecent materials, requiring a descrambler or decryptor possessed only by permitted users.

  The exact text of the regulation is in the appendix.

- Be familiar with the ways that pornographic materials might show up on the system. These could include text files, graphic files, message threads, private mail, online chats, animated loops, multimedia, and sound files.

- Post a notice upon user registration, and periodically afterwards in the form of all-user bulletins, telling users that obscene materials will not be tolerated. If any obscene messages or wrongly placed indecent messages are found, the system operator should consider deleting them immediately, cancel access by the uploader, and post a very public message regarding that file, its uploader, and his or her fate.

- The system operator might consider monitoring private areas to protect himself or herself against users trafficking in obscene materials. While it certainly limits the likelihood that obscene materials are present, this brute force approach would be considered going too far in terms of intruding on user activities.

- Operators of adult systems are notorious for fooling themselves about their legal risks. Don't fall for their old wives' tales. Major fallacies include:

> **Operators of adult systems are notorious for fooling themselves about their legal risks. Don't fall for their old wives' tales.**

- The local video store or adult bookstore doesn't get in trouble, so my adult online system is safe.

- If I verify users' ages, then I can put anything I want on the system.

- Pictures of normal sexual activities that healthy, decent people perform privately at home can never be considered obscene.

- The adult online systems don't get in trouble, so I won't either.

- Pictures from CD-ROMs advertised in national computer magazines are never obscene.

- If I post bulletins on the system saying that all adult materials are for "educational" purposes only, this will give them serious scientific value, and they cannot be found obscene.

- Freedom of speech means I can put any adult materials that I want on the system.

Wrong. Each and every statement above is wrong. To understand the legal status of adult materials, read this book and other texts on the laws of pornography.

The First Amendment does protect system operators in their capacity as distributors, when they inadvertently carry occasional obscene materials as part of the large volume of messages and files moving continuously through their systems. This protection is described more fully in the first chapter. But it is not a license to carry obscene materials knowingly, or to ignore suspicious activities indicating obscene materials are passing through the system. Some system operators might believe they have an absolute First Amendment shield for knowingly distributing obscene materials—but they may be headed for a big fall.

Sample Contracts

Following are sample contracts for four of the most common deals today between those doing business online:

- User Agreement for Online Services
- System Operator Agreement
- Information Provider Agreement
- Online Space and Services Agreement

These examples demonstrate many important contract provisions. This is by no means, however, a complete collection of contracts relating to online services.

Everybody's situation is unique, so it is not recommended that readers use any of these samples in "plain vanilla" form as their own contracts. If you do want to use one of these contracts as a starting point or source of ideas, ask a lawyer comfortable with online activities to review it and recommend any changes necessary for your particular situation. Be aware that some actual contracts are far more ornate than these examples, and others far shorter. There is no one "right approach." Whatever makes sense to those making the deal is the right approach for that deal.

Sample Contract 1: User Agreement for Online Services

(for display to users as part of online registration to use an online system)

A. Introduction

We start every new caller relationship with a contract. It spells out what you can expect from us, and what we expect from you. We do not know each caller personally, so it is important to set out the ground rules clearly in advance.

If you agree to what you read below, welcome to our system! An instruction screen at the end of the contract will show you how to sign up.

If you have any questions about any part of the contract, please send us an e-mail about it! We will be glad to explain why these contract provisions are important for our system. We are willing to work with you on making changes if you can show us you have a better approach.

Please remember—until you and we have an agreement in place, you will not receive full access to our system.

B. Access and Services

(1) Access—We will give you full access to all file and message areas on our system. Currently, these include:

- Public message areas—reading and posting messages. We also carry Usenet and Fidonet conferences, which means you can join in public discussions with others around the world.

- File transfer areas—uploading, downloading files and browsing files.

- Local e-mail—sending and receiving messages (please see the section on privacy, below).

- Chat areas—real-time discussions with other callers who are online at the same time as you.

- Internet e-mail—permitting you to send e-mail to systems on other computer networks.

(2) Services—We offer a variety of services to our callers, and are adding more all the time. Our current services include:

- Daily electronic news from nationally syndicated news services.

- Free classified advertising for our callers, in many different product categories.

- Virus hotline—an area with frequently updated news on computer virus outbreaks, new forms of virus detected, new ways to protect your computer, and other matters of interest.

- Batch mail services, allowing you to upload and download all messages of interest for reading and writing offline.

If you would like to set up a private discussion area on our system for a group, we will be glad to do so for fees and terms to be discussed.

(3) We may change or discontinue certain access or services on our system from time to time. We will try to let you know about such changes a month or more in advance.

C. Price and Payment

(1) We will charge you a monthly fee for using our system. For $15 per month, you can use our system each month for up to 40 hours of connect time, and you can send up to 200 electronic mail messages. For additional use, you will be required to pay additional charges of 50 cents an hour, and 10 cents per electronic mail message.

(2) Certain services on our system require additional fees. Please review the complete price list in the Caller Information area before signing up for any such services. The price list will tell you which services are included in the standard monthly fee, and which are extra.

(3) You may pay by check or by credit card. You will be given the opportunity to choose the payment method when you sign up.

- If you choose to pay by credit card, we will automatically bill the amount due to your credit card account at the end of every month.

- If you choose to pay by check, we will send you an invoice at the end of every month. Payment is due within twenty days after we send your invoice.

(4) We can change the prices and fees at any time, except that our existing customers will receive two months notice of any change. All price changes will be announced in opening screen bulletins.

D. System Rules

In order to keep this system attractive and useful for all users, we need you to follow the rules we set for use of the system. You will find some of our rules here in this contract, and the rest in bulletins posted at various points in the system.

Here are some of the basic rules for our system:

- Respect other callers of the system. Feel free to express yourself, but do not do anything to injure or harm others. In particular, if you dislike someone else's ideas, you can attack the ideas, but not the person.

- We want people to speak freely on our system. But if you misuse that freedom to abuse others, we will take the liberty of cutting that discussion short.

- Do not use our system for anything that might be illegal. This system may not be used to encourage anything to do with illegal drugs, gambling, pornography, prostitution, child pornography, robbery, spreading computer viruses, cracking into private computer systems, software infringement, trafficking in credit card codes, or other crimes.

- People sometimes have trouble figuring out whether certain activities are illegal. It's usually not that hard. If it's illegal out there, it's illegal in here!

- Using a bulletin board system to commit a crime does not make it less of a crime. In fact, if you use a bulletin board system to commit a crime, you're exposing others on the system to legal risks that should be yours alone.

- If you genuinely do not know whether something you'd like to do is legal or illegal, discuss it with us before you proceed. And if we tell you we do not want you to pursue your plans on our system, you must respect our decision.

- Respect the security of our system. Do not try to gain access to system areas private to ourselves, or to other callers. Some callers try to crack system security just to show it can be done. Don't try to demonstrate this on our system.

E. Privacy

We offer private electronic mail on our system as a service to our callers. We will endeavor to keep all of your e-mail private, viewable only by you and the person to whom you address it, except:

- We, as system operators, may need to look at your electronic mail if we believe it is necessary to protect ourselves or other callers from injury or damage. For example, if we have reason to believe a caller is involved in illegal activities, which could lead the authorities to seize or search our system, we may review his or her electronic mail for our own protection. We will not, however, monitor electronic mail unless we believe it is being misused.

- We will not deliberately disclose electronic mail to other callers. If we believe certain electronic mail is connected with illegal activities, we may disclose it to the authorities to protect our system, ourselves and other callers.

- Remember that the person to whom you send electronic mail is not legally required to keep it secret. The sender or receiver of electronic mail has the right to make it public.

- If the authorities ever search or seize our system, they may gain access to your private electronic mail. In that case, we cannot assure they will not review it. Remember that you have personal rights of privacy that even the government cannot legally violate, though you may have to go to court to enforce those rights.

F. Editorial Control

We want our system to be a worthwhile place for all of our callers. This does not mean everyone can do whatever they choose on this system, regardless of its effect on others. It is our job to accommodate the common needs of all callers while we strive to meet our own goals for the system.

We will not monitor all messages and file transfers. We want to keep the message and file traffic moving quickly and smoothly—this goal would be defeated if we monitored everything on the system. However, if we see (or hear about) messages or other activities that violate the rules, threaten the order or security of the system, or use the system in ways we do not agree with, we will take appropriate action.

Our editorial control includes normal housekeeping activities like changing subject headers and deleting profanities in public messages and selecting among uploaded files for those we wish to make available for download. It also goes beyond that.

If a caller persists in posting messages or transferring files that we previously warned should not be on the system, those messages will be deleted, and he or she may be locked out. If we discover any caller violating the rules, especially the prohibition against illegal activities, we will act firmly and swiftly. Depending on the circumstances, the caller involved will be warned, or simply locked out. If the caller has done anything to put us or other callers in jeopardy, we may contact the authorities.

We do not plan on doing any of these things. If all callers act with respect and regard for us and for other callers, there will never be any problems. But if problems arise, we will assert control over our system against any caller who threatens it. And in this Agreement, you acknowledge that control.

G. Ownership of Materials

You shall retain all rights to all original messages you post and all original files you upload. Likewise, you must respect the ownership rights of others in their own messages and files. You may not post or upload any messages or files unless you own them, or you have full authority to transmit them to this system.

We own certain things you will find on this system, including the "look and feel" of the system, the name of our system, and the collective work copyright in sequences of public messages on our system. You cannot reproduce any message thread from our system, either electronically or in print, without our permission and the permission of all participants in the thread. This is not a complete list—other things on the system are also our property. Before you copy anything from our system with plans of reproducing it or distributing it, contact us about it.

H. Limitation of Liability and Indemnity

The great danger for us, and for all operators of online systems, is that we might be held accountable for the wrongful actions of our callers. If one caller libels another caller, the injured caller might blame us, even though the first caller was really at fault. If a caller uploads a program with a computer virus, and other callers' computers are damaged, we might be blamed even though the virus was left on our board by a caller. If a caller transfers illegal credit card information to another caller through private electronic mail, we might be blamed even though we did nothing more than unknowingly carry the message from one caller to another.

We did not start this system to take the blame for others' actions, and we cannot afford to operate it if we must take that blame. Accordingly, we need all callers to accept responsibility for their own acts, and to accept that an act by another caller that damages them must not be blamed on us, but on the other caller. These needs are accomplished by the following paragraph:

You agree that we will not be responsible to you for any indirect, consequential, special or punitive damages or losses you may incur in connection with our system or any of the data or other materials transmitted through or residing on our system, even if we have been advised of the possibility of such damage or loss. In addition, you agree to defend and indemnify us and

hold us harmless from and against any and all claims, proceedings, damages, injuries, liabilities, losses, costs and expenses (including reasonable attorneys fees) relating to any acts by you or materials or information transmitted by you in connection with our system leading wholly or partially to claims against us or our system by other callers or third parties.

I. Choice of Law

Our bulletin board system can be reached by callers from all fifty states, and around the world. Each of these places has a different set of laws. Since we cannot keep track of all these laws and their requirements, you agree that the law of our own state and country, *[fill in names of state and country]*, will apply to all matters relating to this Agreement and to our bulletin board system. In addition, you agree and consent that if there is ever any legal action against us, the courts of our own state and country, *[fill in names of state and country]*, will have exclusive jurisdiction and be the exclusive venue for any such legal actions.

J. General

This agreement is the entire understanding between you and us regarding your relationship to our bulletin board system. If either you or we fail to notify the other of any violations of this agreement, this will not mean that you or we cannot notify the other of future violations of any part of this agreement.

[At this point, the system initiates the contract sign-up process. For example, the user is given a choice of typing in "I agree to the terms of the [system name] User Agreement for Online Services", or exiting the system without gaining registered user privileges.]

Sample Contract 2: System Operator Agreement

System Operator Agreement

Agreement, dated _____, between _____,

with an address at _____ ("Owner"), and

_____, with an address at

_____ ("Operator").

1. ENGAGEMENT OF SERVICES

1.1 *Project Description.* Operator will provide the following services (the "Services") within Owner's [Name of System] system (the "Online Service"), as follows:

- Operator shall set up and continuously maintain the _____ area (the "Area") on the Online Service, and shall organize the Area as appropriate and in accord with any instructions given by Owner.

- Operator shall manage and edit the messages, file areas and other contents of the Area according to Owner's standard policies and procedures. Operator shall use reasonable caution to keep the Area free of illegal materials of any kind. Owner shall include disclaimers of both Owner's and Operator's liability in agreements with users of the Online Service.

- Operator shall use best efforts to promote the Area and maximize user participation in the Area.

1.2 *Personal Performance of Services.* Owner selected Operator to perform the services set forth in the Project Description in reliance on Owner receiving Operator's personal services. Operator therefore may not subcontract or otherwise delegate its obligations under this Agreement without Owner's prior written consent.

2. COMPENSATION

(a) As compensation for the Services rendered by Operator under this Agreement, Owner will pay Operator an amount equal to ____% of the amount Owner collects from use of the Area managed by Operator.

   In addition, Owner provide Operator with free access to the Area and the Online Service for puposes of performing this Agreement.

(b) Operator shall be entitled to no other compensation for the Services except as specifically set forth in this Agreement. Operator will be reimbursed for expenses in connection with this Agreement, only if approved in advance and in writing by Owner. Upon termination of this Agreement for any reason, Operator will be paid fees and expenses on a proportional basis for work to and including the effective date of the termination.

3. OWNERSHIP AND CONFIDENTIALITY

3.1 *Ownership.* Owner is and shall remain the sole and exclusive owner of all rights, title, and interest in and to all lists, libraries, databases, software, files and other works created within the Area or created by Operator for inclusion in the Area, and all modifications and enhancements thereof by or on behalf of either Owner or Operator (including ownership of all trade secrets and copyrights pertaining thereto) (collectively, the "Works"). Operator hereby assigns to Owner all of Operator's ownership and other interests of any kind in the Works and all other materials provided or created hereunder now and in the future, and shall promptly execute and return to Owner all documents deemed necessary or desirable by Owner to perfect or document such assignment for any and all purposes. Operator must keep the Works free and clear of all claims, liens and encumbrances.

Operator may use, copy, modify, distribute and transmit the Works only as part of Operator's perfomance of Services for Owner under this Agreement. Owner reserves all other rights in the Works.

3.2 *Confidentiality.* Operator acknowledges that the following comprise valuable trade secrets and other confidential information exclusively owned by Owner ("Confidential Information"): (i) the internal structure and operation of the Area not apparent to users, and all Owner business operations related to or based on use of the Area, (ii) the identities of Owner's distributors, customers and other business contacts, and (iii) any other information disclosed by Owner to Operator under conditions indicating that it is confidential. In no event may Operator disclose any Confidential Information to third parties, nor use any Confidential Information for purposes outside of this Agreement. Operator shall be fully responsible to Owner for any use or disclosure of Confidential Information by any person receiving Confidential Information in Operator's possession, without limiting any other remedies available to Owner. Operator's confidentiality obligations shall continue for ten (10) years after the termination or expiration of this Agreement.

3.3 *Return of Owner Property.* When this Agreement with Owner is terminated, or at any other time upon Owner's request, Operator will promptly deliver to Owner, all Confidential Information, Works, and other documents and materials in any form received or prepared by Operator in connection with the Services.

4. TERMINATION AND NONINTERFERENCE WITH BUSINESS

4.1 *Termination.* Either party may terminate this Agreement with or without cause at any time upon one month's written notice to the other. In the event a party breaches of the contract, the other party may terminate immediately following written notice of breach and failure by the other party to remedy the breach within ten days following such notice.

4.2 *Non-solicitation.* Operator agrees that during this Agreement and for a one (1) year period following the expiration or termination of this Agreement, Operator will not directly or indirectly solicit, or assist others in soliciting, the employees, agents or representatives of Owner on behalf of any person, including Operator.

5. INDEPENDENT CONTRACTOR RELATIONSHIP

5.1 *Nature of Relationship.* Operator's relationship with Owner will be that of an independent contractor and nothing in this Agreement should be construed to create a partnership, joint venture, or employer-employee relationship. Operator is not an agent of Owner and is not authorized to make any representation, contract, or commitment on behalf of Owner unless specifically requested or authorized to do so by Owner.

5.2 *Taxes and Records.* Operator will be solely responsible for all tax returns and payments required to be filed with or made to any federal, state or local tax authority with regard to Operator's performance of services and receipt of fees under this Agreement.

6. INDEMNITY

Operator shall defend and indemnify Owner and hold Owner harmless against and from any and all claims, actions, proceedings, judgments, damages, injuries, orders, losses, liabilities, costs and expenses of any kind (including reasonable attorneys fees) related to or based on: (a) any violation or infringement of the intellectual property rights or other rights of third parties by Operator, or (b) any grossly negligent, reckless, or intentional acts or omissions by Operator.

7. LIMITATION OF LIABILITY

In no event shall either party be liable to the other party for any incidental, special, exemplary or consequential damages, even if advised of the possibility of such damages.

8. WARRANTIES

8.1 *Right to Enter Into Agreement.* Operator warrants that its entry into this Agreement is rightful and does not violate any other Agreement to which it is a party.

8.2 *Lawful Conduct.* Operator warrants that it will conform, and cause the Area to conform, to all applicable and valid laws and regulations.

8.3 *Illegal Materials.* Operator warrants and agrees that it will use best efforts to keep the Area and the Works free of any materials or messages that may infringe or violate any copyright, patent, trade secret, or other third party right.

9. GENERAL PROVISIONS

9.1 *Law.* This Agreement will be governed and construed in accordance with the laws of _____, except for its choice of law provisions.

9.2 *Entire Agreement.* This Agreement sets forth the entire understanding and agreement of the parties as to the subject matter of this Agreement, and merges and supersedes all prior or verbal understandings, promises, agreements, arrangements, and representations between the parties. It may be changed only by a writing signed by both parties.

9.3 *Severability; Waiver.* If any provision of this Agreement is held to be invalid or unenforceable, the remaining provisions will continue in full force without being impaired or invalidated in any way. The waiver by Owner of a breach of any provision by Operator will not operate or be interpreted as a waiver of any other or subsequent breach by Operator.

9.4 *Successors and Assigns.* Neither this Agreement nor any of the rights or obligations of Operator arising under this Agreement may be assigned or transferred without Owner's prior written consent.

9.5 *Notices.* All notices must be in writing, and must be mailed by registered or certified mail, postage prepaid and return receipt requested, or delivered by hand to the party to whom the notice is required or permitted to be given.

9.6 *Survival of Promises.* The promises in Section 3 (Ownership and Confidentiality) will survive any termination or expiration of this Agreement.

9.7 *Forum and Jurisdiction.* Exclusive jurisdiction and venue for any and all actions or proceedings relating to this Agreement can be brought only in courts located within _____ County, State of _____. The parties hereby consent to such jurisdiction and agree to such venue.

9.8 *Headings.* The headings in this Agreement are intended solely for convenience and shall be given no effect in the construction or interpretation of this Agreement.

OPERATOR: **OWNER:**

By: _____   By: _____

Title: _____   Title: _____

Sample Contract 3: Information Provider Agreement

Information Provider Agreement

This Agreement dated _____, 199__, between _____, with an address at _____ ("Online Service") and_____, with an address at _____ ("Owner").

Owner owns and updates regularly an electronic database of publications relating to the [Name of Industry] service industry (the "Database"). Online Service owns and operates _____, a computerized system for data communications (the "System"), and wishes to offer users of the System ("Users") access to the Database. In consideration of the above and the promises set forth below, Online Service and Owner hereby agree as follows:

1. License

(a) *Basic Grant.* Subject to the terms and conditions of this Agreement, Owner hereby grants Online Service a nonexclusive, worldwide right and license to copy, modify, distribute, transmit and provide access to the Database on the System, for use by Users of the System.

(b) *Reformatting.* Online Service has the right to reformat the information in the Database as deemed appropriate by Online Service for distribution on the System. Owner's prior consent is necessary for any changes to the content of the Database, including all additions, changes or deletions to or of any of the data or publications in the Database.

(c) *Permitted Use.* Online Service shall not sell, license or distribute the Database other than to Users of the System, in their capacity as end users. Online Service shall permit each User to store, manipulate, analyze, reformat, print and display material from the Database only on a single personal computer under such User's direct control. Online Service shall not permit Users to distribute or redistribute the Database or any such derived materials, in whole or in part, in any form or medium.

(d) *Reservation of Rights.* All rights and licenses in the Database and its contents not expressly granted herein are reserved entirely to the Owner.

2. Price and Payment

(a) *Price.* Online Service will pay Owner a percentage of total revenues collected by Online Service from use of the Database by Users as set forth in Exhibit B.

(b) *Payment.* Online Service will pay Owner the royalties due on revenues collected in each calendar month within 30 days after the end of that calendar month. Together with such payments, Online Service will include a report of all usage of the Database, including all information necessary to show the basis on which payments are calculated in accord with this Agreement.

(c) Taxes. Online Service shall be responsible for the proper payment of all taxes which may be levied or assessed on the provision of the Database or on any payments by Online Service to Owner hereunder, other than income taxes of Owner.

3. Delivery of Database to Owner

(a) *Manner of Delivery and Timing.* Owner shall provide Online Service the Database and daily updates to the Database via electronic transmission. Daily updates shall be delivered between 12:00 a.m. and 8:00 a.m. EST every day.

(b) *Delivery Format.* Owner shall provide Online Service with all information necessary to properly receive the Database and all updates delivered by Owner, and integrate same into Online Service's own database management system. Owner may make changes in content formats and organization from time to time, upon 90 days' notice to Online Service.

4. Audit

(a) *Books and Records.* Online Service agrees to keep complete, clear and accurate books and records documenting all activities relating to the Database and payments to Owner. During the term of this Agreement and for one year afterwards, Owner may examine such books and records at any time on reasonable notice during normal business hours through an independent certified public accountant. Online Service shall sign a reasonable nondisclosure agreement relating to such books and records if requested by Owner. All audits and inspections shall be conducted at Owner's expense, unless it demonstrates an underpayment exceeding 5% for the period covered by the inspection, in which event Online Service shall bear all expenses of the examination.

(b) *Service Monitoring.* Online Service shall give Owner one free User account for the purpose of monitoring Online Service's provision of the Database to Users under this Agreement.

5. Online Service Responsibilities

(a) *Providing Database Access to Users.* Online Service shall provide access to the Database to all Users who desire such access, in accordance with this Agreement and upon such other terms as are specified by Online Service.

(b) *User Contracts.* Online Service shall obtain a legally enforceable contract with each User, prior to providing such User with access to the Database, which protects Owner from all liability, expressly places restrictions on each User's use of the Database at least as great as those specified in this Agreement, and fully protects all of Owner's proprietary rights in the Database and its contents as specified in this Agreement. Online Service shall be responsible for collecting all amounts due from Users for use of the Database.

(c) *Support.* Online Service shall provide all reasonable telephone support requested by Users in use of the Database. Owner's support personnel shall be available to Online Service during normal business hours to provide any information on the Database needed by Online Service in order to support Users.

6. Marketing and Promotion

(a) *By Online Service.* Online Service will use reasonable efforts throughout the term of this Agreement to market, advertise and promote the Database as a part of the System, build market awareness of the Database as part of the System, and maximize use of the Database on the System.

(b) *Approval of Materials.* Online Service and Owner each may promote the Database as provided on the System. The parties agree that the creation of advertising, promotion or other marketing materials using the other party's trademarks, services marks or trade names shall be subject to the other party's prior approval, which approval shall not be unreasonably withheld or delayed.

7. Ownership

(a) *Ownership by Owner.* As between Online Service and Owner, all copyrights and other interests in the Database, in any and all forms, are exclusively owned by Owner.

(b) *Protection of Database Rights.* Online Service shall not infringe, violate, or impair, or knowingly permit any infringement, violation or impairment of any of Owner's rights in the Database. Online Service shall notify Owner of any suspected infringement or violation of such rights. Online Service shall retain all copyright notices and other proprietary notices of Owner and others contained in the Database and updates as provided by Owner, and add any other proprietary notices to the Database as reasonably requested by Owner.

8. Representations and Warranties

(a) *Authority.* Each party represents and warrants that it has the power and authority to enter into and perform this Agreement and to grant the rights granted herein.

(b) *Non-Infringement.* Owner warrants that the Database does not infringe any patent known to Owner, nor infringe or violate any copyright, trade secret or any other proprietary or other right of any third party. Online Service warrants that changes to the Database by Online Service hereunder, and only such changes, do not infringe any patent known to Owner, nor infringe or violate any copyright, trade secret or any other proprietary or other right of any third party.

9. Liability Limitations and Indemnification

(a) *Warranty Disclaimer and Liability Limitation.* EACH PARTY HEREBY DISCLAIMS ANY AND ALL WARRANTIES, EXPRESS OR IMPLIED, IN REGARD TO ANY INFORMATION, PRODUCT OR SERVICE FURNISHED BY IT HEREUNDER, INCLUDING WITHOUT LIMITATION ANY AND ALL IMPLIED WARRANTIES OF MERCHANTABILITY OR FITNESS FOR A PARTICULAR PURPOSE. NEITHER PARTY SHALL BE LIABLE UNDER ANY CIRCUMSTANCES FOR LOSS OF PROFITS OR ANY INCIDENTAL, SPECIAL, EXEMPLARY, PUNITIVE OR CONSEQUENTIAL DAMAGES, EVEN IF IT HAS

BEEN ADVISED OF THE POSSIBILITY OF SUCH DAMAGES, EXCEPT FOR ANY EX-PRESS INDEMNITY OBLIGATIONS HEREUNDER.

(b) *Indemnification.* Each party shall defend, indemnify and hold harmless the other party and its officers, directors, owners, and employees, from and against any and all loss, liability, claims, damage, cost or expense (including attorneys' fees and costs) relating to breach of any warranties or representations by the indemnifying party herein, or any claims which, if true, would contradict any warranties or representations by the indemnifying party herein, provided that the indemnified party must give the indemnifying party prompt notice of any claims covered by this indemnity, and the indemnifying party shall control defense and settlement of all claims hereunder.

10. Term and Termination

(a) *Term.* The initial term of this Agreement shall be two years from the date first written above. The Agreement shall renew automatically thereafter on a year to year basis for successive one year renewal terms, until and unless either party provides written notice of non-renewal to the other party 90 days or more prior to the expiration of the then-current term.

(b) *Termination.*

   (i) *For Cause.* In the event either party commits a material breach of one or more of the terms of this Agreement, and does not cure such breach within 30 days after written notice of such breach from the other party, then the notifying party may terminate this Agreement immediately by written notice.

   (ii) *Bankruptcy or Insolvency.* If either party makes an assignment for the benefit of creditors, files a petition under the bankruptcy or insolvency laws of any jurisdiction, appoints a trustee or receiver for its property or business, or is adjudicated bankrupt or insolvent, then the other party may terminate this Agreement immediately upon notice.

   (iii) *Proprietary Rights.* If either party violates the proprietary rights of the other hereunder, then the other party may terminate this Agreement immediately upon notice.

(c) *Post-Termination Obligations.* Upon any termination or expiration of this Agreement: (i) Online Service shall promptly delete the Database from the System, and shall not use the Database or any part of the Database thereafter under authority of this Agreement, and (ii) except for termination by Online Service due to breach by Owner, Online Service shall promptly provide Owner with a complete and accurate final account of all transactions subsequent to those shown in the statement last submitted to Owner, and shall pay to Owner all amounts due as provided in this Agreement.

(d) *Survival.* The following provisions shall survive any termination or expiration of this Agreement: 2(c), 4(a), 9(b), 10(c).

11. Other

(a) *Assignability.* This Agreement shall not be assigned, sublicensed or transferred by either party, without the prior written consent of the other party, which shall not be unreasonably withheld.

(b) *Notice.* All notices hereunder shall be given in writing at the addresses set forth above. The parties shall promptly notify each other in writing of any change in address. Notice given by express courier requiring signature upon delivery shall be deemed delivered on the day of receipt by notified party or someone who purports to sign on behalf of notified party.

(c) *Force Majeure.* Neither party shall be responsible for delays or failures in performance resulting from acts beyond its control, such as acts of God, acts of war, epidemics, power outages, fire, earthquakes and other disasters.

(d) *Severability.* If any of the provisions of this Agreement shall be held invalid, illegal or unenforceable, the validity, legality or enforceability of the remaining provisions of this Agreement shall not be affected thereby.

(e) *Law.* This Agreement shall be interpreted, construed and enforced in accordance with the laws of the State of _____, without regard to _____ choice of law rules.

(f) *Forum and Jurisdiction.* Exclusive jurisdiction and venue for any and all actions or proceedings relating to this Agreement can be brought only in courts located within _____ County, State of _____. The parties hereby consent to such jurisdiction and agree to such venue.

(g) *Headings.* The headings in this Agreement are intended solely for convenience and shall be given no effect in the construction or interpretation of this Agreement.

(h) *Entire Agreement.* This Agreement sets forth the entire understanding and agreement of the parties as to the subject matter of this Agreement, and merges and supersedes all prior or verbal understandings, promises, agreements, arrangements, and representations between the parties. It may be changed only by a writing signed by both parties.

(i) *Waiver.* The waiver by either party of a breach of any provision by the other party will not operate or be interpreted as a waiver of any other or subsequent breach caused by the other party.

[Online Service]   **[Provider]**

By: _____   By: _____

Title: _____   Title: _____

Sample Contract 4:
Online Space and Services Agreement

Online Space and Services Agreement

AGREEMENT, dated _____, between _____ ("System Owner") and
_____ ("Vendor").

Purpose:

1. System Owner operates an electronic information system (the "System"), and offers others the opportunity to provide their own online systems and services within the System (the System area provided to Vendor under this Agreement shall be called the "Vendor Area"), and

2. Vendor desires to operate a Vendor Area on the System to provide services to its customers and/or the general public (all System and Vendor Area participants are called "Callers").

Accordingly, System Owner and Vendor agree:

1. Resources and Services Provided by System Owner

(a) System Owner shall provide Vendor with a Vendor Area on the System with the following features:

   (i) The Vendor Area can support up to:

      ____ public message areas

      ____ file library areas

      ____ live discussion areas

      ____ Caller electronic mail accounts

     Vendor shall also have complete access to System Owner's existing computer network gateways for purposes of electronic mail, and any other general gateways System Owner may establish in the future for Callers. System Owner may charge an additional fee for certain network gateway services. System Owner may enhance the capabilities or capacities of the System from time to time at its sole discretion.

   (ii) Up to _____ Callers may participate in the Vendor Area simultaneously, and an unlimited number of Callers may be registered for use of the Vendor Area. The Vendor Area configuration and requirements desired by Vendor may reduce the number of Callers that can be handled simultaneously.

   (iii) Vendor shall have _____bytes of basic disk storage space standard for the Vendor Area; more storage space is available for additional charges.

(iv) If Vendor requires additional capacity for the Vendor Area, System Owner will provide such capacity at a reasonable price to be mutually agreed, subject to availability and the technical and practical limits of the System.

(b) System Owner shall provide the following services:

(i) System Owner shall authorize and remove authorization of Callers as requested by Vendor. Authorization and removal of authorization shall occur within one (1) business day after each request by Vendor, except for bona fide emergencies, such as removal of authorization of Callers who are misusing or damaging System resources or data.

(ii) System Owner shall maintain, and provide to Vendor within thirty (30) days after the end of each month, records of access times and connect times for all Callers to the Vendor Area for that month.

(iii) System Owner intends to back up all messages and files regularly as part of System Owner's general system backup. However, Vendor is solely responsible for maintaining complete backup records of all information in the Vendor area, and shall not rely upon System Owner for such backups.

(iv) System Owner shall provide Vendor with security for Callers, messages and files equivalent to the security provided for the System generally. If Vendor or its Callers deem any of their materials maintained on the System or transmitted through the System to be highly confidential, then Vendor or its callers are solely responsible to protect their confidentiality through the use of encryption or other security techniques. System Owner does not guarantee that such materials are safe from interception or alteration by third parties.

(v) System Owner shall provide Vendor with reasonable assistance in setting up and maintaining the Vendor Area, and with system operator level access to the System. Vendor shall perform all system operator functions, unless indicated otherwise in Exhibit A.

(vi) System Owner shall have in force maintenance contracts providing for maintenance of all computer equipment and systems necessary to support the Vendor Area as described herein. Vendor shall pay any costs where emergency maintenance is required for the Vendor Area and no other part of the System, or is made necessary due to the activities of Vendor or its callers.

(vii) System Owner may change user interface, transmission, or other System specifications upon sixty (60) days notice to Vendor, except that such changes may be made without notice where required by emergency or external circumstances. If Vendor objects to any such change, System Owner shall attempt to accommodate Vendor's needs.

(c) Other services provided by System Owner are described in Exhibit A.

2. Price and Payment

Vendor shall pay System Owner the setup fees, connect time charges and other charges indicated in Exhibit B. All charges payable on invoice shall be due within ten (10) business days after delivery of each invoice. Prices and terms for additional services shall be separately agreed between System Owner and Vendor.

3. Setup of Vendor Area

System Owner shall make the Vendor Area ready for production use by Vendor within thirty (30) days after the date of this Agreement. Vendor will be given access to the System to begin setup of the Vendor Area within ten (10) days after the date of this Agreement.

4. System Rules

(a) *Daily Operations.* Vendor shall comply fully with all System Rules for daily operation on the System, as set or changed by System Owner from time to time. In the event of any conflict between the express terms of this Agreement and the System Rules, the express terms of this Agreement shall govern.

(b) *No Brokering.* Vendor shall not broker, resell or provide to third parties the online services capability provided by System Owner to Vendor under this Agreement. Vendor shall use the Vendor Area provided hereunder solely to provide end user services to Callers. Vendor's Callers may not set up their own online Systems using the System except under direct agreements with System Owner.

5. Term and Termination

(a) *Term.* This Agreement shall become effective on the date first written above, and remain in force for an initial term of one (1) year. Thereafter, the Agreement shall automatically renew for successive one-year renewal terms, until and unless either party gives the other party notice of non-renewal at least sixty (60) days prior to the end of the initial term or then-current renewal term.

(b) *Termination.* Either party can terminate this Agreement immediately following breach of this Agreement by the other party and failure of the breaching party to cure within thirty (30) days after written notice of the breach, except that in the event of non-payment by Vendor, System Owner may terminate upon failure of Vendor to fully cure the non-payment within five (5)days after notice. In addition, in the event of any breach of security or confidentiality obligations by Vendor, or in the event Vendor's activities create a serious risk to the System, System Owner's property rights or any Callers, in System Owner's sole judgment, then System Owner can suspend or terminate Vendor's participation in the System immediately upon notice.

6. Confidentiality

(a) *Electronic mail.* System Owner shall maintain all electronic mail sent to or by Vendor's Callers reasonably confidential and shall not review such electronic mail, provided that System Owner may review the contents of one or more such electronic mail messages in the event System Owner reasonably believes that such messages may be illegal or injurious to System

Owner, the System or others. System Owner intends to give Vendor reasonable notice before engaging in any such review.

(b) *Confidential Information.* Each party agrees not to disclose any Confidential Information (as hereinafter defined) concerning the other party or any Caller, customer, client or business associate of the other party (collectively, "Associated Entities") to any person, corporation or other organization, nor use any Confidential Information other than in performance of this Agreement, at all times during the term of this Agreement and for ten years thereafter. Each party's "Confidential Information" includes, but is not limited to, its and its Associated Entities' business and marketing plans, programs, patents, know-how, customer lists, business methods, electronic mail and any other information or materials not listed above which is confidentially disclosed by such party or any of its Associated Entities to the other party.

(c) *Encrypted Materials.* Vendor and its Callers may transmit and maintain encrypted materials in the Vendor Area. However, System Owner reserves the right to request the decryption of any or all such materials if it believes or suspects in good faith that some or all such materials may be injurious or pose other risks to System Owner, the System or others. If Vendor or any Vendor Caller refuses to decrypt any such materials, or to provide reliable proof that plain text provided by Vendor to System Owner is truly the decrypted form of the encrypted materials in question, then System Owner may at its sole option terminate this Agreement immediately for cause, shut down and/or eliminate all or any part of the Vendor Area, pursue all available remedies at law or equity, or take any other action System Owner believes in good faith is necessary to protect System Owner, the System or others, all without any liability or responsibility to Vendor or any Vendor Callers.

7. Representations and Disclaimers

(a) Each party represents and agrees that its conduct in relation to the System conforms and will conform to all applicable laws and regulations, and does not and will not violate the rights of any third parties.

(b) Vendor represents and agrees that it shall enter into an agreement with each of its Callers expressly disclaiming all express and implied warranties from Vendor or System Owner to Callers, expressly limiting the Caller's damages for any reason against either Vendor or System Owner to direct damages only, and with a full indemnity from each Caller to both Vendor and System Owner against any legal actions, judicial orders, costs, losses or expenses of any kind relating to illegal or injurious activities by such Caller or to any materials or information placed on or transmitted through the System or the Vendor Area by such Caller. In addition, Vendor's contract with each Vendor Caller shall include an agreement by that Caller that: (i) only Vendor, and not System Owner, is obligated to that Caller under that agreement, and (ii) any actions by that Caller in relation to the Vendor, the Vendor Area or the System shall be against Vendor, and not System Owner.

(c) **System Owner does not give Vendor any warranties, express or implied, including but not limited to the implied warranties of merchantability or fitness for a particular purpose. The System and all other services and materials are provided by System Owner "AS IS." Vendor acknowledges and agrees that it is wholly and solely respon-**

ible for all information transmitted to and through the System by Vendor or its Callers, and that the System has no responsibility for the accuracy, completeness or legality of that information.

8. Indemnity

Vendor shall defend and indemnify System Owner and hold System Owner harmless from and against any and all claims, actions, proceedings, judgments, losses, liabilities, costs and expenses (including reasonable attorneys fees) arising from or related to: (i) Vendor's failure to perform correctly any of Vendor's obligations under this Agreement, (ii) failure of any representation by Vendor in this Agreement to be entirely true, (iii) Vendor's incorrect maintenance of the Vendor area, or any data on or off the System, (iv) any legal action or other action against System Owner by any Vendor Caller, or (v) any actions or omissions by Vendor in its operation of the Vendor Area that lead to any claims against System Owner.

9. Limitation of Liability

Neither party shall be liable to the other party for any indirect, consequential, incidental, special or punitive damages, even if advised in advance of the possibility of same, except for damages due under the express indemnity provisions of this Agreement.

10. Non-Hiring

During the term of this Agreement and for two years thereafter, neither party shall solicit, recruit or attempt to employ or induce employment of any employee or consultant of the other party for itself or for any other company or individual.

11. Independent Contractors

The parties shall perform all of their duties under this Agreement as independent contractors, not as principal-agent, joint venturers or partners. Neither party shall hold itself out to third parties as a principal, agent, partner or joint venturer of the other party or as having any power to bind the other party.

12. General

(a) This Agreement contains the entire agreement of the parties with respect to its subject matter and supersedes all existing agreements and all oral, written or other communications between them concerning its subject matter. This Agreement shall not be modified in any way except by a writing signed by both parties. There are no third party beneficiaries of this Agreement, including but not limited to Callers.

(b) If any provision of the Agreement (or any portion thereof) shall be held to be invalid, illegal or unenforceable, the validity, legality or enforceability of the remainder of this Agreement shall not in any way be affected or impaired thereby.

(c) This Agreement and its validity, construction and performance shall be governed in all respects by the laws of the State of _____, without regard to _____'s choice of law rules. Exclusive jurisdiction and venue for all matters relating to this Agreement shall be in the State of _____, and the parties hereby agree and consent to such jurisdiction and venue.

(d) Except as otherwise specifically set forth herein, all notices shall be in writing and shall be forwarded by registered or certified mail or by overnight express courier requiring signature of the recipient to complete delivery, and sent to the parties at the addresses set forth at the top of this Agreement or to any other addresses designated in writing hereafter, ATT: President. Notices sent by registered or certified mail shall be deemed delivered seven (7) business days after mailing; notices sent by express courier as described above shall be deemed delivered the day after they are given to the courier by the notifying party.

(e) The headings in this Agreement are intended for convenience of reference and shall not affect its interpretation.

(f) The failure of either Vendor or System Owner to insist upon strict performance of any of the provisions contained herein shall in no way constitute a waiver of future violations of the same or any other provision.

(g) Neither this Agreement, nor any duties or obligations under this Agreement, may be assigned by either party without the prior consent of the other, except that either party may assign its rights and obligations under this Agreement without consent to any person or entity that succeeds to all or substantially all of such party's business. This agreement is fully binding on System Owner's and Vendor's permitted successors in interest, agents, servants, heirs, executors and administrators.

(h) The provisions of this Agreement relating to confidentiality, warranties and indemnities shall survive any termination or expiration of this Agreement.

System Owner: _____   **Vendor:** _____

By: _____   By: _____

Title:_____   Title:_____

Electronic Communications Privacy Act

Wire and Electronic Communications Interception and Interception of Oral Communications

18 USCS 2510 (1988)

§ 2510. Definitions

As used in this chapter [18 USCS §§ 2510 et seq.]-

(1) "wire communication" means any aural transfer made in whole or in part through the use of facilities for the transmission of communications by the aid of wire, cable, or other like connection between the point of origin and the point of reception (including the use of such connection in a switching station) furnished or operated by any person engaged in providing or operating such facilities for the transmission of interstate or foreign communications or communications affecting interstate or foreign commerce and such term includes any electronic storage of such communication, but such term does not include the radio portion of a cordless telephone communication that is transmitted between the cordless telephone handset and the base unit;

(2) "oral communication" means any oral communication uttered by a person exhibiting an expectation that such communication is not subject to interception under circumstances justifying such expectation, but such term does not include any electronic communication;

(3) "State" means any State of the United States, the District of Columbia, the Commonwealth of Puerto Rico, and any territory or possession of the United States;

(4) "intercept" means the aural or other acquisition of the contents of any wire, electronic, or oral communication through the use of any electronic, mechanical, or other device.

(5) "electronic, mechanical, or other device" means any device or apparatus which can be used to intercept a wire, oral, or electronic communication other than-

(a) any telephone or telegraph instrument, equipment or facility, or any component thereof, (i) furnished to the subscriber or user by a provider of wire or electronic communication service in the ordinary course of its business and being used by the subscriber or user in the ordinary course of its business or furnished by such subscriber or user for connection to the facilities of such service and used in the ordinary course of its business; or (ii) being used by a provider of wire or electronic communication service in the ordinary course of its business, or by an investigative or law enforcement officer in the ordinary course of his duties;

(b) a hearing aid or similar device being used to correct subnormal hearing to not better than normal;

(6) "person" means any employee, or agent of the United States or any State or political subdivision thereof, and any individual, partnership, association, joint stock company, trust, or corporation;

(7) "Investigative or law enforcement officer" means any officer of the United States or of a State or political subdivision thereof, who is empowered by law to conduct investigations of or to make arrests for offenses enumerated in this chapter [18 USCS §§ 2510 et seq.], and any attorney authorized by law to prosecute or participate in the prosecution of such offenses;

(8) "contents," when used with respect to any wire, oral, or electronic communication, includes any information concerning the substance, purport, or meaning of that communication;

(9) "Judge of competent jurisdiction" means-

(a) a judge of a United States district court or a United States court of appeals; and

(b) a judge of any court of general criminal jurisdiction of a State who is authorized by a statute of that State to enter orders authorizing interceptions of wire, oral, or electronic communications;

(10) "communication common carrier" shall have the same meaning which is given the term "common carrier" by section 153(h) of title 47 of the United States Code;

(11) "aggrieved person" means a person who was a party to any intercepted wire, oral, or electronic communication or a person against whom the interception was directed;

(12) "electronic communication" means any transfer of signs, signals, writing, images, sounds, data, or intelligence of any nature transmitted in whole or in part by a wire, radio, electromagnetic, photoelectronic or photooptical system that affects interstate or foreign commerce, but does not include-

(A) the radio portion of a cordless telephone communication that is transmitted between the cordless telephone handset and the base unit;

(B) any wire or oral communication;

(C) any communication made through a tone-only paging device; or

(D) any communication from a tracking device (as defined in section 3117 of this title);

(13) "user" means any person or entity who-

(A) uses an electronic communication service; and

(B) is duly authorized by the provider of such service to engage in such use;

(14) "electronic communications system" means any wire, radio, electromagnetic, photooptical or photoelectronic facilities for the transmission of electronic communications, and any computer facilities or related electronic equipment for the electronic storage of such communications;

(15) "electronic communication service" means any service which provides to users thereof the ability to send or receive wire or electronic communications;

(16) "readily accessible to the general public" means, with respect to a radio communication, that such communication is not-

(A) scrambled or encrypted;

(B) transmitted using modulation techniques whose essential parameters have been withheld from the public with the intention of preserving the privacy of such communication;

(C) carried on a subcarrier or other signal subsidiary to a radio transmission;

(D) transmitted over a communication system provided by a common carrier, unless the communication is a tone only paging system communication; or

(E) transmitted on frequencies allocated under part 25, subpart D, E, or F of part 74, or part 94 of the Rules of the Federal Communications Commission, unless, in the case of a communication transmitted on a frequency allocated under part 74 that is not exclusively allocated to broadcast auxiliary services, the communication is a two-way voice communication by radio;

(17) "electronic storage" means-

(A) any temporary, intermediate storage of a wire or electronic communication incidental to the electronic transmission thereof; and

(B) any storage of such communication by an electronic communication service for purposes of backup protection of such communication; and

(18) "aural transfer" means a transfer containing the human voice at any point between and including the point of origin and the point of reception.

§ 2511. Interception and disclosure of wire, oral, or electronic communications prohibited

(1) Except as otherwise specifically provided in this chapter [18 USCS §§ 2510 et seq.] any person who—

(a) intentionally intercepts, endeavors to intercept, or procures any other person to intercept or endeavor to intercept, any wire, oral, or electronic communication;

(b) intentionally uses, endeavors to use, or procures any other person to use or endeavor to use any electronic, mechanical, or other device to intercept any oral communication when-

(i) such device is affixed to, or otherwise transmits a signal through, a wire, cable, or other like connection used in wire communication; or

(ii) such device transmits communications by radio, or interferes with the transmission of such communication; or

(iii) such person knows, or has reason to know, that such device or any component thereof has been sent through the mail or transported in interstate or foreign commerce; or

(iv) such use or endeavor to use (A) takes place on the premises of any business or other commercial establishment the operations of which affect interstate or foreign commerce; or (B) obtains or is for the purpose of obtaining information relating to the operations of any business or other commercial establishment the operations of which affect interstate or foreign commerce; or

(v) such person acts in the District of Columbia, the Commonwealth of Puerto Rico, or any territory or possession of the United States;

(c) intentionally discloses, or endeavors to disclose, to any other person the contents of any wire, oral, or electronic communication, knowing or having reason to know that the information was obtained through the interception of a wire, oral, or electronic communication in violation of this subsection;

(d) intentionally uses, or endeavors to use, the contents of any wire, oral, or electronic communication, knowing or having reason to know that the information was obtained through the interception of a wire, oral, or electronic communication in violation of this subsection; or

(e)(i) intentionally discloses, or endeavors to disclose, to any other person the contents of any wire, oral, or electronic communication, intercepted by means authorized by sections 2511(2)(A)(ii), 2511(b)-(c), 2511(e), 2516, and 2518 of this subchapter, (ii) knowing or having reason to know that the information was obtained through the interception of such a communication in connection with a criminal investigation, (iii) having obtained or received the information in connection with a criminal investigation, and (iv) with intent to improperly obstruct, impede, or interfere with a duly authorized criminal investigation,

shall be punished as provided in subsection (4) or shall be subject to suit as provided in subsection (5).

(2) (a) (i) It shall not be unlawful under this chapter for an operator of a switchboard, or an officer, employee, or agent of a provider of wire or electronic communication service, whose facilities are used in the transmission of a wire communication, to intercept, disclose, or use that communication in the normal course of his employment while engaged in any activity which is a necessary incident to the rendition of his service or to the protection of the rights or property of the provider of that service, except that a provider of wire communication service to the public shall not utilize service observing or random monitoring except for mechanical or service quality control checks.

(ii) Notwithstanding any other law, providers of wire or electronic communication service, their officers, employees, and agents, landlords, custodians, or other persons, are authorized to provide information, facilities, or technical assistance to persons authorized by law to intercept wire, oral, or electronic communications or to conduct electronic surveillance, as defined in section 101 of the Foreign Intelligence Surveillance Act of 1978 if such provider, its officers, employees, or agents, landlord, custodian, or other specified person, has been provided with-

(A) a court order directing such assistance signed by the authorizing judge, or

(B) a certification in writing by a person specified in section 2518(7) of this title [18 USCS § 2518(7)] or the Attorney General of the United States that no warrant or court order is required by law, that all statutory requirements have been met, and that the specified assistance is required, setting forth the period of time during which the provision of the information, facilities, or technical assistance is authorized and specifying the information, facilities, or technical assistance required. No provider of wire or electronic communication service, officer, employee, or agent thereof, or landlord, custodian, or other specified person shall disclose the existence of any interception or surveillance or the device used to accomplish the interception or surveillance with respect to which the person has been furnished an order or certification under this subparagraph, except as may otherwise be required by legal process and then only after prior notification to the Attorney General or to the principal prosecuting attorney of a State or any political subdivision of a State, as may be appropriate. Any such disclosure, shall render such person liable for the civil damages provided for in section 2520. No cause of action shall lie in any court against any provider of wire or electronic communication service, its officers, employees, or agents, landlord, custodian, or other specified person for providing information, facilities, or assistance in accordance with the terms of a court order or certification under this chapter.

(b) It shall not be unlawful under this chapter for an officer, employee, or agent of the Federal Communications Commission, in the normal course of his employment and in discharge of the monitoring responsibilities exercised by the Commission in the enforcement of chapter 5 of title 47 of the United States Code, to intercept a wire or electronic communication, or oral communication transmitted by radio, or to disclose or use the information thereby obtained.

(c) It shall not be unlawful under this chapter for a person acting under color of law to intercept a wire, oral, or electronic communication, where such person is a party to the communication or one of the parties to the communication has given prior consent to such interception.

(d) It shall not be unlawful under this chapter for a person not acting under color of law to intercept a wire or oral communication where such person is a party to the communication or where one of the parties to the communication has given prior consent to such interception unless such communication is intercepted for the purpose of committing any criminal or tortious act in violation of the Constitution or laws of the United States or of any State.

(e) Notwithstanding any other provision of this title [18 USCS §§ 1 et seq.] or section 705 or 706 of the Communications Act of 1934 [47 USCS § 605 or 606], it shall not be unlawful for an officer, employee, or agent of the United States in the normal course of his official duty to conduct electronic surveillance, as defined in section 101 of the Foreign Intelligence Surveillance Act of 1978 [50 USCS § 1801], as authorized by that Act [50 USCS §§ 1801 et seq.].

(f) Nothing contained in this chapter [18 USCS §§ 2510 et seq.] or chapter 121, or section 705 of the Communications Act of 1934 [47 USCS § 605], shall be deemed to affect the acquisition by the United States Government of foreign intelligence information from international or foreign communications, or foreign intelligence activities conducted in accordance with otherwise applicable Federal law involving a foreign electronic communications system, utilizing a means other than electronic surveillance as defined in section 101 of the Foreign Intelligence Surveillance Act of 1978 [50 USCS § 1801], and procedures in this chapter [18 USCS §§ 2510 et seq.] and the Foreign Intelligence Surveillance Act of 1978 [50 USCS §§ 1801 et seq.] shall be the exclusive means by which electronic surveillance, as defined in section 101 of such Act [50 USCS § 1801], and the interception of domestic wire, oral, or electronic communications may be conducted.

(g) It shall not be unlawful under this chapter or chapter 121 of this title for any person-

(i) to intercept or access an electronic communication made through an electronic communication system that is configured so that such electronic communication is readily accessible to the general public;

(ii) to intercept any radio communication which is transmitted-

(I) by any station for the use of the general public, or that relates to ships, aircraft, vehicles, or persons in distress;

(II) by any governmental, law enforcement, civil defense, private land mobile, or public safety communications system, including police and fire, readily accessible to the general public;

(III) by a station operating on an authorized frequency within the bands allocated to the amateur, citizens band, or general mobile radio services; or

(IV) by any marine or aeronautical communications system;

(iii) to engage in any conduct which-

(I) is prohibited by section 633 of the Communications Act of 1934; or

(II) is excepted from the application of section 705(a) of the Communications Act of 1934 by section 705(b) of that Act;

(iv) to intercept any wire or electronic communication the transmission of which is causing harmful interference to any lawfully operating station or consumer electronic equipment, to the extent necessary to identify the source of such interference; or

(v) for other users of the same frequency to intercept any radio communication made through a system that utilizes frequencies monitored by individuals engaged in the provision or the use of such system, if such communication is not scrambled or encrypted.

(h) It shall not be unlawful under this chapter-

(i) to use a pen register or a trap and trace device (as those terms are defined for the purposes of chapter 206 (relating to pen registers and trap and trace devices) of this title); or

(ii) for a provider of electronic communication service to record the fact that a wire or electronic communication was initiated or completed in order to protect such provider, another provider furnishing service toward the completion of the wire or electronic communication, or a user of that service, from fraudulent, unlawful or abusive use of such service.

(3) (a) Except as provided in paragraph (b) of this subsection, a person or entity providing an electronic communication service to the public shall not intentionally divulge the contents of any communication (other than one to such person or entity, or an agent thereof) while in transmission on that service to any person or entity other than an addressee or intended recipient of such communication or an agent of such addressee or intended recipient.

(b) A person or entity providing electronic communication service to the public may divulge the contents of any such communication-

(i) as otherwise authorized in section 2511(2)(a) or 2517 of this title;

(ii) with the lawful consent of the originator or any addressee or intended recipient of such communication;

(iii) to a person employed or authorized, or whose facilities are used, to forward such communication to its destination; or

(iv) which were inadvertently obtained by the Owner and which appear to pertain to the commission of a crime, if such divulgence is made to a law enforcement agency.

(4) (a) Except as provided in paragraph (b) of this subsection or in subsection (5), whoever violates subsection (1) of this section shall be fined under this title or imprisoned not more than five years, or both.

(b) If the offense is a first offense under paragraph (a) of this subsection and is not for a tortious or illegal purpose or for purposes of direct or indirect commercial advantage or private commercial gain, and the wire or electronic communication with respect to which the offense under paragraph (a) is a radio communication that is not scrambled or encrypted, then-

(i) if the communication is not the radio portion of a cellular telephone communication, a public land mobile radio service communication or a paging service communication, and the conduct is not that described in subsection (5), the offender shall be fined under this title or imprisoned not more than one year, or both; and

(ii) if the communication is the radio portion of a cellular telephone communication, a public land mobile radio service communication or a paging service communication, the offender shall be fined under this title.

(c) Conduct otherwise an offense under this subsection that consists of or relates to the interception of a satellite transmission that is not encrypted or scrambled and that is transmitted-

(i) to a broadcasting station for purposes of retransmission to the general public; or

(ii) as an audio subcarrier intended for redistribution to facilities open to the public, but not including data transmissions or telephone calls, is not an offense under this subsection unless the conduct is for the purposes of direct or indirect commercial advantage or private financial gain.

(5) (a) (i) If the communication is-

(A) a private satellite video communication that is not scrambled or encrypted and the conduct in violation of this chapter is the private viewing of that communication and is not for a tortious or illegal purpose or for purposes of direct or indirect commercial advantage or private commercial gain; or

(B) a radio communication that is transmitted on frequencies allocated under subpart D of part 74 of the rules of the Federal Communications Commission that is not scrambled or encrypted and the conduct in violation of this chapter is not for a tortious or illegal purpose or for purposes of direct or indirect commercial advantage or private commercial gain,

then the person who engages in such conduct shall be subject to suit by the Federal Government in a court of competent jurisdiction.

(ii) In an action under this subsection-

(A) if the violation of this chapter is a first offense for the person under paragraph (a) of subsection (4) and such person has not been found liable in a civil action under section 2520 of this title, the Federal Government shall be entitled to appropriate injunctive relief; and

(B) if the violation of this chapter is a second or subsequent offense under paragraph (a) of subsection (4) or such person has been found liable in any prior civil action under section 2520,

the person shall be subject to a mandatory $500 civil fine.

(b) The court may use any means within its authority to enforce an injunction issued under paragraph (ii)(A), and shall impose a civil fine of not less than $500 for each violation of such an injunction.

§ 2512. Manufacture, distribution, possession, and advertising of wire, oral, or electronic communication intercepting devices prohibited

(1) Except as otherwise specifically provided in this chapter, any person who intentionally—

(a) sends through the mail, or sends or carries in interstate or foreign commerce, any electronic, mechanical, or other device, knowing or having reason to know that the design of such device renders it primarily useful for the purpose of the surreptitious interception of wire, oral, or electronic communications;

(b) manufactures, assembles, possesses, or sells any electronic, mechanical, or other device, knowing or having reason to know that the design of such device renders it primarily useful for the purpose of the surreptitious interception of wire, oral, or electronic communications, and that such device or any component thereof has been or will be sent through the mail or transported in interstate or foreign commerce; or

(c) places in any newspaper, magazine, handbill, or other publication any advertisement of-

(i) any electronic, mechanical, or other device knowing or having reason to know that the design of such device renders it primarily useful for the purpose of the surreptitious interception of wire, oral, or electronic communications; or

(ii) any other electronic, mechanical, or other device, where such advertisement promotes the use of such device for the purpose of the surreptitious interception of wire, oral, or electronic communications,

knowing or having reason to know that such advertisement will be sent through the mail or transported in interstate or foreign commerce, shall be fined under this title or imprisoned not more than five years, or both.

(2) It shall not be unlawful under this section for-

(a) a provider of wire or electronic communication service or an officer, agent, or employee of, or a person under contract with, such a provider, in the normal course of the business of providing that wire or electronic communication service, or

(b) an officer, agent, or employee of, or a person under contract with, the United States, a State, or a political subdivision thereof, in the normal course of the activities of the United States, a State, or a political subdivision thereof, to send through the mail, send or carry in interstate or foreign commerce, or manufacture, assemble, possess, or sell any electronic, mechanical, or other device knowing or having reason to know that the design of such device renders it primarily useful for the purpose of the surreptitious interception of wire, oral, or electronic communications.

§ 2513. Confiscation of wire, oral, or electronic communication intercepting devices

Any electronic, mechanical, or other device used, sent, carried, manufactured, assembled, possessed, sold, or advertised in violation of section 2511 or section 2512 of this chapter [18 USCS §§ 2511 or 2512] may be seized and forfeited to the United States. All provisions of law relating to (1) the seizure, summary and judicial forfeiture, and condemnation of vessels, vehicles, merchandise, and baggage for violations of the customs laws contained in title 19 of the United States Code [19 USCS §§ 1 et seq.], (2) the disposition of such vessels, vehicles, merchandise, and baggage or the proceeds from the sale thereof, (3) the remission or mitigation of such forfeiture, (4) the compromise of claims, and (5) the award of compensation to informers in respect of such forfeitures, shall apply to seizures and forfeitures incurred, or alleged to have been incurred, under the provisions of this section, insofar as applicable and not inconsistent with the provisions of this section; except that such duties as are imposed upon the collector of customs or any other person with respect to the seizure and forfeiture of vessels, vehicles, merchandise, and baggage under the provisions of the customs laws contained in title 19 of the United States Code [19 USCS §§ 1 et seq.] shall be performed with respect to seizure and forfeiture of electronic, mechanical, or other intercepting devices under this section by such officers, agents, or other persons as may be authorized or designated for that purpose by the Attorney General.

§ 2514. [Repealed]

§ 2515. Prohibition of use as evidence of intercepted wire or oral communications

Whenever any wire or oral communication has been intercepted, no part of the contents of such communication and no evidence derived therefrom may be received in evidence in any trial, hearing, or other proceeding in or before any court, grand jury, department, officer, agency, regulatory body, legislative committee, or other authority of the United States, a State, or a political subdivision thereof if the disclosure of that information would be in violation of this chapter [18 USCS §§ 2510 et seq.].

§ 2516. Authorization for interception of wire, oral, or electronic communications

(1) The Attorney General, Deputy Attorney General, Associate Attorney General, any Assistant Attorney General, any acting Assistant Attorney General, or any Deputy Assistant Attorney General in the Criminal Division specially designated by the Attorney General, may authorize an application to a Federal judge of competent jurisdiction for, and such judge may grant in conformity with section 2518 of this chapter [18 USCS § 2518] an order authorizing or approving the interception of wire or oral communications by the Federal Bureau of Investigation, or a Federal agency having responsibility for the investigation of the offense as to which the application is made, when such interception may provide or has provided evidence of-

(a) any offense punishable by death or by imprisonment for more than one year under sections 2274 through 2277 of title 42 of the United States Code (relating to the enforcement of the Atomic Energy Act of 1954), section 2284 of title 42 of the United States Code (relating to sabotage of nuclear facilities or fuel), or under the following chapters of this title: chapter 37 [18 USCS §§ 791 et seq.] (relating to espionage), chapter 105 [18 USCS §§ 2151 et seq.] (relating to sabotage), chapter 115 [18 USCS §§ 2381 et seq.] (relating to treason), chapter 102 [18 USCS §§ 2101 et seq.]; (relating to riots) chapter 65 [18 USCS §§ 1361 et seq.] (relating to malicious mischief), chapter 111 [18 USCS §§ 2271 et seq.] (relating to destruction of vessels), or chapter 81 [18 USCS §§ 1621 et seq.] (relating to piracy);

(b) a violation of section 186 or section 501(c) of title 29, United States Code [29 USCS § 186 or 501(c)] (dealing with restrictions on payments and loans to labor organizations), or any offense which involves murder, kidnapping, robbery, or extortion, and which is punishable under this title [18 USCS §§ 1 et seq.];

(c) any offense which is punishable under the following sections of this title [18 USCS §§ 1 et seq.] : section 201 (bribery of public officials and witnesses), section 224 (bribery in sporting contests), subsection (d), (e), (f), (g), (h), or (i) of section 844 (unlawful use of explosives), section 1032 (relating to concealment of assets), section 1084 (transmission of wagering information), section 751 (relating to escape), sections 1503, 1512, and 1513 (influencing or injuring an officer, juror, or witness generally), section 1510 (obstruction of criminal investigations), section 1511 (obstruction of State or local law enforcement), section 1751 (Presidential and Presidential staff assassination, kidnaping, and assault), section 1951 (interference with commerce by threats or violence), section 1952 (interstate and foreign travel or transportation in aid of racketeering enterprises), section 1954 (offer, acceptance, or solicitation to influence operations of employee benefit plan), section 1955 (prohibition of business enterprises of gambling), section 1956 (laundering of monetary instruments), section 1957 (relating to engaging in monetary transactions in property derived from specified unlawful activity), section 659 (theft from interstate shipment), section 664 (embezzlement from pension and welfare funds), section 1343 (fraud by wire, radio, or television), section 1344 (relating to bank fraud), sections 2251 and 2252 (sexual exploitation of children), sections 2312, 2313, 2314, and 2315 (interstate transportation of stolen property), section 2321 (relating to trafficking in certain motor vehicles or motor vehicle parts), section 1203 (relating to hostage taking), section 1029 (relating to fraud and related activity in connection with access devices), section 3146 (relating to penalty for failure to appear), section 3521(b)(3) (relating to witness relocation and assistance), section 32 (relating to destruction of aircraft or aircraft facilities), section 1963 (violations with respect to racketeer influenced and corrupt organizations), section 115 (relating to threatening or retaliating against a Federal official), the section in chapter 65 relating to destruction of an energy facility, and section 1341 (relating to mail fraud), or section 351 (violations with respect to congressional, Cabinet, or Supreme Court assassinations, kidnaping, and assault), section 831 (relating to prohibited transactions involving nuclear materials), section 33 (relating to destruction of motor vehicles or motor vehicle facilities), section 175 (relating to biological weapons) or section 1992 (relating to wrecking trains)

(d) any offense involving counterfeiting punishable under section 471, 472, or 473 of this title [18 USCS § 471, 472, or 473];

(e) any offense involving fraud connected with a case under title 11 [11 USCS §§ 1 et seq.] or the manufacture, importation, receiving, concealment, buying, selling, or otherwise dealing in narcotic drugs, marihuana, or other dangerous drugs, punishable under any law of the United States;

(f) any offense including extortionate credit transactions under sections 892, 893, or 894 of this title [18 USCS § 892, 893, or 894];

(g) a violation of section 5322 of title 31, United States Code [31 USCS § 5322] (dealing with the reporting of currency transactions);

(h) any felony violation of sections 2511 and 2512 (relating to interception and disclosure of certain communications and to certain intercepting devices) of this title;

(i) any violation of section 60123(b) (relating to destruction of a natural gas pipeline) or 46502 (relating to aircraft piracy) of title 49;

(j) any criminal violation of section 2778 of title 22 (relating to the Arms Export Control Act); or

(k) the location of any fugitive from justice from an offense described in this section;

(l) any conspiracy to commit any of the foregoing offenses.

(2) The principal prosecuting attorney of any State, or the principal prosecuting attorney of any political subdivision thereof, if such attorney is authorized by a statute of that State to make application to a State court judge of competent jurisdiction for an order authorizing or approving the interception of wire or oral communications, may apply to such judge for, and such judge may grant in conformity with section 2518 of this chapter [18 USCS § 2518] and with the applicable State statute an order authorizing, or approving the interception of wire or oral communications by investigative or law enforcement officers having responsibility for the investigation of the offense as to which the application is made, when such interception may provide or has provided evidence of the commission of the offense of murder, kidnapping, gambling, robbery, bribery, extortion, or dealing in narcotic drugs, marihuana or other dangerous drugs, or other crime dangerous to life, limb, or property, and punishable by imprisonment for more than one year, designated in any applicable State statute authorizing such interception, or any conspiracy to commit any of the foregoing offenses.

(3) Any attorney for the Government (as such term is defined for the purposes of the Federal Rules of Criminal Procedure) may authorize an application to a Federal judge of competent jurisdiction for, and such judge may grant, in conformity with section 2518 of this title, an order authorizing or approving the interception of electronic communications by an investigative or law enforcement officer having responsibility for the investigation of the offense as to which the application is made, when such interception may provide or has provided evidence of any Federal felony.

§ 2517. Authorization for disclosure and use of intercepted wire, oral, or electronic communications

(1) Any investigative or law enforcement officer who, by any means authorized by this chapter, has obtained knowledge of the contents of any wire, oral, or electronic communication, or evidence derived therefrom, may disclose such contents to another investigative or law enforcement officer to the extent that such disclosure is appropriate to the proper performance of the official duties of the officer making or receiving the disclosure.

(2) Any investigative or law enforcement officer who, by any means authorized by this chapter, has obtained knowledge of the contents of any wire, oral, or electronic communication or evidence derived therefrom may use such contents to the extent such use is appropriate to the proper performance of his official duties.

(3) Any person who has received, by any means authorized by this chapter, any information concerning a wire, oral, or electronic communication, or evidence derived therefrom intercepted in accordance with the provisions of this chapter may disclose the contents of that communication or such derivative evidence while giving testimony under oath or affirmation in any proceeding held under the authority of the United States or of any State or political subdivision thereof.

(4) No otherwise privileged wire, oral, or electronic communication intercepted in accordance with, or in violation of, the provisions of this chapter shall lose its privileged character.

(5) When an investigative or law enforcement officer, while engaged in intercepting wire, oral, or electronic communications in the manner authorized herein, intercepts wire, oral, or electronic communications relating to offenses other than those specified in the order of authorization or approval, the contents thereof, and evidence derived therefrom, may be disclosed or used as provided in subsections (1) and (2) of this section. Such contents and any evidence derived therefrom may be used under subsection (3) of this section when authorized or approved by a judge of competent jurisdiction where such judge finds on subsequent application that the contents were otherwise intercepted in accordance with the provisions of this chapter. Such application shall be made as soon as practicable.

§ 2518. Procedure for interception of wire, oral, or electronic communications

(1) Each application for an order authorizing or approving the interception of a wire, oral, or electronic communication under this chapter shall be made in writing upon oath or affirmation to a judge of competent jurisdiction and shall state the applicant's authority to make such application. Each application shall include the following information:

(a) the identity of the investigative or law enforcement officer the application, and the officer authorizing the application;

(b) a full and complete statement of the facts and circumstances relied upon by the applicant, to justify his belief that an order should be issued, including (i) details as to the particular offense that has been, is being, or is about to be committed, (ii) except as provided in subsection (11), a particular description of the nature and location of the facilities from which or the place where the communication is to be intercepted, (iii) a particular description of the type of communications sought to be intercepted, (iv) the identity of the person, if known, committing the offense and whose communications are to be intercepted;

(c) a full and complete statement as to whether or not other investigative procedures have been tried and failed or why they reasonably appear to be unlikely to succeed if tried or to be too dangerous;

(d) a statement of the period of time for which the interception is required to be maintained. If the nature of the investigation is such that the authorization for interception should not automatically terminate when the described type of communication has been first obtained, a particular description of facts establishing probable cause to believe that additional communications of the same type will occur thereafter;

(e) a full and complete statement of the facts concerning all previous applications known to the individual authorizing and making the application, made to any judge for authorization to intercept, or for approval of interceptions of, wire, oral, or electronic communications involving any of the same persons, facilities or places specified in the application, and the action taken by the judge on each such application; and

(f) where the application is for the extension of an order, a statement setting forth the results thus far obtained from the interception, or a reasonable explanation of the failure to obtain such results.

(2) The judge may require the applicant to furnish additional testimony or documentary evidence in support of the application.

(3) Upon such application the judge may enter an ex parte order, as requested or as modified, authorizing or approving interception of wire, oral, or electronic communications within the territorial jurisdiction of the court in which the judge is sitting (and outside that jurisdiction but within the United States in the case of a mobile interception device authorized by a Federal court within such jurisdiction), if the judge determines on the basis of the facts submitted by the applicant that-

(a) there is probable cause for belief that an individual is committing, has committed, or is about to commit a particular offense enumerated in section 2516 of this chapter [18 USCS § 2516];

(b) there is probable cause for belief that particular communications concerning that offense will be obtained through such interception;

(c) normal investigative procedures have been tried and have failed or reasonably appear to be unlikely to succeed if tried or to be too dangerous;

(d) except as provided in subsection (11), there is probable cause for belief that the facilities from which, or the place where, the wire, oral, or electronic communications are to be intercepted are being used, or are about to be used, in connection with the commission of such offense, or are leased to, listed in the name of, or commonly used by such person.

(4) Each order authorizing or approving the interception of any wire, oral, or electronic communication under this chapter shall specify-

(a) the identity of the person, if known, whose communications are to be intercepted;

(b) the nature and location of the communications facilities as to which, or the place where, authority to intercept is granted;

(c) a particular description of the type of communication sought to be intercepted, and a statement of the particular offense to which it relates;

(d) the identity of the agency authorized to intercept the communications, and of the person authorizing the application; and

(e) the period of time during which such interception is authorized, including a statement as to whether or not the interception shall automatically terminate when the described communication has been first obtained.

An order authorizing the interception of a wire, oral, or electronic communication under this chapter shall, upon request of the applicant, direct that a provider of wire or electronic communication service, landlord, custodian or other person shall furnish the applicant forthwith all information, facilities, and technical assistance necessary to accomplish the interception unobtrusively and with a minimum of interference with the services that such Owner, landlord, custodian, or person is according the person whose communications are to be intercepted. Any provider of wire or electronic communication service, landlord, custodian or other person furnishing such facilities or technical assistance shall be compensated therefor by the applicant for reasonable expenses incurred in providing such facilities or assistance.

(5) No order entered under this section may authorize or approve the interception of any wire, oral, or electronic communication for any period longer than is necessary to achieve the objective of the authorization, nor in any event longer than thirty days. Such thirty-day period begins on the earlier of the day on which the investigative or law enforcement officer first begins to conduct an interception under the order or ten days after the order is entered. Extensions of an order may be granted, but only upon application for an extension made in accordance with subsection (1) of this section and the court making the findings required by subsection (3) of this section. The period of extension shall be no longer than the authorizing judge deems necessary to achieve the purposes for which it was granted and in no event for longer than thirty days. Every order and extension thereof shall contain a provision that the authorization to intercept shall be executed as soon as practicable, shall be conducted in such a way as to minimize the interception of communications not otherwise subject to interception under this chapter [18 USCS §§ 2510 et seq.], and must terminate upon attainment of the authorized objective, or in any event in thirty days. In the event the intercepted communication is in a code or foreign language, and an expert in that foreign language or code is not reasonably available during the interception period, minimization may be accomplished as soon as practicable after such interception. An interception under this chapter may be conducted in whole or in part by Government personnel, or by an individual operating under a contract with the Government, acting under the supervision of an investigative or law enforcement officer authorized to conduct the interception.

(6) Whenever an order authorizing interception is entered pursuant to this chapter [18 USCS §§ 2510 et seq.], the order may require reports to be made to the judge who issued the order showing what progress has been made toward achievement of the authorized objective and the need for continued interception. Such reports shall be made at such intervals as the judge may require.

(7) Notwithstanding any other provision of this chapter [18 USCS §§ 2510 et seq.], any investigative or law enforcement officer, specially designated by the Attorney General, the Deputy Attorney General, the Associate Attorney General, or by the principal prosecuting attorney of any State or subdivision thereof acting pursuant to a statute of that State, who reasonably determines that-

(a) an emergency situation exists that involves-

(i) immediate danger of death or serious physical injury to any person,

(ii) conspiratorial activities threatening the national security interest, or

(iii) conspiratorial activities characteristic of organized crime,

that requires a wire, oral, or electronic communication to be intercepted before an order authorizing such interception can, with due diligence, be obtained, and

(b) there are grounds upon which an order could be entered under this chapter [18 USCS §§ 2510 et seq.] to authorize such interception, may intercept such wire, oral, or electronic communication if an application for an order approving the interception is made in accordance with this section within forty-eight hours after the interception has occurred, or begins to occur. In the absence of an order, such interception shall immediately terminate when the communication sought is obtained or when the application for the order is denied, whichever is earlier. In the event such application for approval is denied, or in any other case where the interception is terminated without an order having been issued, the contents of any wire, oral, or electronic communication intercepted shall be treated as having been obtained in violation of this chapter [18 USCS §§ 2510 et seq.], and an inventory shall be served as provided for in subsection (d) of this section on the person named in the application.

(8) (a) The contents of any wire, oral, or electronic communication intercepted by any means authorized by this chapter shall, if possible, be recorded on tape or wire or other comparable device. The recording of the contents of any wire, oral, or electronic communication under this subsection shall be done in such way as will protect the recording from editing or other alterations. Immediately upon the expiration of the period of the order, or extensions thereof, such recordings shall be made available to the judge issuing such order and sealed under his directions.

Custody of the recordings shall be wherever the judge orders. They shall not be destroyed except upon an order of the issuing or denying judge and in any event shall be kept for ten years. Duplicate recordings may be made for use or disclosure pursuant to the provisions of subsections (1) and (2) of section 2517 of this chapter for investigations. The presence of the seal provided for by this subsection, or a satisfactory explanation for the absence thereof, shall be a prerequisite for the use or disclosure of the contents of any wire, oral, or electronic communication or evidence derived therefrom under subsection (3) of section 2517.

(b) Applications made and orders granted under this chapter [18 USCS §§ 2510 et seq.] shall be sealed by the judge. Custody of the applications and orders shall be wherever the judge directs. Such applications and orders shall be disclosed only upon a showing of good cause before a judge of competent jurisdiction and shall not be destroyed except on order of the issuing or denying judge, and in any event shall be kept for ten years.

(c) Any violation of the provisions of this subsection may be punished as contempt of the issuing or denying judge.

(d) Within a reasonable time but not later than ninety days after the filing of an application for an order of approval under section 2518(7)(b) [18 USCS § 2518(7)(b)] which is denied or the termination of the period of an order or extensions thereof, the issuing or denying judge shall cause to be served, on the persons named in the order or the application, and such other parties to intercepted communications as the judge may determine in his discretion that is in the interest of justice, an inventory which shall include notice of-

(1) the fact of the entry of the order or the application;

(2) the date of the entry and the period of authorized, approved or disapproved interception, or the denial of the application; and

(3) the fact that during the period wire or oral communications were or were not intercepted.

The judge, upon the filing of a motion, may in his discretion make available to such person or his counsel for inspection such portions of the intercepted communications, applications and orders as the judge determines to be in the interest of justice. On an ex parte showing of good cause to a judge of competent jurisdiction the serving of the inventory required by this subsection may be postponed.

(9) The contents of any wire, oral, or electronic communication intercepted pursuant to this chapter or evidence derived therefrom shall not be received in evidence or otherwise disclosed in any trial, hearing, or other proceeding in a Federal or State court unless each party, not less than ten days before the trial, hearing, or proceeding, has been furnished with a copy of the court order, and accompanying application, under which the interception was authorized or approved. This ten-day period may be waived by the judge if he finds that it was not possible to furnish the party with the above information ten days before the trial, hearing, or proceeding and that the party will not be prejudiced by the delay in receiving such information.

(10) (a) Any aggrieved person in any trial, hearing, or proceeding in or before any court, department, officer, agency, regulatory body, or other authority of the United States, a State, or a political subdivision thereof, may move to suppress the contents of any wire or oral communication intercepted pursuant to this chapter [18 USCS §§ 2510 et seq.], or evidence derived therefrom, on the grounds that-

(i) the communication was unlawfully intercepted;

(ii) the order of authorization or approval under which it was intercepted is insufficient on its face; or

(iii) the interception was not made in conformity with the order of authorization or approval.

Such motion shall be made before the trial, hearing, or proceeding unless there was no opportunity to make such motion or the person was not aware of the grounds of the motion. If the motion is granted, the contents of the intercepted wire or oral communication, or evidence derived therefrom, shall be treated as having been obtained in violation of this chapter [18 USCS §§ 2510 et seq.]. The judge, upon the filing of such motion by the aggrieved person, may in his discretion make available to the aggrieved person or his counsel for inspection such portions of the intercepted communication or evidence derived therefrom as the judge determines to be in the interests of justice.

(b) In addition to any other right to appeal, the United States shall have the right to appeal from an order granting a motion to suppress made under paragraph (a) of this subsection, or the denial of an application for an order of approval, if the United States attorney shall certify to the judge or other official granting such motion or denying such application that the appeal is not taken for purposes of delay. Such appeal shall be taken within thirty days after the date the order was entered and shall be diligently prosecuted.

(c) The remedies and sanctions described in this chapter with respect to the interception of electronic communications are the only judicial remedies and sanctions for nonconstitutional violations of this chapter involving such communications.

(11) The requirements of subsections (1)(b)(ii) and (3)(d) of this section relating to the specification of the facilities from which, or the place where, the communication is to be intercepted do not apply if-

(a) in the case of an application with respect to the interception of an oral communication-

(i) the application is by a Federal investigative or law enforcement officer and is approved by the Attorney General, the Deputy Attorney General, the Associate Attorney General, an Assistant Attorney General, or an acting Assistant Attorney General;

(ii) the application contains a full and complete statement as to why such specification is not practical and identifies the person committing the offense and whose communications are to be intercepted; and

(iii) the judge finds that such specification is not practical; and

(b) in the case of an application with respect to a wire or electronic communication-

(i) the application is by a Federal investigative or law enforcement officer and is approved by the Attorney General, the Deputy Attorney General, the Associate Attorney General, an Assistant Attorney General, or an acting Assistant Attorney General;

(ii) the application identifies the person believed to be committing the offense and whose communications are to be intercepted and the applicant makes a showing of a purpose, on the part of that person, to thwart interception by changing facilities; and

(iii) the judge finds that such purpose has been adequately shown.

(12) An interception of a communication under an order with respect to which the requirements of subsections (1)(b)(ii) and (3)(d) of this section do not apply by reason of subsection (11) shall not begin until the facilities from which, or the place where, the communication is to be intercepted is ascertained by the person implementing the interception order. A provider of wire or electronic communications service that has received an order as provided for in subsection (11)(b) may move the court to modify or quash the order on the ground that its assistance with respect to the interception cannot be performed in a timely or reasonable fashion. The court, upon notice to the government, shall decide such a motion expeditiously.

§ 2519. Reports concerning intercepted wire, oral, or electronic communications

(1) Within thirty days after the expiration of an order (or each extension thereof) entered under section 2518 [18 USCS § 2518], or the denial of an order approving an interception, the issuing or denying judge shall report to the Administrative Office of the United States Courts-

(a) the fact that an order or extension was applied for;

(b) the kind of order or extension applied for (including whether or not the order was an order with respect to which the requirements of sections 2518(1)(b)(ii) and 2518(3)(d) of this title did not apply by reason of section 2518(11) of this title);

(c) the fact that the order or extension was granted as applied for, was modified, or was denied;

(d) the period of interceptions authorized by the order, and the number and duration of any extensions of the order;

(e) the offense specified in the order or application, or extension of an order;

(f) the identity of the applying investigative or law enforcement officer and agency making the application and the person authorizing the application; and

(g) the nature of the facilities from which or the place where communications were to be intercepted.

(2) In January of each year the Attorney General, an Assistant Attorney General specially designated by the Attorney General, or the principal prosecuting attorney of a State, or the principal prosecuting attorney for any political subdivision of a State, shall report to the Administrative Office of the United States Courts-

(a) the information required by paragraphs (a) through (g) of subsection (1) of this section with respect to each application for an order or extension made during the preceding calendar year;

(b) a general description of the interceptions made under such order or extension, including (i) the approximate nature and frequency of incriminating communications intercepted, (ii) the approximate nature and frequency of other communications intercepted, (iii) the approximate number of persons whose communications were intercepted, and (iv) the approximate nature, amount, and cost of the manpower and other resources used in the interceptions;

(c) the number of arrests resulting from interceptions made under such order or extension, and the offenses for which arrests were made;

(d) the number of trials resulting from such interceptions;

(e) the number of motions to suppress made with respect to such interceptions, and the number granted or denied;

(f) the number of convictions resulting from such interceptions and the offenses for which the convictions were obtained and a general assessment of the importance of the interceptions; and

(g) the information required by paragraphs (b) through (f) of this subsection with respect to orders or extensions obtained in a preceding calendar year.

(3) In April of each year the Director of the Administrative Office of the United States Courts shall transmit to the Congress a full and complete report concerning the number of applications for orders authorizing or approving the interception of wire, oral, or electronic communications pursuant to this chapter and the number of orders and extensions granted or denied pursuant to this chapter during the preceding calendar year. Such report shall include a summary and analysis of the data required to be filed with the Administrative Office by subsections (1) and (2) of this section. The Director of the Administrative Office of the United States Courts is authorized to issue binding regulations dealing with the content and form of the reports required to be filed by subsections (1) and (2) of this section.

§ 2520. Recovery of civil damages authorized

(a) In general. Except as provided in section 2511(2)(a)(ii), any person whose wire, oral, or electronic communication is intercepted, disclosed, or intentionally used in violation of this chapter may in a civil action recover from the person or entity which engaged in that violation such relief as may be appropriate.

(b) Relief. In an action under this section, appropriate relief includes-

(1) such preliminary and other equitable or declaratory relief as may be appropriate;

(2) damages under subsection (c) and punitive damages in appropriate cases; and

(3) a reasonable attorney's fee and other litigation costs reasonably incurred.

(c) Computation of damages.

(1) In an action under this section, if the conduct in violation of this chapter, is the private viewing of a private satellite video communication that is not scrambled or encrypted or if the communication is a radio communication that is transmitted on frequencies allocated under subpart D of part 74 of the rules of the Federal Communications Commission that is not scrambled or encrypted and the conduct is not for a tortious or illegal purpose or for purposes of direct or indirect commercial advantage or private commercial gain, then the court shall assess damages as follows:

(A) If the person who engaged in that conduct has not previously been enjoined under section 2511(5) and has not been found liable in a prior civil action under this section, the court shall assess the greater of the sum of actual damages suffered by the plaintiff, or statutory damages of not less than $50 and not more than $500.

(B) If, on one prior occasion, the person who engaged in that conduct has been enjoined under section 2511(5) or has been found liable in a civil action under this section, the court shall assess the greater of the sum of actual damages suffered by the plaintiff, or statutory damages of not less than $100 and not more than $1000.

(2) In any other action under this section, the court may assess as damages whichever is the greater of-

(A) the sum of the actual damages suffered by the plaintiff and any profits made by the violator as a result of the violation; or

(B) statutory damages of whichever is the greater of $100 a day for each day of violation or $10,000.

(d) Defense. A good faith reliance on-

(1) a court warrant or order, a grand jury subpoena, a legislative authorization, or a statutory authorization;

(2) a request of an investigative or law enforcement officer under section 2518(7) of this title; or

(3) a good faith determination that section 2511(3) of this title permitted the conduct complained of; is a complete defense against any civil or criminal action brought under this chapter or any other law.

(e) Limitation. A civil action under this section may not be commenced later than two years after the date upon which the claimant first has a reasonable opportunity to discover the violation.

§ 2521. Injunction against illegal interception

Whenever it shall appear that any person is engaged or is about to engage in any act which constitutes or will constitute a felony violation of this chapter [18 USCS §§ 2510 et seq.], the Attorney General may initiate a civil action in a district court of the United States to enjoin such violation. The court shall proceed as soon as practicable to the hearing and determination of such an action, and may, at any time before final determination, enter such a restraining order or prohibition, or take such other action, as is warranted to prevent a continuing and substantial injury to the United States or to any person or class of persons for whose protection the action is brought. A proceeding under this section is governed by the Federal Rules of Civil Procedure, except that, if an indictment has been returned against the respondent, discovery is governed by the Federal Rules of Criminal Procedure.

§ 2701. Unlawful access to stored communications

(a) Offense. Except as provided in subsection (c) of this section whoever-

(1) intentionally accesses without authorization a facility through which an electronic communication service is provided; or

(2) intentionally exceeds an authorization to access that facility; and thereby obtains, alters, or prevents authorized access to a wire or electronic communication while it is in electronic storage in such system shall be punished as provided in subsection (b) of this section.

(b) Punishment. The punishment for an offense under subsection (a) of this section is-

(1) if the offense is committed for purposes of commercial advantage, malicious destruction or damage, or private commercial gain-

(A) a fine of [sic] under this title or imprisonment for not more than one year, or both, in the case of a first offense under this subparagraph; and

(B) a fine under this title or imprisonment for not more than two years, or both, for any subsequent offense under this subparagraph; and

(2) a fine of [sic] under this title or imprisonment for not more than six months, or both, in any other case.

(c) Exceptions. Subsection (a) of this section does not apply with respect to conduct authorized-

(1) by the person or entity providing a wire or electronic communications service;

(2) by a user of that service with respect to a communication of or intended for that user; or

(3) in section 2703, 2704 or 2518 of this title.

§ 2702. Disclosure of contents

(a) Prohibitions. Except as provided in subsection (b)-

(1) a person or entity providing an electronic communication service to the public shall not knowingly divulge to any person or entity the contents of a communication while in electronic storage by that service; and

(2) a person or entity providing remote computing service to the public shall not knowingly divulge to any person or entity the contents of any communication which is carried or maintained on that service-

(A) on behalf of, and received by means of electronic transmission from (or created by means of computer processing of communications received by means of electronic transmission from), a subscriber or customer of such service; and

(B) solely for the purpose of providing storage or computer processing services to such subscriber or customer, if the provider is not authorized to access the contents of any such communications for purposes of providing any services other than storage or computer processing.

(b) Exceptions. A person or entity may divulge the contents of a communication-

(1) to an addressee or intended recipient of such communication or an agent of such addressee or intended recipient;

(2) as otherwise authorized in section 2516, 2511(2)(a), or 2703 of this title;

(3) with the lawful consent of the originator or an addressee or intended recipient of such communication, or the subscriber in the case of remote computing service;

(4) to a person employed or authorized or whose facilities are used to forward such communication to its destination;

(5) as may be necessarily incident to the rendition of the service or to the protection of the rights or property of the provider of that service; or

(6) to a law enforcement agency, if such contents-

  (A) were inadvertently obtained by the Owner; and

  (B) appear to pertain to the commission of a crime.

§ 2703. Requirements for governmental access

(a) Contents of electronic communications in electronic storage. A governmental entity may require the disclosure by a provider of electronic communication service of the contents of an electronic communication, that is in electronic storage in an electronic communications system for one hundred and eighty days or less, only pursuant to a warrant issued under the Federal Rules of Criminal Procedure or equivalent State warrant. A governmental entity may require the disclosure by a provider of electronic communications services of the contents of an electronic communication that has been in electronic storage in an electronic communications system for more than one hundred and eighty days by the means available under subsection (b) of this section.

(b) Contents of electronic communications in a remote computing service.

  (1) A governmental entity may require a provider of remote computing service to disclose the contents of any electronic communication to which this paragraph is made applicable by paragraph (2) of this subsection-

    (A) without required notice to the subscriber or customer, if the governmental entity obtains a warrant issued under the Federal Rules of Criminal Procedure or equivalent State warrant; or

    (B) with prior notice from the governmental entity to the subscriber or customer if the governmental entity-

      (i) uses an administrative subpoena authorized by a Federal or State statute or a Federal or State grand jury subpoena; or

      (ii) obtains a court order for such disclosure under subsection (d) of this section;

    except that delayed notice may be given pursuant to section 2705 of this title.

  (2) Paragraph (1) is applicable with respect to any electronic communication that is held or maintained on that service-

(A) on behalf of, and received by means of electronic transmission from (or created by means of computer processing of communications received by means of electronic transmission from), a subscriber or customer of such remote computing service; and

(B) solely for the purpose of providing storage or computer processing services to such subscriber or customer, if the provider is not authorized to access the contents of any such communications for purposes of providing any services other than storage or computer processing.

(c) Records concerning electronic communication service or remote computing service.

(1) (A) Except as provided in subparagraph (B), a provider of electronic communication service or remote computing service may disclose a record or other information pertaining to a subscriber to or customer of such service (not including the contents of communications covered by subsection (a) or (b) of this section) to any person other than a governmental entity.

(B) A provider of electronic communication service or remote computing service shall disclose a record or other information pertaining to a subscriber to or customer of such service (not including the contents of communications covered by subsection (a) or (b) of this section) to a governmental entity only when the governmental entity-

(i) obtains a warrant issued under the Federal Rules of Criminal Procedure or equivalent State warrant;

(ii) obtains a court order for such disclosure under subsection (d) of this section; or

(iii) has the consent of the subscriber or customer to such disclosure.

(C) A provider of electronic communication service or remote computing service shall disclose to a governmental entity the name, billing address, and length of service of a subscriber to or customer of such service and the types of services the subscriber or customer utilized, when the governmental entity uses an administrative subpoena authorized by a Federal or State statute or a Federal or State grand jury or trial subpoena or any means available under subparagraph (B).

(2) A governmental entity receiving records or information under this subsection is not required to provide notice to a subscriber or customer.

(d) Requirements for court order. A court order for disclosure under subsection (b) or (c) may be issued by any court that is a court of competent jurisdiction described in section 3126(2)(A) and shall issue only if the governmental entity offers specific and articulable facts showing that there are reasonable grounds to believe that the contents of a wire or electronic communication, or the records or other information sought, are relevant and material to an ongoing criminal investigation. In the case of a State governmental authority, such a court order shall not issue if prohibited by the law of such State. A court issuing an order pursuant to this section, on a motion made promptly by the Owner, may quash or modify such order, if the information or records requested are unusually voluminous in nature or compliance with such order otherwise would cause an undue burden on such provider.

(e) No cause of action against a provider disclosing information under this chapter [18 USCS §§ 2701 et seq.]. No cause of action shall lie in any court against any provider of wire or electronic communication service, its officers, employees, agents, or other specified persons for providing information, facilities, or assistance in accordance with the terms of a court order, warrant, subpoena, or certification under this chapter [18 USCS §§ 2701 et seq.].

§ 2704. Backup preservation

(a) Backup preservation.

(1) A governmental entity acting under section 2703(b)(2) may include in its sub-poena or court order a requirement that the Owner to whom the request is directed create a backup copy of the contents of the electronic communications sought in order to preserve those communications. Without notifying the subscriber or customer of such subpoena or court order, such Owner shall create such backup copy as soon as practicable consistent with its regular business practices and shall confirm to the governmental entity that such backup copy has been made. Such backup copy shall be created within two business days after receipt by the Owner of the subpoena or court order.

(2) Notice to the subscriber or customer shall be made by the governmental entity within three days after receipt of such confirmation, unless such notice is delayed pursuant to section 2705(a).

(3) The Owner shall not destroy such backup copy until the later of-

(A) the delivery of the information; or

(B) the resolution of any proceedings (including appeals of any proceeding) concerning the government's subpoena or court order.

(4) The Owner shall release such backup copy to the requesting governmental entity no sooner than fourteen days after the governmental entity's notice to the subscriber or customer if such Owner-

(A) has not received notice from the subscriber or customer that the subscriber or customer has challenged the governmental entity's request; and

(B) has not initiated proceedings to challenge the request of the governmental entity.

(5) A governmental entity may seek to require the creation of a backup copy under subsection (a)(1) of this section if in its sole discretion such entity determines that there is reason to believe that notification under section 2703 of this title of the existence of the subpoena or court order may result in destruction of or tampering with evidence. This determination is not subject to challenge by the subscriber or customer or Owner.

(b) Customer challenges.

(1) Within fourteen days after notice by the governmental entity to the subscriber or customer under subsection (a)(2) of this section, such subscriber or customer may file a motion to quash such subpoena or vacate such court order, with copies served upon the governmental entity and with written notice of such challenge to the Owner. A motion to vacate a court order shall be filed in the court which issued such order. A motion to quash a subpoena shall be filed in the appropriate United States district court or State court. Such motion or application shall contain an affidavit or sworn statement-

(A) stating that the applicant is a customer or subscriber to the service from which the contents of electronic communications maintained for him have been sought; and

(B) stating the applicant's reasons for believing that the records sought are not relevant to a legitimate law enforcement inquiry or that there has not been substantial compliance with the provisions of this chapter in some other respect.

(2) Service shall be made under this section upon a governmental entity by delivering or mailing by registered or certified mail a copy of the papers to the person, office, or department specified in the notice which the customer has received pursuant to this chapter [18 USCS §§ 2701 et seq.]. For the purposes of this section, the term "delivery" has the meaning given that term in the Federal Rules of Civil Procedure.

(3) If the court finds that the customer has complied with paragraphs (1) and (2) of this subsection, the court shall order the governmental entity to file a sworn response, which may be filed in camera if the governmental entity includes in its response the reasons which make in camera review appropriate. If the court is unable to determine the motion or application on the basis of the parties' initial allegations and response, the court may conduct such additional proceedings as it deems appropriate. All such proceedings shall be completed and the motion or application decided as soon as practicable after the filing of the governmental entity's response.

(4) If the court finds that the applicant is not the subscriber or customer for whom the communications sought by the governmental entity are maintained, or that there is a reason to believe that the law enforcement inquiry is legitimate and that the communications sought are relevant to that inquiry, it shall deny the motion or application and order such process enforced. If the court finds that the applicant is the subscriber or customer for whom the communications sought by the governmental entity are maintained, and that there is not a reason to believe that the communications sought are relevant to a legitimate law enforcement inquiry, or that there has not been substantial compliance with the provisions of this chapter, it shall order the process quashed.

(5) A court order denying a motion or application under this section shall not be deemed a final order and no interlocutory appeal may be taken therefrom by the customer.

§ 2705. Delayed notice

(a) Delay of notification.

(1) A governmental entity acting under section 2703(b) of this title may-

(A) where a court order is sought, include in the application a request, which the court shall grant, for an order delaying the notification required under section 2703(b) of this title for a period not to exceed ninety days, if the court determines that there is reason to believe that notification of the existence of the court order may have an adverse result described in paragraph (2) of this subsection; or

(B) where an administrative subpoena authorized by a Federal or State statute or a Federal or State grand jury subpoena is obtained, delay the notification required under section 2703(b) of this title for a period not to exceed ninety days upon the execution of a written certification of a supervisory official that there is reason to believe that notification of the existence of the subpoena may have an adverse result described in paragraph (2) of this subsection.

(2) An adverse result for the purposes of paragraph (1) of this subsection is-

(A) endangering the life or physical safety of an individual;

(B) flight from prosecution;

(C) destruction of or tampering with evidence;

(D) intimidation of potential witnesses; or

(E) otherwise seriously jeopardizing an investigation or unduly delaying a trial.

(3) The governmental entity shall maintain a true copy of certification under paragraph (1)(B).

(4) Extensions of the delay of notification provided in section 2703 of up to ninety days each may be granted by the court upon application, or by certification by a governmental entity, but only in accordance with subsection (b) of this section.

(5) Upon expiration of the period of delay of notification under paragraph (1) or (4) of this subsection, the governmental entity shall serve upon, or deliver by registered or first-class mail to, the customer or subscriber a copy of the process or request together with notice that-

(A) states with reasonable specificity the nature of the law enforcement inquiry; and

(B) informs such customer or subscriber-

(i) that information maintained for such customer or subscriber by the Owner named in such process or request was supplied to or requested by that governmental authority and the date on which the supplying or request took place;

(ii) that notification of such customer or subscriber was delayed;

(iii) what governmental entity or court made the certification or determination pursuant to which that delay was made; and

(iv) which provision of this chapter allowed such delay.

(6) As used in this subsection, the term "supervisory official" means the investigative agent in charge or assistant investigative agent in charge or an equivalent of an investigating agency's headquarters or regional office, or the chief prosecuting attorney or the first assistant prosecuting attorney or an equivalent of a prosecuting attorney's headquarters or regional office.

(b) Preclusion of notice to subject of governmental access. A governmental entity acting under section 2703, when it is not required to notify the subscriber or customer under section 2703(b)(1), or to the extent that it may delay such notice pursuant to subsection (a) of this section, may apply to a court for an order commanding a provider of electronic communications service or remote computing service to whom a warrant, subpoena, or court order is directed, for such period as the court deems appropriate, not to notify any other person of the existence of the warrant, subpoena, or court order. The court shall enter such an order if it determines that there is reason to believe that notification of the existence of the warrant, subpoena, or court order will result in-

(1) endangering the life or physical safety of an individual;

(2) flight from prosecution;

(3) destruction of or tampering with evidence;

(4) intimidation of potential witnesses; or

(5) otherwise seriously jeopardizing an investigation or unduly delaying a trial.

§ 2706. Cost reimbursement

(a) Payment. Except as otherwise provided in subsection (c), a governmental entity obtaining the contents of communications, records, or other information under section 2702, 2703, or 2704 of this title shall pay to the person or entity assembling or providing such information a fee for reimbursement for such costs as are reasonably necessary and which have been directly incurred in searching for, assembling, reproducing, or otherwise providing such information. Such reimbursable costs shall include any costs due to necessary disruption of normal operations of any electronic communication service or remote computing service in which such information may be stored.

(b) Amount. The amount of the fee provided by subsection (a) shall be as mutually agreed by the governmental entity and the person or entity providing the information, or, in the absence of agreement, shall be as determined by the court which issued the order for production of such information (or the court before which a criminal prosecution relating to such information would be brought, if no court order was issued for production of the information).

(c) The requirement of subsection (a) of this section does not apply with respect to records or other information maintained by a communications common carrier that relate to telephone toll records and telephone listings obtained under section 2703 of this title. The court may, however, order a payment as described in subsection (a) if the court determines the information required is unusually voluminous in nature or otherwise caused an undue burden on the provider. : (Added Oct. 21, 1986, P. L. 99-508, Title II, § 201(a), 100 Stat. 1866.)

§ 2707. Civil action

(a) Cause of action. Except as provided in section 2703(e), any provider of electronic communication service, subscriber, or customer aggrieved by any violation of this chapter in which the conduct constituting the violation is engaged in with a knowing or intentional state of mind may, in a civil action, recover from the person or entity which engaged in that violation such relief as may be appropriate.

(b) Relief. In a civil action under this section, appropriate relief includes-

(1) such preliminary and other equitable or declaratory relief as may be appropriate;

(2) damages under subsection (c); and

(3) a reasonable attorney's fee and other litigation costs reasonably incurred.

(c) Damages. The court may assess as damages in a civil action under this section the sum of the actual damages suffered by the plaintiff and any profits made by the violator as a result of the violation, but in no case shall a person entitled to recover receive less than the sum of $1,000.

(d) Defense. A good faith reliance on-

(1) a court warrant or order, a grand jury subpoena, a legislative authorization, or a statutory authorization;

(2) a request of an investigative or law enforcement officer under section 2518(7) of this title; or

(3) a good faith determination that section 2511(3) of this title permitted the conduct complained of; is a complete defense to any civil or criminal action brought under this chapter [18 USCS §§ 2701 et seq.] or any other law.

(e) Limitation. A civil action under this section may not be commenced later than two years after the date upon which the claimant first discovered or had a reasonable opportunity to discover the violation.

§ 2708. Exclusivity of remedies

The remedies and sanctions described in this chapter [18 USCS §§ 2701 et seq.] are the only judicial remedies and sanctions for nonconstitutional violations of this chapter [18 USCS §§ 2701 et seq.].

§ 2709. Counterintelligence access to telephone toll and transactional records

(a) Duty to provide. A wire or electronic communication Owner shall comply with a request for subscriber information and toll billing records information, or electronic communication transactional records in its custody or possession made by the Director of the Federal Bureau of Investigation under subsection (b) of this section.

(b) Required certification. The Director of the Federal Bureau of Investigation (or an individual within the Federal Bureau of Investigation designated for this purpose by the

Director) may request any such information and records if the Director (or the Director's designee) certifies in writing to the wire or electronic communication Owner to which the request is made that-

(1) the information sought is relevant to an authorized foreign counterintelligence investigation; and

(2) there are specific and articulable facts giving reason to believe that the person or entity to whom the information sought pertains is a foreign power or an agent of a foreign power as defined in section 101 of the Foreign Intelligence Surveillance Act of 1978 (50 U.S.C. 1801).

(c) Prohibition of certain disclosure. No wire or electronic communication Owner, or officer, employee, or agent thereof, shall disclose to any person that the Federal Bureau of Investigation has sought or obtained access to information or records under this section.

(d) Dissemination by bureau. The Federal Bureau of Investigation may disseminate information and records obtained under this section only as provided in guidelines approved by the Attorney General for foreign intelligence collection and foreign counterintelligence investigations conducted by the Federal Bureau of Investigation, and, with respect to dissemination to an agency of the United States, only if such information is clearly relevant to the authorized responsibilities of such agency.

(e) Requirement that certain Congressional bodies be informed. On a semiannual basis the Director of the Federal Bureau of Investigation shall fully inform the Permanent Select Committee on Intelligence of the House of Representatives and the Select Committee on Intelligence of the Senate concerning all requests made under subsection (b) of this section.

§ 2710. Definitions for chapter

As used in this chapter [18 USCS §§ 2701 et seq.]-

(1) the terms defined in section 2510 of this title have, respectively, the definitions given such terms in that section; and

(2) the term "remote computing service" means the provision to the public of computer storage or processing services by means of an electronic communications system.

Computer Fraud and Abuse Act

18 USCS § 1030 (1991)

§1030. Fraud and related activity in connection with computers

(a) Whoever—

(1) knowingly accesses a computer without authorization or exceeds authorized access, and by means of such conduct obtains information that has been determined by the United States Government pursuant to an Executive order or statute to require protection against unauthorized disclosure for reasons of national defense or foreign relations, or any restricted data, as defined in paragraph y[(y)][.] of section 11 of the Atomic Energy Act of 1954 [42 USCS 2014(y)], with the intent or reason to believe that such information so obtained is to be used to the injury of the United States, or to the advantage of any foreign nation;

(2) intentionally accesses a computer without authorization or exceeds authorized access, and thereby obtains information contained in a financial record of a financial institution, or of a card issuer as defined in section 1602(n) of title 15, or contained in a file of a consumer reporting agency on a consumer, as such terms are defined in the Fair Credit Reporting Act (15 U.S.C. 1681 et seq.);

(3) intentionally, without authorization to access any computer of a department or agency of the United States, accesses such a computer of that department or agency that is exclusively for the use of the Government of the United States or, in the case of a computer not exclusively for such use, is used by or for the Government of the United States and such conduct adversely affects the use of the Government's operation of such computer;

(4) knowingly and with intent to defraud, accesses a Federal interest computer without authorization, or exceeds authorized access, and by means of such conduct furthers the intended fraud and obtains anything of value, unless the object of the fraud and the thing obtained consists only of the use of the computer;

(5) (A) through means of a computer used in interstate commerce or communications, knowingly causes the transmission of a program, information, code, or command to a computer or a computer system if—

(i) the person causing the transmission intends that such a transmission will—

(I) damage, or cause damage to, a computer, computer system, network, information, data, or program; or

(II) withhold or deny, or cause the withholding or denial, of the use of a computer, computer services, system or network, information, data or program; and

(ii) the transmission of the harmful component of the program, information, code or command—

(I) occurred without the authorization of the persons or entities who own or are responsible for the computer system receiving the program, information, code or command; and

(II) (aa) causes loss or damage to one or more other persons of value aggregating $1,000 or more during any 1-year period; or

(bb) modifies or impairs, or potentially modifies or impairs, the medical examination, medical diagnosis, medical treatment, or medical care of one or more individuals; or

(B) through means of a computer used in interstate commerce or communication, knowingly causes the transmission of a program, information, code, or command to a computer or computer system—

(i) with reckless disregard of a substantial and unjustifiable risk that the transmission will—

(I) damage, or cause damage to, a computer, computer system, network information, data or program; or

(II) withhold or deny or cause the withholding or denial of the use of a computer, computer services, system, network, information, data or program; and

(ii) if the transmission of the harmful component of the program, information, code or command—

(I) occurred without the authorization of the persons or entities who own or are responsible for the computer system receiving the program, information, code, or command; and

(II) (aa) causes loss or damage to one or more other persons of a value aggregating $1,000 or more during any 1-year period; or (bb) modifies or impairs, or potentially modifies or impairs, the medical examination, medical diagnosis, medical treatment, or medical care of one or more individuals;

(6) knowingly and with intent to defraud traffics (as defined in section 1029) in any password or similar information through which a computer may be accessed without authorization, if—

(A) such trafficking affects interstate or foreign commerce; or

(B) such computer is used by or for the Government of the United States; shall be punished as provided in subsection (c) of this section.

(b) Whoever attempts to commit an offense under subsection (a) of this section shall be punished as provided in subsection (c) of this section.

(c) The punishment for an offense under subsection (a) or (b) of this section is—

(1)(A) a fine under this title or imprisonment for not more than ten years, or both, in the case of an offense under subsection (a)(1) of this section which does not occur after a conviction for another offense under such subsection, or an attempt to commit an offense punishable under this subparagraph; and

(B) a fine under this title or imprisonment for not more than twenty years, or both, in the case of an offense under subsection (a)(1) of this section which occurs after a conviction for another offense under such subsection; or an attempt to commit an offense punishable under this subparagraph; and

(2)(A) a fine under this title or imprisonment for not more than one year, or both, in the case of an offense under subsection (a)(2), (a)(3) or (a)(6) of this section which does not occur after a conviction for another offense under such subsection, or an attempt to commit an offense punishable under this subparagraph; and

(B) a fine under this title or imprisonment for not more than ten years, or both, in the case of an offense under subsection (a)(2), (a)(3) or (a)(6) of this section which occurs after a conviction for another offense under such subsection, or an attempt to commit an offense punishable under this subparagraph; and

(3)(A) a fine under this title or imprisonment for not more than five years, or both, in the case of an offense under subsection (a)(4) or (a)(5) of this section which does not occur after a conviction for another offense under such subsection, or an attempt to commit an offense punishable under this subparagraph; and

(B) a fine under this title or imprisonment for not more than ten years, or both, in the case of an offense under subsection (a)(4) or (a)(5) of this section which occurs after a conviction for another offense under such subsection, or an attempt to commit an offense punishable under this subparagraph; and

(4) a fine under this title or imprisonment for not more than 1 year, or both in case of an offense under subsection (a)(5)(B).

(d) The United States Secret Service shall, in addition to any other agency having such authority, have the authority to investigate offenses under this section. Such authority of the United States Secret Service shall be exercised in accordance with an agreement which shall be entered into by the Secretary of the Treasury and the Attorney General.

(e) As used in this section—

(1) the term "computer" means an electronic, magnetic, optical, electrochemical, or other high speed data processing device performing logical, arithmetic, or storage functions, and includes any data storage facility or communications facility directly related to or operating in conjunction with such device, but such term does not include an automated typewriter or typesetter, a portable hand held calculator, or other similar device;

(2) the term "Federal interest computer" means a computer—

(A) exclusively for the use of a financial institution or the United States Government, or, in the case of a computer not exclusively for such use, used by or for a financial institution or the United States Government and the conduct constituting the offense affects the use of the financial institution's operation or the Government's operation of such computer; or

(B) which is one of two or more computers used in committing the offense, not all of which are located in the same State;

(3) the term "State" includes the District of Columbia, the Commonwealth of Puerto Rico, and any other commonwealth, possession or territory of the United States;

(4) the term "financial institution" means—

(A) an institution, with deposits insured by the Federal Deposit Insurance Corporation;

(B) the Federal Reserve or a member of the Federal Reserve including any Federal Reserve Bank;

(C) a credit union with accounts insured by the National Credit Union Administration;

(D) a member of the Federal home loan bank system and any home loan bank;

(E) any institution of the Farm Credit System under the Farm Credit Act of 1971;

(F) a broker-dealer registered with the Securities and Exchange Commission pursuant to section 15 of the Securities Exchange Act of 1934;

(G) the Securities Investor Protection Corporation;

(H) a branch or agency of a foreign bank (as such terms are defined in paragraphs (1) and (3) of section 1(b) of the International Banking Act of 1978 [12 USCS § 3101(1), (3)]); and

(I) an organization operating under section 25 or section 25(a) of the Federal Reserve Act.

(5) the term "financial record" means information derived from any record held by a financial institution pertaining to a customer's relationship with the financial institution;

(6) the term "exceeds authorized access" means to access a computer with authorization and to use such access to obtain or alter information in the computer that the accesser is not entitled so to obtain or alter; and

(7) the term "department of the United States" means the legislative or judicial branch of the Government or one of the executive department enumerated in section 101 of title 5.

(f) This section does not prohibit any lawfully authorized investigative, protective, or intelligence activity of a law enforcement agency of the United States, a State, or a political subdivision of a State, or of an intelligence agency of the United States.

(g) Any person who suffers damage or loss by reason of a violation of this section, other than a violation of subsection (a)(5)(B), may maintain a civil action against the violator to obtain compensatory damages and injunctive relief or other equitable relief. Damages for violations of any subsection other than (a)(5)(A)(ii)(II)(bb) or (a)(5)(B)(ii)(bb) are limited to economic damages. No action may be brought under this subsection unless such action is begun within 2 years of the date of the act complained of or the date of the discovery of the damage.

(h) The Attorney General and the Secretary of the Treasury shall report to Congress annually, during the first 3 years following the date of the enactment of this subsection, concerning investigations and prosecutions under section (a)(5) of title 18, United States Code [sic].

Credit Card Abuse

18 USCS § 1029 (1991)

§ 1029. Fraud and related activity in connection with access devices

(a) Whoever—

(1) knowingly and with intent to defraud produces, uses, or traffics in one or more counterfeit access devices;

(2) knowingly and with intent to defraud traffics in or uses one or more unauthorized access devises during any one-year period, and by such conduct obtains anything of value aggregating $ 1,000 or more during that period;

(3) knowingly and with intent to defraud possesses fifteen or more devices which are counterfeit or unauthorized access devices; or

(4) knowingly, and with intent to defraud, produces, traffics in, has control or custody of, or possesses device-making equipment;

(5) knowingly and with intent to defraud effects transactions, with 1 or more access devices issued to another person or persons, to receive payment or any other thing of value during any 1-year period the aggregate value of which is equal to or greater than $1,000;

(6) without the authorization of the issuer of the access device, knowingly and with intent to defraud solicits a person for the purpose of—

(A) offering an access device; or

(B) selling information regarding or an application to obtain an access device; or

(7) without the authorization of the credit card system member or its agent, knowingly and with intent to defraud causes or arranges for another person to present to the member or its agent, for payment, 1 or more evidences or records of transactions made by an access device;

shall, if the offense affects interstate or foreign commerce, be punished as provided in subsection (c) of this section.

(b)(1) Whoever attempts to commit an offense under subsection (a) of this section shall be punished as provided in subsection (c) of this section.

(2) Whoever is a party to a conspiracy of two or more persons to commit an offense under subsection (a) of this section, if any of the parties engages in any conduct in furtherance of such offense, shall be fined an amount not greater than the amount provided as the maximum fine for such offense under subsection (c) of this section or imprisoned not longer than one-half the period provided as the maximum imprisonment for such offense under subsection (c) of this section, or both.

(c) The punishment for an offense under subsection (a) or (b)(1) of this section is—

(1) a fine under this title or twice the value obtained by the offense, whichever is greater, or imprisonment for not more than ten years, or both, in the case of an offense under subsection (a)(2), (3), (5), (6), or (7) of this section which does not occur after a conviction for another offense under either such subsection, or an attempt to commit an offense punishable under this paragraph;

(2) a fine under this title or twice the value obtained by the offense, whichever is greater, or imprisonment for not more than fifteen years, or both, in the case of an offense under subsection (a)(1) or (a)(4) of this section which does not occur after a conviction for another offense under either such subsection, or an attempt to commit an offense punishable under this paragraph; and

(3) a fine under this title or twice the value obtained by the offense, whichever is greater, or imprisonment for not more than twenty years, or both, in the case of an offense under subsection (a) of this section which occurs after a conviction for another offense under such subsection, or an attempt to commit an offense punishable under this paragraph.

(d) The United States Secret Service shall, in addition to any other agency having such authority, have the authority to investigate offenses under this section. Such authority of the United States Secret Service shall be exercised in accordance with an agreement which shall be entered into by the Secretary of the Treasury and the Attorney General.

(e) As used in this section—

(1) the term "access device" means any card, plate, code, account number, or other means of account access that can be used, alone or in conjunction with another access device, to obtain money, goods, services, or any other thing of value, or that can be used to initiate a transfer of funds (other than a transfer originated solely by paper instrument);

(2) the term "counterfeit access device" means any access device that is counterfeit, fictitious, altered, or forged, or an identifiable component of an access device or a counterfeit access device;

(3) the term "unauthorized access device" means any access device that is lost, stolen, expired, revoked, canceled, or obtained with intent to defraud;

(4) the term "produce" includes design, alter, authenticate, duplicate, or assemble;

(5) the term "traffic" means transfer, or otherwise dispose of, to another, or obtain control of with intent to transfer or dispose of;

(6) the term "device-making equipment" means any equipment, mechanism, or impression designed or primarily used for making an access device or a counterfeit access device; and

(7) The term "credit card system member" means a financial institution or other entity that is a member of a credit card system, including an entity, whether affiliated with or identical to the credit card issuer, that is the sole member of a credit card system.

(f) This section does not prohibit any lawfully authorized investigative, protective, or intelligence activity of a law enforcement agency of the United States, a State, or a political subdivision of a State, or of an intelligence agency of the United States, or any activity authorized under chapter 224 of this title. For purposes of this subsection, the term "State" includes a State of the United States, the District of Columbia, and any commonwealth, territory, or possession of the United States.

New York Computer Crime Statute

ARTICLE 156. Offenses Involving Computers; Definition of Terms

NY CLS Penal §156.00 (1992)

§156.00. Offenses involving computers; definition of terms

The following definitions are applicable to this chapter except where different meanings are expressly specified:

1. "Computer" means a device or group of devices which, by manipulation of electronic, magnetic, optical or electrochemical impulses, pursuant to a computer program, can automatically perform arithmetic, logical, storage or retrieval operations with or on computer data, and includes any connected or directly related device, equipment or facility which enables such computer to store, retrieve or communicate to or from a person, another computer or another device the results of computer operations, computer programs or computer data.

2. "Computer program" is property and means an ordered set of data representing coded instructions or statements that, when executed by computer, cause the computer to process data or direct the computer to perform one or more computer operations or both and may be in any form, including magnetic storage media, punched cards, or stored internally in the memory of the computer.

3. "Computer data" is property and means a representation of information, knowledge, facts, concepts or instructions which are being processed, or have been processed in a computer

and may be in any form, including magnetic storage media, punched cards, or stored internally in the memory of the computer.

4. "Computer service" means any and all services provided by or through the facilities of any computer communication system allowing the input, output, examination, or transfer, of computer data or computer programs from one computer to another.

5. "Computer material" is property and means any computer data or computer program which:

(a) contains records of the medical history or medical treatment of an identified or readily identifiable individual or individuals. This term shall not apply to the gaining access to or duplication solely of the medical history or medical treatment records of a person by that person or by another, specifically authorized by the person whose records are gained access to or duplicated; or

(b) contains records maintained by the state or any political subdivision thereof or any governmental instrumentality within the state which contains any information concerning a person, as defined in subdivision seven of section 10.00 of this chapter, which because of name, number, symbol, mark or other identifier, can be used to identify the person and which is otherwise prohibited by law from being disclosed. This term shall not apply to the gaining access to or duplication solely of records of a person by that person or by another specifically authorized by the person whose records are gained access to or duplicated; or

(c) is not and is not intended to be available to anyone other than the person or persons rightfully in possession thereof or selected persons having access thereto with his or their consent and which accords or may accord such rightful possessors an advantage over competitors or other persons who do not have knowledge or the benefit thereof.

6. "Uses a computer or computer service without authorization" means the use of a computer or computer service without the permission of, or in excess of the permission of, the owner or lessor or someone licensed or privileged by the owner or lessor after notice to that effect to the user of the computer or computer service has been given by:

(a) giving actual notice in writing or orally to the user; or

(b) prominently posting written notice adjacent to the computer being utilized by the user; or

(c) a notice that is displayed on, printed out on or announced by the computer being utilized by the user. Proof that the computer is programmed to automatically display, print or announce such notice or a notice prohibiting copying, reproduction or duplication shall be presumptive evidence that such notice was displayed, printed or announced.

7. "Felony" as used in this article means any felony defined in the laws of this state or any offense defined in the laws of any other jurisdiction for which a sentence to a term of imprisonment in excess of one year is authorized in this state.

§156.05. Unauthorized use of a computer

A person is guilty of unauthorized use of a computer when he knowingly uses or causes to be used a computer or computer service without authorization and the computer utilized is equipped or programmed with any device or coding system, a function of which is to prevent the unauthorized use of said computer or computer system.

Unauthorized use of a computer is a class A misdemeanor.

§156.10. Computer trespass

A person is guilty of computer trespass when he knowingly uses or causes to be used a computer or computer service without authorization and:

1. he does so with an intent to commit or attempt to commit or further the commission of any felony; or

2. he thereby knowingly gains access to computer material. Computer trespass is a class E felony.

§156.20. Computer tampering in the fourth degree

A person is guilty of computer tampering in the fourth degree when he uses or causes to be used a computer or computer service and having no right to do so he intentionally alters in any manner or destroys computer data or a computer program of another person.

Computer tampering in the fourth degree is a class A misdemeanor.

§156.25. Computer tampering in the third degree

A person is guilty of computer tampering in the third degree when he commits the crime of computer tampering in the fourth degree and:

1. he does so with an intent to commit or attempt to commit or further the commission of any felony; or

2. he has been previously convicted of any crime under this article or subdivision ten of section 165.15 of this chapter; or

3. he intentionally alters in any manner or destroys computer material; or

4. he intentionally alters in any manner or destroys computer data or a computer program so as to cause damages in an aggregate amount exceeding one thousand dollars.

Computer tampering in the third degree is a class E felony.

§156.26. Computer tampering in the second degree

A person is guilty of computer tampering in the second degree when he commits the crime of computer tampering in the fourth degree and he intentionally alters in any manner or destroys computer data or a computer program so as to cause damages in an aggregate amount exceeding three thousand dollars.

Computer tampering in the second degree is a class D felony.

§156.27. Computer tampering in the first degree

A person is guilty of computer tampering in the first degree when he commits the crime of computer tampering in the fourth degree and he intentionally alters in any manner or destroys computer data or a computer program so as to cause damages in an aggregate amount exceeding fifty thousand dollars.

Computer tampering in the first degree is a class C felony.

§156.30. Unlawful duplication of computer related material

A person is guilty of unlawful duplication of computer related material when having no right to do so, he copies, reproduces or duplicates in any manner:

1. any computer data or computer program and thereby intentionally and wrongfully deprives or appropriates from an owner thereof an economic value or benefit in excess of two thousand five hundred dollars; or

2. any computer data or computer program with an intent to commit or attempt to commit or further the commission of any felony.

Unlawful duplication of computer related material is a class E felony.

§156.35. Criminal possession of computer related material

A person is guilty of criminal possession of computer related material when having no right to do so, he knowingly possesses, in any form, any copy, reproduction or duplicate of any computer data or computer program which was copied, reproduced or duplicated in violation of section 156.30 of this article, with intent to benefit himself or a person other than an owner thereof.

Criminal possession of computer related material is a class E felony.

§156.50. Offenses involving computers; defenses

In any prosecution:

1. under section 156.05 or 156.10 of this article, it shall be a defense that the defendant had reasonable grounds to believe that he had authorization to use the computer;

2. under section 156.20, 156.25, 156.26 or 156.27 of this article it shall be a defense that the defendant had reasonable grounds to believe that he had the right to alter in any manner or destroy the computer data or the computer program;

3. under section 156.30 of this article it shall be a defense that the defendant had reasonable grounds to believe that he had the right to copy, reproduce or duplicate in any manner the computer data or the computer program.

First Amendment Privacy Protection (Privacy Protection Act)

42 USCS § 2000aa (1991)

§ 2000aa. Search or seizure of work product materials

(a) Notwithstanding any other law, it shall be unlawful for a government officer or employee, in connection with the investigation or prosecution of a criminal offense, to search for or seize any work product materials possessed by a person reasonably believed to have a purpose to disseminate to the public a newspaper, book, broadcast, or other similar form of public communication, in or affecting interstate or foreign commerce; but this provision shall not impair or affect the ability of any government officer or employee, pursuant to otherwise applicable law, to search for or seize such materials, if-

(1) there is probable cause to believe that the person possessing such materials has committed or is committing the criminal offense to which the materials relate: Provided, however, That a government officer or employee may not search for or seize such materials under the provisions of this paragraph if the offense to which the materials relate consists of the receipt, possession, communication, or withholding of such materials or the information contained therein (but such a search or seizure may be conducted under the provisions of this paragraph if the offense consists of the receipt, possession, or communication of information relating to the national defense, classified information, or restricted data under the provisions of section 793, 794, 797, or 798 of title 18, United States Code [18 USCS § 793, 794, 797, or 798], or section 224, 225, or 227 of the Atomic Energy Act of 1954 (42 U.S.C. 2274, 2275, 2277) [42 USCS § 2274, 2275, or 2277], or section 4 of the Subversive Activities Control Act of 1950 (50 U.S.C. 783) [50 USCS § 783]); or

(2) there is reason to believe that the immediate seizure of such materials is necessary to prevent the death of, or serious bodily injury to, a human being.

(b) Notwithstanding any other law, it shall be unlawful for a government officer or employee, in connection with the investigation or prosecution of a criminal offense, to search for or seize documentary materials, other than work product materials, possessed by a person in connection with a purpose to disseminate to the public a newspaper, book, broadcast, or other similar form of public communication, in or affecting interstate or foreign commerce; but this provision shall not impair or affect the ability of any government officer or employee, pursuant to otherwise applicable law, to search for or seize such materials, if-

(1) there is probable cause to believe that the person possessing such materials has committed or is committing the criminal offense to which the materials relate: Provided, however, That a government officer or employee may not search for or seize such materials under the provisions of this paragraph if the offense to which the materials relate consists of the receipt, possession, communication, or withholding of such materials or the information contained therein (but such a search or seizure may be conducted under the provisions of this paragraph if the offense consists of the receipt, possession, or communication of information relating to the national defense, classified information, or restricted data under the provisions of section 793, 794, 797, or 798 of title 18, United States Code [18 USCS § 793, 794, 797, or 798], or section 224, 225, or 227 of the Atomic Energy Act of 1954 (42 U.S.C. 2274, 2275, 2277) [42 USCS § 2274, 2275 or 2277], or section 4 of the Subversive Activities Control Act of 1950 (50 U.S.C. 783) [50 USCS § 783]);

(2) there is reason to believe that the immediate seizure of such materials is necessary to prevent the death of, or serious bodily injury to, a human being;

(3) there is reason to believe that the giving of notice pursuant to a subpena duces tecum would result in the destruction, alteration, or concealment of such materials; or

(4) such materials have not been produced in response to a court order directing compliance with a subpena duces tecum, and-

(A) all appellate remedies have been exhausted; or

(B) there is reason to believe that the delay in an investigation or trial occasioned by further proceedings relating to the subpena would threaten the interests of justice.

(c) In the event a search warrant is sought pursuant to paragraph (4)(B) of subsection (b), the person possessing the materials shall be afforded adequate opportunity to submit an affidavit setting forth the basis for any contention that the materials sought are not subject to seizure.

§ 2000aa-6. Damages; civil actions

(a) Action against United States, State or other governmental unit. A person aggrieved by a search for or seizure of materials in violation of this Act [42 USCS §§ 2000aa et seq.] shall have a civil cause of action for damages for such search or seizure-

(1) against the United States, against a State which has waived its sovereign immunity under the Constitution to a claim for damages resulting from a violation of this Act [42 USCS §§ 2000aa et

seq.], or against any other governmental unit, all of which shall be liable for violations of this Act [42 USCS §§ 2000aa et seq.] by their officers or employees while acting within the scope or under color of their office or employment; and

(2) against an officer or employee of a State who has violated this Act [42 USCS § 2000aa et seq.] while acting within the scope or under color of his office or employment, if such State has not waived its sovereign immunity as provided in paragraph (1).

(b) Defense. It shall be a complete defense to a civil action brought under paragraph (2) of subsection (a) that the officer or employee had a reasonable good faith belief in the lawfulness of his conduct.

(c) Assertion of defense; exception. The United States, a State, or any other governmental unit liable for violations of this Act [42 USCS §§ 2000aa et seq.] under subsection (a)(1), may not assert as a defense to a claim arising under this Act [42 USCS §§ 2000aa et seq.] the immunity of the officer or employee whose violation is complained of or his reasonable good faith belief in the lawfulness of his conduct, except that such a defense may be asserted if the violation complained of is that of a judicial officer.

(d) Exclusive remedy. The remedy provided by subsection (a)(1) against the United States, a State, or any other governmental unit is exclusive of any other civil action or proceeding for conduct constituting a violation of this Act [42 USCS §§ 2000aa et seq.], against the officer or employee whose violation gave rise to the claim, or against the estate of such officer or employee.

(e) Evidence. Evidence otherwise admissible in a proceeding shall not be excluded on the basis of a violation of this Act [42 USCS §§ 2000aa et seq.].

(f) Damage recovery. A person having a cause of action under this section shall be entitled to recover actual damages but not less than liquidated damages of $ 1,000, and such reasonable attorneys' fees and other litigation costs reasonably incurred as the court, in its discretion, may award: Provided, however, That the United States, a State, or any other governmental unit shall not be liable for interest prior to judgment.

(g) Attorney General; claims settlement; regulations. The Attorney General may settle a claim for damages brought against the United States under this section, and shall promulgate regulations to provide for the commencement of an administrative inquiry following a determination of a violation of this Act [42 USCS §§ 2000aa et seq.] by an officer or employee of the United States and for the imposition of administrative sanctions against such officer or employee, if warranted.

(h) Jurisdiction. The district courts shall have original jurisdiction of all civil actions arising under this section.

§ 2000aa-7. Definitions

(a) "Documentary materials", as used in this Act [42 USCS §§ 2000aa et seq.], means materials upon which information is recorded, and includes, but is not limited to, written or printed materials, photographs, motion picture films, negatives, video tapes, audio tapes, and other mechanically, magnetically or electronically recorded cards, tapes, or discs, but does not include contraband or the fruits of a crime or things otherwise criminally possessed, or property designed or intended for use, or which is or has been used as, the means of committing a criminal offense.

(b) "Work product materials", as used in this Act [42 USCS §§ 2000aa et seq.], means materials, other than contraband or the fruits of a crime or things otherwise criminally possessed, or property designed or intended for use, or which is or has been used, as the means of committing a criminal offense, and-

(1) in anticipation of communicating such materials to the public, are prepared, produced, authored, or created, whether by the person in possession of the materials or by any other person;

(2) are possessed for the purposes of communicating such materials to the public; and

(3) include mental impressions, conclusions, opinions, or theories of the person who prepared, produced, authored, or created such material.

(c) "Any other governmental unit", as used in this Act [42 USCS §§ 2000aa et seq.], includes the District of Columbia, the Commonwealth of Puerto Rico, any territory or possession of the United States, and any local government, unit of local government, or any unit of State government.

§ 2000aa-11. Attorney General guidelines

(a) Procedure to obtain documentary materials in private possession. The Attorney General shall, within six months of date of enactment of this Act [enacted Oct. 13, 1980], issue guidelines for the procedures to be employed by any Federal officer or employee, in connection with the investigation or prosecution of an offense, to obtain documentary materials in the private possession of a person when the person is not reasonably believed to be a suspect in such offense or related by blood or marriage to such a suspect, and when the materials sought are not contraband or the fruits or instrumentalities of an offense. The Attorney General shall incorporate in such guidelines-

(1) a recognition of the personal privacy interests of the person in possession of such documentary materials;

(2) a requirement that the least intrusive method or means of obtaining such materials be used which do not substantially jeopardize the availability or usefulness of the materials sought to be obtained;

(3) a recognition of special concern for privacy interests in cases in which a search or seizure for such documents would intrude upon a known confidential relationship such as that which may exist between clergyman and parishioner; lawyer and client; or doctor and patient; and

(4) a requirement that an application for a warrant to conduct a search governed by this title be approved by an attorney for the government, except that in an emergency situation the application may be approved by another appropriate supervisory official if within 24 hours of such emergency the appropriate United States Attorney is notified.

(b) Report to Congressional committees. The Attorney General shall collect and compile information on, and report annually to the Committees on the Judiciary of the Senate and the House of

Representatives on the use of search warrants by Federal officers and employees for documentary materials described in subsection (a)(3).

§ 2000aa-12. Effect of guidelines; violations

Guidelines issued by the Attorney General under this title [42 USCS §§ 2000aa-11 et seq.] shall have the full force and effect of Department of Justice regulations and any violation of these guidelines shall make the employee or officer involved subject to appropriate administrative disciplinary action. However, an issue relating to the compliance, or the failure to comply, with guidelines issued pursuant to this title [42 USCS §§ 2000aa-11 et seq.] may not be litigated, and a court may not entertain such an issue as the basis for the suppression or exclusion of evidence.

Child Pornography Statute

Sexual Exploitation of Children

18 USCS § 2252 (1991)

§ 2252. Certain activities relating to material involving the sexual exploitation of minors

(a) Any person who—

(1) knowingly transports or ships in interstate or foreign commerce by any means including by computer or mails, any visual depiction, if—

(A) the producing of such visual depiction involves the use of a minor engaging in sexually explicit conduct; and

(B) such visual depiction is of such conduct;

(2) knowingly receives, or distributes any visual depiction that has been mailed, or has been shipped or transported in interstate or foreign commerce, or which contains materials which have been mailed or so shipped or transported, by any means including by computer, or knowingly reproduces any visual depiction for distribution in interstate or foreign commerce or through the mails, if—

(A) the producing of such visual depiction involves the use of a minor engaging in sexually explicit conduct; and

(B) such visual depiction is of such conduct;

shall be punished as provided in subsection (b) of this section.

(3) either—

(A) in the special maritime and territorial jurisdiction of the United States, or on any land or building owned by, leased to, or otherwise used by or under the control of the Government of the United States, or in the Indian country as defined in section 1151 of this title, knowingly sells or possesses with intent to sell any visual depiction; or

(B) knowingly sells or possesses with intent to sell any visual depiction that has been mailed, or has been shipped or transported in interstate or foreign commerce, or which was produced using materials which have been mailed or so shipped or transported, by any means, including by computer, if—

(i) the producing of such visual depiction involves the use of a minor engaging in sexually explicit conduct; and

(ii) such visual depiction is of such conduct; or

(4) either—

(A) in the special maritime and territorial jurisdiction of the United States, or on any land or building owned by, leased to, or otherwise used by or under the control of the Government of the United States, or in the Indian country as defined in section 1151 of this title, knowingly possesses 3 or more books, magazines, periodicals, films, video tapes, or other matter which contain any visual depiction; or

(B) knowingly possesses 3 or more books, magazines, periodicals, films, video tapes, or other matter which contain any visual depiction that has been mailed, or has been shipped or transported in interstate or foreign commerce, or which was produced using materials which have been mailed or so shipped or transported, by any means including by computer, if—

(i) the producing of such visual depiction involves the use of a minor engaging in sexually explicit conduct; and

(ii) such visual depiction is of such conduct;

shall be punished as provided in subsection (b) of this section.

(b)(1) Whoever violates paragraph (1), (2), or (3) of subsection (a) shall be fined under this title or imprisoned not more than ten years, or both, but, if such person has a prior conviction under this chapter or chapter 109A, such person shall be fined under this title and imprisoned for not less than five years nor more than fifteen years.

(2) Whoever violates paragraph (4) of subsection (a) shall be fined under this title or imprisoned for not more than five years, or both.

§ 2253. Criminal forfeiture

(a) Property subject to criminal forfeiture. A person who is convicted of an offense under this chapter [18 USCS §§ 2251 et seq.] involving a visual depiction described in section 2251, 2251A, or 2252 of this chapter shall forfeit to the United States such person's interest in—

(1) any visual depiction described in sections 2251, 2251A, or 2252 of this chapter, or any book, magazine, periodical, film, videotape, or other matter which contains any such visual depiction, which was produced, transported, mailed, shipped or received in violation of this chapter [18 USCS §§ 2251 et seq.];

(2) any property, real or personal, constituting or traceable to gross profits or other proceeds obtained from such offense; and

(3) any property, real or personal, used or intended to be used to commit or to promote the commission of such offense.

(b) Third party transfers. All right, title, and interest in property described in subsection (a) of this section vests in the United States upon the commission of the act giving rise to forfeiture under this section. Any such property that is subsequently transferred to a person other than the defendant may be the subject of a special verdict of forfeiture and thereafter shall be ordered forfeited to the United States, unless the transferee establishes in a hearing pursuant to subsection (m) of this section that he is a bona fide purchaser for value of such property who at the time of purchase was reasonably without cause to believe that the property was subject to forfeiture under this section.

(c) Protective orders. (1) Upon application of the United States, the court may enter a restraining order or injunction, require the execution of a satisfactory performance bond, or take any other action to preserve the availability of property described in subsection (a) of this section for forfeiture under this section—

(A) upon the filing of an indictment or information charging a violation of this chapter [18 USCS §§ 2251 et seq.] for which criminal forfeiture may be ordered under this section and alleging that the property with respect to which the order is sought would, in the event of conviction, be subject to forfeiture under this section; or

(B) prior to the filing of such an indictment or information, if, after notice to persons appearing to have an interest in the property and opportunity for a hearing, the court determines that—

(i) there is a substantial probability that the United States will prevail on the issue of forfeiture and that failure to enter the order will result in the property being destroyed, removed from the jurisdiction of the court, or otherwise made unavailable for forfeiture; and

(ii) the need to preserve the availability of the property through the entry of the requested order outweighs the hardship on any party against whom the order is to be entered;

except that an order entered pursuant to subparagraph (B) shall be effective for not more than 90 days, unless extended by the court for good cause shown or unless an indictment or information described in subparagraph (A) has been filed.

(2) A temporary restraining order under this subsection may be entered upon application of the United States without notice or opportunity for a hearing when an information or indictment has not yet been filed with respect to the property, if the United States demonstrates that there is probable cause to believe that the property with respect to which the order is sought would, in the event of conviction, be subject to forfeiture under this section and that provision of notice will

jeopardize the availability of the property for forfeiture. Such a temporary order shall expire not more than 10 days after the date on which it is entered, unless extended for good cause shown or unless the party against whom it is entered consents to an extension for a longer period. A hearing requested concerning an order entered under this paragraph shall be held at the earliest possible time and prior to the expiration of the temporary order.

(3) The court may receive and consider, at a hearing held pursuant to this subsection, evidence and information that would be inadmissible under the Federal Rules of Evidence.

(d) Warrant of seizure. The Government may request the issuance of a warrant authorizing the seizure of property subject to forfeiture under this section in the same manner as provided for a search warrant. If the court determines that there is probable cause to believe that the property to be seized would, in the event of conviction, be subject to forfeiture and that an order under subsection (c) of this section may not be sufficient to assure the availability of the property for forfeiture, the court shall issue a warrant authorizing the seizure of such property.

(e) Order of forfeiture. The court shall order forfeiture of property referred to in subsection (a) if the trier of fact determines, beyond a reasonable doubt, that such property is subject to forfeiture.

(f) Execution. Upon entry of an order of forfeiture under this section, the court shall authorize the Attorney General to seize all property ordered forfeited upon such terms and conditions as the court shall deem proper. Following entry of an order declaring the property forfeited, the court may, upon application of the United States, enter such appropriate restraining orders or injunctions, require the execution of satisfactory performance bonds, appoint receivers, conservators, appraisers, accountants, or trustees, or take any other action to protect the interest of the United States in the property ordered forfeited. Any income accruing to or derived from property ordered forfeited under this section may be used to offset ordinary and necessary expenses to the property which are required by law, or which are necessary to protect the interests of the United States or third parties.

(g) Disposition of property. Following the seizure of property ordered forfeited under this section, the Attorney General shall destroy or retain for official use any article described in paragraph (1) of subsection (a), and shall retain for official use or direct the disposition of any property described in paragraph (2) or (3) of subsection (a) by sale or any other commercially feasible means, making due provision for the rights of any innocent persons. Any property right or interest not exercisable by, or transferable for value to, the United States shall expire and shall not revert to the defendant, nor shall the defendant or any person acting in concert with him or on his behalf be eligible to purchase forfeited property at any sale held by the United States. Upon application of a person, other than the defendant or person acting in concert with him or on his behalf, the court may restrain or stay the sale or disposition of the property pending the conclusion of any appeal of the criminal case giving rise to the forfeiture, if the applicant demonstrates that proceeding with the sale or disposition of the property will result in irreparable injury, harm, or loss to him.

(h) Authority of Attorney General. With respect to property ordered forfeited under this section, the Attorney General is authorized to—

(1) grant petitions for mitigation or remission of forfeiture, restore forfeited property to victims of a violation of this chapter [18 USCS §§ 2251 et seq.], or take any other action to protect the rights of innocent persons which is in the interest of justice and which is not inconsistent with the provisions of this section;

(2) compromise claims arising under this section;

(3) award compensation to persons providing information resulting in a forfeiture under this section; apply to a criminal forfeiture under this section.

(4) direct the disposition by the United States, under section 616 of the Tariff Act of 1930 [19 USCS § 1616], of all property ordered forfeited under this section by public sale or any other commercially feasible means, making due provision for the rights of innocent persons; and

(5) take appropriate measures necessary to safeguard and maintain property ordered forfeited under this section pending its disposition.

(i) Applicability of civil forfeiture provisions. Except to the extent that they are inconsistent with the provisions of this section, the provisions of section 2254(d) of this title (18 U.S.C. 2254(d)) shall . . .

(j) Bar on intervention. Except as provided in subsection (m) of this section, no party claiming an interest in property subject to forfeiture under this section may—

(1) intervene in a trial or appeal of a criminal case involving the forfeiture of such property under this section; or

(2) commence an action at law or equity against the United States concerning the validity of his alleged interest in the property subsequent to the filing of an indictment or information alleging that the property is subject to forfeiture under this section.

(k) Jurisdiction to enter orders. The district courts of the United States shall have jurisdiction to enter orders as provided in this section without regard to the location of any property which may be subject to forfeiture under this section or which has been ordered forfeited under this section.

(l) Depositions. In order to facilitate the identification and location of property declared forfeited and to facilitate the disposition of petitions for remission or mitigation of forfeiture, after the entry of an order declaring property forfeited to the United States, the court may, upon application of the United States, order that the testimony of any witness relating to the property forfeited be taken by deposition and that any designated book, paper, document, record, recording, or other material not privileged be produced at the same time and place, in the same manner as provided for the taking of depositions under rule 15 of the Federal Rules of Criminal Procedure.

(m) Third party interests.

(1) Following the entry of an order of forfeiture under this section, the United States shall publish notice of the order and of its intent to dispose of the property in such manner as the Attorney General may direct. The Government may also, to the extent practicable, provide direct written

notice to any person known to have alleged an interest in the property that is the subject of the order of forfeiture as a substitute for published notice as to those persons so notified.

(2) Any person, other than the defendant, asserting a legal interest in property which has been ordered forfeited to the United States pursuant to this section may, within 30 days of the final publication of notice or his receipt of notice under paragraph (1), whichever is earlier, petition the court for a hearing to adjudicate the validity of his alleged interest in the property. The hearing shall be held before the court alone, without a jury.

(3) The petition shall be signed by the petitioner under penalty of perjury and shall set forth the nature and extent of the petitioner's right, title, or interest in the property, the time and circum-stances of the petitioner's acquisition of the right, title, or interest in the property, any additional facts supporting the petitioner's claim, and the relief sought.

(4) The hearing on the petition shall, to the extent practicable and consistent with the interests of justice, be held within 30 days of the filing of the petition. The court may consolidate the hearing on the petition with a hearing on any other petition filed by a person other than the defendant under this subsection.

(5) At the hearing, the petitioner may testify and present evidence and witnesses on his own behalf, and cross-examine witnesses who appear at the hearing. The United States may present evidence and witnesses in rebuttal and in defense of its claim to the property and cross-examine witnesses who appear at the hearing. In addition to testimony and evidence presented at the hearing, the court shall consider the relevant portions of the record of the criminal case which resulted in the order of forfeiture.

(6) If, after the hearing, the court determines that the petitioner has established by a preponderance of the evidence that—

(A) the petitioner has a legal right, title, or interest in the property, and such right, title, or interest renders the order of forfeiture invalid in whole or in part because the right, title, or interest was vested in the petitioner rather than the defendant or was superior to any right, title, or interest of the defendant at the time of the commission of the acts which gave rise to the forfeiture of the property under this section; or

(B) the petitioner is a bona fide purchaser for value of the right, title, or interest in the property and was at the time of purchase reasonably without cause to believe that the property was subject to forfeiture under this section;

the court shall amend the order of forfeiture in accordance with its determination.

(7) Following the court's disposition of all petitions filed under this subsection, or if no such petitions are filed following the expiration of the period provided in paragraph (2) for the filing of such petitions, the United States shall have clear title to property that is the subject of the order of forfeiture and may warrant good title to any subsequent purchaser or transferee.

(n) Construction. This section shall be liberally construed to effectuate its remedial purposes.

(o) Substitute assets. If any of the property described in subsection (a), as a result of any act or omission of the defendant—

(1) cannot be located upon the exercise of due diligence;

(2) has been transferred or sold to, or deposited with, a third party;

(3) has been placed beyond the jurisdiction of the court;

(4) has been substantially diminished in value; or

(5) has been commingled with other property which cannot be divided without difficulty;

the court shall order the forfeiture of any other property of the defendant up to the value of any property described in paragraphs (1) through (5).

§ 2254. Civil forfeiture

(a) Property subject to civil forfeiture. The following property shall be subject to forfeiture by the United States:

(1) Any visual depiction described in section 2251, 2251A, or 2252 of this chapter, or any book, magazine, periodical, film, videotape or other matter which contains any such visual depiction, which was produced, transported, mailed, shipped, or received in violation of this chapter [18 USCS §§ 2251 et seq.].

(2) Any property, real or personal, used or intended to be used to commit or to promote the commission of an offense under this chapter [18 USCS §§ 2251 et seq.] involving a visual depiction described in section 2251, 2251A, or 2252 of this chapter, except that no property shall be forfeited under this paragraph, to the extent of the interest of an owner, by reason of any act or omission established by that owner to have been committed or omitted without the knowledge or consent of that owner.

(3) Any property, real or personal, constituting or traceable to gross profits or other proceeds obtained from a violation of this chapter involving a visual depiction described in section 2251, 2251A, or 2252 of this chapter, except that no property shall be forfeited under this paragraph, to the extent of the interest of an owner, by reason of any act or omission established by that owner to have been committed or omitted without the knowledge or consent of that owner.

(b) Seizure pursuant to Supplemental Rules for Certain Admiralty and Maritime Claims. Any property subject to forfeiture to the United States under this section may be seized by the Attorney General, the Secretary of the Treasury, or the United States Postal Service upon process issued pursuant to the Supplemental Rules for Certain Admiralty and Maritime Claims by any district court of the United States having jurisdiction over the property, except that seizure without such process may be made when the seizure is pursuant to a search under a search warrant or incident to an arrest. The Government may request the issuance of a warrant authorizing the seizure of property subject to forfeiture under this section in the same manner as provided for a search warrant under the Federal Rules of Criminal Procedure.

(c) Custody of Federal official. Property taken or detained under this section shall not be repleviable, but shall be deemed to be in the custody of the Attorney General, Secretary of the Treasury, or the United States Postal Service subject only to the orders and decrees of the court or the official having jurisdiction thereof. Whenever property is seized under any of the provisions of this subchapter, the Attorney General, Secretary of the Treasury, or the United States Postal Service may—

(1) place the property under seal;

(2) remove the property to a place designated by the official or agency; or

(3) require that the General Services Administration take custody of the property and remove it, if practicable, to an appropriate location for disposition in accordance with law.

(d) Other laws and proceedings applicable. All provisions of the customs laws relating to the seizure, summary and judicial forfeiture, and condemnation of property for violation of the customs laws, the disposition of such property or the proceeds from the sale thereof, the remission or mitigation of such forfeitures, and the compromise of claims, shall apply to seizures and forfeitures incurred, or alleged to have been incurred, under this section, insofar as applicable and not inconsistent with the provisions of this section, except that such duties as are imposed upon the customs officer or any other person with respect to the seizure and forfeiture of property under the customs laws shall be performed with respect to seizures and forfeitures of property under this section by such officers, agents, or other persons as may be authorized or designated for that purpose by the Attorney General, the Secretary of the Treasury, or the Postal Service, except to the extent that such duties arise from seizures and forfeitures affected by any customs officer.

(e) Inapplicability of certain sections. Sections 1606, 1613, 1614, 1617, and 1618 of title 19, United States Code, shall not apply with respect to any visual depiction or any matter containing a visual depiction subject to forfeiture under subsection (a)(1) of this section.

(f) Disposition of forfeited property. Whenever property is forfeited under this section the Attorney General shall destroy or retain for official use any property described in paragraph (1) of subsection (a) and, with respect to property described in paragraph (2) or (3) of subsection (a), may—

(1) retain the property for official use or transfer the custody or ownership of any forfeited property to a Federal, State, or local agency under section 616 of the Tariff Act of 1930 [19 USCS § 1616a];

(2) sell, by public sale or any other commercially feasible means, any forfeited property which is not required to be destroyed by law and which is not harmful to the public; or

(3) require that the General Services Administration take custody of the property and dispose of it in accordance with law.

The Attorney General, Secretary of the Treasury, or the United States Postal Service shall ensure the equitable transfer pursuant to paragraph (1) of any forfeited property to the appropriate State or local law enforcement agency so as to reflect generally the contribution of any such agency participating directly in any of the acts which led to the seizure or forfeiture of such property. A decision by an official or agency pursuant to paragraph (1) shall not be subject to judicial review. With respect to a forfeiture conducted by the Attorney General, the Attorney General shall forward to the Treasurer of the United States for deposit in accordance with section 524(c) of title 28 the proceeds from any sale under paragraph (2) and any moneys forfeited under this section. With respect to a forfeiture conducted by the Postal Service, the proceeds from any sale under paragraph (2) and any moneys forfeited under this subchapter shall be deposited in the Postal Service Fund as required by section 2003(b)(7) of title 39.

(g) Title to property. All right, title, and interest in property described in subsection (a) of this section shall vest in the United States upon commission of the act giving rise to forfeiture under this section.

(h) Stay of proceedings. The filing of an indictment or information alleging a violation of this chapter which is also related to a civil forfeiture proceeding under this section shall, upon motion of the United States and for good cause shown, stay the civil forfeiture proceeding.

(i) Venue. In addition to the venue provided for in section 1395 of title 28 or any other provision of law, in the case of property of a defendant charged with a violation that is the basis for forfeiture of the property under this section, a proceeding for forfeiture under this section may be brought in the judicial district in which the defendant owning such property is found or in the judicial district in which the criminal prosecution is brought.

§ 2256. Definitions for chapter

For the purposes of this chapter [18 USCS §§ 2251 et seq.], the term—

(1) "minor" means any person under the age of eighteen years;

(2) "sexually explicit conduct" means actual or simulated—

(A) sexual intercourse, including genital-genital, oral-genital, anal-genital, or oral-anal, whether between persons of the same or opposite sex;

(B) bestiality;

(C) masturbation;

(D) sadistic or masochistic abuse (for the purpose of sexual stimulation);

or

(E) lascivious exhibition of the genitals or pubic area of any person;

(3) "producing" means producing, directing, manufacturing, issuing, publishing, or advertising;

(4) "organization" means a person other than an individual;

(5) "visual depiction" includes undeveloped film and videotape;

(6) "computer" has the meaning given that term in section 1030 of this title; and

(7) "custody or control" includes temporary supervision over or responsibility for a minor whether legally or illegally obtained.

§ 2257. Record keeping requirements

(a) Whoever produces any book, magazine, periodical, film, videotape, or other matter which—

(1) contains one or more visual depictions made after November 1, 1990 of actual sexually explicit conduct; and

(2) is produced in whole or in part with materials which have been mailed or shipped in interstate or foreign commerce, or is shipped or transported or is intended for shipment or transportation in interstate or foreign commerce; shall create and maintain individually identifiable records pertaining to every performer portrayed in such a visual depiction.

(b) Any person to whom subsection (a) applies shall, with respect to every performer portrayed in a visual depiction of actual sexually explicit conduct—

(1) ascertain, by examination of an identification document containing such information, the performer's name and date of birth, and require the performer to provide such other indicia of his or her identity as may be prescribed by regulations;

(2) ascertain any name, other than the performer's present and correct name, ever used by the performer including maiden name, alias, nickname, stage, or professional name; and

(3) record in the records required by subsection (a) the information required by paragraphs (1) and (2) of this subsection and such other identifying information as may be prescribed by regulation.

(c) Any person to whom subsection (a) applies shall maintain the records required by this section at his business premises, or at such other place as the Attorney General may by regulation prescribe and shall make such records available to the Attorney General for inspection at all reasonable times.

(d)(1) No information or evidence obtained from records required to be created or maintained by this section shall, except as provided in this section, directly or indirectly, be used as evidence against any person with respect to any violation of law

(2) Paragraph (1) of this subsection shall not preclude the use of such information or evidence in a prosecution or other action for a violation of this section or for a violation of any applicable provision of law with respect to the furnishing of false information.

(e)(1) Any person to whom subsection (a) applies shall cause to be affixed to every copy of any matter described in paragraph (1) of subsection (a) of this section, in such manner and in such form as the Attorney General shall by regulations prescribe, a statement describing where the records required by this section with respect to all performers depicted in that copy of the matter may be located.

(2) If the person to whom subsection (a) of this section applies is an organization the statement required by this subsection shall include the name, title, and business address of the individual employed by such organization responsible for maintaining the records required by this section.

(f) It shall be unlawful—

(1) for any person to whom subsection (a) applies to fail to create or maintain the records as required by subsections (a) and (c) or by any regulation promulgated under this section;

(2) for any person to whom subsection (a) applies knowingly to make any false entry in or knowingly to fail to make an appropriate entry in, any record required by subsection (b) of this section or any regulation promulgated under this section;

(3) for any person to whom subsection (a) applies knowingly to fail to comply with the provisions of subsection (e) or any regulation promulgated pursuant to that subsection; and

(4) for any person knowingly to sell or otherwise transfer, or offer for sale or transfer, any book, magazine, periodical, film, video, or other matter, produce in whole or in part with materials which have been mailed or shipped in interstate or foreign commerce or which is intended for shipment in interstate or foreign commerce, which—

(A) contains one or more visual depictions made after the effective date of this subsection of actual sexually explicit conduct; and

(B) is produced in whole or in part with materials which have been mailed or shipped in interstate or foreign commerce, or is shipped or transported or is intended for shipment or transportation in interstate or foreign commerce;

which does not have affixed thereto, in a manner prescribed as set forth in subsection (e)(1), a statement describing where the records required by this section may be located, but such person shall have no duty to determine the accuracy of the contents of the statement or the records required to be kept.

(g) The Attorney General shall issue appropriate regulations to carry out this section.

(h) As used in this section—

(1) the term "actual sexually explicit conduct" means actual but not simulated conduct as defined in subparagraphs (A) through (D) of paragraph (2) of section 2256 of this title;

(2) "identification document" has the meaning given that term in section 1028(d) of this title;

(3) the term "produces" means to produce, manufacture, or publish any book, magazine, periodical, film, video tape or other similar matter and includes the duplication, reproduction, or reissuing of any such matter, but does not include mere distribution or any other activity which does not involve hiring, contracting for managing, or otherwise arranging for the participation of the performers depicted; and

(4) the term "performer" includes any person portrayed in a visual depiction engaging in, or assisting another person to engage in, actual sexually explicit conduct.

(i) Whoever violates this section shall be imprisoned for not more than 2 years, and fined in accordance with the provisions of this title, or both. Whoever violates this section after having been convicted of a violation punishable under this section shall be imprisoned for any period of years not more than 5 years but not less than 2 years, and fined in accordance with the provisions of this title, or both.

FCC Restrictions on Obscene and Indecent Telephone Transmissions

A. STATUTE—Title 47, Section 223 of the United States Code (rev. 1989)

§ 223. Obscene or harassing telephone calls in the District of Columbia or in interstate or foreign communications

(a) Whoever—

(1) in the District of Columbia or in interstate or foreign communication by means of telephone—

(A) makes any comment, request, suggestion or proposal which is obscene, lewd, lascivious, filthy, or indecent;

(B) makes a telephone call, whether or not conversation ensues, without disclosing his identity and with intent to annoy, abuse, threaten, or harass any person at the called number;

(C) makes or causes the telephone of another repeatedly or continuously to ring, with intent to harass any person at the called number; or

(D) makes repeated telephone calls, during which conversation ensues, solely to harass any person at the called number; or

(2) knowingly permits any telephone facility under his control to be used for any purpose prohibited by this section, shall be fined not more than $50,000 or imprisoned not more than six months, or both.

(b)(1) Whoever knowingly—

(A) within the United States, by means of telephone, makes (directly or by recording device) any obscene communication for commercial purposes to any person, regardless of whether the maker of such communication placed the call; or

(B) permits any telephone facility under such person's control to be used for an activity prohibited by subparagraph (A), shall be fined in accordance with title 18, United States Code, or imprisoned not more than two years, or both.

(2) Whoever knowingly—

(A) within the United States, by means of telephone, makes (directly or by recording device) any indecent communication for commercial purposes which is available to any person under 18 years of age or to any other person without that person's consent, regardless of whether the maker of such communication placed the call; or

(B) permits any telephone facility under such person's control to be used for an activity prohibited by subparagraph (A), shall be fined not more than $50,000 or imprisoned not more than six months, or both.

(3) It is a defense to prosecution under paragraph (2) of this subsection that the defendant restrict access to the prohibited communication to persons 18 years of age or older in accordance with subsection (c) of this section and with such procedures as the Commission may prescribe by regulation.

(4) In addition to the penalties under paragraph (1), whoever, within the United States, intentionally violates paragraph (1) or (2) shall be subject to a fine of not more than $ 50,000 for each violation. For purposes of this paragraph, each day of violation shall constitute a separate violation.

(5)(A) In addition to the penalties under paragraphs (1), (2), and (5), whoever, within the United States, violates paragraph (1) or (2) shall be subject to a civil fine of not more than $ 50,000 for each violation. For purposes of this paragraph, each day of violation shall constitute a separate violation.

(B) A fine under this paragraph may be assessed either—

(i) by a court, pursuant to civil action by the Commission or any attorney employed by the Commission who is designated by the Commission for such purposes, or

(ii) by the Commission after appropriate administrative proceedings.

(6) The Attorney General may bring a suit in the appropriate district court of the United States to enjoin any act or practice which violates paragraph (1) or (2). An injunction may be granted in accordance with the Federal Rules of Civil Procedure.

(c)(1) A common carrier within the District of Columbia or within any State, or in interstate or foreign commerce, shall not, to the extent technically feasible, provide access to a communication specified in subsection (b) from the telephone of any subscriber who has not previously requested in writing the carrier to provide access to such communication if the carrier collects from subscribers an identifiable charge for such communication that the carrier remits, in whole or in part, to the provider of such communication.

(2) Except as provided in paragraph (3), no cause of action may be brought in any court or administrative agency against any common carrier, or any of its affiliates, including their officers, directors, employees, agents, or authorized representatives on account of—

(A) any action which the carrier demonstrates was taken in good faith to restrict access pursuant to paragraph (1) of this subsection;

or

(B) any access permitted—

(i) in good faith reliance upon the lack of any representation by a provider of communications that communications provided by that provider are communications specified in subsection (b), or

(ii) because a specific representation by the provider did not allow the carrier, acting in good faith, a sufficient period to restrict access to communications described in subsection (b).

(3) Notwithstanding paragraph (2) of this subsection, a provider of communications services to which subscribers are denied access pursuant to paragraph (1) of this subsection may bring an action for a declaratory judgment or similar action in a court. Any such action shall be limited to the question of whether the communications which the provider seeks to provide fall within the category of communications to which the carrier will provide access only to subscribers who have previously requested such access.

B. FCC REGULATION—Title 47, Section 64.201 of the Code of Federal Regulations

Restrictions on obscene or indecent telephone message services.

47 CFR 64.201

It is a defense to prosecution under section 223(b) of the Communications Act of 1934, as amended, 47 U.S.C. 223(b), that the defendant has taken one of the actions set forth in paragraph (a), (b), or (c) of this section to restrict access to prohibited communications to persons eighteen years of age or older, and has additionally complied with paragraph (d) of this section, where applicable:

(a) Requires payment by credit card before transmission of the message; or

(b) Requires an authorized access or identification code before transmission of the message, and where the defendant has:

(1) Issued the code by mailing it to the applicant after reasonably ascertaining through receipt of a written application that the applicant is not under eighteen years of age; and

(2) Established a procedure to cancel immediately the code of any person upon written, telephonic or other notice to the defendant's business office that such code has been lost, stolen, or used by a person or persons under the age of eighteen, or that such code is no longer desired; or

(c) Scrambles the message using frequency inversion techniques so that it is unintelligible and incomprehensible to the calling party without use of a descrambler by the calling party; and

(d) Where the defendant is a message sponsor or subscriber to mass announcement services tariffed at this Commission and such defendant prior to the transmission of the message has requested in writing to the carrier providing the public announcement service that calls to his message service be subject to billing notification as an adult telephone message service.

State Computer Crime Laws

Following is a list of computer crime laws of the 50 states. These laws change every now and then, possibly with new numbering, so it's a good idea to double-check recent legislation as well.

Alabama—Code of Alabama
    Sections 13A-8-100 to 103
Alaska—Statutes
    Section 11.46.200(a)
    Section 11.46.484
    Section 11.46.740
    Section 11.46.985
    Section 11.46.990
Arizona—Revised Statutes
    Section 13-2301
    Section 13-2316
Arkansas
    Sections 5-41-101 to 107
California—Penal Code
    Section 502
    Sections 1203.047, 48
Colorado—Revised Statutes
    Sections 18-5.5-101, 102
Connecticut—General Statutes
    Section 52-570b
    Sections 53a-250 to 261
Delaware—Code, Title 11
    Sections 931 to 939

Florida—Statutes Annotated
    Sections 815.01 to .07
    Sections 934.01 to 43
Georgia—Codes Annotated
    Sections 16-9-90 to 95
Hawaii—Revised Statutes
    Sections 708-890 to 896
Idaho—Code, Chapter 22, Title 18
    Sections 18-2201 to 2202
Illinois—Criminal Code, Chapter 38
    Section 15-1
    Section 16-9
Indiana
    Section 35-43-1-4
    Section 35-43-2-3
Iowa—Statutes
    Sections 716A.1 to .16
Kansas—Statutes Annotated
    Section 21-3755
Kentucky—Revised Statutes
    Sections 434.840 to .860
Louisiana—Revised Statutes, Title 14
    Sections 73.1—73.5

Maine—Revised Statutes, Title 17A
Section 357
Maryland—Annotated Code of
Maryland, Art. 27
Section 45A
Section 146
Massachusetts—General Laws, Chapter 266
Section 30
Michigan—Statutes Annotated
Section 752.791 et seq.
Minnesota—Criminal Code
Sections 609.87 to .89
Mississippi—Code Annotated
Sections 97-45-1 to 13
Missouri—Revised Statutes
Sections 569.093 to .099
Montana—Code Annotated
Section 45-2-101
Section 45-6-310
Section 45-6-311
Nebraska—Revised Statutes
Sections 28-1343 to 1348
Nevada—Revised Statutes
Sections 205.473 to .477
Section 205.480
New Hampshire—Revised Statutes,
Annotated
Sections 638.16 to 638.19
New Jersey—Statutes
Title 2C, Sections 20-23 to 20-35
Title 2A, Sections 38A-1 to 38A-3
New Mexico—Criminal Offenses
Sections 30-16A-1k to 30-16A-4
Sections 30-45-1 to 30-45-7
New York—Penal Law
Sections 156 to 156.5
Section 165.15
North Carolina—General Statutes
Sections 14-453 to 457
North Dakota—Century Code
Section 12.1-06.1-01, subsection 3
Section 12.1-06.1-08

Ohio—Revised Code Annotated
Sections 2901.01(J)(1),(2)
Sections 2913.01(E),(F),(L)-(Q)
Section 2913.04
Oklahoma—Session Laws, Title 21
Section 1124
Sections 1951-1956
Oregon—Revised Statutes
Section 164.125
Sections 164.345 to 365
Section 164.377
Pennsylvania—Consolidated Statutes of
Crimes and Offenses
Section 3933
Rhode Island—Criminal Offenses
Sections 11-52-1 to 4
South Carolina—Code of Laws
Sections 16-16-10 to 40
South Dakota—Codified Laws
Sections 43-43B-1 to 8
Tennessee—Code Annotated
Sections 39-3-1401 to 1406
Texas—Penal Code, Title 7
Sections 33.01 to 33.05
Utah—Code Annotated
Sections 76-6-701 to 705
Vermont
No computer crime statute
Virginia—Code of Virginia
Sections 18.2-152.1 to 152.14
Washington—Revised Code of
Washington Annotated
Section 9A.48.100
Sections 9A.52.110 to 130
West Virginia—Code
Sections 61-3C-1 to 21
Wisconsin—Statutes Annotated
Section 943.70
Wyoming—Statutes
Sections 6-3-501 to 505

Sources of Further Information

Ready for more information on the legal side of online systems and networks? Here are some of the places you will find it. Some of these resources are easy to lay hands on; others require mailing, e-mailing, use of the World Wide Web, or access to law libraries. There is no chance of putting a comprehensive list in a book, because the number of resources is growing all the time. Nonetheless, anyone who actually reads everything listed here will be one of the best-informed people about online law on the face of the planet.

In addition to the resources listed below, which have a particular focus on the online world or online law, you can keep up with many online legal developments in the general media these days. This wasn't always the case; just a couple of years ago, in order to keep up you needed to monitor key newsgroups, mailing lists, and bulletin board discussion groups. Now, enough reporters have tuned into the online world that news of its development is starting to blanket the older media, especially the daily newspapers and business and computer magazines.

Magazines

- *Boardwatch Magazine*. 8500 W. Bowles Avenue, Suite 210, Littleton, Colorado 80123. Subscriptions: Voice (800)933-6038, BBS (303)973-4222 (8N1).
  The leading magazine for online systems and the Internet. It broadly covers current cultural, technical, and business issues, as well as legal and regulatory developments affecting BBSs. Offers insights and strong opinions on online affairs you won't find anywhere else.

- *WIRED*. 520 Third Street, Fourth Floor, San Francisco, California 94107, Voice: (415)222-6200, Internet: info@wired.com.
  Subscriptions: P.O. Box 191826, San Francisco, California 94119-9866, $39.95/year (12 issues).
  Monthly explorations of the exploding Information Age culture, done with style and wild graphics. Tracks important online trends such as cryptography, privacy, online commerce, government regulation, and online property rights.

- ***Morph's Outpost on the Digital Frontier***. Morphs Outpost, Inc., P.O. Box 578, Orinda, CA 94563, Voice: (510)210-8170.
  Subscriptions: $39.95/year (12 issues).
  Focuses on the world of multimedia and VR developers. A lot of information on emerging online developments, a good regular column on practical legal issues, and lots of insight on how to structure and grow new media businesses and products.

- ***Internet World***. Mecklermedia, 20 Ketchum Street, Westport, Connecticut 06880, Voice: (800)632-5537 or (203)226-6967.
  Subscriptions: P.O. Box 713, Mt. Morris, Illinois 61054-9965, $29/year (10 issues).
  Covers the Internet beat of cyberspace, with special attention to business development and opportunities, plus a good regular legal column.

- ***Upside***. Upside Publishing Company, 2015 Pioneer Court, San Mateo, CA 94403, Voice: (415)377-0950
  Subscriptions: $48/year (12 issues).
  For those interested in the investment and financial side of computer-related high tech industries, although its focus is shifting increasingly to online affairs. Well-written feature articles on developing online businesses, and revealing interviews with the men and women shaping modern industry on the broad scale.

- ***Red Herring***. Flipside Communications Inc., 2055 Woodside Road, Suite 240, Redwood City, CA 94061, Voice: (415)780-0158.
  Subscriptions: $180/year (12 issues).
  Directed at high-tech investors, it gives a panoramic view of developing online industries and profiles software and online industry leaders.

- ***Information Law Alert***. Voorhees Reports, 411 First Street, Brooklyn, New York 11215-2507, Voice: (800)369-4840, Internet: markvoor@phantom.com.
  Subscriptions: $350/year (20 issues).
  Newsletter that astutely follows cutting-edge legal and regulatory developments in the online and related arenas. Often gets to the heart of issues just hinted at elsewhere.

- ***RELease 1.0***. EDventure Holdings Inc., 104 Fifth Avenue, 20th Floor, New York, New York 10011, Voice: (212)924-8800, Internet: 0005113705@mcimail.com.
  Subscriptions: $495/year (12 issues).
  Under new editor Gerald Michalski, RELease 1.0, long a standard reference newsletter for computer industry strategists, now regularly examines the business and cultural implications of developing online technologies and industries. It does not dwell on the legal aspects, but it does provide an enlightened context for understanding the developing online world(s).

- ***Interactive Content***. Jupiter Communications, 594 Broadway Suite 1003, New York, New York 10012, Voice: (212)941-9252.
  Subscriptions: $495/year (12 issues).
  Newsletter focusing on the online and interactive services industry. Does a good job of emphasizing the important new trends and analyzing the various business models being tried out by online businesses.

- *Online Access.* 900 N. Franklin, Suite 1310, Chicago, Illinois 60610, Voice: (312)573-1700. Subscriptions: $29.70/year (10 issues).
  Covers developments in the online world generally. Contains a lot of material to help newer cyberspace explorers get their bearings as they venture online.

- *NetGuide.* 600 Community Drive, Manhasset, New York 11030, Voice: (516)562-5000, Internet: mail@netguide.cmp.com, WWW: http://www.cmp.com/NetGuide/home.html. Subscriptions: P.O. Box 420355, Palm Coast, Florida 32142-9371, $14.97/year (12 issues).
  Newly released as this book goes to press, NetGuide explores the emerging world of cyberspace for the general public. Covers a broad range of cutting-edge Net issues, and tells you about a lot of cool places on the Net.

- *Privacy Journal.* P.O. Box 28577, Providence, Rhode Island 02908, Voice: (401)274-7861.
  This is a newsletter covering privacy issues in all facets of society, including areas most people never even think to look.

Online Resources

- **EduPage.** Educom, 1112 16th Street NW, Washington, DC 20036, Voice: (202)872-4200, Internet: info@educom.edu, WWW: http://educom.edu.
  Subscriptions: listproc@educom.edu (text: subscribe edupage Your Name), free, twice weekly.
  An indispensable electronic newswire that covers news and events in online and information technology. The single best way to keep current, and possibly the best free resource on the Net today.

- **Electronic Privacy Information Center.** 666 Pennsylvania Avenue SE, Suite 301, Washington, DC 20003, Voice: (202)547-5482, Internet: epic@cpsr.org, CompuServe: GO NCSA-FORUM, EPIC section.
  The leading high technology privacy group in Washington, D.C., which aggressively takes on government and corporate intrusions into our private affairs. Much of their focus is on privacy in communications environments. They recently started publishing their own online newsletter, EPIC ALERT.

- **Electronic Frontier Foundation (EFF).** 1667 K Street NW, Suite 801, Washington, DC 20006-1605, Voice: (202)347-5400, BBS (202)638-6119, Internet: eff@eff.org. Membership organization.
  The EFF is an advocacy group promoting online civil rights and public interest legislation. It publishes an electronic newsletter of online legal developments called EFFector, available on many networks and the large commercial information services. It also runs various online public discussion areas, including the comp.org.eff.talk newsgroup on Usenet, the EFF Conference on the Well, the EFF forum on CompuServe (GO EFFSIG), and the EFF area on America Online. Archives of legal and regulatory materials are available on the World Wide Web at http://www.eff.org, and by gopher at gopher.eff.org.

- **Association of Online Professionals (AOP)**. 1818 Wyoming Avenue NW, Washington, DC 20009, Voice: (202)265-1266, E-mail: 70631.266@compuserve.com, CompuServe: GO IBMBBS, AOL Section.

  Advocacy and resource organization for smaller online and bulletin board systems, newly formed as this book goes to press. Intends to act as voice for smaller online systems in national policy and affairs, coordinate responses to local regulation of online activities, and maintain resources of use to those who operate online systems.

- *Computer Underground Digest (CuD)*. Usenet: alt.society.cu-digest

  CuD *is a weekly electronic newsletter covering a broad scope of online legal and cultural issues, with contributions from all over the network. A lot of material from hackers, activists, and other non-mainstream sources. It can be found on the network and on various online systems, and in its own Usenet newsgroup at alt.society.cu-digest.*

- **Society for Electronic Access**. P.O. Box 7081, New York, New York 10116-7081, Voice: (212)592-3801, Internet: sea-info@sea.org (for information message), sea@sea.org (for inquiries).

  EFF-Austin. P.O. Box 18957, Austin, Texas 78760, Voice: (512)465-7871, Internet: eff-austin@zilker.net.

  Electronic Frontiers Houston. 2476 Bolsover #145, Houston, Texas 77005, Voice: (713)661-1561 (Ed Cavazos), Internet: efh@blkbox.com, BBS: (713)665-4656.

  Local and regional groups devoted to furthering civil liberties in cyberspace, creating greater means of access to online resources, and promoting online culture, among other things. A great way not only to be involved in the development of the online world, but meet regularly with others involved in related efforts.

Books

- *Technologies of Freedom*, by Ithiel de Sola Pool. Harvard University Press, 1983.

  The primary reference work on 1st Amendment rights for electronic media. It traces the history of U.S. regulation of print and electronic media, and the development of the concept of freedom of speech and of the press. Don't be fooled by the publication date—it's still ahead of its time today.

- *Contracts in the Information Industry II*, published by the Information Industry Association, 555 New Jersey Avenue NW, Suite 800, Washington, DC 20001, 1990.

  This book is filled with sample form contracts from corporate members of the Information Industry Association, covering all sorts of information services deals. By thumbing through these contracts, online services can get some pretty good ideas on how to structure their own contracts, and the kinds of expectations that prevail in the large-scale commercial marketplace for information services.

- *Law of Electronic Commerce*, by Benjamin Wright. Little, Brown & Co., 1992.

  Written by an expert in electronic commerce and Electronic Data Interchange, this book explores broadly and deeply the legal matters that have arisen and will arise among those who do business online.

- *The Copyright Handbook: How to Protect and Use Written Works*, by Stephen Fishman. Nolo Press, 1994.

  Basics of copyright, and how to secure and protect your rights.

- *Access to and Use and Disclosure of Electronic Mail on Company Computer Systems: A Tool Kit for Formulating Your Company's Policy*, by David R. Johnson and John Podesta. Published by the Electronic Mail Association.
  A detailed handbook for corporate employee e-mail policies. Provides a Chinese menu approach to building a corporate policy that gives employees the desired amount of privacy and freedom on the company e-mail system. It is also useful for private BBS operators wishing to explore e-mail privacy options in more detail.

- *Cyberpunk: Outlaws and Hackers on the Computer Frontier*, by Katie Hafner and John Markoff. Simon & Schuster, 1991.
  True, fascinating stories of three celebrated "computer crime" episodes on the networks. Detailed accounts of lives, technology, and legal maneuvers. Provides a visceral sense of how network crime happens, for those of us who have not brushed up against it personally.

- *Rogue Programs: Viruses, Worms, and Trojan Horses*, edited by Lance J. Hoffman. Van Nostrand Reinhold, 1990.
  An anthology of articles by various writers on technical, legal, and cultural aspects of computer viruses and other dangerous code.

- *Who Owns Information?: From Privacy to Public Access*, by Anne Wells Branscomb. Basic Books, 1994.
  Explores new concepts of "ownership" as applied to information. Fascinating case studies of people and businesses struggling for control over such emergent forms of information property as telephone numbers and health records.

- *Privacy for Sale: How Computerization Has Made Everyone's Private Life an Open Secret*, by Jeffrey Rothfeder. Simon & Schuster, 1992.

- *Girls Lean Back Everywhere: The Law of Obscenity and the Assault on Genius*, by Edward De Grazia. Random House, 1992.
  General exploration of the development of obscenity law. No particular attention to online materials, but the motives behind obscenity laws and prosecutions have not changed.

- *Cyberspace and the Law: Your Rights and Duties in the On-Line World*, by Edward A. Cavazos and Gavino Morin. MIT Press, 1994.
  Guidebook to many of the legal issues in the online world.

- *The Hacker Crackdown: Law and Disorder on the Electronic Frontier*, by Bruce Sterling. Bantam Books, 1993.
  Powerful true account of the world of hackers and cops. Part sociology, part journalism, part first-person descent into hackerdom.

- *The Virtual Community: Homesteading on the Electronic Frontier*, by Howard Rheingold. Harperperennial, 1994.
  The title of this book gets to the heart of the matter. Rheingold explores the new kinds of communities enabled by online services.

- *Approaching Zero: The Extraordinary Underworld of Hackers, Phreakers, Virus Writers, and Keyboard Criminals*, by Paul Mungo and Bryan Clough. Random House, 1993.
  A book about network outlaws, with a strong focus on virus writers.

Software

- **Online Subscriber Agreement Toolkit**. Invisible Hand Software, 3847 Whitman Road, Annandale, VA 22003, Voice: (703)207-9353
  Software that automates the design of user agreements for online systems. Fill in the blanks and out pops an agreement tailored to your services and the kind of relationship you want with your users. The language of the forms is lawyerly, but there is a feature enabling attorneys to adjust the phrasing for user-friendliness and other purposes.

Conferences

- **Computers, Freedom and Privacy (CFP)**. Held in March each year. No fixed address; changes locations year to year. For yearly announcements, subscribe to the CPSR-announce mailing list (subscribe: listserv@cpsr.org [text: subscribe cpsr-announce Your Name]).
  The premiere yearly gathering of those with a shared interest in network policies and community. Hackers, Internet professors, civil libertarians, policy makers, spies, cypherpunks, and others in a festive setting.

- **ONE BBSCON**. ONE, Inc., 4255 South Buckley Road, Suite 308, Aurora, Colorado 80013, Voice: (303)693-5253, BBS: (303)693-5432. Every August.
  The most important yearly event for small online systems and businesses. Innumerable sessions on social, business, legal, and technical matters.

- **Internet World**. Mecklermedia, 20 Ketchum Street, Westport, Connecticut 06880, Voice: (800)632-5537 or (203)226-6967. Several times yearly, various locations.
  The main trade show and convention specifically for the Internet.

- **Online Developers Conference**. Jupiter Communications, 594 Broadway, Suite 1003, New York, New York 10012, Voice: (212)941-9252.
  Important conference for online businesses.

Law Review Articles

- Barron, Jerome A. "The Telco, the Common Carrier Model and the First Amendment—the Dial-a-Porn Precedent." *Rutgers Computer and Technology Law Journal* 19 (Winter 1993): 371-404.

- Becker, Loftus E. Jr. "The Liability of Computer Bulletin Board Operators for Defamation Posted by Others." 22 *Connecticut Law Review*, 203 (1989).

- Cavazos, Edward A. "Computer Bulletin Board Systems and the Right of Reply: Redefining Defamation Liability for a New Technology." *Review of Litigation* 12 (Fall 1992): 231-248.

- Cutera, Terri A. "Computer Networks, Libel and the First Amendment." *Computer-Law Journal* 11 (December 1992): 555-583.

- Cutera, Terri A. "The Constitution in Cyberspace: the Fundamental Rights of Computer Users." *University of Missouri at Kansas City Law Review* 60 (Fall 1991): 139-167.

- Dierks, Michael P. "Computer Network Abuse." *Harvard Journal of Law and Technology* 6 (Spring 1993): 307-342.

- DiLello, Edward V. "Functional Equivalency and its Application to Freedom of Speech on Computer Bulletin Boards." *Columbia Journal of Legal and Social Problems* 26 (Winter 1993): 199-247.

- Faucher, John D. "Let the Chips Fall Where They May: Choice of Law in Computer Bulletin Board Defamation Cases." *University of California at Davis Law Review* 26 (Summer 1993): 1045-1078.

- Hardy, Trotter. "The Proper Legal Regime For Cyberspace." 55 *University of Pittsburgh Law Review*, 993 (1994).

- Jensen, Eric. "An Electronic Soapbox: Computer Bulletin Boards and the First Amendment." 39 *Federal Communications Law Journal* 217 (1987).

- Johnson, David R. and Kevin A. Marks. "Mapping Electronic Data Communications onto Existing Legal Metaphors: Should We Let Our Conscience (and Our Contracts) Be Our Guide?" *Villanova Law Review* 38 (April 1993): 487-515.

- Katsh, M. Ethan. "Law in a Digital World: Computer Networks and Cyberspace." *Villanova Law Review* 38 (April 1993): 403-485.

- Lyman, Susan C. "Civil Remedies for the Victims of Computer Viruses." *Southwestern Law Review* 21 (Summer 1992): 1169-1197.

- "The Message Is the Medium: The First Amendment on the Information Superhighway." *Harvard Law Review* 107 (March 1994): 1062-1098.

- Miller, Philip H. "New Technology, Old Problems: Determining the First Amendment Status of Electronic Information Services." *Fordham Law Review* 61 (April 1993): 1147-1201.

- Naughton, Edward J. "Is Cyberspace a Public Forum? Computer Bulletin Boards, Free Speech and State Action." *Georgetown Law Journal* 81 (December 1992): 409-441.

- Perritt, Henry H. Jr. "The Congress, the Courts and Computer Based Communications Networks: Answering Questions About Access and Content Control." *Villanova Law Review* 38 (April 1993): 319-348.

- Reidenberg, Joel R. "Rules of the Road for Global Electronic Highways: Merging the Trade and Technical Paradigms." *Harvard Journal of Law and Technology* 6 (Spring 1993): 287-305.

- Schlachter, Eric. "Cyberspace, the Free Market and the Free Marketplace of Ideas: Recognizing Legal Differences in Computer Bulletin Board Functions." 16 *Hastings Comm. & Ent. L. J.* 87 (1993).

- Walter, Priscilla A. and Eric H. Sussman. "Protecting Commercially Developed Information on the NREN." *The Computer Lawyer* 10 (April 1993): 1-11.

- Yin, Tung. "Post-Modern Printing Presses: Extending Freedom of Press to Protect Electronic Information Services." 8 *High Tech Law Journal*, 311 (1993).

Relevant Cases

Here are the some of the most important cases relating to online law. There's just a handful so far. Some cases discussed in the text are not included here because they were settled, are still going on, or the judge just didn't make any rulings for the law books.

- Bourke v. Nissan Motor Corp., No. B068705 (Cal.App. 2d Dist., Div. 5, 1993)
  Shoars v. Epson America, Inc., No. B073234 (Cal.App. 2d Dist., Div. 2, 1993)
  These two cases refused to recognize e-mail privacy rights in the worklace in California.

- Braun v. Soldier of Fortune Magazine, 968 F.2d 1110 (11th Cir., 1992)
  Refused to hold magazine liable for negligently publishing classified ad for contract killer.

- CompuServe Incorporated v. Patterson, Case No. C2-94-91 (S.D.Ohio, Aug. 11. 1994)
  Held that using an online service does not automatically subject the user to lawsuit anywhere that service may be offered.

- Cubby, Inc. v. CompuServe, Inc., 776 F. Supp. 135 (S.D.N.Y. 1991)
  Currently the leading case on First Amendment protection of online services.

- Daniel v. Dow Jones & Company, Inc., 520 N.Y.S. 2d 334, 137 Misc. 2d 94 (Civ.Ct. N.Y.C., N.Y. Co. 1987)
  Limited the liability of online publisher for publishing erroneous information.

- Dial Information v. Thornburgh, 938 F.2d 1535 (2nd Cir. 1991)
  Information Provider's Coalition v. FCC, 928 F.2d 866 (9th Cir. 1991)
  These cases established the constitutionality of the current dial-a-porn regulation.

- Eimann v. Soldier of Fortune Magazine, 880 F.2d 830 (5th Cir. 1989), *cert. denied*, 493 U.S. 1024, 110 S. Ct. 729, 107 L. Ed. 2d 748 (1990)
  Held magazine liable for negligently publishing classified ad for contract killer.

- FCC v. Pacifica Foundation, 438 U. S. 726, 98 S. Ct. 3026 (1978)
  Established legal category of "indecent materials," which are protected by First Amendment but may be barred from access by minors.

- Feist v. Rural Telephone, 111 S. Ct. 1282 (1991)
  Declared there can be no copyright in facts, or in fact databases, unless there is original selection, coordination, or arrangement of the facts.

- Grand Upright Music v. Warner Brothers, 780 F. Supp. 182 (S.D.N.Y. 1991)
  Held that the use of small, digitized sample of pop song within a hiphop song can infringe copyright.

- Miller v. California, 413 U.S. 15, 93 S. Ct. 2607, 37 L. Ed. 2d 419 (1973), *reh'g denied* 414 U.S. 881, 94 S. Ct. 26, 38 L. Ed. 2d 128 (1973)
  Established current balance in U.S. between First Amendment freedom of speech and government right to prosecute obscenity in name of public morality.

- NAACP v. Alabama, ex rel Patterson, 357 U.S. 449, 78 S. Ct. 1163, 2 L. Ed. 2d 1488 (1958), *on remand* 268 Ala. 531, 109 So. 2d 138 (1959)
  Established right to privacy of members of association under First Amendment.

- Playboy Enterprises, Inc. v. Frena, 839 F. Supp. 1552 (M.D. Fla. 1993)
  Recognized full copyright protection for digitized magazine pictures.

- Sable Communications v. FCC, 492 U.S. 115, 109 S. Ct. 2829 (1989)
  Struck down earlier version of dial-a-porn law, and demonstrates legal balancing between First Amendment and goal of protecting children from indecent materials.

- Sega Enterprises Ltd. v. Maphia, 30 U.S.P.Q. 2d 1921 (N.D. Cal. 1994)
  Used copyright law to support civil seizure of online system involved in pirating video game software.

- Stanley v. Georgia, 399 U.S. 557, 89 S. Ct. 1243 (1969)
  Established First Amendment right of privacy to read what you want within your own home.

- State of Oklahoma v. Anthony Davis, No. CF-93-4859 (Dist. Ct. Okla. County 1994)
  Found online system operator guilty of distributing obscene materials on system.

- Steve Jackson Games, Inc. v. U.S. Secret Service, 816 F. Supp. 432 (W.D. Texas 1993), *aff'd* Steve Jackson Games, Inc. v. U.S. Secret Service, No. 93-8661 (5th Cir., Oct. 31, 1994)
  Recognized that Electronic Communications Privacy Act and Privacy Protection Act set limits on government search and seizure of online systems.

- The T. J. Hooper, 60 F.2d 737 (2d Cir. 1932)
  Famous holding articulating standard of care for high risk situations under negligence law, where customary practices do not provide state of the art protection.

- United States v. Fernandez, 1993 U.S. Dist. LEXIS 3590, (S.D.N.Y. 1993)
  Pre-trial decision discussing defenses raised in an intrusive hacker case.

- U.S. v. LaMacchia, No. 94-10092-RGS (D.Mass. 1994)
  Held that federal wire fraud law cannot be used to prosecute a pirate BBS operator for copyright infringement.

- United States v. Morris, 928 F.2d 504 (2d Cir., 1991)
  Held that release of worm program that brought down the Internet violated the Computer Fraud and Abuse Act.

- United States v. Riggs, 743 F. Supp. 556 (N.D. IL. 1990)
  Pre-trial decision discussing causes of action in an intrusive hacker case.

- U.S. v. Thomas, Case No. 94-20019-G (W.D. Tenn. 1994)
  Held that California-based online system operators were guilty of violating Tennessee obscenity law.

Index

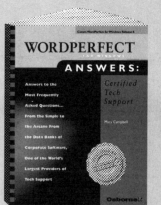

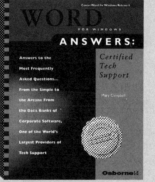

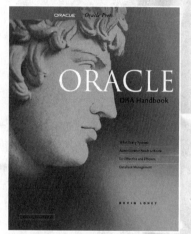

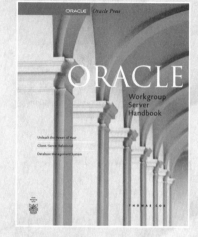
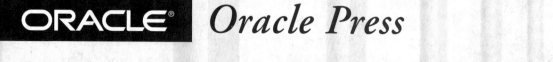

Secret Recipes

FOR THE SERIOUS CODE CHEF

BYTE's Mac Programmer's Cookbook
by Rob Terrell
Includes One 3.5-Inch Disk
$29.95 U.S.A., ISBN: 0-07-882062-6

No longer underground...the best-kept secrets and profound programming tips have been liberated! You'll find them all in the new BYTE Programmer's Cookbook series – the hottest hacks, facts, and tricks for veterans and rookies alike. These books are accompanied by a CD-ROM or disk packed with code from the books plus utilities and plenty of other software tools you'll relish.

BYTE's Windows Programmer's Cookbook
by L. John Ribar
Includes
One CD-ROM
$34.95 U.S.A.
ISBN: 0-07-882037-5

BYTE's DOS Programmer's Cookbook
by Craig Menefee, Lenny Bailes, and Nick Anis
Includes
One CD-ROM
$34.95 U.S.A.
ISBN: 0-07-882048-0

BYTE's OS/2 Programmer's Cookbook
by Kathy Ivens and Bruce Hallberg
Includes
One CD-ROM
$34.95 U.S.A.
ISBN: 0-07-882039-1

BYTE Guide to CD-ROM
by Michael Nadeau
Includes
One CD-ROM
$39.95 U.S.A.
ISBN: 0-07-881982-2

BC640SL

ORDER BOOKS DIRECTLY FROM OSBORNE/MC GRAW-HILL.

For a complete catalog of Osborne's books, call 510-549-6600 or write to us at 2600 Tenth Street, Berkeley, CA 94710

Call Toll-Free: *1-800-822-8158*
24 hours a day, 7 days a week
in U.S. and Canada

Mail this order form to:
McGraw-Hill, Inc.
Blue Ridge Summit, PA 17294-0840

Fax this order form to:
717-794-5291

EMAIL
7007.1531@COMPUSERVE.COM
COMPUSERVE GO MH

Ship to:

Name _____

Company _____

Address _____

City / State / Zip _____

Daytime Telephone: _____
(We'll contact you if there's a question about your order.)

ISBN #	BOOK TITLE	Quantity	Price	Total
0-07-88				
0-07-88				
0-07-88				
0-07-88				
0-07-88				
0-07088				
0-07-88				
0-07-88				
0-07-88				
0-07-88				
0-07-88				
0-07-88				
0-07-88				

Shipping & Handling Charge from Chart Below	
Subtotal	
Please Add Applicable State & Local Sales Tax	
TOTAL	

Shipping & Handling Charges

Order Amount	U.S.	Outside U.S.
Less than $15	$3.45	$5.25
$15.00 - $24.99	$3.95	$5.95
$25.00 - $49.99	$4.95	$6.95
$50.00 - and up	$5.95	$7.95

METHOD OF PAYMENT

☐ Check or money order enclosed (payable to Osborne/McGraw-Hill)

☐ AMERICAN EXPRESS ☐ DISCOVER ☐ MasterCard ☐ VISA

Account No. ☐☐☐☐☐☐☐☐☐☐☐☐☐☐☐☐

Expiration Date _____

Signature _____

In a hurry? Call 1-800-822-8158 anytime, day or night, or visit your local bookstore.

Thank you for your order

Code BC640SL